PASSING GAME

PASSING GAME

Benny Friedman
and the Transformation of Football

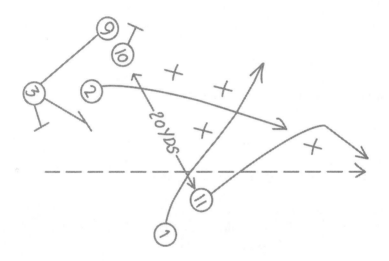

MURRAY GREENBERG

PublicAffairs • New York

Published in the United States by PublicAffairs™,
a member of the Perseus Books Group.

PublicAffairs books are available at special discounts for bulk pur-
chases in the U.S. by corporations, institutions, and other organizations. For more information, please contact the Special Markets
Department at the Perseus Books Group, 2300 Chestnut Street,
Suite 200, Philadelphia, PA 19103, call (800) 810-4145, ext. 5000, or
e-mail special.markets@perseusbooks.com.

Designed by Pauline Brown
Text set in 11.5 point Garamond

Library of Congress Cataloging-in-Publication Data

Greenberg, Murray.
    Passing game : Benny Friedman and the transformation of
football / Murray Greenberg. — 1st ed.
        p.   cm.
    Includes bibliographical references and index.
    ISBN 978-1-58648-477-4 (alk. paper)
    1. Friedman, Benny, 1905–1982. 2. Football players—United
States—Biography. 3. Michigan Wolverines (Football team)—
History. I. Title.
    GV939.F75 2008
    796.33092—dc22
    [B]
                                                    2008033117

First Edition

10 9 8 7 6 5 4 3 2 1

For my Mom, Bea Greenberg, who never missed a game,
and my Dad, Ted Greenberg, who taught me how to play.

And for my wife, Andrea, and
my daughters, Allie and Samantha,
who were there from the beginning
and who rooted for me every day.

CONTENTS

Introduction

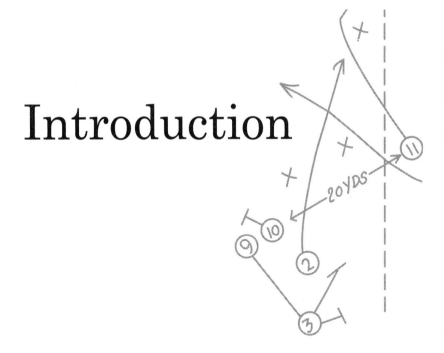

Football wasn't always a game dominated by strong-armed quarterbacks flinging the ball sixty yards downfield. In its beginnings football was mostly a messy affair in which brave men with altogether insufficient protective equipment would carry the melon-shaped ball into an angry thicket of defenders and scratch and plod and push for yardage. Rarely was football real estate acquired by way of the forward pass. The ball was so large that most players couldn't grip and throw it; the best they could do was hold it in their palm and heave it. That's why photographs of quarterbacks posing as if to pass in those early days evoked the image of a shot-putter in football pants.

Herman Maisin recalled those Neanderthal times. For more than seven decades, Maisin was the editor of the instructional magazine *Scholastic Coach,* a how-to bible for coaches and athletes filled with pictorial essays and articles featuring some of the sporting world's great performers. He was ninety-four years old when I met him in his Manhattan apartment to talk about Benny Friedman. They had first met in *Scholastic*'s offices, where Benny had come to discuss doing a photo shoot on the art of the forward pass. "When he introduced himself, I went crazy," Maisin recalled enthusiastically, as if the meeting had taken place forty-five minutes rather than forty-five years ago. "He'd been a sort of idol of mine . . . a Jewish kid, the greatest quarterback that ever was, all that sort of stuff."

Friedman did the photo shoot for *Scholastic,* throwing pass after pass to a group of high-school receivers until the camera had captured what it needed. Maisin recalled that every one of Benny's passes was "on the button," not especially remarkable for an experienced quarterback—until you consider that the quarterback was sixty years old at the time, forty years past his all-American days at the University of Michigan, and thirty-five years past a groundbreaking professional career during which he and Red Grange carried a fledgling enterprise called the National Football League on their backs.

Friedman and Maisin became good friends after that *Scholastic* photo shoot, often dining together and reminiscing about Benny's glorious days at Michigan and with the New York Giants, with Friedman, never in short supply of ego, doing most of the reminiscing. One day, Maisin recalled, Benny stopped him in his tracks with a question.

"Herman," Benny queried, "do you think anyone would want to write a book about me?"

Maisin's initial reaction wasn't what Benny had hoped for. Benny was without question a major star, a celebrity, in his heyday, but Maisin told him that too much time had passed since then, that, in essence, it was too late for a book.

On reflection, Herman's response discomfited him. He realized that Friedman's story was eminently worthy of a book, regardless of the passage of time. Indeed, in the case of a prominent, influential life that over time has, for whatever reason, been overlooked, that has fallen through history's cracks, the passage of time compels the retelling. Benny Friedman's life was such a life.

At Michigan, beginning in 1924, the uniquely talented Friedman startled defenses with his spectacular passes. At that time defenses stacked their players at the line of scrimmage to smother the run, all but ignoring the threat of a pass. But Friedman's passes came on any down and from anywhere on the field. Then Benny went to the nascent NFL—where fan interest and press coverage were scant in the shadow of the sporting behemoth called college football—and stunned the pros. Coaches devised formations to thwart Benny's passing attack; defenders were forced to play off the line and spread the field. "Benny Friedman was responsible for changing the entire concept of defense," insisted the great Grange, Benny's frequent rival.

Friedman's talents thrilled fans, and NFL owners realized that the popularity and growth of their league depended on the exciting brand of football that a vibrant passing game would bring. They slimmed down the ball, making it easier to throw, and eliminated rules that had discouraged passing. Thus did Benny Friedman help launch football toward the passing-dominated modern era during which the NFL became an American obsession. He revolutionized his sport, much as Babe Ruth (Benny's Roaring Twenties contemporary) revolutionized baseball with his towering home runs and Bobby Orr revolutionized hockey by popularizing the "offensive defenseman."

Friedman emerged at a time of rising anti-Semitism, when Jews were struggling to become a part of the fabric of America. The handsome son of working-class Orthodox Russian immigrants was in his day as inspirational to American Jews as were the two most celebrated Jewish-American athletes, Hank Greenberg and Sandy Koufax. He was hugely popular in his prime and the highest-paid footballer of his day: the New York Giants paid him $10,000 a season when most players were lucky to make $150 a game.

But though Greenberg and Koufax are well-remembered, as are Grange and other football stars of Benny's time, Benny has been largely forgotten. It is not entirely clear how that came to pass, but almost certainly Friedman's personality had something to do with it. He had an ego nearly equal to his prodigious talent, and such a degree of self-appreciation is generally not one's best friend. His efforts later in life to remind others of his greatness seemed only to hasten, and deepen, the fading of his star. In 1982, sick and anguished and feeling forgotten, he took his own life.

Benny Friedman was a complex man, blessed with otherworldly talent but also afflicted with human frailties. On the football field, however, he was always at home. "Has Mike Ditka been tipped off to the fact that ever since Benny Friedman set the league on fire, you've got to be able to throw the ball to win?" Paul Zimmerman, the eminent football writer, asked in evaluating the Ditka-coached, passing-challenged New Orleans Saints. Zimmerman wrote those words in 1999, more than six decades after Friedman threw his last NFL pass.

Here is the story of the man who inspired Zimmerman's jab at Mike Ditka, the man whom legendary sportswriter Paul Gallico called, at the peak of America's Golden Age of Sport, "the greatest football player in the world." As Benny himself would say, it's a story worth telling.

ONE

The Kid from Glenville

Between 1880 and 1920, Cleveland, Ohio, like other American cities, became home to thousands of Russian Jewish immigrants desperate to flee the suffocating poverty of their homeland and the pogroms that periodically ripped through their lives. They came to Cleveland, primarily to the Woodland section, east of the Cuyahoga River, and became peddlers and bakers, shopkeepers and tailors, teachers and rabbis and homemakers. They wanted freedom from oppression. They yearned for that little bit of prosperity that was possible in America.

But they wanted just as badly to maintain their religious and cultural traditions that had been forged over so many centuries. And so their neighborhoods became insular ghettos, comfortable shelters from the American storm. They spoke mostly Yiddish, not English. Shuls dotted every corner. Butcher shops and tailor shops were everywhere. Bakeries and delicatessens served kosher foods that were as popular with non-Jewish Clevelanders as they were with the neighborhood residents.

The *Yiddishe Velt* told you what was happening in the world, if you could read and understand Yiddish. For entertainment there was the Yiddish theater, where the patrons could retreat to their homeland for an hour or two without the fear of a soldier crashing through the door in the middle of the night. For those who liked to exercise their writing muscles and powers of persuasion, there were literary societies and debating societies.

And there was the Jewish Center, the fulcrum of Jewish life for immigrants in early-twentieth-century Cleveland, and, for that matter, in most urban Jewish communities of the day. Part synagogue, part lecture hall, and part gymnasium, the Jewish Center offered a smorgasbord of facilities that met a variety of religious, intellectual, and recreational needs. You could pray there on Shabbat. You could read in the library. You could hear prominent community members speak in the lecture hall. If you wanted to relax by shooting a few baskets, you could do that too. You could even go swimming at the Jewish Center, or, as it was known in the vernacular of the day, the "shul with a pool."

Lewis Friedman was one of the many Orthodox immigrants who made his home in Woodland. He'd come from Russia in 1890 and, with his skill as a tailor, found a small place in Cleveland's booming garment industry. Lewis also found a wife, Mayme Atlevonik, who had arrived in America with her Orthodox family in 1894 after fleeing the czar's oppression and forsaking a prosperous life in Russia.

The Friedmans began raising a family in their small home on Scovill Avenue, a few blocks west of Woodland Cemetery and north of Woodland Avenue. They would have six children: daughters Betty and Florence and sons Harry, Jerry, Sydney, and their fourth child overall, Benjamin, "son of the right hand" in colloquial Hebrew, born on March 18, 1905.

It's safe to say there was no toy football placed in the newborn child's crib for him to swat around. Lewis and Mayme knew almost nothing about football, and the hardworking tailor and equally hardworking young homemaker, like their fellow immigrants, had neither the time nor the inclination to learn. What they did know about football was that it was violent. The seemingly random slamming of bodies into the ground or into one another didn't resonate with their notions of appropriate leisure-time pursuits. Sometimes—too many times—the violence of the sport would take a life. Eighteen men died from football-related injuries the year Benjamin was born. Benny's parents and their contemporaries were in no rush to embrace such mayhem.

The same couldn't be said for the children of these immigrants. Cleveland's youngest Jews weren't set in the ways of the Russian shtetl as their parents were. They lacked their elders' built-in resistance to cultural change. In large part due to their enrollment in Cleveland's public schools, they gradually became exposed to a more secular world than their parents had ever known, and they wanted a place in it.

The growing popularity of football in turn-of-the-century Cleveland coincided with the explosive growth of the city's Jewish population. Local press coverage of the football-crazed Ivy League helped the sport gain traction in the city by the lake. Cleveland high schools began fielding teams. Cleveland schoolboys began reading about the teams' exploits in the sports sections of local papers. If you were a kid at East High or East Tech or Central High or the University School or other high schools comprising the Athletic Senate, a league organized by Cleveland school administrators, playing football had become a very cool thing to do.

For Jewish boys in Cleveland and other cities, football had an added element of cool. Playing football was a great way to fit in. It was also a perfect antidote to the anti-Semitism and vulgar stereotypes that accompanied the influx of European Jews into American cities. Jews were "the polar opposites of our pioneer breed," wrote E. A. Ross, a noted sociologist of the day. "Not only are they undersized and weak-muscled, but they also shun bodily activity and are extremely sensitive to pain." What better way to debunk such venomous stereotypes than to embrace the physicality and violence that football offered? No matter that the violence of the game was precisely what the parents of these boys found most offensive. Shooting a few baskets or taking a casual swim at the Jewish Center was fine as far as it went, but these boys needed more.

The football genie began to woo young Benjamin Friedman while he was in grammar school, just another neighborhood runt with grandiose dreams of all-American glory. For him and other inner city boys, because fields and

parks weren't always available, the road to the all-American team sometimes began, quite literally, on a road. On narrow side streets, in the cold
mist blowing in off Lake Erie just a mile or so uptown, the boys practiced
the moves they imagined had been used by such college football legends
as the University of Chicago's Walter Eckersall and Michigan Wolverine
Willie Heston. Depending on the particular street, sometimes the best interference, or blocking, for these future stars was a tree trunk sitting on a
lawn on the side of the road.

Poor facilities weren't the only obstacles these young Jewish kids had
to deal with. Unlike their gentile counterparts who were more or less free to
grab a football the moment school let out, Jewish boys spent the better part
of their afternoons in Hebrew school—*cheder* in Yiddish. Hebrew school provided the kids, who were quickly adapting to secular culture, with a little
religious balance. But many of them, Benny included, weren't particularly
interested in that, as he recalled years later: "I couldn't wait to get over
[Hebrew school] so that I could be free and play with the rest of the kids."
What active adolescent boy wouldn't prefer pickup football to cramming
into a small, unventilated room to learn Hebrew from a rabbi who tended
to discipline misbehaving students with the business end of a stick?

Benny's Hebrew school crucible ended mercifully, if somewhat painfully,
when he was twelve, thanks to a fellow student's prank. One day, as the
class stood up to recite prayers, a loud thud interrupted the proceedings.
The kid next to Benny had knocked his prayer book out of his hand. A
moment later there was the sound of another thud. It wasn't another book.
It was the sound of the teacher's stick smashing into Benny's back.

"Pick it up," the teacher barked at Benny.

"I didn't knock it down," Benny said.

Benny's reply didn't mollify the old rabbi. Once again his stick crashed
against the boy's back. "Pick it up," he again commanded.

Benny wouldn't give in, despite the two painful blows and the promise
of more to come.

"I won't pick it up," the boy cried. The old man rained down his stick
on Benny's back a third time.

The rabbi's brutality didn't persuade Benny to pick up the book. But the three welts that Lewis and Mayme saw on their son's back when he came home persuaded them to remove him from the Hebrew school.

If Benny had known that the rabbi's corporal punishment would have prematurely ended his formal religious education, he gladly would have taken another three cracks to the back. Now he had more time for after-school football.

He also had more time to pursue his other passion—bodybuilding. Becoming the next Jim Thorpe, the Olympic track and field champion and superstar footballer, wasn't enough of a dream for young Friedman. He also wanted to become the world's strongest man. The boy was a fanatic. He read magazines on bodybuilding techniques. He attended traveling strongman shows. He entered and won local strongman tournaments.

Mostly, though, Benny exercised indefatigably, crafting a unique regimen that included but went far beyond the usual barbells and dumbbells and medicine balls. "We had an iron brick that weighed forty-nine pounds and it was a trick to be able to pick that up by the side and turn it over and hang onto it and muscle it up," Benny said later. The other part of the "we" was a big Irishman named Sweeney, a janitor in Benny's grammar school. Sweeney worked with Benny in the school's cellar and taught Benny the trick.

Benny also learned to lift a heavy chair by the tip of a leg and toss the chair from hand to hand. Sometimes he'd lift a heavy broom from the tip of the handle. One particularly unorthodox move in Benny's repertoire involved his right hand and a one-armed desk. "I'd stretch my hand and stretch my hand till I could get it all the way across [the desk] so that I was able to make a 180-degree spread between my thumb and my little finger and have this big spread between my first finger and my thumb," Benny said later.

Benny liked these unusual exercises not only because they began to produce a strongman's power and muscles, but also because—maybe more so because—there was an intellectual component to them. He was a smart kid and liked figuring out the "tricks" involved, in thinking through the leverage and angles that were as necessary to the performance of the maneuvers as was brute strength.

When Benny entered Fairmount Junior High, he received some formal football instruction for the first time. There was no football team at Fairmount, but there was Howard Gehrke, a gym teacher who was happy to teach the boys certain fundamentals that in later years he'd display as a Harvard fullback. Gehrke gave Benny and his classmates their first lessons on how to fall on the football, how to tackle, and other fine points they'd given little or no thought to while playing in the street. (Less than a decade later, another Fairmount student named Jesse Owens would catch the eye of a Fairmount coach and receive his first instruction in his chosen sport.)

Gehrke's emphasis on fundamentals literally and figuratively took the game off of the street for Benny. The gym teacher gave Benny his first glimpse at the technique and strategy of the game. The boy began to understand that football, as violent and physical as it is, was also a thinking man's game, and he liked that. The game was far more intellectually stimulating than the challenges involved in becoming a strongman, which, aside from a creative exercise here and there, were limited to endless chin-ups and the repetitive hoisting of heavy weights. As high school beckoned, Benny abandoned his strongman ambitions to devote himself to football. He entered the ninth grade at East Tech High, and he entered a new world when he came out for coach Sam Willaman's football team.

Willaman's football pedigree was impressive. He'd been a star fullback for the mighty Ohio State Buckeyes. Now, as East Tech's coach, he played professionally in his spare time with the Canton Bulldogs alongside none other than Jim Thorpe. "Sad" Sam Willaman (so known for the naturally dour expression branded on his face) had built East Tech into the scourge of the Senate, and he had multiple championship trophies sitting in his office to prove it. And his 1919 group had enough talent to field two all-star teams.

It didn't take Benny long to realize that the East Tech football scene wasn't Mr. Gehrke's gym class. The second coming of Walter Eckersall and Pudge Heffelfinger and Jim Thorpe and Willie Heston would have to wait. Friedman would need to watch and learn, and he'd have to grow, too, because even with his strength he was still, as he would say, "just a little kid," about five foot six and not even 150 pounds. So Benny spent his ninth and tenth grade seasons on the scrub team, watching East Tech's talented varsity players, eagerly learning fundamentals, and building up his body.

With the wisdom of a dedicated apprentice and a bit more size and muscle, Benny, now a junior, reported for tryouts for East Tech's 1921 team. He was developing into a fast and agile player, clever with the ball, and strong, much stronger and tougher than his modest frame suggested. He was also good, unusually good, at passing the big round watermelon they called a football in those days. All the weight training and chair tossing and hand stretching he'd done had unwittingly paid off: Benny could wrap his hand around the ball, cock it behind his ear, and throw it, accurately. He didn't merely place the ball in his palm and heave it like most everyone else.

Unfortunately, Sam Willaman couldn't see past Benny's size, or, more to the point, lack of size. A year earlier, Willaman's undefeated team had steamrolled its way to the Cleveland city championship and into a national championship game against Washington state's Everett High School. The boys from Washington were bigger than the invaders from Ohio by about twenty pounds per player, and they asserted that advantage to bang out a bruising 16–7 victory. Willaman was determined to "get bigger" for the following season. The still-undersized Friedman wasn't what the coach had in mind.

"You're too small to play for us," he told Friedman. "You should transfer to Glenville High if you want to play football."

Willaman might have thought he was doing the youngster a favor by steering the young Jewish player to Glenville, a far weaker team than East Tech with a roster liberally sprinkled with Jewish players.

Sad Sam Willaman didn't realize he'd also just made the biggest mistake of his coaching life. Many years later, a high-school basketball coach in North Carolina would make a similar mistake, cutting a sophomore who was "too small" to play. The boy's name was Michael Jordan.

• • •

As 1920 approached, Woodland's Jews crept eastward, out of their increasingly dilapidated neighborhood and into the newer neighborhoods of Glenville and Mount Pleasant/Kinsman.

Kinsman, slightly south of Woodland, was an ethnically mixed area that grew into a center for working-class Jewish families. Glenville, almost exclusively Jewish, was literally and figuratively further uptown. Located just north and west of the prestigious schools and hospitals of the University Circle area, Glenville became home to a burgeoning Cleveland Jewish middle class. The Friedmans joined the exodus, moving "uptown" into the lower half of a two-family house on Ostend Avenue, just off 105th Street, Glenville's main thoroughfare and home to Glenville's massive Jewish Center.

A short cable-car ride up 105th Street from the Jewish Center, at the corner of Parkwood and Everton, were the ivy-swathed brick walls of Glenville High School. The school with a predominantly Jewish student body had a reputation for academic excellence and for training future artists and writers and musicians and Nobel Prize winners.

The school's football team also had a reputation, and it wasn't for excellence. The Glenville High Tarblooders weren't nearly as imposing as their bold black-and-red uniforms suggested. East Tech and Central High and the other powers of the Senate had routinely thrashed the Glenville boys in the years before Benny's arrival. With all-stars in the classroom and also-rans on the football field, Glenville was an ideal example for those looking to perpetuate the stereotype that Jews were talented academically but lacked heart athletically.

Benny was hopeful that his fortunes would improve with a change of scenery and Erling Theller, his new coach. Theller didn't quite have Sam Willaman's football pedigree. He'd played in college for tiny Oberlin, and he didn't spend his spare time playing pro ball with Jim Thorpe. But the man was plenty tough—he had displayed his grit in the trenches during World War I.

Benny got off to a good start with Theller; he made the varsity and started Glenville's first game in 1921. Maybe Glenville, less selective about its players than powerful East Tech, was Benny's best bet after all. But Theller benched Benny after the first game. Had Sam Willaman gotten to him? The coaches had run into each other at a dinner, and Willaman didn't mince words about Benny. "Bet you a dinner for all the high school coaches in Cleveland you will never make a football player out of Benny Friedman," Willaman told Theller.

It didn't look like Theller was going to try very hard to prove Willaman wrong. Benny's demotion didn't stop at the varsity bench; he soon was sent down to the scrub team. Not cutting it at East Tech, with its tradition of excellence, was one thing. Demotion in your junior year to the scrub team of a losing program was quite another. Benny needed something good to happen, quickly.

Then Theller took a leave of absence from the team with four games left to play. It seems the coach needed time off to attend to lingering effects from exposure to gas suffered during the war.

Theller's assistant took over and immediately installed Benny as half-back for the game at Wadsworth High, about twenty-five miles south of Cleveland. Benny almost single-handedly administered a 35–0 thrashing to the suburban school, which just couldn't cope with his passes or his tough, speedy running. Benny would later describe his coming-out party succinctly and with no hint of false modesty: "I had a field day; I ran all over the field scoring touchdowns."

Friedman did much the same in the next three games. Theller returned to coach the season finale and apologized to Benny for dropping him, explaining that his poor health had clouded his judgment. The coach was now so enthralled with Benny that he would have moved him to quarterback had it not been the Glenville senior quarterback's final high-school game, which the Tarbloodders won handily.

The 1921 Cleveland high-school football season ended with East Tech at the top of the Senate for the sixth straight year. But Benny's emergence and Glenville's season-ending streak gave the Tarblooders great hope for the 1922 season. Their optimism wasn't hurt any by the news that Sam

Willaman was leaving East Tech to become the head coach at Iowa State University. East Tech's loss of their longtime coach had to make every school in the Senate feel better about its chances in 1922.

By this time Benny had developed into an outstanding all-around athlete, starring for Glenville's baseball and basketball teams. If his election as captain of the football team was a foregone conclusion, his election as basketball captain was further testament to the young man's leadership skills. And if his outstanding academic record wasn't unique at Glenville, his striking physical appearance was another story. A shock of black hair framing the dark Semitic features of his face and a chiseled jaw set him apart. The popular Friedman was elected 1922 class president.

If Gilbert Patten had had a Jew in mind when he created Frank Merriwell, it could have been Benny.

· · ·

Which school was going to evict East Tech from the Senate penthouse in 1922? It wasn't expected to be Glenville. The Tarblooders were impressive in the second half of the 1921 season, but a few strong games weren't enough to overcome the perception created by their legacy of mediocrity. Their reputation didn't change much even after they won their first three games in 1922, with Friedman now starring at quarterback and his good friend, Saul Mielziner, anchoring the lines. After all, they still hadn't beaten the best of the Senate.

Their fourth game, against East Tech, would give them that chance. Considering East Tech's upset loss the previous week to a Lincoln team that Glenville had trounced 31–0, a Glenville victory over the defending champs wouldn't have been a shock. But the 31–0 slaughter that Benny orchestrated was.

It was only too bad for Benny that Sam Willaman wasn't on the East Tech sideline to witness the payback that oozed from the still-open wound Willaman had inflicted. Friedman humbled his old team with passes, embarrassed it with trick plays, and buried it with four touchdown runs that included jaunts of forty-two and thirty-five yards. The long scoring runs dazzled East Tech, but for pure devastation there was his shortest touchdown, a one-yard exclamation point to a ninety-nine-yard drive that saw the Tarblooders bully the six-time Senate champs from goal line to goal line. It was the drive that signified a change in the balance of power in Cleveland high-school football, a drive that just a year earlier would have been unthinkable. But Benny Friedman wasn't running the Glenville show a year earlier.

Benny's performance once and for all debunked Sam Willaman's gloomy forecast of his football future. It also erased any lingering doubts about the Tarblooders' bona fides. They were for real, undefeated and nearly unscored upon, and in first place in the Senate.

Powerful East High, Glenville's next foe, was cruising on a streak of five shutout victories following a disappointing opening game tie. Glenville hadn't defeated East High in fifteen contests dating back to 1908. And while they'd been a pushover for most teams during those years, the Tarblooders saved their worst form for East High—in those fifteen losses, they'd managed to score the grand total of nine points. First place in the Senate, as important as that was, seemed almost secondary to the opportunity for Glenville to purge this streak of futility.

Benny had, once and for all, knocked East Tech from its championship perch. Now his coreligionists in Glenville and football fanatics and the press throughout the Cleveland area would see if he could outplay East High.

The anticipation produced a stadium packed at kickoff with fifteen thousand fans. No other local football contest had ever attracted as large an audience. A healthy number of the spectators were Glenville residents, brimming with pride in their young quarterback who was proving that Jews could be lithe and agile and strong physically as well as intellectually. And if you were just a plain old Cleveland area sports fan on November 3, 1922, and you were at Dunn Field, you were where you were supposed to be.

Offense was in short supply as the game unfolded, no real surprise for two teams with a ream of shutouts on their resumes. The East High defense squelched Benny's running and passing forays most of the day and, as the fourth quarter began, Benny brought his mates to the line at the Glenville 34, needing something special to crack the scoreless stalemate. He found it, not in any single spectacular play, but in his steady, consistent running and his self-assured leadership that sent the message to everyone—to the fans, to his Glenville mates, and, most significantly, to the East High defense— that East High would be the first to give way. When Benny crossed the goal line on a one-yard smash, East High's shutout streak was finished. When he scampered forty yards for a second touchdown and a 13–0 Glenville lead with only minutes to play, East High's undefeated season, its supremacy over Glenville, and its shot at the Senate title were finished too.

Glenville coasted to victory in its final two regular season games, scoring ninety-one points with Benny driving them, and the transformation was complete. In one season Friedman had changed the school in the heart of the Jewish ghetto from Senate *schlep* to Senate *shtarker* (a "big shot" in Yiddish). Undefeated, untied, and nearly unscored upon, Benny and the Tarblooders also captured the overall city championship of Cleveland. Next for the kid who was too small to play for East Tech would be a game against longtime Illinois power Oak Park for the mythical national high-school championship.

Actually, several of these "national championship" games were played each year. They weren't officially sanctioned as such by any football governing body or association. The games evolved from a desire on the part of the best from given areas of the country to test themselves against the best from other areas. The teams themselves arranged the games. But even if somewhat informally organized, these contests were serious business. Red Grange, the sensational Illinois halfback, would readily attest to that. In his senior year at Wheaton (Illinois) High in 1921, he led his undefeated team into one of these games against legendary Toledo Scott High. "We went into the game scared to death," Grange wrote. It showed. Grange was knocked unconscious as he and his mates received a 38–0 trouncing.

Glenville faced a similar challenge against Oak Park. In the century's first decade, coach Bob Zuppke had built the suburban Chicago school into a football beast. Zuppke was now the head coach at the University of Illinois, having left Oak Park in 1913. But despite the loss of Zuppke's services, Oak Park was still a national force. Glenville was new to such rarified air and had every reason to be skittish. But they didn't play that way. Oak Park had won several of these championship games, but this day they weren't going to add Glenville to their list of the vanquished. The scoreboard at the end of the hard-fought game read Glenville 13, Oak Park 7. Benny had done what the great Red Grange of Wheaton couldn't do. The upstart school from the Jewish ghetto was a national champion.

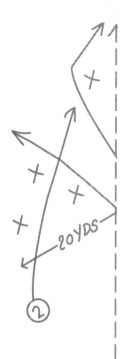

TWO

Michigan

In the first decade of the twentieth century, intercollegiate football wasn't much more than a half-step up from intramurals. Teams had part-time coaches and played part-time schedules, sometimes no more than four or five games a season. By the early 1920s, though, most schools had become more committed to football as an important part of the overall college experience. Schedules were expanded to ten or eleven games per season. Schools hired, on a full-time basis, colorful, innovative coaches who knew not only how to coach the game but also how to promote it with the fans and the press. Some of these mentors—such as Bob Zuppke at Illinois, Knute Rockne at Notre Dame, and Fielding Yost at Michigan—were in the process of crafting what would ultimately become legendary careers. Rivalries captivated the public in all parts of the country—Michigan-Illinois in the Western Conference, Harvard-Yale in the East, Vanderbilt-Tennessee in the South, and the intersectional battles between Notre Dame and Army, to name a few. Tension between proponents of eastern football, which generally featured strictly conservative offensive play, and western football, which offered a bit more offensive flare and, on rare occasion, a forward pass or two, stimulated debate as to which brand of football was superior and kept columnists' typewriters humming.

And college football had nothing to fear from its professional counterpart. The National Football League that Joe Carr and a few of his friends created in an automobile showroom in 1921 hadn't yet learned to crawl, let alone walk. Some former college players and even an occasional active college player would now and then submit to the lure of a quick fifty bucks or so and play in a pro game. But professional football was still largely a refuge for "just good-sized, rough customers" from wherever a given game happened to be played. Looking in the newspaper for the story of a pro game was a little like driving through a one-stoplight town—if you blinked while turning the pages, you'd miss the story, which was usually a blurb that contained not much more than the names of the teams and the final score. Meanwhile, most papers devoted multiple pages to the college game, and not just in postgame coverage. Stories and columns abounded all week leading up to any given Saturday—pieces about star players, coaches, a team's progress in practice that week, and just about anything else connected to the upcoming weekend action.

And so 1923 was a great time to be a college football player, or, like Benny Friedman, a high-school star about to become a college football player. But the sport hadn't reached that place without having endured some difficulty that threatened its vitality.

Around the turn of the century and into the first few years of the 1900s, ringers—professionals masquerading as students—populated many college football rosters. And some players who were actually enrolled as students had no qualifications for college beyond the ability to block and tackle. The absence of any recruiting or academic guidelines to speak of, or a regulatory body with jurisdiction over the sport, made it easy for coaches to enlist such players, and it was an open secret that even such prominent coaches as Fielding Yost, Amos Alonzo Stagg, and Walter Camp played along.

An even bigger problem had been the unmitigated brutality of the game. Originally loosely modeled after rugby, the sport was, in its worst light, not much different than legalized assault. The rules permitted, if not encouraged, multiple defenders to pile on a ball carrier, not merely to smash him to the ground but, once there, to grind him into it. Crippling injuries were practically routine, and deaths weren't unexpected.

Eventually, the frequency of the deaths and serious injuries to young men was such that even the president of the United States took notice. Teddy Roosevelt, the old Spanish-American War veteran and noted out-doorsman, was certainly no pantywaist, but when eighteen players died on America's football fields in 1905, he had had enough. The president blud-geoned the coaches and administrators of Harvard, Yale, Princeton, and many other leading schools into rule changes designed to eliminate the barbarism from the gridiron. Gang-tackling was banished. Also banned were mass offensive formations such as the flying wedge, where multiple offensive players linked together and overran opposing players like a tsunami while possessing, at most, an incidental interest in gaining yardage.

The rule change that had the potential to dilute football's ferocity most dramatically was the legalization of the forward pass.

John Heisman—he of the Heisman trophy—had been advocating the forward pass since the 1890s, arguing that it would open up the game and thus relieve it of some of its gratuitous violence. The prospect of a team gaining large chunks of yardage upon the mere fling of the ball down the field would also appeal to the fan looking for some relief from the hypnosis that a slogging running game could induce. Heisman's pleas had been viewed by Walter Camp, Glenn "Pop" Warner, and other stewards of the game as nothing short of heresy. These men weren't thrilled with crippling injuries and fatalities on the football field, but their philosophy was that football is a violent game and, well, stuff happens. There was no need to sissify the game with the forward pass. Such traditionalist thinking had warded off the change for years, but with Roosevelt getting involved, the time for change had finally arrived. The forward pass was legalized in 1906.

However, being legal and actually being used to any significant degree were two different things. Most teams approached the pass with the timidity of a child wading into a swimming pool for the first time without a float. Aside from an instinctive aversion to change, the apprehension was in large part due to the draconian conditions the football lawmakers had attached to the use of the pass. A passer had to be at least five yards behind the line of scrimmage when throwing the pass. This rule severely compromised a passer's ability to improvise. When a ballcarrier was knocked out of bounds, the ball was placed one step inside the sideline for the next play, eliminating an entire side of the field for passing. An incomplete pass resulted in an immediate change of possession. A receiver was not permitted to catch the ball while standing in the end zone; if he did, the play was a touchback rather than a touchdown. And then there was the ball itself, round and heavy and next to impossible to throw more than a few yards downfield with much accuracy.

There were a few adventurers, though. The first was Eddie Cochems, the coach of the St. Louis University eleven. Cochems had his boys work on pass plays in practice before the 1906 season, and the work paid dividends in an early season tussle with Carroll College. Mired in a scoreless tie and impatient with a running game that was running nowhere, Cochems ordered a player named Bradbury Robinson to attempt what has come to be acknowledged as football's first forward pass in competition. Walter Camp would have been pleased at the result had he seen the play— the pass fell incomplete, and Carroll College took possession. But Cochems didn't give up. He had Bradbury pass again the next time St. Louis had possession, and this time, his receiver, Jack Schneider, caught the ball and waltzed into the end zone untouched by Carroll players who, needless to say, hadn't practiced much pass defense. For the rest of the game, Bradbury kept passing, the receivers kept catching, and St. Louis had a 22–0 victory and a new offensive game plan.

Other coaches around the country, especially in the Midwest, gradually began experimenting with the forward pass. Fielding Yost at Michigan, Amos Alonzo Stagg at Chicago, and Bob Zuppke of Illinois were among the first to do so. Mostly they used it to keep opponents honest; Eddie

Cochems and his St. Louis eleven aside, rarely during the early part of the century's second decade did a team try to dominate a game through the air.

That it could be done, though, was illustrated on a November 1, 1913, afternoon in West Point, New York, when the University of Notre Dame's football team took the field against a bigger, stronger Army squad. Not that Notre Dame was any easy touch; the Irish came into the game undefeated, with recent wins over some of western college football's elite teams. Never before, though, had the Irish challenged an eastern power on its home turf. The dope on the game said the Cadets would push Notre Dame around with their powerful running attack and win going away.

The pundits got it half-right; the game was a one-sided affair. But they had the winner and loser all wrong. The Irish shocked the Army, 35–13, and the real story wasn't the score so much as it was the way the Irish had pulled off the upset. They hadn't pounded out a victory with the running game. Instead, they'd surprised the Cadets with the passes of quarterback Gus Dorais, who repeatedly found a skinny Notre Dame end named Knute Rockne downfield for huge chunks of yardage that ripped the heart out of the powerful Army machine.

The Notre Dame explosion didn't engender an immediate conversion of football's traditionalists. The running game continued its domination of team playbooks as the second decade of the twentieth century wore on and gave way to the 1920s. But resistance to the notion that the forward pass could play more than a token role in a team's offense was ever so slowly ebbing, particularly with western schools, which weren't quite as steeped in the traditions of the game as schools like Harvard, Yale, and Pennsylvania.

While college football rosters weren't flooded with Jewish players, the prospects for Jewish high-school footballers looking to play in college were fairly bright. There had already been more than ample precedent. In 1893 and 1894, the star of the Princeton University football team was a Jew by the name of Phil King. In 1903 and 1904, the University of Minnesota football team was led by Sigmund "Sig" Harris, a five-foot-five-inch dynamo who, when he wasn't punting, returning punts, and playing defensive safety, was earning two-time all-American honors while quarterbacking the

Gophers to a 27–0–1 record and a Big Ten title. Eastern power Syracuse University was anchored by Joseph Alexander, an all-American in 1917, 1918, and 1919. John Alexander, no relation to Joseph, was a mountain of a man whose roving defensive style at Rutgers was regarded as the template for the latter-day outside linebacker position. Brothers Ralph and Arnold Horween were all-Americans at Harvard, and Arnold was the Crimson's first Jewish captain.

The presence, if not prevalence, of star Jewish players at a variety of schools, particularly such blue-blood schools as Harvard and Princeton, was a reflection of the growing importance in college life of a strong foot-ball program. In the world at large, the world outside the gridiron, the spectre of anti-Semitism was growing ever more visible. The massive Jewish migration from Eastern Europe was creating resentment, and that resentment was increasingly manifesting itself in the form of well-worn anti-Semitic stereotypes. But within the cocoon of college football, that gilded place where heroes were made on Saturday afternoons and worshipped every other day of the week, a player's religion didn't seem to matter too much. College administrators, coaches, players, and fans wanted—needed—a thriving football program. If you were good enough, you could play, even if your name was Alexander or Horween or Saul Mielziner—or Benjamin Friedman.

Was Benny Friedman good enough? A number of college football coaches and scouts had seen him perform gridiron heroics for Glenville High. But because of his relatively modest size, his outstanding play didn't arouse the widespread interest it otherwise might have. Glenn Killinger, who'd just completed an all-American football career at Penn State, scouted Benny for his alma mater and liked what he saw. But Killinger ultimately passed on Friedman, declaring him too small to play. Ohio State, just a few hours from Benny's home in Cleveland, also passed on Benny.

The school that seemed to show the most interest in Friedman was Dartmouth. Several people at Glenville with New England connections helped arrange for Benny to receive a scholarship from the New Hampshire school—an *academic* scholarship. Dartmouth offered Benny three hundred dollars per year, conditioned upon his receiving straight-A grades. Should Benny receive lower grades, the amount of scholarship money would decrease proportionately. Recognizing that the scholarship alone wouldn't enable Benny to pay for tuition, the school also promised Friedman a job waiting tables in the campus dining hall. Playing football for the Big Green wasn't even part of the deal—that would be entirely up to Benny.

Friedman wasn't keen on attending school in the East, far from home. But Dartmouth appealed to his studious side, he needed the financial help the school was offering, and he didn't have many attractive alternatives—until, just before he committed to Dartmouth, one possibility materialized. "The Michigan alumni in Cleveland decided that maybe I was some kind of material," Benny said later. "They asked if I'd like to go up to Ann Arbor to see the school, and I said yes, and so I went up to Ann Arbor and I met Coach Yost."

Benny liked what he saw in Ann Arbor. A few of his friends from home were already students there. The school was much closer to home than Dartmouth. The football program was one of the best anywhere. And in a workout with four other prospects, he showed Fielding Yost that he was good enough to become a part of that program. Dartmouth couldn't measure up to a chance for Benny to play where Michigan greats of the past had played and, just maybe, to secure his own hallowed spot in Wolverine lore.

The catch for Benny, with his precarious financial position, was that Michigan didn't offer him a scholarship. They didn't even guarantee him a job, though they promised to help him find one. Benny was probably going to need to dip into his own very limited resources if he wanted to attend Michigan, and even that wouldn't be enough if he couldn't find work. It was a big risk for the young quarterback.

Benny decided to take it. He wanted to play football for Fielding Harris Yost.

. . .

One day in 1901, four years before Benny Friedman was born, Fielding Yost arrived by train in Ann Arbor, Michigan, a state that wouldn't have been considered friendly by Yost's father, a Confederate army veteran, or by his uncle, who had the misfortune of being on the wrong side of Pickett's charge at Gettysburg. Yost's outlook was a bit different. He hadn't come north to refight the Civil War. He'd come to coach football at the University of Michigan.

Yost was thirty years old the day he ambled off the train and greeted Michigan athletic director Charles Baird with his distinctive West Virginia drawl. Despite his relatively tender years, Yost had already compiled an impressive coaching record. Beginning in the Midwest at Ohio Wesleyan in 1897 and then moving on to Nebraska, Kansas, and Stanford, in that order, Yost compiled a record of 35–5–1. While Yost coached Stanford, he also found the time to coach the Stanford freshman team, San Jose Normal College, and two high-school teams to championships.

For all of Yost's success on the West Coast, he couldn't suppress his wanderlust. He wanted to return to midwestern football, and in 1899 he came east to interview for the head coaching job at the University of Illinois. Unfortunately, Illinois had already hired a coach, but Yost impressed the Illinois athletic director, who recommended him to Baird. The Michigan athletic director asked Yost to come back east to interview for the Wolverines job. Yost agreed, but before he got back on a train, he sent Baird a box of clippings and scrapbooks. The boy who grew up in a West Virginia log cabin wanted Baird to know just how good he was before he even set foot in Ann Arbor. Yost's advance work made the interview a formality; Fielding Harris Yost was hired to lead the Michigan Wolverines into the twentieth century.

Michigan wasn't new to football when Yost arrived; the Wolverines began playing a limited schedule in 1879 and had been playing a full schedule since 1890. And they'd been playing well—their record over the previous three seasons was 25–4–1. But one of those losses had been to bitter rival Chicago, a result that was unacceptable to Baird. In fact, Chicago had won three of the four contests with Michigan over the previous five years. Baird needed someone who could restore order to this rivalry.

Yost was just as keen on reversing Michigan's fortunes against Chicago, but his ambition was far greater than that. "Michigan isn't going to lose a game," the new coach proclaimed on the day he arrived in Ann Arbor, treating the locals to a preview of the Yost arrogance they would very shortly come to know, if not always love.

Fielding Yost had the colloquial manner and twang of a backwoodsman— "Michigan" wasn't in his lexicon; it was "Meeshegan"—that belied a resolute approach to coaching and a consuming love for the game of football. He wasted no time seizing control of the program and of the players, who quickly realized that football practice was a serious business designed to make performance in games as automatic as the next day's sunrise. "I remember Yost when he came to Michigan," said a 1903 Michigan graduate who wrote for the school newspaper. "I can see him coming to football practice in his first year. On that first day, he wore his black Lafayette sweater and his black felt hat. The players didn't know it, but it was a signal that the heat was on. Mr. Yost did not fool."

Mr. Yost didn't stop talking for very long, either, especially when the subject was football, which it usually was where he was concerned. Anyone foolish enough to try to cut his football musings short did so at their peril. "No, my father taught me never to interrupt," said Yost's friend and famed sportswriter Ring Lardner, when asked if he ever spoke to Yost. If the coach couldn't sufficiently explain his most recently concocted play with words, he'd enlist whatever physical props might be at hand. Chairs or silverware or bushes or acorns would become players, maneuvered into place by Yost to illustrate the formation of the play and the genius of its conception.

Even ingenious plays need good players to execute them, a fact Yost grasped firmly from the beginning of his tenure at Ann Arbor. He began by stocking his team with players he'd coached in California. One of these players was Willie Heston, a back Yost had coached at San Jose Normal.

Describing Heston as a back is a little like calling Caruso an opera singer or Einstein a scientist. The description is accurate but woefully incomplete. All anyone needed to do to understand that was to ask Yost. "Willie Heston never had an equal," the coach said. "I have seen thousands of players in all parts of the country, and with the exception of Ted Coy of Yale, I have seen all the players who stand out among the great of all time. Jim Thorpe is the second greatest player I ever saw."

Heston was big for his day at six feet, 190 pounds, and he wasn't bashful about running tacklers into the ground. His arsenal also included a shiftiness and balance uncommon for a relatively big man. The gift that really created the gulf between Heston and defenders who flailed after him, though, was his speed and his ability to reach top speed in a blur. Archie Hahn, a Michigan track star who won multiple Olympic sprinting medals, couldn't stay with Heston at forty yards and needed every bit of his Olympic champion form to run him down beyond that distance. What chance, then, did a mere football defender have against such a burst?

Albion College was the first opponent to experience Yost and his meteor from the coast. In an apparently deliberately understated performance by Heston—one report noted that the player "did not attempt to star"—Michigan humbled Albion, 50–0.

Albion was no football juggernaut and the score logically could have been dismissed as an aberration. Surely, the true barometer for the new Wolverines' coach and Heston would be upcoming contests against bruisers such as Iowa, Case, Ohio State, and Northwestern. Some of these teams did offer resistance, but by the end of the Wolverines' undefeated season, the Albion score proved to be the template—Michigan defeated their eleven opponents, including Yost's former Stanford team in a postseason game that would later be recognized as the first Rose Bowl, by a combined score of 550–0—an average margin of victory of 50–0!

In the Stanford game, Yost demonstrated that despite his reputation for sportsmanship, he wasn't above stepping on an opponent's throat when he had the chance. At halftime, the new Stanford coach nearly begged Yost to

call off the rest of the game to spare his badly outclassed team further embarrassment. "No sirree," Yost said, laughing, "get on with it."

No one on earth relished a Michigan romp as much as Yost, and over
his first five years as the Wolverines' coach—four of which featured the services of Heston—he did a lot of relishing. The Wolverines were an unfathomable 55–1–1 over that five-year stretch, compiling an even more
unfathomable point differential of 2,821 to 42. Chicago was the victim in
four of those victories, by a combined score of 93–12. Given the bludgeoning Yost and his Wolverines had administered to Chicago and everyone else for five years, Michigan supporters could forgive the coach for
the lone blemish on Michigan's complexion—a 2–0 loss to Chicago in a
1905 season-ending stunner.

Any coach producing such a staggering success would have found it
difficult to refrain from at least some boastfulness. For Yost, false modesty
was never a consideration. It wasn't in his nature. He reveled in his success
and in the success of his team. Part cheerleader, part public relations man,
he'd often parade through the streets of Ann Arbor, in and out of stores and
restaurants, lauding his players and Michigan football to anyone who'd lis-
ten, which was just about everyone. And for anyone with the temerity, or
ignorance, to blaspheme that a particular opponent might, just might, actually defeat Michigan on the gridiron, the man from West Virginia offered a stock dismissal. "Who are they," Yost would posit with a laugh,
"that they should beat a Meeshegan team?" It's unlikely that anyone ever
answered the question, and if they did, Yost wouldn't have hung around
long enough to hear it.

Despite his arrogance and boastfulness, even boorishness, Yost was tolerated, indeed revered, in Ann Arbor. Winning fifty-five of fifty-seven games
over a five-year period will tend to ingratiate a coach to his constituents.

But it was more than the winning. There was a purity about the man,
manifested in a variety of ways, that overwhelmed the mischief, even rendered it appealing. Yost arrived on the coaching scene at a time when the
normal physicality of the game was supplemented by hooligans disguised as
players who had little regard for the rules or the safety of their opponents (or

themselves). Yost wouldn't tolerate such mayhem from his charges. He encouraged—demanded—that his boys play hard but clean. Michigan's record demonstrated that clean football was not an oxymoron for winning football, and it was no accident that the Wolverines avoided the tragic deaths and, for the most part, the serious injuries that were plaguing college football.

Just as Yost insisted that his boys play clean on the field, he demanded that they live clean away from the field. The coach didn't drink or smoke or carouse, and neither did his players. "Some people can drink, and it doesn't hurt them," Yost once said. "But it doesn't do them any good. And ye want to be good, don't ye?" The same thinking could have been applied to swearing—there wasn't any of that going on either, at least not within earshot of the coach.

And so, with a program that featured hard-hitting but clean players who stayed healthy and out of trouble on and off the field and who won nearly every game they played, Michigan supporters could endure Yost's ego. And Yost, who came to Michigan with a one-year contract and no preconceived notions about making a career out of coaching the Wolverines, felt quite comfortable in Ann Arbor.

• • •

Michigan's 12–1 season in 1905, the year after Willie Heston graduated, proved that Yost could win even without the great back. It also was the end of an era, the era of Yost's "point-a-minute" teams, so called because their offensive output very nearly averaged one point for every minute played. Yost's teams over the next seventeen seasons leading up to Benny Friedman's arrival in Ann Arbor did not dominate at that level, but they did keep on winning. The Wolverines compiled a record of 88–26–9 over that span, during which they had but one losing season, a 3–4 campaign in 1919.

How did Yost do it? He wasn't thought of as a master football tactician or a pioneering innovator in the mold of Rockne or Zuppke or Stagg or other contemporaries, though he knew the game as well as or better than all of those superb coaches. His prescription for success was simple: play for field position, wait for the opponent's mistake, and capitalize on it when it comes. "Cynics call our method the 'punt, pass, and prayer system,' but we generally have the last laugh," Yost said. It was a system that required a good punter, team discipline, and solid fundamentals—"No good blocker and tackler was ever kept off a football team," Yost liked to say—that could be developed and honed only with slavish dedication to practice, where no matter how quick to the task his players were, they were never quick enough. "Ye think we got all day?" he'd bark at his players. "Hurry up! Hurry up! Hurry Up!" That command, issued far too many times to count, became Yost's nickname.

. . .

When Benny arrived at Michigan, he and about two hundred other freshmen reported to Edwin Mather, the freshman coach. Frosh football at Michigan was informal, in the sense that the team didn't play against other schools. Their season, consisting of workouts and occasional scrimmages against the varsity, was in essence an audition for an invitation to try out for the varsity as sophomores. Generally, only a select few received those invitations, and Benny's impressive workout for Yost on his recruiting visit didn't guarantee one. Like each and every other freshman with dreams of stardom, he was going to have to earn it.

Benny was also going to have to earn his tuition if he wanted to stay in school. He'd come to Ann Arbor with savings of $270, an amount that was immediately trimmed in half when he paid his $135 freshman year tuition. The football staff found him a job as a busboy in the student union cafeteria. After two days of handling dirty dishes, Benny chucked his apron and went looking for other employment. In short order he found not one but two jobs. For the princely sum of eight dollars per week, he became the new evening ticket-taker at an Ann Arbor movie theater; and for forty cents an hour, he worked in between classes at a local bookstore part-time.

Benny's routine was set: classes, work, more classes, football practice, studying, work at night, study some more, a few hours sleep. The heavy load wore on him. His social life was all but nonexistent. Even with his two jobs, he was just barely managing financially. On the field, he had impressed Mather and by season's end had inched toward the top of the fresh-man group. But he couldn't be sure if he'd done enough to secure a varsity tryout invitation for his sophomore year. The big club had just completed an 8–0 season that included a share of the Big Ten title with Illinois. Competition for promotion to the varsity was sure to be fierce. Benny seriously wondered if Michigan had been the right choice for him.

Saul Mielziner, Benny's Glenville teammate and closest high-school friend, was having a far easier time of it at Carnegie Tech in Pittsburgh. The big tackle was receiving room, board, and tuition—a full football scholarship. Carnegie was even throwing in seventy-five bucks a month for expenses. All Mielziner had to do was play football. No washing dishes, no taking tickets, no shelving books. Plenty of time to study and sleep. When Mielziner wired Benny, telling him he could get him the same deal if he transferred to Carnegie, Benny's desire to become a Michigan football legend suddenly seemed less compelling.

Confused and conflicted, Benny approached Yost's assistant coach, George Little, hoping to talk things out. He explained his difficulties and mentioned the arrangement that seemed to be available for him at Carnegie Tech. According to Friedman, if he was looking for some guidance and a sympathetic ear, he didn't get it from his coach.

"Well, Friedman," Little said, "if you think you're getting a dirty deal, why don't you leave?"

Benny was stunned. Little's coarseness seemed intended to give him the final nudge toward the door out of Ann Arbor. Friedman wired his parents in Cleveland and Mielziner in Pittsburgh, telling them he'd be heading there looking to enroll at Carnegie. He thanked the people at the bookstore, told his landlady he was leaving, and went to work for one last night at the theater.

At the conclusion of that evening's film, *Little Old New York*, Benny locked up and walked out onto State Street. George Little was waiting for him. "Do you mind if I walk with you?" the coach asked. The gruffness of their earlier conversation was gone. Little was all smiles as he invited Benny to join him for a waffle in the student union.

Coach and player sat down, munched on waffles, engaged in some small talk, and then Benny got down to the heart of the matter.

"All I want to do is talk to you about whether or not I should stay or leave because I could get this scholarship at Carnegie Tech," he told the coach.

"You think you'd like an engineering degree?"

"I don't know," Benny replied.

Little explored Friedman's equivocation. "Well, do you think you're qualified for it? Is there a desire for it?"

"No, not really," Benny said.

"Well then," Little said, "what are you thinking about it for?"

The coach's questions had revealed a dimension to Benny's idea of transferring that he hadn't thought through.

"You got any other trouble?" Little continued.

"You know, I'm one step ahead of the sheriff," Benny said. "I need a hundred dollars."

"Well, that's not difficult," Little said.

Just one day earlier, it seemed as if Little would have been happy to personally escort Friedman to the train station and pay for his ticket out of Ann Arbor. Benny found Little's apparent change of heart bizarre. Maybe Fielding Yost had talked some sense into Little following the assistant coach's earlier chat with Benny. In any case, with Little's softer side on display, Benny was convinced to stay at Michigan, at least for the spring semester.

The $100 that Little arranged for Benny relieved some of the financial pressure, but otherwise the grind of the fall carried over into the spring. Benny worked, studied, worked, and studied some more. When football season ended, he didn't get a break in his schedule because he couldn't resist the lure of freshman basketball. A good night's sleep was a luxury rarely enjoyed. As the spring semester drew to a close, he was more than ready to go home to Cleveland for the summer. Thanks to his discipline and diligence, he was able to take a slate of good grades home with him.

And Benny had one other item of interest in his pocket as he boarded the train for Cleveland—an invitation to try out in the fall for the University of Michigan's varsity football team.

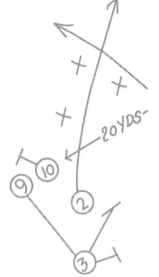

THREE

Grange Opens the Door

B ob Zuppke had Harold "Red" Grange on his team, and in 1924 that fact would have sent most football coaches home for the summer with nothing on their minds but their favorite off-season pursuit. There shouldn't have been much football to worry about, not with the most spectacular ball carrier ever to streak down a sideline in your back pocket.

Zuppke, though, was a different breed. Twenty Red Granges wouldn't have put the Illinois coach's mind at ease that summer. For Zuppke, those lazy days of summer were just days to be endured until the arrival of October 18 and, with it, the arrival in Champaign of the Michigan Wolverines.

Zuppke had always taken any encounter with Michigan and Fielding Yost very personally. But this game promised to elevate the intensity of the rivalry to new heights. The Wolverines and the Illini had shared the 1923 Western Conference championship with identical 5–0 records. Neither team was pleased about being the other's co-champion. The fact that they hadn't played each other in '23 added more spice to the upcoming collision.

So Bob Zuppke, an accomplished and passionate painter, didn't go home to paint his summer away. He went home to worry about football.

He went home to worry about Michigan. And just to make sure his players spent their summers worrying, too, Zuppke inundated them with letters that all but threatened their future firstborn children if the Wolverines should defeat Illinois in October. Zup took particular care to highlight Yost's forecasts of the coming annihilation of Grange, and the football lesson the Illini were about to receive.

Grange and his teammates might have been amused by the letters if they didn't know their coach as well as they did. They knew his fervor was genuine. Whatever else was to happen in Western Conference football in 1924, Bob Zuppke was making sure of one thing—every one of his players would be ready for Michigan on October 18.

One thing Zuppke wouldn't get a chance to do in 1924, at least not on the coaching level, would be to defeat Fielding Yost. When Yost walked off his beloved Ferry Field turf following the Wolverines' 1923 season-ending 10–0 defeat of Minnesota, he carried the scars of nearly twenty-three years at the pinnacle of college football coaching. His doctors had told him he'd had enough, and to the great surprise of nearly everyone who knew the tough old man from the West Virginia hills, Yost relented. That win over Minnesota was to be Yost's last. Yost would now focus on his duties as Michigan's athletic director, a position he had held since 1921, and act in an "advisory capacity" to George Little, his former assistant who would guide Michigan's football fortunes in 1924 as head coach.

Michigan had tried to include Grange in those fortunes. When Red was in high school, the Wolverines, appealing to his real passion, track and field, had sent former Wolverine track star Carl Johnson to Wheaton, Illinois to woo the redheaded sprinter. Johnson might have got him were it not for Red's concern that he couldn't afford to attend a school outside Illinois.

Enter Bob Zuppke. The University of Illinois coach met with Red in his senior year at Wheaton High while Red was competing in the Illinois state track championships, held, conveniently for Zuppke, in Champaign. Zuppke knew all about Red's spectacular high-school football career. He told Red that if he decided to attend Illinois, he'd "stand a good chance of making our football team." Coming from Zuppke, who rarely got carried away over any player, this amounted to lavish praise. Grange appreciated the coach's endorsement, but it was the affordable tuition offered by his home state university that most attracted Red to Illinois.

Getting Grange to Champaign was only the first half of the equation for Zuppke. Still remaining was the chore of persuading him to play football there. Red was a bit intimidated by the Illinois freshman hotshots from the big Chicago high schools, and he was concerned that his six-foot, 170-pound frame was too fragile to handle the punishment of Western Conference football. He figured the speed and moves that had confounded high-school defenders simply wouldn't cut it with the big boys.

It took all of one freshman-varsity scrimmage at the start of the 1922 season for Red to see that he'd figured wrong. He took back a punt sixty-five yards for a touchdown, leaving Zuppke's crack defenders strewn about the field in exhausted bewilderment. Red scored a second touchdown that day for good measure. The only bad news for Zuppke was that he would have to wait a year before he could spring the redhead on the Yosts of the world.

The University of Nebraska painfully discovered in the first game of the 1923 season that for Zuppke, it was worth the wait. Grange shredded the powerful Cornhusker defense for three touchdowns, one on a long punt return, to lead the Illini to victory. Nebraska may have derived some consolation in the weeks that followed, because Grange worked over the Big Ten's best in similar fashion. Twelve touchdowns, a nation's-best 1,260 yards, and an unbeaten Illinois season later, the spectacular sophomore was a first-team all-American—except in the mind of the *Michigan Daily*; the rivalry between Michigan and Illinois seemed to get the best of the Michigan student newspaper's editors, who relegated Grange to their second team.

The accolades and the numbers, impressive as they were, weren't the real story behind Grange. The real story was his style. It was the way he did it—a way that, frankly, hadn't been seen before. Others had been fast. Others had been shifty. Others had the strength to plunge the line. No other—save for Willie Heston, if you were asking Fielding Yost—had ever combined all these things into one elegant, sinewy package. And no other had ever made it look so easy. "Grange runs as Nurmi runs and Jack Dempsey moves, with almost no effort, as a shadow flits and drifts and darts," famed sportswriter Grantland Rice wrote. Red had a unique crossover step that enabled him to suddenly change direction to avoid a hit. His uncanny ability to change speeds would first lull a defender to sleep, then leave the defender a bird's-eye view of his heels after he'd turned on the jets. His most powerful tool, though, might have been his extraordinary vision.

Grange's breathtaking ability and genuine modesty were an irresistible combination. At the dawn of the 1924 season, barely twenty-one years old, he was speeding toward folk-hero status. He was certainly the most famous player Zuppke had yet coached. Ernest Hemingway, who had played for Zuppke at Oak Park a decade earlier, and who in 1924 was a young man floundering around Europe, would one day match if not surpass Grange's fame (though not as a footballer).

Thanks to the vagaries of the 1923 schedule, Michigan had avoided the Grange onslaught. The Wolverines plowed through their own schedule undefeated, earning a share of the Big Ten title with Illinois. What would have happened had the two teams played each other? Not surprisingly, Zuppke and Yost had a difference of opinion. Zup thought the Wolverines should have been offering daily thanks to the football gods for enabling them to avoid his explosive redhead. Yost thought Grange ought to have been thankful that he was spared a Wolverines throttling. Yost was only sorry that come October 18, 1924, he'd be sitting in the stands rather than prowling the Michigan sideline as his Wolverines went about dismantling Red Grange and Illinois.

• • •

Before they'd get their hands on each other, the 1923 co-champs had two games to play to start the 1924 season.

First up for Illinois was none other than Nebraska, the unwitting victims of Red Grange's coming-out party a season earlier. This time the

Cornhuskers were ready and waiting for Red. The Illini should have known Nebraska would be aching for the rematch and should have been ready too. But Zup had dulled their senses with his incessant letters and obsession with Michigan. Nebraska repeatedly smothered Grange behind the line. Red rescued the Illini with a rare touchdown pass, and, with an Earl Britton field goal, the Illini barely managed a 9–6 victory. The unexpected struggle against Nebraska had to be disconcerting to the Illini, especially since the Wolverines were enjoying a 55–0 party at Miami's expense in Ann Arbor that same afternoon.

Unfortunately for Benny, he didn't have an invitation to that party. He had capitalized on his opportunity to try out for the varsity and had made the team, but for some reason, he was so far down on George Little's depth chart that, as Benny would later say, the coach couldn't see him with a telescope. Whatever good will Little had shown toward Benny the previous fall when he'd convinced Benny to stay at Michigan had evaporated. One day in practice, when line coach Tad Weiman had asked Little for two players to join the linemen in a blocking drill, Little motioned toward Benny and Henry Ferenz—both of whom were clearly within earshot—and told Weiman to "take those two dummies." At first, the Wolverine linemen pounded the smaller and basically uninitiated Friedman and Ferenz. But before too long, Benny and Henry figured things out and the linemen were the ones taking the beating. By the end of Benny's five-day stint with the linemen, they were happy to see him leave.

In fact, Benny was about to leave the team altogether. "I'm quitting," Benny told Weiman. "The coach can't see me for dust and there's no point in my going on." Weiman spoke to Benny about previous Michigan players who had endured time on the bench and then seized the opportunity to play when it arose. Benny calmed down and stayed on the team, returning to his reserved seat deep on George Little's bench, from which he couldn't escape even for a few minutes of playing time at the end of Michigan's 55–0 rout of Miami.

. . .

Butler, Illinois's next opponent following their opening struggle with Nebraska, didn't promise to be a picnic either. Two years earlier the Bulldogs had surprised the Illini in a major upset. The tough squad from Indiana didn't figure to be intimidated by Illinois. Unfortunately for Butler, though, they were catching Illinois right off the Nebraska scare. With a very focused Zuppke motivating them, the Illini got back on track with a 40–10 thumping of the Bulldogs. Grange, with improved support from his blockers, returned from his one-game sabbatical from stardom the week before and dazzled the well-meaning but overmatched Butler eleven.

If the tentative performance against Nebraska had cast any doubts on Illinois's readiness for Michigan, the demolition of Butler erased them. It also caught the attention of one particularly interested spectator in the stands that day. For all his bluster about the destruction that awaited Illinois, Fielding Yost knew that Grange presented a clear and present danger, clear and present enough to merit a rare personal scouting visit. In fact, the Butler game was Yost's second Grange reconnaissance mission; he'd also scrutinized Red against Nebraska the previous week. Yost may have retired as the Wolverines' coach, but he remained the overseer of Michigan football.

While Yost was surveilling Grange, the Wolverines were unexpectedly laboring against a very willing Michigan A&G in East Lansing. Maybe the Wolverines were letting down a bit following their romp the week before. Maybe the ferociously hot fall afternoon was slowing them down. For whatever reason, the offense that scored at will against Miami a week earlier could do nothing right.

Benny watched his team from the bench, desperate for a chance to jump-start his struggling mates. Again, Little ignored him. The Wolverines were lucky to avert disaster, squeaking by with a 7–0 victory on a last-minute touchdown.

Benny's relationship with Little, already frayed, took another bad turn at the Wolverines' team dinner that night at their hotel. Bob Brown, Michigan's star center, was seated across from Benny at the U-shaped dinner table. Brown, still unwinding from the tough battle on the field, hadn't had much of an appetite through most of the dinner but finally asked the waitress for some ice cream. "My, I must have put down a half-dozen portions here," the waitress said, apparently thinking that Brown had already had his fill.

Unbeknownst to Benny, who was minding his business across from Brown, Little was about to drag him into the matter.

"Friedman," Little bellowed across the room, "why can't you behave like a gentleman?"

"Why?" Benny said, looking at Little.

"You had a good seat on the sideline, didn't you? You didn't play."

"No."

"Why don't you see that the varsity get his food?"

Benny was seeing red now.

"I didn't take any of his food."

It was getting harder and harder for Benny to accept Tad Weiman's advice that he should wait his turn.

· · ·

The worlds of college football generally and the worlds of Michigan and Illinois football in particular breathed a major sigh of relief. The rivals had given their supporters a couple of major scares, but they each emerged from their first two games unscathed. Now nothing lay in their way, except each other.

Fielding Yost was an intelligent and sophisticated man, but he was nothing if not colloquial. The coach from the West Virginia hills loved malapropisms and odd-sounding expressions that would make today's Yogi Berra fans chuckle. So it was at the outset of Michigan's preparations for Illinois. The mission, Yost said, was "to beat Illinoism." No one, least of all Yost's players, had to be told that "Illinoism" was a synonym for Red Grange. Michigan spent nearly the entire week in closed practices drilling to halt the redhead's rampage through western football. "Every time Grange takes the ball, there will be eleven hard, clean tackling Michigan men headed for him at the same time," Yost declared. "We have made special preparation for Grange." Those special preparations included Yost himself donning practice garb and personally supervising the Wolverines' workouts—not exactly typical conduct for a retired coach. But with the battle against Grange and Zuppke and Illinois approaching, Yost was finding it difficult to stay retired. And nobody—not George Little or anybody else—was about to get in the Michigan legend's way.

Yost's determination to stop Red approached obsessive levels as game day neared. The *Daily Illini,* commenting on reports of Yost's warnings to his players to beware Grange, couldn't resist taking a shot at the fixated coach for stating the obvious. "You can't beat a coach like that," chirped the paper in its sarcastic "Bunking the Line" section.

Still, Grange or no Grange, Michigan rooters were confident. The Wolverines hadn't lost in twenty-two games dating back to a 1922 defeat by Ohio State. In those twenty-two games, most played against first-rate teams, the Ann Arbor boys had yielded only four touchdowns. One of the Wolverines' 1922 victims was Illinois. Grange and his freshman teammates watched that day as the Wolverines outclassed the Zuppkemen, 24–0.

The 1923 schedule hadn't even afforded Illinois the chance to square things. Two years would have been a long time for Zuppke to wait for a rematch under any circumstances. The fact that he was waiting to unleash fury in the person of Red Grange made the wait all the more difficult. With his galloping redheaded time bomb, Zup thought, things would be different.

Still, the "Illinoism" orchestrator was taking no chances. He began the week of practice with strategy sessions and light workouts. By week's end, he was putting the Illini through hard-hitting scrimmages, even as the Wolverines were avoiding scrimmages to reduce the risk of injury. In a long and distinguished career at Illinois, Zuppke had coached many excellent players in many important games. But he'd never coached a player as spectacular as Red Grange, nor had he ever coached in a game where the stakes were this high. This game was going to be Bob Zuppke's perfect storm. If the boys got banged up a little getting ready for it, so be it.

Benny Friedman's perfect storm, however, was still nowhere in sight. The only thing awaiting him in Champaign was his customary seat on the bench, and he'd barely managed that—Benny was the last Wolverine named for the trip to Champaign. George Little didn't seem to care about the sharp forward passes Benny had been throwing in practice, or the speed and strength he'd shown running with the football, or his sure tackling and pass defending. It was eating Benny up—here was maybe the biggest game in Western Conference history, featuring the most acclaimed player in college football, and he'd be no closer to the action than the Michigan water boys. Every bone in his body ached to play. He wanted Illinois. He wanted Red Grange. But with Little calling the shots, the Jewish quarterback was likely to have more action attending synagogue in Champaign on Saturday than he'd get during the football game.

As Benny stared out the window of the train taking the Wolverines to Champaign, the glory days at Glenville High seemed like a century away.

. . .

Not everyone in Michigan had football on their minds on October 18, 1924. On this autumn Saturday, hundreds of white-robed Ku Klux Klansmen marched through the downtown streets, flags waving, marching-band horns blaring, crosses jutting above the crowd on their way to a burning at the city's fairgrounds. The city wasn't in Alabama or Mississippi or some other southern venue. The city was Owosso, Michigan, barely an hour north of Ann Arbor, and the parade was a stark reminder that even in the North the Klan had a thriving market for its racist, anti-Semitic, anti-Catholic hate-mongering.

Anti-Catholic sentiment, though not Klan-related, was indirectly responsible for one of the other college football plums to be played that day. In the first decade of the twentieth century, many top midwestern football teams refused to play Notre Dame, the country's most prominent Catholic university. Notre Dame converted this narrow-mindedness into a blessing; forced to look outside the region for top competition, the school became the first from the Midwest to develop a national schedule that included eastern and western powers. By 1924, Notre Dame was routinely playing such schools as Stanford, Princeton, and Georgia Tech, while other midwestern powers rarely ventured outside the region.

The Ramblers' (Notre Dame wasn't widely known as the "Fighting Irish" until the late 1920s) most notable inter-regional foe was the Army. Their East-West rivalry had developed into one of the game's most intense since its first installment in 1913. West Point had been the site of the game each year until 1923, when its rising popularity forced it to nearby New York City and a stadium that could accommodate a larger audience. At roughly the same time that Michigan and Illinois would commence hostilities in Champaign, the Army and Notre Dame would clash at the Polo Grounds, where coach Knute Rockne's invading backfield of Harry Stuhldreher, Don Miller, Elmer Layden, and "Sleepy" Jim Crowley would be making their first appearance.

But that day, certainly in the Midwest, Illinois-Michigan was the big story. The game would be played in Champaign's new Memorial Stadium, amidst lavish dedication ceremonies and the pomp and circumstance of Illinois homecoming. The stadium would be jammed with fans streaming into Champaign from every direction by every means available, including several thousand Wolverines supporters making the trip from Ann Arbor by train. Last-minute ticket seekers couldn't have been pleased with the *Daily Illini*'s declaration: "There is absolutely no hope for these late applicants."

The lucky ones with tickets were greeted that day by an Indian summer sun that enveloped the gleaming new stadium. If the warm weather promised the fans a comfortable day for spectating, it also promised to make the players warmer than they'd care to be. This unwelcome burst of heat had Zuppke's mind churning as he paced nervously in the locker room during pregame festivities.

"Anything in the rule book that says we can't remove our stockings?" Zup asked an assistant, who promptly scurried for the rulebook to search for an answer.

After months of preparation for the biggest game of their lives, Zup's players weren't expecting to hear him talking about stockings just minutes before kickoff. They were even more surprised at Zup's directive when his assistant replied that the rules didn't require stockings.

"Okay, fellas, let's take off the stockings," Zuppke said. "It's hot out there and without those heavy socks, you'll feel a lot fresher and cooler."

Now the Illini thought their coach had finally gone over the edge. Playing a football game without stockings would leave a player's legs scraped to the bone. The players initially resisted their commander's order, but the mutiny lasted only a moment; one loud reprise of the order from Zuppke initiated the ruffling sound of stockings peeling off legs.

Then Zuppke turned his attention to a penny lying on the locker room floor. Two years earlier Zuppke had found a coin on the locker room floor as his players readied to battle Michigan. He'd pocketed that coin for good luck, then promptly led his boys out for a 22–0 drubbing that, naturally, Zuppke attributed to the malevolent coin. Seeing another coin on the floor moments before a game against Michigan, Zuppke was sure that Yost had planted it. He angrily flung the coin out the window and dispatched the Illini to the field.

The bare-legged Illini charged from the locker room and immediately felt far more comfortable than they had during warm-ups. Yost and Little stared at their opponents' bare legs. The Michigan brain trust would have thought it odd to see any team take the field without stockings. When they saw Bob Zuppke's team do it, they were convinced a scheme was afoot. They must have greased their legs to make low tackling difficult if not impossible.

After Yost and Little protested loudly, it was agreed that the Wolverines' captain, Herb Steger, would inspect the Illinois players' legs to see if Yost's suspicions were warranted. To what had to have been Steger's everlasting embarrassment, he knelt down and rubbed his hands on the greaseless legs of each Illinois player, in full view of thousands of howling Illinois fans.

Finally—stockings removed, legs checked for grease, and evil penny hurled away—captains Steger of Michigan and Rokusek of the Illini walked to midfield for the coin toss. The stadium was overflowing with nearly seventy thousand spectators—the largest audience ever to witness a game in the state of Illinois. Fielding Yost and his wife strode from the locker room to their seats in the stands. Yost had done what he could to prepare the Wolverines to vanquish "Illinoism"; tough as it might be to watch this game as a spectator, he'd follow doctor's orders and leave the heat of the sideline to Little.

Benny made his way to the Wolverines' bench and prepared to endure another excruciating few hours of inactivity. He thought about the conversation he'd had with assistant coach Tad Weiman the night before, when Weiman had asked if he knew the pass plays.

"Yes, I know 'em," Benny had said, not knowing why Weiman would even care to ask. As far as Benny knew, the only place he'd ever get to throw a pass for Michigan would be at practice.

"Well," Weiman had said, "we may need you."

Benny didn't see how that could be, not with George Little commanding the team. Once again he'd sit on the avalanche of firepower he knew he had in his right arm. He'd think about being at Dartmouth or just about anywhere else where he'd have a chance to play. He probably didn't notice the coin toss and its result: Michigan won the toss and elected to kick off.

Herb Steger strode to the forty-yard line with the privilege of kicking off perhaps the most eagerly awaited game in college football history. In his entire career, first at high-school powerhouse Oak Park (where Bob Zuppke once coached) and then in his more than three years at Michigan, this fine player had never lost a game. At the other end of the field, Red Grange waited at the goal line, midway between the goal posts, exactly where the Wolverines expected him to line up. Steger had explicit instructions to kick the ball toward the corner of the field to Grange's left, as far away from Grange as possible.

With the south goal and a slight wind at his back, Steger's toe crashed into the ball, sending it soaring high and straight down the middle of the field. Straight toward a surprised Red Grange, who thought the Wolverines would kick the ball to anyone but him. Had Steger forgotten his instructions? Had he tried to kick the ball to the corner and simply flubbed the kick? Or had his pride compelled him to disregard orders and kick the ball to Grange so that he and his mates could confront the challenge straight away?

Red moved into the ball at the five-yard line and bolted straight upfield. Steaming straight downfield were eleven Michigan Wolverines, each and every one of them intent on bringing the redhead to the ground. Grange and the pack of Wolverines sped toward each other. At the thirty-yard line, Red suddenly veered and sprinted to the right sideline. The Wolverines knew that Grange liked to sprint to his right and then rocket up the sideline, and they angled over to trap him there.

Then Red rewrote the script. In the week leading up to the game, he and Zuppke, figuring that Michigan would be prepared for Red's usual tendencies, worked on cutting back across the grain and then sprinting toward the opposite sideline for daylight. As the Wolverines closed in for Red's usual burst up the right sideline, he suddenly stopped, cut back and dashed toward the left sideline. The stunned Wolverines didn't touch him. Once near the left sideline, Red had only to unleash his trackman's speed and head directly for the goal line. He reached the end zone just ahead of the futile lunge of Michigan's Tod Rockwell. Earl Britton's extra-point kick made the score 7–0.

It's hard to imagine that a team as strong as Michigan, a team that for weeks had done barely anything beyond gird itself to stop Grange, could have been victimized by him so summarily and so quickly. But like the boxer whose elaborate pre-bout plan evaporates the moment his opponent hits him with a telling blow, it took just seconds for the Wolverines to tumble into disorientation. They were down 7–0, and there were sixty thousand maniacal Illini fans howling for more.

And the Wolverines' heavy stockings were soaking up the Indian summer heat in a very unwelcome way.

It wasn't unusual for a team just scored upon to kick off after the touchdown. Field position was the goal—pin the receiving team deep in their own end, force a punt, and take possession with a short field. Grange's spectacular dash might have suggested a different course of action for

Michigan now. But Michigan kicked, Herb Steger aiming the kickoff straight at the man who only seconds earlier had undressed him and ten other would-be tacklers. This time, Steger nailed Grange at the nineteen-yard line after just a ten-yard runback.

The delirium that had engulfed the stadium subsided a bit and then a bit more as the teams exchanged uneventful possessions. The Wolverines had calmed down. They were into the game now. They'd slowed Grange on a couple of runs from scrimmage. They were poised to show the stuff that had earned them twenty-two straight victories. They were ready for Grange when he took a second-down pitch from Rokusek on the Illinois thirty-three-yard line and headed toward his left end. Sensing his path blocked, Red cut back to the right and picked up a devastating block from McIlwain near the line of scrimmage. Grange dispensed with the next Wolverine threat himself with a stiff-arm that launched him into the secondary. Now it was a footrace and Red didn't lose too many of those. Sixty-seven yards and an extra point later, it was Illinois 14, Michigan 0. The Wolverines were getting closer to their target, though; this time at least there had been some contact between a Michigan player and Grange.

Benny squirmed in disgust on the Michigan sideline. For weeks the Wolverines had prepared for Grange, and now, barely five minutes into the game, he had scored half as many touchdowns as the Wolverines had allowed in their twenty-two previous games combined! Friedman was desperate for a shot at Grange and desperate for a chance to move the moribund Michigan offense. George Little's desperation was mounting also, but he ignored Benny.

The good news for Michigan was that the game was still young. There was more than enough time for them to catch up—if they could steady themselves and put a lid on Grange. After a couple of exchanges of possession and a couple of unproductive Grange carries from scrimmage, including one for a seven-yard loss, it once again appeared that Michigan had quieted Illinois and its raucous crowd.

Then, in a blur, Grange went to work again—from the Illinois forty-four-yard line, a pitch back to Grange, a dash to the right end, a sudden cutback toward the middle, a swerve or two to avoid tacklers, an un-impeded sprint into the end zone.

Most people in the stadium probably didn't even notice that Earl Britton missed the extra point. Bob Zuppke, perfectionist that he was, was probably the only person who cared. He had to stay detached from the pandemonium. Red Grange was dismantling Fielding Yost's legendary football machine. But Zuppke had to stay above it all. There were still three and a half quarters of football to play, and Grange couldn't be expected to keep doing what he'd been doing. Surely the redhead would soon be stopped or just plain give out from exhaustion and then the Wolverines would storm back.

The big question on Michigan's mind was whether that would happen before the end of the first quarter. One play after Steger's fourth kickoff of the quarter, a fatigued Grange fumbled a handoff and was dumped for a six-yard loss. If Michigan had to spot Illinois a 20–0 lead in order to tire out Red, they'd take it. They'd still have nearly the whole game to recover.

Fumbling Britton's long punt at their own forty-five-yard line, however, was not Michigan's recipe for recovery. Illinois recovered the loose ball and immediately gave Michigan another chance to stop Red. They ran the same play they'd run a couple of minutes earlier, sending Grange around right end. It was a play the Michigan defense should have been laying in wait for and should have snuffed out. But the Wolverines were traumatized, stunned into near-paralysis by a force the likes of which neither they nor anyone else had seen. Benny seethed as he watched Grange—again—sprint to the end, cut back toward the center, then snake his way through the hapless Wolverines and steam to the end zone. Britton's kick made the score 27–0.

When Red made his fourth long touchdown run in less than twelve minutes, it seemed that the remainder of the game only promised further embarrassment for Michigan. The Wolverines couldn't stop Red. And they weren't about to get any help from the clock, which still showed three minutes left to play in the first quarter. If there had been a "mercy rule," the referee surely would have invoked it.

The Wolverines did receive some mercy, from Grange himself. Red's fourth touchdown run left him exhausted. Only the goalpost he leaned on after he crossed the goal line held him upright. Somehow he managed to carry the ball from scrimmage another couple of times before Illini quarterback Harry Hall called time-out to allow the Illini trainer onto the field to tend to the gasping Grange.

"I'm so dog-tired I can hardly stand up," Red told the trainer. "Better get me outta here."

Red was so clouded by fatigue that he barely heard the crowd's eruption as he trotted off the field. But he heard Zuppke quite clearly when he reached the sideline, and it wasn't the admiring sound of a grateful coach. "Shoulda had another touchdown, Red," Zup barked at his spent star. "You didn't cut at the right time on that last play."

Red was too tired to speak in his own defense. It wouldn't have done any good anyway. Zup kept his players hungry by withholding praise. Not even four long touchdown runs in less than twelve minutes against one of the strongest teams ever assembled could soften this coach.

While a seriously oxygen-depleted Grange repaired to the Illinois bench, a seriously stunned, recently retired football coach stared out from the stands in disbelief. Fielding Yost had seen just about everything there was to see on a football field. After all, he'd coached the great Willie Heston. But not even Heston had ever done what Yost had just seen Red Grange do. Not Jim Thorpe, either, or Chicago's elusive Walter Eckersall or Harvard's Eddie Mahan or Notre Dame's George Gipp. Not anybody. Grange had proved impervious to all of the pregame strategizing, practices, scouting trips, and verbal bluster that Yost had aimed straight at his head. Only a rude shove to the shoulder roused Yost from his near-catatonic state. His wife, Eunice, who normally steered clear of her husband's business, had delivered the blow. "Fielding," she pleaded, "why don't you *do* something about it?"

The old coach didn't need much prompting. He bolted up from his seat and streaked to the Michigan sideline. He couldn't undo the damage already done, but maybe he could spare his Wolverines further embarrassment.

Grange rested the entire second quarter. During Red's absence, the Wolverines actually resembled a competitive football team, and Steger managed a fifteen-yard touchdown run. After the extra point, they were still way behind, but they stumbled into the locker room with a pulse.

Bob Zuppke never needed an excuse to be serious during halftime, and Steger's touchdown eliminated any chance that Zup might lighten up just a bit this time. The Illini coach was all business, reviewing the few mistakes Illinois made in the first half and plotting a defense to thwart an expected Michigan surge.

George Little's halftime mission was quite different. He had to find a way to score a lot of points quickly. Michigan's passing attack didn't seem up to that task. It was a perfect opportunity to give Friedman a chance to shake things up, but there was no sign that Benny was going to get that chance from Little, not now, maybe not ever.

Grange resumed his dissection of the Wolverines in the third quarter. On his way to eighty-five more rushing yards in the quarter, Red scored his fifth touchdown of the day, a twelve-yard scamper that made the score 33–7. Then Red started passing the ball and, not surprisingly, did so with some success.

As the fourth quarter descended and there was no doubt about the outcome, the only question was what the final tally would be. If Zup wasn't trying to run up the score, he didn't seem inclined to sit on it, either. The Illini kept pressing, with Grange alternately threatening to explode for another long run or finding Illini receivers for modest gains with the pass. When Marion Leonard took Red's short toss and rumbled into the end zone from eighteen yards out, the score became 39–7. The Wolverines at long last countered with a touchdown from Steger. The proud Michigan captain, who with a bit of his own Grange-like flair had galloped for a sixty-yard touchdown run in his very first varsity game in 1922, refused to yield to the Illinois onslaught. The extra point made the score Illinois 39, Michigan 14.

With only a few minutes remaining and the game well in hand, Zuppke and Little removed some of their regulars. Surprisingly, though, Red Grange stayed on the field.

"You!" Little bellowed at Benny. "Get in there!" Benny remembered Tad Weiman's alert to him the night before as he ran over to Little.

Benny could barely feel his legs underneath him as he sprinted onto the field to join his teammates on defense. This moment, his first varsity action, was long overdue, but as he reached his teammates on the field and spied Grange huddling with his Illini mates, he wasn't thinking about George Little or holding grudges or transferring to Dartmouth. He was on the field now, across the line of scrimmage from Illinois number 77. Benny had been watching number 77 conduct his own personal track meet at the expense of the Wolverines all day long. Benny believed that Grange had expertly taken advantage of his interference (which meant "blocking" in those days), interference that more than anything else had accounted for Red's performance. The Wolverine tacklers had allowed themselves to be blocked too easily. Friedman wasn't going to let that happen to him. He was going to stop Grange.

The Illinois offense was at the line of scrimmage in a matter of seconds. As Benny set himself, he could see nothing but Grange bent over the back of the line. Benny heard the Illini quarter barking signals but it was just meaningless sound, like the hum from the throng in the stands. He'd forgotten whatever tactics the Wolverines had called for the play at hand. The tactics—his tactics—were simple. Grange was going to get the ball and Benny was going to stop him.

Red took the pitch from the quarter and steamed toward the line behind his guard. Just as Red began to gather speed, Friedman sidestepped the guard and crashed into a stunned Grange. The two of them sprawled to the ground.

On his very first varsity play, Benny had stopped the great Grange cold. It was more than a matter of what he expected to do. In his mind, it was the play's only possible result.

FOUR

Benny Takes Command

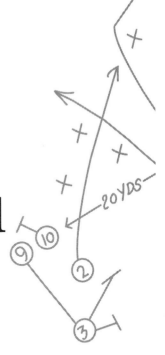

"Give me a redheaded man," Fielding Yost once said, sometime before his encounter with Red Grange, "and I'll give you an athlete." If this was mere opinion when Yost first said it, Grange turned it into fact. Michigan hadn't simply been defeated. They'd been undressed in front of seventy thousand eyewitnesses by the shocking final score of 39–14. With typical modesty, Red disclaimed any credit for the heroics; it was the marvelous interference provided by his teammates, he said, that had escorted him through the Wolverines' defense. Benny had thought just that as he watched from the sideline.

But a breathless national media was having none of that. This was a performance for the ages, and writers from New York to California were going to make sure it was lionized accordingly. "It may be some one else has played as much football and done as much damage against strong opposition in eleven minutes, but there is no official record to prove the case," Grantland Rice wrote in the *New York Herald-Tribune*. The *Brooklyn Standard Union* pronounced Red "the second Jim Thorpe."

"Harold is a red-haired god," the *Daily Illini* proclaimed, and James Crusinberry of the *Chicago Tribune* wrote: "Michigan has some fleet-footed runners on its team in such men as Capt. Steger and Rockwell, but they looked sluggish and slow in their efforts to head off the Illinois wildcat." Rockwell himself all but confirmed Crusinberry's point of view, writing in his own postgame column that the Wolverines hadn't so much as touched Grange on any of his five touchdown runs.

The *New York Sun*'s H. F. Mahoney offered a tribute as dramatic as any of Red's scoring bursts against the Wolverines. "Leading the long caravan [of outstanding performances] by a margin too wide to even hint at comparison," Mahoney wrote, "one finds Harold (Red) Grange of the University of Illinois. This human meteor, against the University of Michigan eleven, spread upon the Urbana gridiron one of the most dazzling carpets of super football ability ever woven by man."

Yost wasn't feeling quite so romantic about things. Rarely had his Wolverines failed to perform in big games, and never had they been so shamefully routed. The pain would have been unbearable even if the coach on the other sideline hadn't been Zuppke. Things were going to change in Ann Arbor—right away—and it wasn't going to be minor tinkering. Yost and Little began charting an offensive and defensive overhaul of the Wolverines' lineup almost before the final whistle in Champaign. Benny figured prominently in the discussion, at least Yost's end of it.

Yost liked what he had seen from Benny in the last minutes of the game. He liked the kid's brassy stop of Grange and his three forward passes, one completed, the other two thrown perfectly but dropped, including a drop by Steger with an open field to the end zone ahead of him. The thing that intrigued the old coach the most about Friedman, though, was his command. The Cleveland boy had never before seen any varsity action, yet he seemed in control of himself and his teammates from the moment he stepped on the field. Yost was thinking that maybe the kid who almost didn't even make the trip to Champaign deserved a longer look.

Benny arrived for practice the following Monday prepared to take his customary position with the scrubs. He had no idea that the coaches had been thinking about looking at him with the first unit. As far as he knew, the few minutes he'd played in Champaign were more of a tease than anything else. But Little installed him at right halfback, just as he and Yost had discussed.

After practice, Benny blurted out the news of his reversal of fortune to his roommate. "Bill, I'm on the varsity!"

Given how far down the depth chart Benny had been, the news was nothing short of shocking. Bill wasn't buying it. He grabbed Benny by the arm.

"Let's go to the infirmary," he told the new right halfback, only half-joking.

"No, Bill, honestly, I'm on the varsity."

When Benny practiced with the first team at right halfback the following day and the day after that and the day after that, the promotion was beyond debate. He was on the varsity, preparing to start at right halfback on Saturday at Ferry Field against the University of Wisconsin.

• • •

If the Wolverines could have handpicked their next conference opponent following the Illinois debacle, they might have chosen the Badgers. Wisconsin was 2–0–2, but the victories had come against weak non-conference teams, and one of the ties came against tiny Coe College. Wisconsin looked to be just the soft touch the Wolverines needed to begin their resurgence. But a tragedy, an unsettled score, and the Badgers' most recent game might have suggested otherwise.

The tragedy was the freakish death two days before the game of Wisconsin fullback Herbert Opitz. The young man was electrocuted while conducting an experiment in an electrical engineering class. If the Wisconsin players needed a rallying cry, their teammate's horrible fate certainly provided one.

The unsettled score related back to the previous year's contest between the Badgers and Wolverines, a contest that nearly cost Michigan its share of the 1923 Big Ten title while nearly costing game referee Walter Eckersall his health, if not his life. Late in that game in Madison, with Wisconsin ahead 3–0, Michigan's Tod Rockwell had been brought to the ground and apparently stopped by the Badgers after a punt return. But Rockwell got up, took a couple of tentative steps, and then continued to the end zone.

Eckersall ruled that Rockwell hadn't been held down long enough, as the rule then required, and credited him with the touchdown that gave the Wolverines a 6–3 victory.

At game's end, hundreds of bloodthirsty Wisconsin fans rushed Eckersall, and one lunatic struck the former Chicago star. Eckersall might not have left the field alive had the Wisconsin players not escorted him to safety while the Badgers' athletic director dispersed the crowd with a wave of his pistol.

Yost's less-than-gracious analysis of the incident didn't help matters. "Yes, Rockwell may have been downed, the officials may have made a mistake, but ten years from now, who will care about that?" the coach said. "The record will read: 'Michigan 6, Wisconsin 3.'"

If Opitz's death and the scandal perpetrated by Eckersall weren't sufficient inspiration, the Badgers could draw on their fine effort against a difficult Minnesota team the week before they would meet Michigan. An intense effort had earned the Badgers a 7–7 tie with the Gophers in Minneapolis.

The Wolverines were plenty motivated as well. Michigan had not lost to Wisconsin in ten games at Ferry Field, and as another conference loss would all but end the Wolverines' Big Ten title chase, this would not be a good time for that streak to end. Moreover, listening to Fielding Yost all week following the most humiliating loss of his long career could motivate a dead man to score four touchdowns. The Wolverines badly needed a rebound from the Illinois debacle.

Benny had his own personal motivation. The game represented the moment he thought would never come, at least not at Michigan. He was finally getting a chance to show what he could do, and there wasn't much room for error. He'd been buried on the bench too long, and the road back to the bench was too short for him to approach this game as a trial with the promise of more games to come.

George Little had treated Benny like a piece of excess baggage from the day the kid had arrived in Ann Arbor. But now, thanks to Red Grange, Friedman had Fielding Yost's attention. He couldn't afford to lose it.

• • •

Sitting amidst the throng in Ferry Field's packed east end-zone stands as the game was about to begin was a man named Edwin "Ty" Tyson. Two things distinguished the otherwise unobtrusive Tyson from the thousands of fans around him. One was his hat, a wide-rimmed white number sharply contrasted with a black band. The other was the radio microphone sitting in front of him.

The twenty-first-century football fan no doubt takes for granted the pleasures of television and radio that broadcast live presentations of his favorite games and teams. Of course, it wasn't always that way. As of the morning of the Michigan-Wisconsin game in 1924, if you wanted to see a football game, you had to be at the game. And if you wanted to hear the game, you couldn't, at least not a fully live broadcast. The closest thing to a live radio broadcast of a game was a "re-creation." Working on a delay, a radio announcer would broadcast each play after receiving an account of it by telephone or wire from a reporter at the game. Fans had listened to just such a re-creation of the Michigan-Illinois contest only a week earlier.

That morning at Ferry Field, television was still years away. But Tyson, of Detroit radio station WWJ, was there to broadcast a college football game live from the stadium for the first time.

Unfortunately, there wasn't much excitement for Tyson to convey as the first quarter unfolded. Yost and Little had decided to pound away at Wisconsin early, thinking Michigan's superior line play would wear down the Badgers and open up the middle of the field. The Badgers didn't cooperate; they smothered Steger and Rockwell and turned the first quarter into a dull punting contest.

Then, in the second quarter, Benny introduced himself to the Ferry Field legions, the fans in the WWJ listening area, and the world of college football.

At the Wisconsin forty-six-yard line, Friedman took the snap from center and set himself to pass. Herb Steger was sprinting downfield from his end position looking for open space. He didn't need much of it. Benny drew back his arm, stepped toward his target, brought his arm forward, and released the ball with a powerful flick of his wrist. Steger grabbed the perfectly thrown ball near the fifteen-yard line and steamed toward the end zone. He was just a yard short of it when the Badger defenders dragged him down.

Wisconsin had never seen Friedman before, had barely heard of Friedman before, but they had just watched him instantaneously change the tone of the game. The Badgers had suddenly, jarringly been thrown from the safety of the middle of the field to the shadow of their end zone.

Wisconsin then surprised everyone in the stadium by repelling Michigan on five successive tries to smash the ball into the end zone (a Wisconsin penalty gave the Wolverines an extra down). But the gallant goal-line stand was almost beside the point. Benny had found the recipe for a Wolverines victory; it was just a matter of time before the scoreboard would reflect it.

The Wolverines kept the Badgers pinned to their goal line and forced them to punt from the end zone. Michigan took possession at the Badger 35. Benny went to work on the first play, again sending Steger downfield, again placing a perfect pass in the Wolverine captain's hands, this time at the five-yard line. There would be no goal-line stand this time; the crowd at Ferry Field erupted as Steger cruised into the end zone. The extra point gave Michigan a 7–0 lead.

This was Benny's game, and he played it with the guile and skill of a master magician who is always a step ahead of his audience. Every Michigan play became a guessing game for the Badgers' defense. When would Friedman throw long again? When would he run the ball?

Who is this *Friedman?*

The Badgers never seemed to come up with the answers, and Benny made them pay for their uncertainty.

In the third quarter he smashed through left tackle, and then weaved his way through the secondary for a twenty-six-yard scoring run. In the fourth quarter he hit another long pass, this time finding end Charles Grube at the Wisconsin twelve-yard line. The Wolverines scored two plays later with a bit of deception from Tod Rockwell. As the Wolverines called signals at the line, Rockwell motioned as if to stop the play, drawing the attention of the Wisconsin defenders just long enough to allow fullback Phil

Marion to plunge through the center of the line, untouched, into the end zone. And Rockwell wasn't through sticking it to the Badgers. He took the ball from Marion and gave it a celebratory flip over the cross bar. Then he kicked the extra point.

Wisconsin couldn't penetrate the Wolverines defense on their next possession. The final score was 21–0, and except for the first quarter, the game hadn't been even that close.

Benny used whatever energy he had left to struggle to the locker room, with help from Michigan trainer Chuck Hoyt. The kid had played all sixty minutes, had been a standout on defense, punts, and kickoffs as well as offense, and he was spent. But he felt good. He'd performed brilliantly when the Wolverines, looking to rebound from their worst loss ever, were desperate for a win.

As Benny sat sprawled against the lockers while Hoyt helped him remove his shoes, George Little ambled over. Looking up, Benny hoped the coach might toss him some kind words. He should have known better. When Little had something to say to Benny, it almost always meant trouble for the youngster. Despite the fact—or maybe because of the fact—that Benny had just all but single-handedly rescued Michigan's season, this occasion would be no exception.

"Friedman," Little sneered from the corner of his mouth, "we got a bigger and a tougher game next week, so forget about this one."

Just like that, the coach shattered the kid's quiet reverie. Perhaps from another coach, Benny might have taken the remark as a motivational tactic to prevent him from feeling too full of himself. But coming from Little, it didn't seem tactical to Benny. It was mean-spirited.

"Is that what you get for coming through?" Benny implored of Hoyt, tears filling his eyes, as the trainer pulled at Benny's shoes.

"You just keep your feet on the ground," Hoyt said, with a pat to Benny's leg.

The raves that Benny's performance garnered in the national press would have made it difficult for any nineteen-year-old kid to stay grounded. "Michigan Finds New Star in Friedman," proclaimed the *New*

York Herald-Tribune. The *Daily Illini*, of all papers, led with the Michigan-Wisconsin game under the banner headline "FRIEDMAN STAR OF TILT." The Associated Press fairly gushed over Benny's performance and even favorably compared the new Wolverine hero to a certain redheaded running back from Illinois: "Michigan whipped Wisconsin, 21–0, today, and found a new and dazzling gridiron meteor. Just as 'Red' Grange of Illinois almost single-handed defeated the Wolverines a week ago, Ben Friedman of Cleveland, Ohio, beat Wisconsin today."

Not even George Little could keep Benny down now.

. . .

Benny was an unknown when he took the field against Wisconsin, but with his performance against the Badgers and the rave notices it received, there would be no sneaking up on Michigan's next opponent, Minnesota. It didn't matter. The scrap in Minneapolis mirrored the Wisconsin game. Benny confused the defense with the same smorgasbord of passing and running that had mystified the Badgers. Steger missed the game with an ankle injury suffered against Wisconsin, but it didn't much matter to Benny—he simply found other targets. Benny's working knowledge of Yiddish also forced Minnesota's two standout defenders, George Abramson and Louis Gross, who were Jewish, to abandon their practice of calling signals in Yiddish, something they ordinarily did without fear of tipping off the opposing offense. The Gophers' own offense managed to move the ball somewhat behind their physical forwards, but the Wolverines stiffened on defense when it counted. In the end, the score was Michigan 13, Minnesota 0.

Two weeks earlier, as the Wolverines staggered off the field in Champaign, there had been more than a few writers and fans who were sure they'd just seen a sorry and premature end to Michigan's 1924 season. But they hadn't known about Ben Friedman then.

. . .

The Wolverines hoped to continue their post-Grange recovery and preserve their Big Ten title chances as they prepared for Northwestern's visit to

Ferry Field on November 8. Northwestern had a bit of momentum going with a 4–1 record, including conference wins in its last two games over Indiana and Michigan State. And as Michigan now had Benny, Northwestern had a budding star of their own: halfback Ralph "Moon" Baker. They also had a new nickname, having shed the colorful but uninspiring "Purple" in favor of the intimidating "Wildcats."

Neither Baker nor the ferocious new nickname was much help. As good as Friedman had been against Wisconsin and Minnesota, Northwestern saw an even better performance. Benny baffled the Wildcats with his accurate long passes, including three for touchdowns. The decisive sequence featured another Friedman variety show. With Michigan cradling a hard-fought 7–0 lead in the second quarter, Benny launched a perfect twenty-nine-yard scoring pass to Rockwell. Following Michigan's kickoff, Moon Baker heaved a pass of his own downfield, not to be outdone by his Wolverine sophomore counterpart—or so he hoped. Friedman intercepted the pass and returned it to the Wildcats' twenty-one-yard line. On the next play, Phil Marion was blowing kisses to the Wildcat defenders as he crossed the goal line with Benny's second scoring strike. Three plays, two touchdowns, game over—all courtesy of George Little's former blocking dummy. Benny's long fourth-quarter touchdown pass was beautiful but academic; Michigan's defense was stifling the Wildcats, who came no closer to scoring than two missed field-goal tries from long range by Baker. Final score: Michigan 27, Northwestern 0.

Had Las Vegas sports books been in business in 1924, they would have offered very long odds on a Michigan Big Ten championship following the Illinois debacle. Friedman had revived the Michigan title hopes that Grange had trampled, but they still had to deal with struggling Ohio State in Columbus and then pesky Iowa in Ann Arbor to have any chance.

. . .

Michigan had had things pretty much their own way in Benny's first three games as a regular, thanks to his outstanding play and a Wolverine defense that teased its opponents before ultimately suffocating them. But the underdog Buckeyes immediately knocked Michigan from its comfort zone. The sellout crowd at the Horseshoe was still getting settled when, two plays after the kickoff, Ohio State connected on a sixty-five-yard touchdown pass.

The play shocked a defense that hadn't been scored upon in three games. But against a Buckeye team meandering through a poor season, including a loss to weak Indiana the previous week, it shouldn't have been much to overcome.

Then Benny's receivers started dropping his passes as if the ball had suddenly acquired some dread communicable disease. First it was Steger. The captain, back in action after injuring his foot against Wisconsin, dropped three perfect throws, flinching on his foot each time he reached for the ball. Friedman started throwing to other receivers, but the drops continued, sometimes with a clear path to the end zone awaiting the receiver.

Benny's impatience was growing with each pass that fell harmlessly to the turf. His attitude didn't improve when he took a shot in the ribs from three gang-tackling Buckeyes that left him writhing in pain and gasping for air. He stayed in the game with taped ribs and an assist from guard Edliff Slaughter, who lifted him each time he was knocked to the ground by placing his hands behind Benny's head and standing him up, like a plank. With the third quarter winding down, the pain wracking his body, and the Buckeyes still leading, the Wolverines botched another pass.

"To hell with you guys!" Friedman shrieked as he slammed his helmet to the turf. "If you're not going to catch them, I'm not going to take this licking."

Benny wasn't kidding. He started to walk off the field.

His stunned teammates ran after him and convinced him to stay. Then they began catching some passes and pounding the Buckeyes with their running attack. Somehow, the scoreboard at the end of the game read Michigan 16, Ohio State 6. A work of art it wasn't, but it was a win.

Benny's outburst on the field had seemed to ignite the Wolverines, waking them from their slumber just in time. But Coach Little wasn't impressed. At the team's weekly meeting a couple of days later, Little made it clear that, for him, the game's victorious end didn't justify Benny's means. Little tore into Friedman right in the middle of the team meeting.

"Friedman, don't ever let me see you playing for the grandstand again," the coach said, jabbing his finger at Benny. "Don't ever let me see you slam your helmet down." Little went on and on with the upbraiding.

The coach had a point. Benny had gone too far with his histrionics. Friedman's response to his first serious adversity on the field since cracking the lineup was a self-absorbed impulse to do the unpardonable—quit on his teammates. It was a sign that the sophomore's emotional maturity hadn't yet caught up with the precociousness of his skills.

Sitting at that team meeting, absorbing yet another flogging from his coach, Benny didn't quite see it that way. Had the criticism come from Yost or Tad Weiman or just about anybody else, it probably would have registered with Benny. But the coach's relentless hostility had blinded Friedman to anything he said, even when it had merit. Benny still wasn't sure why it had been this way with the coach almost from the day the season began. But as that team meeting ended and Benny walked up to Little, he *did* know that the abuse was going to end, finally, right there.

"You no-good son of a bitch," Friedman said. "You can take my suit and shove it. I don't want to play for you."

Little probably wouldn't have cared if Benny never played another down for the Wolverines. But Fielding Yost cared. A lot. It had been the old coach who'd first intrigued Benny with the idea of attending Michigan, who'd first worked out the Cleveland boy and filled his head with romantic notions of playing on the hallowed Ferry Field turf where Willie Heston had tread. Yost might have lost sight of Benny during his freshman year in 1923, but that was before a five-game winning streak and the revelation of a new star in 1924. George Little was the coach, but Fielding Yost was still Michigan football, and Benny Friedman wasn't going anywhere.

The Wolverines would play Iowa in the final game of the season. Iowa, like Wisconsin, had lost to Michigan in 1923 on a bitterly disputed play. A punt by Michigan captain Harry Kipke late in that game with the score tied 3–3 rolled into the end zone for what appeared to be a touchback. But when Michigan's Jack Blott pounced on the ball, the referee awarded the

Wolverines a touchdown that gave them a 9–3 victory. The Iowa safety who let the ball roll into the end zone hadn't realized that a teammate had nicked the punted ball at the line of scrimmage, making it a live ball. Of course, as Fielding Yost might have said, the record book showed Michigan 9, Iowa 3, nicked punt or not.

Michigan's 1924 rematch with Iowa involved big stakes in the Big Ten thanks to the pounding Minnesota handed Illinois on November 15. The Gophers assaulted Grange with a zeal that knocked the redhead out of the game and out for the season. Some reports even declared that the mauling had killed Grange. Red had a good laugh at that, but the torn arm and shoulder ligaments he sustained were no laughing matter. In any case, the Illinois loss delivered the Big Ten title to the Michigan-Iowa winner—if Chicago cooperated by losing their finale to Wisconsin.

Even though Iowa had played strong ball on their way to a 5–1–1 record, they looked to have a tall task ahead at Ferry Field against the streaking Wolverines and their recently unearthed forward-passing marvel. Benny had started just four games, but, according to the *Michigan Daily*, he had already acquired the reputation as "the leading student of the forward pass in the country." All Benny and the Wolverines needed to complete their storybook comeback from Illinois massacre victim to Big Ten champ was one more quality game.

They didn't get it. Iowa's physical line clamped down on Benny early and never loosened the vise. A steady mist and wet turf didn't do much for Benny's passing, either, as the incompletions piled up. Michigan's running attack fared no better. On offense, Iowa's talented back, Leland Parker, controlled the game and produced nine points, seven more than Michigan managed.

The only consolation Michigan could draw from its loss was that it didn't cost them the Big Ten title—Chicago won it by eking out a tie with Wisconsin.

FIVE

"We Got the Little Badgers' Skins to Wrap the Baby Bunting In"

The good news about the Iowa game, at least for Benny, was that it would be the last for George Little as the coach of the Wolverines. In January 1925, Little was hired as the new athletic director at Wisconsin. Shortly thereafter, Little was also named as Wisconsin's new football coach. The union of Little and the Badgers seemed to make sense: Wisconsin wanted to revitalize its football program, which had been mediocre at best for several seasons, and Little wanted to emerge from Fielding Yost's very large shadow. Benny's performance in Michigan's 21–0 wipeout of the Badgers undoubtedly, and ironically, boosted his tormentor Little's stock in the eyes of Wisconsin's board of regents.

In the fall of 1924, Benny had been a mere eyelash from leaving Ann Arbor himself. It seemed to be the only way to escape Little's oppression and give himself a chance to develop into the player he knew he could become. But he had stuck it out, and a season that had started in obscurity for him had ended with a starring role and a spot on several experts' all-Big-Ten second and third teams. There had even been some mention of Benny being worthy of all-American status. Now, in an added bonus, Little was gone—and Michigan's football patriarch was returning to the sidelines. Fielding Yost had decided to "unretire" and resume his head coaching duties. In Benny, he certainly had strong incentive to return. Yost had had Willie Heston and Boss Weeks and more than two decades at the top of football's coaching hierarchy, but he'd never had a quarterback with the complete package Benny seemed to have. Friedman couldn't have written a better script as he prepared to hit his stride in 1925.

Just a few miles east of Ferry Field, in the offices of the *Dearborn Independent*, Henry Ford was at the peak of *his* stride as arguably the country's most prominent and influential anti-Semite. The *Independent* had been giving voice to the auto magnate's malice toward Jews since 1920, when its May 22 issue revealed Ford's long-held prejudice to the world with the headline, "The International Jew: The World's Problem." Over the next five years, that issue of the *Independent* was followed by ninety others that parroted the bigotry of the fictional *Protocols of the Elders of Zion*, castigating Jews for their alleged plan to take over the world through domination of its finances. Henry Ford's organ of intolerance blamed "the Jew" for World War I, economic inequality, and anything else wicked that his ghostwriter, William Cameron, could craft.

The *Independent*'s campaign of hatred coincided with a tide of anti-Semitism in the United States that began rising in the second decade of the twentieth century and was swelling in earnest in the early 1920s. The massive Jewish emigration from Russia and Eastern Europe that had begun in the 1880s reached its zenith in 1920, when some 120,000 European Jews entered the country. Most drifted into the cities, increasing an urban workforce already beset by too many workers and too few jobs. With the Jewish population in the country approaching 3.5 million in the early 1920s, both the government and certain segments of a citizenry anxious to curtail what they saw as Jewish malevolence geared up their operations. Congress enacted legislation limiting immigration. "Nativists" looking to preserve and protect the purity of a white Anglo-Saxon America promoted eugenics. A small but passionate group of Jewish immigrants with socialist sympathies ignited a national "red scare," inflaming the bigotry of anti-Semites throughout the country.

The Ku Klux Klan, in particular, was enjoying a banner period. By 1923 it could boast approximately five million members nationwide. Curiously, Michigan featured the largest membership of any single state; in 1921 there were some 875,000 members, many based in or near Detroit. The Klan's profound influence in that city moved Supreme Court Justice Louis Brandeis to remark, upon a visit to Detroit: "Anti-Semitism seems to have reached its American pinnacle here."

Henry Ford was certainly one Detroiter who might have proudly embraced Brandeis's assessment. Despite increasingly frequent and sharp objections from Jewish groups, the carmaker showed no inclination to stop the bile that oozed from the pages of the *Independent*. The paper, which had been on the brink of extinction before beginning its anti-Semitic crusade in 1920, saw its subscriber numbers soar with the publication of anti-Jewish articles, revealing a disturbing public appetite for this type of fare. Ford wasn't about to abandon this successful formula, and besides, the articles were more than good business: they expressed personal sentiments he'd long held but had been reluctant to publicize. As 1925 arrived, not even a $1 million libel suit filed against Ford by Aaron Sapiro, a Jewish lawyer viciously attacked in the *Independent* for his efforts to create farming cooperatives in Detroit, gave Ford any pause.

Colleges and universities weren't immune to the crawl of anti-Semitism in the 1920s. In fact, many of them were all too willing to do their part to rein in the perceived excessive Jewish influence.

Beginning in the late-nineteenth century, the promise of a better life offered by a college education spurred a dramatic increase in the number of young men and women attending colleges and universities. Jews enthusiastically embraced this trend—a bit too enthusiastically for the administrators at many prominent schools, who bristled at what they perceived to be a disproportionately high percentage of Jewish students. One such school was Harvard, where in 1922 Jews constituted 22 percent of the undergraduate student body. This was unacceptable to Harvard president A. Lawrence Lowell, who instituted practices such as character and psychological testing that would identify and help limit the number of Jews accepted to the university. When Lowell's actions, intended to be implemented discreetly, became public, Harvard absorbed a fair amount of criticism, but Lowell had accomplished his mission—the establishment of a de facto quota limiting Jewish attendance at Harvard. Methods similar to those used at Harvard were employed to establish quotas limiting Jewish enrollment at Yale, Columbia, Cornell, and many other schools.

The Jewish students who filled these anti-Semitic quotas weren't exactly welcomed into their respective college communities with open arms. Barriers, some subtle, some not so subtle, impeded the Jewish student's path to a truly equal college experience. In varying degrees at various schools, Jewish students encountered difficulty in joining fraternities and societies, participating in campus political activities, even attending school dances.

Yet despite the increased anti-Semitic fervor, the number of Jewish players on college football rosters continued to rise. "Never before in the history of football have so many Jewish boys occupied regular places in the line-ups of their college teams," Sidney Cohen wrote in the *Jewish Advocate*. A good number of these players were stars who figured prominently in their team's plans. Harvard back Al Miller was a track star who was thought to be the fastest back in the country. Harry Kaplan would make important contributions at the quarterback position for Columbia. In 1924, Syracuse University's football roster included nine Jewish players, among them "Bus" Friedman (no relation to Benny), a standout lineman who would lead the Orangemen to an upset victory over powerful Penn State in 1925.

This apparent paradox—the rising number of Jewish football players at a time when schools were systematically winnowing Jews from their student bodies at large—can be explained by the growing importance to American society of sports in general and of college football in particular. In this context, it is easy to understand why Jews on college football rosters were accepted, if not eagerly embraced. If you could play—Jewish or not—there was a jersey waiting for you.

In a twisted sort of way, the inclusive attitude toward the Jewish footballer served the interests of both Jews and the institutions of higher learning that were scheming to exclude them, at least those who were not athletically inclined, from their leafy campuses. For the Jewish athlete and Jews around the country who followed their Saturday afternoon exploits, football, the roughest, most physical sport, undercut the stereotype of the Jew as weakling. Even more than that, football—the most American of American games—was a Jewish vehicle for assimilation into the mainstream of American society. And for the mildly intolerant if not outright anti-Semitic college and university administrations, the presence of Jews on their football teams provided a rejoinder to the notion that they were discriminating against them.

• • •

The 1925 Michigan Wolverines didn't feature nine Jewish players, like Syracuse, but they did have one other to go along with Friedman. Ray Baer, a sophomore lineman from Louisville, Kentucky, had been an all-state football and basketball player who was also the Kentucky high-school high-jump champion. The outstanding athlete had enjoyed a promising season with the Wolverine freshman team in 1924, and the varsity was now expecting Baer to provide Benny with the time he'd need to throw the ball downfield. But there was another sophomore, an end, who was attracting Benny's attention in early season workouts far more than Baer. His name was Bennie Oosterbaan.

From a purely physical standpoint, it would have been hard not to notice Oosterbaan. With about 185 pounds distributed in perfect proportion on a six-foot-two-inch frame, the young man from Muskegon, Michigan, looked like a born athlete. His speed, lithe movement, and leaping ability were uncanny. It was little wonder that Oosterbaan had arrived in Ann Arbor after one of the most spectacular schoolboy athletic careers in Michigan high-school sports history: all-State in football and baseball, all-American on Muskegon High's state champion basketball squad, and state champ in the discus throw. After a year on the Wolverines' freshman football team, he earned an invitation to the 1925 varsity tryouts.

But the Muskegon standout got off to a poor start with line coach Tad Weiman in early season workouts. On one particular play, Oosterbaan lined up in an unorthodox fashion, and Weiman exploded.

"You don't even know how to take the position of an end!" the coach said. "Turn in your suit." As far as Weiman was concerned, the big end was wasting his time with football; he told Oosterbaan to concentrate on basketball.

This wasn't the first time someone had urged Bennie to abandon football. Several years earlier, his parents wanted their athletic son to give up all sports, though for reasons that were entirely different and far more serious than those offered by Tad Weiman. Bennie's older brother, Guy, had died of tuberculosis in 1917 at the age of twenty-four. Just two years later, another brother, Andy, the captain of Muskegon High's basketball team, died from a bacterial infection that had set in following a knee injury he suffered on the court. Bennie's parents feared that a similar tragedy would befall him if he continued with his sports. But ultimately, they couldn't keep their talented son from playing.

With a little help from Fielding Yost, Oosterbaan wasn't about to let Tad Weiman derail him, either. Yost had already seen enough of Oosterbaan on the football field to know that he belonged there. The coach dispensed with Weiman's plan for Bennie as soon as he caught wind of it.

Yost had his own plan for Oosterbaan, and it didn't include basketball. Bennie was going to be one of the many underclassmen that Yost would rely on in 1925 to fill the void left by the graduation of captain Herb Steger, Tod Rockwell, and all-American lineman Edliff Slaughter. The others would include Bo Molenda, the big fullback from Detroit; end Bill Flora, who'd been Oosterbaan's teammate at Muskegon High; the swift halfback Louis Gilbert; Ray Baer; and, of course, Benny Friedman.

Preseason workouts in 1925 were unlike any other Friedman had experienced since coming to Michigan. The young quarterback was in a completely different place now and there would be no place to hide, not that he was looking to. Benny's days as a scrub were over. Senior Wolverines center Robert "Bob" Brown was the team captain, but Michigan's chances of fulfilling Fielding Yost's goals—a Big Ten championship that would include avenging the embarrassing rout in Champaign at the hands of Grange and Zuppke—rested primarily on Benny's shoulders.

Like Yost, Benny was anxious for the upcoming shot at Grange, but he had another goal driving him. A week before they'd get Red Grange again, the Wolverines would be visiting Camp Randall for a reunion of sorts with George Little. The showdown with Grange would have its own unique intrigue for Benny, because it would give him the chance to show, against the best, that he was the best. The confrontation with Little would be different. It would be—for Benny, if not for his former coach— a personal matter.

Life at Michigan was looking pretty good for Benny all the way around now. The serious young man had had difficulty connecting socially during his freshman year. Seeking refuge in his studies, he'd spent more time thinking about his hometown friends at Dartmouth than he did trying to make friends in Ann Arbor. The reality was that his heavy course load, two jobs, and football didn't leave him much time for socializing.

The improvement in Benny's football fortunes seemed to loosen up the young man. It's amazing what a promotion from obscure benchwarmer to budding star quarterback will do for a college man's social prospects, especially when the star quarterback had Benny's good looks. In addition to his weekly course work reading, Benny was now wading through stacks of perfumed letters from female admirers. He began to attend school dances and parties, where it wasn't unusual for him to dance with the prettiest girl in the room. The more-at-ease Friedman was enjoying Ann Arbor now, hanging out at popular student haunts such as the Pretzel Bell, where he reveled in his newfound celebrity. And at the Jewish fraternity Sigma Alpha Mu,

Benny's growing popularity propelled him to the position of fraternity house manager.

University officials and influential alumni began to realize that the bright, well-spoken, good-looking, and, now, more outgoing young football star could be an important goodwill ambassador for the football program and the school. They booked the young quarterback to speak at local banquets, luncheons, and other functions. Somehow Benny found time to do it, and discovered he was a natural.

. . .

The Wolverines' first victim of the 1925 season figured to be Michigan State College in the season opener. The school with a new name (it had previously been known as Michigan Agricultural College) may have been a bit short of the Wolverines' talent, but they were expected to put up a fight similar to the one waged a year earlier, when the Wolverines were all out to steal a 7–0 win.

Yost wasn't in the mood for such desperation this time. The Wolverines treated the largest opening-day crowd ever at Ferry Field to a 39–0 pasting of State, which, by game's end, had the feel of an exalted dress rehearsal rather than a real contest. The *Syracuse Herald*'s observation that "Benny Friedman appeared to be the whole works" was probably a bit overstated; Yost substituted liberally throughout the game, looking for combinations that might be effective against tougher opponents to come. No combination pleased the coach more than Benny's passes to Oosterbaan. The big end grabbed two of Friedman's throws for touchdowns, showing off soft hands, a quickness that was startling for such a big receiver, and an enthusiasm for running over tacklers.

But as at least one writer was quick to observe, these were Michigan State tacklers. "Michigan's 39–0 victory cannot be assumed as the harbinger of another conference championship, as State College failed to put up the resistance expected," bleated the *Detroit Free Press*. Yost didn't need to be told not to celebrate too much. The Wolverines' performance wasn't without its glitches, and Yost began remedying them at practice the following Monday.

Up next were the Indiana Hoosiers. Coach Bill Ingram worked his boys each day from 1:30 to 7:00 during the week leading up to the game in Ann Arbor. It was as if the coach was trying to elevate the traditionally weak Hoosiers to the level of the perennially strong Wolverines with one week of relentless practice, primarily on their defense.

Friedman showed Ingram that the coach's concern for his team's defense was well-founded. With a virtuoso performance, the young quarterback's running, kicking, and passing single-handedly walloped the Hoosiers, 63–0. It was the kind of waxing that Yost's Willie Heston–led "point-a-minute" teams used to administer routinely. Fans couldn't decide which of Benny's feats was most impressive. Was it the five touchdown passes? The eight extra points? Or perhaps his fifty-five-yard touchdown run, during which he cut through and sped past the entire defense. In praising Benny for his destruction of the Hoosiers, some accounts of the game invoked a certain noted redhead's name. "Benny Friedman was the big noise for Michigan, his passing and running equaling anything Grange has shown in the last two years," one report read. But it was a *Cleveland News* headline, which made no mention of Grange, that may have best capsulized the performance: "Benny Is Team By Himself."

Poor Indiana didn't have much good to take from this debacle, but the student newspaper, the *Indiana Daily Student,* tried gamely to find a helpful nugget with its headline: "Statistics Show Wolverines Made Only Three More First Downs Than Crimson Warriors." If this statistic provided some comfort to the routed Hoosiers, it also illustrated the wisdom of a football philosophy that Yost preached and Benny willingly followed: think touchdowns, not first downs.

Some were unwilling to attribute the 63–0 tally to the talents of an extraordinary player. W. C. Richards of the *Detroit Free Press* wrote: "The [Michigan State and Indiana] games have shown the inadequacy of the opposition rather than any lordship of Michigan. Michigan State showed little. Indiana was puerility itself. Navy and other conference teams won't be." Richards barely mentioned Friedman in his piece; it was as if the young quarterback had no hand in the 102 points Michigan scored in its first two games. Had Red Grange been half as prominent in compiling one-third as many points, Richards and most any other scribe likely would have lionized him. For Michigan and the Wolverines' Jewish star, this kind of praise would have to await the outcome of sterner tests. And they wouldn't have long to wait for the first such battle. The Wolverines' trip to Wisconsin and Benny's reunion with George Little was just a week away.

• • •

A persistent wariness had hovered over the relationship between George Little and Fielding Yost during Little's tenure in Ann Arbor. Yost wasn't like most former coaches; he was a Michigan living legend, the patriarch of the football program, and a restless one at that. He wasn't always able, or willing, to stay out of Little's coaching space. Little, it seems, felt underappreciated when the Wolverines won and unfairly criticized when they lost.

As the third week of action in the 1925 season approached, Little's move to Wisconsin seemed to have invigorated both men. Yost was two productive wins into his personal quest for vengeance against Illinois. Little arrived in Madison determined to cure the indifference that had afflicted Badgers' football over the previous few seasons, and one-sided romps in their first two games, albeit over lesser opponents, were a step in the right direction for the Badgers.

Beating Michigan would be an entirely different matter. Homecoming weekend in Madison and a sea of red-clad fans who were expected to cram into Camp Randall (Wisconsin's stadium) would help. So would assistant coaches Edliff Slaughter and Irwin Uteritz, recent ex-Michigan stars who knew Yost and his strategies. But Little didn't need any inside information to figure out that the Wolverines' main strategy was Benny Friedman. Nor did it take much imagination on the coach's part to deduce that his former blocking dummy was approaching the game with an extra incentive. Little drove his Badgers relentlessly in practice, striving, as reported in the Wisconsin *Daily Cardinal,* to perfect "an impregnable defense for Benny Friedman and his flashy brand of offense play."

Yost, for his part, relished the opportunity to spank his former assistant. But the old coach's priority remained his meeting one week down the road with Bob Zuppke, Red Grange, and Illinois. The Wolverines practiced diligently for Wisconsin, but Yost made sure to avoid overdoing things; contact scrimmages were avoided. The Wolverines spent much of their time strengthening a short passing defense that had allowed Indiana its only glimmer of success during the 63–0 romp.

Of course, Yost didn't neglect his offense, an offense now led by an exciting new quarterback whose ability to pass the football was stimulating the coach to change his conservative "punt, pass, and prayer" approach a bit. The shellacking of Michigan State and Indiana showed that Yost was now less inclined to grind out first downs and more inclined to look for the big strike—for the touchdown. Invoking this philosophy, Yost and Benny prepared a big pass play to deliver an early knockout blow to Wisconsin, a new play that Little and Slaughter and Uteritz likely hadn't seen. Benny planned to call the play on Michigan's first snap, which, as it developed following the opening kickoff from Wisconsin, would come from Michigan's own thirty-two-yard line. It mattered not at all to Friedman that passing on first down, particularly from your own half of the field, was a phenomenon about as common as a solar eclipse. His performance in previous games illustrated that the conventional wisdom about the forward pass didn't apply to him.

As the Wolverines approached the line of scrimmage, Bennie Oosterbaan suddenly sprinted from his left end position to right end, just outside Bill Flora. On the snap, Oosterbaan and Flora sprinted straight downfield. Halfback Bruce Gregory followed them before cutting at a forty-five-degree angle into the middle of the field. Oosterbaan's surprise shift and sprint downfield with Flora so confused the Wisconsin secondary that Gregory found himself unguarded. Benny then coolly found Gregory with an elegant pass that hit the receiver in stride. The halfback sailed sixty yards downfield into the end zone untouched.

It had taken Benny about ten seconds to shred George Little's entire week of preparation. It was a beautiful play, incorporating the hallmarks of a Fielding Yost team that was fast looking like something very special: surprise and deception; Bennie Oosterbaan's speed and mere presence (this time as a decoy); the desire to hit the big play; and the quarterback to execute it all with just the right signal calling, timing, and passing skill.

Friedman's big pass play apparently disoriented Little. The coach elected to kick off to Michigan, playing for field position. It was a decision eerily similar to the one Little had made against Illinois the year before, when the Wolverines kicked the ball to the Illini following Grange's opening kickoff touchdown jaunt. In no time, Illinois had taken that gift and transformed it into a 14–0 lead. Maybe Little, this time with no Grange to deal with, felt more secure with his strategy. If so, the coach shouldn't have felt so sanguine. Friedman was about to show his former antagonist, a flock of bewildered Badger players, and the largest crowd ever to witness a Wisconsin home game that he could do much more than pass the football.

Looking very much like a man with something to prove, Benny scooped up the ball at the Wolverines' fifteen-yard line and twisted, spun, and sprinted eighty-five yards past the Wisconsin defenders. The *Detroit Free Press* reported that no Badger so much as even touched Friedman before he crossed the goal line with the points that surely put the game beyond all argument.

The two lightning-quick scores prompted one of Benny's teammates, caught in the hysteria of the moment, to scream out to Little. "Hey, Coach," bellowed the frenzied Wolverine, "ever seen a point-a-*second* team before?" The Wisconsin coach likely was too astonished to hear the rhetorical question or much of anything else. Benny would later reveal just how personal the game had been to him, saying, "In less than a minute, we had fourteen points up on the board and had scuttled Mr. Little."

Yost wasn't known for sitting on a lead—"point-a-minute" isn't a sobriquet associated with teams that loosen the throttle—but there was good cause this time to pull back. The early Wolverine barrage convinced him the team could score more points if they needed to, and his strong defense convinced him that such a need wasn't likely to arise. Under those circumstances, and wanting to keep his players fresh for the Illinois showdown, Yost felt no compulsion to force the issue. He felt no desire, either, to preview his full assortment of plays for the several Illini scouts in attendance. Benny did loosen the reins slightly in the second quarter, long enough to hit Oosterbaan with a touchdown pass that, with Benny's third extra-point placement (and eleventh in a row for the season), made the score 21–0. Neither team scored in the uneventful second half: Wisconsin because they couldn't, and Michigan because they wouldn't, in order to save themselves for Illinois.

The game was quite a coup for Benny and for Yost. Friedman had laid low the coach who had tormented him, and Yost had shown his former assistant that he still had a few football lessons to learn. In the process they had done away with Michigan's first serious threat to their hopes for a Big Ten title. And they had done so with a restrained performance that kept the Wolverines healthy and fresh and kept Illinois and the rest of the Big Ten guessing just how good they really were.

Essentially co-opting the streets of Madison that night, Michigan fans serenaded the locals wallowing in the Badgers' defeat with a chant of "Benny Friedman, Benny Friedman." On the train ride back to Ann Arbor, Benny savored the day's events, particularly his kickoff return, the play he'd one day label his most thrilling as a college player. And Yost chanted a little ditty of his own for the entertainment of his players and the press. "We got the little Badgers' skins to wrap the baby bunting in," Yost chortled as he engaged in his favorite pastime—the savoring of a Michigan triumph.

Years later, Little's reminiscences of the game and the quarterback who had demolished his Badgers were a lot less gleeful: "[I] left Ann Arbor a year too early. I should have waited until Bennie was gone . . . [The game] was a nightmare."

Friedman, of course, was thrilled that Little hadn't stuck around Michigan for another year. At times during his difficulties with Little, Benny had suspicions that the coach was anti-Semitic. At some point in time, probably before Little left Ann Arbor for Wisconsin, Benny had become convinced of it.

• • •

Benny's impressive showing in the second half of 1924 hadn't been noticed much by the national Jewish press. But he'd established a platform, and as he led Michigan to victories early in 1925, the Jewish papers began paying attention.

"Ben Friedman of Michigan proved that his brilliant play of 1924 was no flash in the pan," Harry Conzel wrote in his "Sporting Column," syndicated in Jewish papers throughout the country, following the Michigan State game. The columnist shone his spotlight on Benny again following the Wisconsin game: "Benny Friedman, Michigan's quarterback, is simply running wild this season," Conzel proclaimed. The *Brooklyn Jewish Chronicle* went a step further with its declaration following the Wisconsin game: "Benny Friedman of Michigan Is All-American Bound."

As the most prominent Jewish footballer, Benny was the prime example of a Jew strong enough and good enough to excel in the toughest of games. Perhaps a stronger indication of the Jewish community's burgeoning pride in Friedman could be found in an editorial in the *Chicago Chronicle* following the Wisconsin game. The *Chronicle,* a self-described "American Weekly Paper for the Modern Jewish Home," did not have a sports section. Its editorial page was typically reserved for prominent American Jewish leaders, such as Supreme Court Justice Louis Brandeis, and serious political and social subjects, such as the editorial in the October 23, 1925, issue entitled "The American Jewish Congress and the German Jews." Yet immediately below that piece appeared an editorial entitled "Benny Friedman."

"A new hero has come into the limelight," the editorial began. "He is Benny Friedman, the dashing quarterback of the championship-aspiring University of Michigan football eleven. Benny is largely responsible for the twenty-one-to-nothing victory which Michigan won over Wisconsin last Saturday, and his name has become a campus shibboleth . . .

"What interests us is that Friedman, the fleet-footed, is a Jewish lad, a Cleveland boy who is an excellent student as well as a superb forward passer; that he is earning his own livelihood at the same time that he is bringing glory to his Alma Mater. Benny is an all-around fellow and a great athlete—one more proof that the Jew can be a striking success in sports."

At the same time that the *Chronicle* praised Friedman as a hero for shattering the stereotype, it acknowledged—equivocally—its embrace of the prominently expressed beliefs of Maurice Samuel and Ludwig Lewisohn, two leading Jewish intellectuals of the day. Their feeling was that Jews and sports didn't mix well. The *Chronicle* stated: "The background, heredity, history and environment of the Jew have developed in him a serious-mindedness and self-consciousness which do not go well with a whole-hearted surrender to the joys of sport and athletics. But when a Benny Friedman comes to the fore, we begin to doubt and wonder whether or not our theory is sound."

The Jewish press wasn't alone in calling attention to Benny's Jewishness; general circulation papers often noted Benny's ethnicity, though they typically avoided the kind of socio-religious hand-wringing that the *Chronicle* engaged in. "Benny, short, stocky, 19, and Jewish, almost single handed ruined Wisconsin's hope for a Big Ten football championship this year," declared the *Chicago Tribune*. Writers covering Red Grange and his breathtaking destruction of Michigan in 1924 employed a myriad of adjectives in an attempt to capture the essence of the great back, but "Christian" wasn't one of them. The *Tribune* piece was kind toward Friedman, and so its reference to his Jewishness could be viewed as complimentary, in the sense that a Jew wasn't supposed to be able to do what Benny had done to the Badgers. But it was also a reminder that Benny was a Jewish football player in a Gentile sport and a Gentile world.

Apart from its religious overtones, the *Tribune* piece also had some advice for Grange and Illinois: "If Mr. Red Grange and his pals are not careful the same name [Benny's] may again be on all tongues in Champaign a week from tonight."

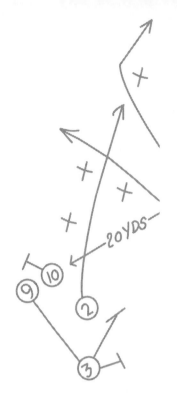

SIX

Benny to Bennie

It was bold, if not temporarily insane, to suggest that Red Grange had anything to fear from Benny Friedman or any other mere mortal. But with the 1925 season under way, there was good cause for concern about the Illini's and Grange's prospects. Graduation and injuries had depleted Illinois's line. Grange may have been the most spectacular runner ever to carry a football, but even he needed interference. The Illini had lost two of their first three games. Now powerful Michigan loomed, confident, healthy, and eager to invade Champaign to avenge last year's massacre.

The dynamic preceding this Michigan-Illinois encounter was different than it had been a year earlier. Then, Grange and Illinois had been peaking; Michigan was playing for the first time in nearly twenty-five years for a coach other than Fielding Yost; and the Wolverines had no star of their own to counter or at least mitigate the mighty redhead. Now, the Illini were reeling while the Wolverines were peaking; Yost was back, and not in a merciful frame of mind; and Michigan appeared to have the anti-Grange in Benny Friedman. The Wolverines were also without distraction, thoroughly focused on what for them was more a mission than a game.

Whether the same could be said for Grange was debatable. The prospect of playing pro football had been tantalizing him since the beginning of the season. The pro ball suitors, particularly George Halas of the Chicago Bears, were ratcheting up the pressure on the redhead with every passing week, waiting to pounce on him with a contract at the earliest possible moment.

There Red was, though, with his Illini teammates as they ran onto the Memorial Stadium turf for another joust with the Wolverines, one that would be played under markedly different conditions than in 1924. Then, the players rushing out of their respective locker rooms were greeted by Indian summer skies and a fast track of a field that promised lots of scoring. This day, cool autumn air and a rain-soaked patch of mud awaited the Wolverines and the Illini.

Bennie Oosterbaan was too nervous to pay much attention to the field conditions. The sophomore had thrashed around in bed the night before, the prospect of Grange sweeping past him rendering sleep all but impossible. Now, minutes before kickoff, the seventy thousand Illini fans crammed into the stadium weren't exactly soothing Bennie's jitters. Oosterbaan spotted Friedman calmly surveying the surroundings. The big end ambled over to his quarterback, looking for comfort.

"Benny," Oosterbaan said in a tone barely above a whisper, "I'm scared to death."

Friedman eyed his standout pass catcher with the same placid gaze he'd been casting about the stadium before answering.

"Hell, Bennie, so am I."

Perhaps Friedman's admission was calculated to relax Oosterbaan. In any case, it quickly became clear that the poor field conditions would render Grange far less a threat than Bennie feared he'd be. The muck was hampering Benny's passing game—one report would describe the ball that day as "a sponge full of mud" and speak of Benny's receivers "doing the backstroke" while trying to catch it—and Red was having difficulty running. Grange's troubles weren't due solely to the wet conditions. Yost's specially designed defensive formation—a seven-man front line backed by a diamond-formation secondary—hounded Grange relentlessly. Friedman was on top of his foe like a noontime sun, leading the Wolverines' defensive charge and often slamming Red into the mire himself.

With the second quarter evaporating, neither team had come close to scoring. Benny had so far shut down Red; now he had to find some way to score some points. After maneuvering the Wolverines to the Illini 15, Benny brought his team up to the line of scrimmage. Then he retreated to the twenty-four-yard line, poised to try a field goal with Louie Gilbert to hold. The massive crowd hushed as Benny awaited Bob Brown's snap. Gilbert grabbed Brown's perfect offering and placed the ball down. Across the line of scrimmage, in the Illinois secondary, Red Grange watched helplessly as Friedman's foot slammed into the ball, driving it out of the mud and through the uprights for what would be the only points scored all afternoon. Red would say later that Benny "outsmarted us to make the play which put his team in position" for the winning kick. Despite his best efforts, Red couldn't shake Benny and his mates in the second half, and Illinois's desperation passes at the end proved futile.

Friedman and Grange and the legions of fans anxiously anticipating their showdown deserved better than a three-hour tug-of-war. But that's what the elements presented to the two team leaders, and in the end, Benny earned the headline in the *Washington Post*: "Wolverine's Star Bests Grange."

In a note that Yost had written for the Illinois official game program, the Wolverines mentor had stressed sportsmanship, insisting that "the score [of the upcoming game] is relatively unimportant." But during Michigan's postgame celebration, a jubilant Yost, having avenged the previous year's 39–14 massacre, seemed to be of a different mind. "Grange didn't gain enough ground to bury him in, y'know," Yost roared gleefully. "Even if they'd buried him head daown!"

Years later, Grange would be far more sporting than the old Wolverines mentor in his analysis of that frustrating day. "I particularly remember

Benny Friedman, Michigan's great quarterback, sticking to me that entire afternoon like flypaper," Grange wrote.

. . .

The Wolverines couldn't have scripted a better start to their season. They were 4–0, Red Grange had been disposed of, and a palpable sensation that this 1925 group was crafting something very special prevailed in Ann Arbor. Their suffocating defense was still unscored upon. Their forwards weren't the biggest, but they consistently outplayed opposing linemen with a combination of strength and quickness and guile. They had unearthed Oosterbaan, a receiver with uncommon skills who was also a demon at defensive end. And they featured a quarterback who had emerged as a true triple threat while exhibiting such calm and smarts in running the team that he was, in essence, an extension of Yost on the field.

Benny had begun the season still somewhat of a secret notwithstanding his fine showing late in the '24 campaign. Now his multiple talents and field generalship were fast becoming the major story of the college football world. Sportswriters everywhere were hammering out pieces extolling Friedman. Walter Eckersall, the former University of Chicago hero, joined in the hullabaloo:

> Friedman's worth to the Michigan team has become more apparent with each game . . . It is his cleverness in directing the team's attack which makes him most valuable. He is cool and deliberate, selects plays with rare judgment and does not overplay himself. He can carry the ball from scrimmage as well as any back in the Middle West, while his forward passing is very accurate. He is a splendid catcher of punts and handles a football in much the same manner as an experienced ball player tosses the horsehide.

. . .

The Wolverines' next opponent was the Navy. The game would bring the Midshipmen farther west than any Navy team had ever ventured, and they'd be steaming into Ann Arbor in impressive shape. The only miscue on their 3–0–1 record was a 10–10 tie against a troublesome Princeton outfit that Knute Rockne's Four Horsemen of Notre Dame had struggled mightily to defeat only a year earlier. With star back Alan Shapley, a defense that had yielded no points other than the ten scored by Princeton, and a physically imposing squad that outweighed the Wolverines by roughly fifteen pounds per man, the Navy was poised to make a powerful statement for eastern football.

For the Wolverines, after four Big Ten contests, the battle against one of the East's strongest squads would be a welcome, albeit challenging change of pace. A solid week of practice left them injury-free and eager to play on Ferry Field again after two consecutive road games.

The Wolverines were also pregnant with an arsenal of talent that, for all of their success in the first four games, hadn't yet fully emerged. Would it, finally, against the bruisers from Annapolis?

Shortly before kickoff, Yost issued an unusual directive to Benny. "Pour it on today," the coach instructed his quarterback. "Pour it on and over." The coach was still seething over an incident with the Navy coach, Jack Owsley, at a breakfast earlier that week. Owsley had spoken poorly of Yost's good friend Walter Camp, provoking a heated exchange between Yost and the Navy coach. Yost's orders to Benny suggested that the coach intended to teach Owsley some manners.

· · ·

The Navy went nowhere after receiving the opening kickoff and was forced to launch a punt into the crystal clear, blue Michigan sky. The Wolverines crossed the Navy's goal line only minutes later, commencing an onslaught that no one, not even the staunchest Michigan booster, could have predicted.

For the next three and a half quarters, Benny tortured the visitors with his passing, running, punt returning, kicking, and field generalship. Benny and his teammates kept the Navy guessing wrong all day, repeatedly fooling the Midshipmen with trick plays that devoured huge chunks of yardage.

When the score was 35–0 with less than a quarter to play, Benny called "Old 83," a classic Yostian piece of deception. With the ball on the Navy 11, tight to the left sideline, Oosterbaan lined up at left end. Benny called signals with tailback Bill Herrnstein behind him. On the snap, Oosterbaan came hard into the backfield from left end to the right, while Herrnstein faked right and darted back to his left, behind Friedman. The Navy's right tackle flew in pursuit of Oosterbaan with such force that Benny *heard* the defender pass by him as he was faking a handoff to Oosterbaan. The Navy's right end was a step behind his teammate and, unsure if Benny had handed the ball to Oosterbaan, yanked Benny by the neck and leg as the quarterback pitched the ball to Herrnstein, who was flying behind Friedman toward the short left sideline. Herrnstein had no interference leading his way, but the Midshipmen had been so bamboozled that any fan in the stadium could have steamed into the end zone untouched.

Friedman was usually careful to move out of harm's way once he had released the ball on such a play, but on this occasion he stood still, transfixed at the sight of Yost's jubilation—the old man was urging Herrnstein on with frantic waves of his hat.

Was Benny piling on a bit when he called "Old 83" against the Navy? Maybe. The score was 35–0 at the time, there was a little less than a quarter to play, and Michigan didn't need to score more points. But Benny had his orders to "pour it on," and as the quarterback stood there, reveling in his coach's joy, he wasn't worried about running up the score. He only thought of how the play embodied the mantra that Yost had drilled into his head on all those strolls around Ferry Field: look over the defense, play for position, find the defense's sucker, or, as Yost liked to say, the "disciple of Barnum," and mercilessly exploit him.

The Navy's offense matched its defense's haplessness. The Michigan thirty-eight-yard line was as close as the Middies got to the Wolverines' goal. If a team could consider itself fortunate to have lost a game by only 54–0, the Navy was such a team that day—and not because Benny, for the first time all season, missed an extra-point placement (actually two).

Michigan's rout of Indiana, impressive as it was, had shocked almost no one; Indiana was no powerhouse. The Navy, on the other hand, had stormed into Ann Arbor with a record and group of players that justified its reputation as one of the nation's finest outfits. Friedman, plain and simple, had humbled them. "The Navy, like every team which preceded it on the Michigan schedule, spent weeks planning a defense for the Cleveland boy's passes, yet it could not hold him in check," declared the *Detroit Free Press.*

Congratulatory telegrams poured into Ann Arbor from Yost's friends and Michigan alumni. One was a single-line note from famed sportswriter and Michigan alum Ring Lardner. "Haven't you any respect for Uncle Sam?" Lardner wanted to know.

Yost was equally brief in his response. "The forward pass is a useful thing," Yost wrote, "when Benny Friedman does the fling."

· · ·

The writers called it the "feather ball." It was a forward pass that was somewhere between a bullet and a lob, and it was Benny's weapon of choice because he felt it was the easiest pass for a receiver to handle. "The secret of the feather ball," Benny wrote, "is to have the ball reach the high point of flight just before reaching the receiver so that the ball will drop into the receiver's hands." Friedman also favored the feather ball because it was a highly accurate pass, far more so than the fast pass or the lob.

That it was desirable to throw an accurate, easy-to-handle pass was hardly a state secret, but perfecting the technique to do so was quite another matter. Friedman's road to owning that technique began in Glenville, with the countless hours he spent performing those unusual exercises that stretched and strengthened his hand. Friedman's expansive hand enabled him to grip the melon of a football, cock the ball behind his right ear, his elbow close to his body, and deliver the ball with wrist snap for power and spin of the fingers for touch and accuracy. In other words, Benny trained himself to throw the ball while nearly all other passers couldn't do much more than place the ball in their palm and push it downfield.

But the grip was only the first half of Benny's recipe. Consistent accuracy also required a proper follow-through of the arm, extending out in direct line with the target. That particular technique wasn't especially unique, but Benny's emphasis on following through with his body certainly was.

Friedman's right side would swing around in pursuit of his arm, the right leg unwinding and the right foot planting in line with the targeted receiver. At the conclusion of the delivery, Benny's right hand nearly touched his left shoe. He looked more like a baseball pitcher than a quarterback. In the spring of 1926, Princeton's highly successful head football coach, Bill Roper, journeyed to Ann Arbor for a close look at Benny's passing motion to see where his astounding accuracy came from. After Roper and Fielding Yost watched Benny throw, "They concluded that all of the elements of my form combined to provide a mathematical certainty that the football would travel accurately," Benny wrote later.

Mathematical certainty or not, there was no question that Benny's peculiar motion worked. And, at least to Benny's thinking, his exaggerated follow-through made him not only more accurate, but also safer. Onrushing defensive linemen typically attack the quarterback by rushing to the spot where the pass is released. Benny's peculiar motion carried him forward a step or two from that spot and a step or two ahead of, as he once put it, "annihilation." When the defenders did get in a shot on Friedman, he was rarely in an exposed position; his follow-through carried him into a strong, braced crouch that allowed him to absorb punishing blows with minimal damage.

Friedman's unusual passing technique wasn't developed by accident; it was well thought out with the express purpose of satisfying two prerequisites to successful passing—accuracy and durability. It was a cerebral approach to a brutal game that was perfectly suited to Fielding Yost, a coach who wasn't so much interested in beating up opponents as he was in outsmarting them.

For all the pleasure Benny derived from the cerebral aspects of the game, he did not play football in a protective cocoon. Although of modest size at five feet ten inches and 180 pounds, he had a body of iron and wasn't afraid to use it. On open field runs, tacklers would pay a price to bring him to the ground. On pass plays, the great quarterback was a marked man for linemen desperately trying to deliver a blow that would knock him out of the game. Yet Friedman would stand amidst the chaos, ball firmly in his big hand, and wait for a receiver to break free before throwing, ready to take the pounding that such patience invited. On defense he got to even things out a bit, delivering tackles from his free safety position with ferocity. Red Grange played with and against the toughest football players in the land—the Minnesota bunch that nearly wrecked his shoulder in 1924, the great Ernie Nevers, the rambunctious George Trafton, and the massive Cal Hubbard to mention just a few. Benny Friedman, Grange said, was the toughest man he ever played against.

. . .

A couple of days after Benny's destruction of the Navy, the Chicago *Southtown Economist* observed: "Michigan, mighty Michigan, has produced yet another fast and furious football star in the person of Benny Friedman, a go-getting Jewish boy.

"We understand Henry Ford has an army of sleuths and detectives working on this latest Semitic conspiracy."

The writer's tongue-in-cheek shot at Ford was a reminder that Benny was performing his heroics amidst the hovering spectre of anti-Semitism. Even as the "go-getting Jewish boy" was demolishing the Navy, a vivid example of the growing intolerance toward his religion was mushrooming back in Cleveland, just minutes from his Glenville home.

In January 1925, the Cleveland Jewish Orphan Home, looking to move the five hundred or so young Jewish orphans housed in its dilapidated building in the center of Cleveland, bought thirty acres on which to build a new orphanage in University Heights, a small village just outside the Cleveland city limits. The construction plans conformed in every respect with the village zoning ordinance's building requirements. The cottages that would house the orphans would be aesthetically pleasing, and all parties concerned agreed that the proposed facility would be first-rate in all respects.

But University Heights had recently amended the zoning ordinance to grant itself broad discretion to reject a use that didn't serve the "public convenience and welfare." Citing this amendment—which had been enacted just as the home had selected the site for the orphanage—the village rejected the plan.

In what manner would the orphanage offend the "public convenience and welfare"? The village proffered three arguments. First, the tax-free status of the orphanage as a public institution would deplete the village's revenues. Second, the small village, with no existing public school, would be burdened with providing school facilities for the five hundred orphans. The third reason exposed the village's true, malevolent motivation. It seems that University Heights was of the opinion that "a school in any community, predominantly attended by the children of a single race, creed or nationality, is hurtful to the community."

The home didn't shrink from the village's blatant anti-Semitism. In May, it sued University Heights in federal court in Cleveland, asking the court to declare the ordinance and amendment illegal and to block its enforcement. Thus began the country's first federal lawsuit involving religious discrimination in zoning.

As the case proceeded into November and Benny began preparing for Northwestern, back in Friedman's hometown, the home's lawyers were preparing a brief that would simply yet eloquently disarm any pretext of legitimacy on the part of the village's actions. "[University Heights]," the lawyers wrote, "does not want a Jewish orphanage, no matter how beautiful, sanitary, safe and moral it may be." Nearly four years later, after the home prevailed in federal district court, the United States Court of Appeals, and the United States Supreme Court, and after it survived University Heights's post-litigation efforts to block the orphanage, the orphanage finally opened.

· · ·

Northwestern had already experienced Benny's passing wizardry, absorbing a 37–0 pasting when the quarterback was a sophomore. Now the Wildcats would get Friedman in full bloom—a year wiser and stronger, throwing passes behind a brick wall of a line, bursting with confidence after laying waste to a very strong Navy team that looked vastly superior to Northwestern.

Difficult as the upcoming task appeared, however, Northwestern had a recent history of responding well to adversity. A year earlier, Knute Rockne and his Four Horsemen of Notre Dame had rolled into Chicago with their 6–0 record for an expected feast against the Wildcats. But Northwestern confronted the Irish with a ferocity that had Rockne praying for the final whistle. Notre Dame was blessed to limp back to South Bend with a 13–6 victory.

The Wolverines and Wildcats woke up that Saturday, November 7, to gale-force winds, rain, and subfreezing temperatures. An entire week of rain had already transformed the Soldier Field turf into a quagmire. Game cancellations were rare, but with rain continuing to knife down and the wind threatening to blow half of Lake Michigan into the stadium, this game was a cancellation candidate.

At that moment, nothing would have pleased Fielding Yost more. Yost sensed—knew—that his high-powered offense would never shift out of neutral in these abysmal conditions. The old coach had returned this season looking for one more shot at glory and, just as he thought he might, he'd struck gold with a sensation at quarterback and a dynamic supporting cast that had the Wolverines barreling toward their best season ever. Yost saw his fairy tale season about to vanish in a wind-blown sea of mud, against a team that on a normal day would likely be of little concern, and he had to at least try to stop it. With kickoff looming, Yost pulled aside Tug Wilson, Northwestern's athletic director.

"Tug," Yost drawled, "I coach a football team, not a swimming team. How can I tell them to play a game on a field they can hardly see?"

"We've already sold 40,000 tickets to the game," Wilson responded. "You know we can't afford to call it off."

Wilson had a legitimate point. He also had a team with almost no chance to beat Michigan under normal playing conditions. The mire would more than compensate Northwestern for the absence of their star back, Moon Baker, who was still nursing an injured leg. This game was going to be played.

No one in Chicago in his right mind should have ventured outside on that Saturday. Yet about twenty thousand people slogged their way into Soldier Field for the Michigan-Northwestern game.

From the moment the players emerged from the locker rooms and took their first steps in the field's ankle-high mud, it was obvious that there would be little if any offensive movement by either team. The Wildcats confirmed as much when they received the opening kickoff and, on the first play from scrimmage from their own forty-yard line and the wind at their back, they punted. No probing of the Michigan line. No thought of sweeping the end. And certainly no thought of a forward pass attempt. The only thought was to get rid of the ball, as far downfield as possible, and let Michigan figure out something from the bowels of their own territory with the rain and sleet whipping at their faces at fifty-five miles per hour.

Benny, waiting deep downfield for the punt, bent to scoop up the ball as it rolled toward him. But nature got the better of the quarterback's usually dependable hands. The ball squirted from Benny's grasp, igniting a melee in the muck as the Wolverines and Wildcats desperately pursued the ball just a few steps from the Michigan goal line. When the thrashing stopped, Northwestern's Barney Matthews had the ball on Michigan's three-yard line. Matthews likely would have scored had Wildcat captain Tim Lowry, believing the mud-caked Matthews to be a Michigan player, not tackled him.

No opponent had sniffed territory so close to the Wolverines' end zone in Michigan's first four contests. Now, just two plays into the game, there were the Wildcats, three yards from recording the first points against the Wolverines all year. And it was a rare lapse in judgment by Benny that had put them there; Friedman shouldn't have tried to field the punt so close to his goal in such abominable conditions.

But Northwestern still had three yards to cover, no easy task against the Wolverines defense on the mildest, driest of days, and on this day, the three yards might as well have been thirty. Three Wildcat plunges into the line garnered negative yardage, leaving Northwestern one last down to cash in on

Benny's gift. They couldn't run it in. They wouldn't even think of trying to pass it in. They'd have to try a field goal.

Northwestern fullback Leland Lewis, who just a few plays earlier had punted to Friedman, stood in the muck at the eighteen-yard line, waiting for the snap. The typhoon and slop made just getting a kick airborne a long shot. But Lewis dug the ball out of the mud and drove it in the general direction of the goalposts. The kick was weak but the squall at the Wildcats' back barely blew the ball over the crossbar, just inside the upright: 3–0, Northwestern.

For the remainder of the game, the teams engaged in a punting contest, booting the waterlogged ball back and forth. Most times they didn't wait for fourth down to punt. Benny threw just one pass, incomplete, and the Wolverines' longest gain from scrimmage was eleven yards. Michigan's best hope for getting those three points back was to punt the Wildcats back to their goal line, hold them there, and then take possession.

Toward the end of the third quarter, it appeared that the Wolverines' patience was about to bear fruit. With the gale now howling in their faces, the Wildcats were trapped with the ball on their own one-yard line. They couldn't advance the ball by running or passing. A punt seemed to be called for, but there was a huge risk that a punt would be mishandled or blocked in the end zone and recovered by Michigan for a touchdown.

Huddling in the mire of their end zone, the Wildcats listened in as captain Lowry barked instructions: "Call a punt—Lewis, drop on the ball—a safety, see?" Lewis did what he was told, and Benny touched him down. The score was now Northwestern 3, Michigan 2.

The Wolverines had an entire quarter to score again. Michigan might have scored thirty points in a quarter on almost any other day, but on this day, the Wolverines were in a strange place full of sleet and wind and sludge and a Northwestern team that smelled a major upset.

The safety rule in effect at the time called for the team taking the safety to keep possession of the ball at their own thirty-yard line. From there, no longer confronted with the perils of punting from his end zone, Lewis launched a punt deep into Michigan territory. The punt-for-field-position game resumed, but the Wolverines never again approached the Wildcats goal line.

Yost's worst fear had been realized. An ordinary Northwestern team—a team that only a week earlier had defeated by a mere three points the same Indiana team that Benny had manhandled 63–0—had beaten mighty Michigan by the baseball score of 3–2. Gone was the Wolverines' undefeated and unscored-upon season and smooth sailing toward the Big Ten crown. Yost was livid—at the result, at the conditions, at the rule that allowed Northwestern to take the safety knowing they'd get the ball at their own thirty-yard line. Ultimately, Yost's protests would prompt a rule change requiring the team taking the safety to kick to the opposing team rather than keep possession.

But that would be for another day. On this day, Lowry was praised as a genius for calling for the safety (though given Northwestern's dire position at the time, it hardly required a genius to realize the intentional safety was the only reasonable play). Yost was left to rail at the godforsaken weather and field conditions that rendered his powerful team impotent. Of course, Yost hadn't complained about the difficult field conditions that had helped the Wolverines halt Grange two weeks earlier. The truth is, though, that the conditions in the Illinois game were temperate compared to the typhoon and mire at Soldier Field, and one needed to look to no less an authority than the great Walter Eckersall—the man who refereed both games—for confirmation. "In my twenty-five years of football, I have never seen worse conditions," Eckersall wrote of the Soldier Field maelstrom.

Poor weather pelted stadiums throughout the Midwest that day, though not with quite the ferocity of the Chicago storm. In some areas around the country, however, decent conditions permitted talented players to display their wares. In a game between two unbeaten teams, Dartmouth's Andy "Swede" Oberlander put on an exhibition against Cornell that rivaled Benny's wizardry against the Navy and Indiana. All year long the Dartmouth star had been the other quarterback mentioned with Benny in any conversation about the country's best passers. Like Benny, Oberlander blended outstanding running ability with superlative passing skills, and while Benny was floundering in the Soldier Field swamp, Oberlander was devastating Cornell with a two-pronged attack that yielded extraordinary results. The Swede rushed and passed for a total of five hundred yards, give or take a few depending on the various statistical accounts of the game. Six of Oberlander's passes went for touchdowns in Dartmouth's 62–13 blitz of Cornell. After the game, Cornell's coach, Gil Dobie, an intense sort known for his disdain of forward passing and a grumpiness even on good days, made it defiantly clear that he was unimpressed by Oberlander's aerial circus.

Seemingly oblivious to the bombardment the Big Red had just absorbed, Dobie told reporters after the game that Cornell had actually won, 13–0, since passing, which in essence accounted for all of Dartmouth's points, wasn't part of football.

Maybe in Ithaca it wasn't. But in Ann Arbor, Benny was fast making Dobie's traditionalist philosophy obsolete.

. . .

Michigan's Chicago misadventure against Northwestern marked more than the end of their unbeaten and unscored-upon streaks. It also seriously dented the veneer of Wolverine invincibility that had been building steadily on Big Ten campuses. Mother Nature, with an assist from Northwestern, had flung the conference championship race wide open. Michigan was now one of five teams in the conference with one loss, the others being Ohio State, Iowa, Minnesota, and Wisconsin. With Ohio State coming to Ferry Field on November 14, the feeling in Ann Arbor wasn't quite as heady as it had been in the afterglow of the Navy game.

The Buckeyes, aided by Benny's second straight subpar performance, threw a scare into the Wolverines. Friedman had been banged up a bit in the Northwestern game and it showed; his trademark accuracy took the day off. Benny also uncharacteristically squandered a prime scoring chance; with Michigan poised to steam into the Buckeyes' end zone, a Friedman pass was picked off at the Ohio State one-yard line. But the Wolverines, sluggish as they were, still had a little too much for the Buckeyes. A

Molenda one-yard scoring plunge, Benny's extra point and his thirty-eight-yard field goal, and an unwavering defense delivered a 10–0 triumph to the Wolverines.

Despite the win, Friedman's performance against Ohio State rankled him. For the second straight week, his passing game had stalled, and while the horrendous conditions in Chicago could excuse his performance there, the decent weather, firm turf, and friendly crowd at Ferry Field should have added up to a big day against the Buckeyes. Benny would get one more chance in 1925 to have such a day. Minnesota, the team from up north, was coming to Ann Arbor.

SEVEN

"The Greatest Team I Ever Coached"

The University of Minnesota was one tough customer of a football team. In 1924 they beat Illinois and they beat up Red Grange, enhancing a well-earned reputation for physical play. In '25 they hadn't played the harshest schedule while compiling their 5–1–1 record, but they'd defeated the teams they should have defeated, with authority. Their two blemishes, a 19–7 loss to Rockne's Fighting Irish and a bitterly contested 12–12 tie with Wisconsin, were hardly disgraces. If there was any doubt as to their bona fides, their 33–0 demolition of a talented Iowa team on November 14 should have erased it. Minnesota confounded the Hawkeyes with their "shift" offense, and the young Gophers lineup, composed mostly of sophomores, played with the swagger of seasoned upperclassmen. Bruising fullback Herb Joesting, in the middle of a season that would see him earn all Big Ten honors, led this precocious group that had every intention of leaving Ferry Field with the 1925 Big Ten championship.

. . .

Indian summer joined the Minnesota Gophers on their visit to Ann Arbor on Saturday, November 21. Aside from a bit more heat than a footballer might want, playing conditions at Ferry Field were ideal. Benny would have no excuses, not with forty-seven thousand Michigan fans and a healthy team supporting him.

Michigan immediately grabbed this game by the throat, like a team spoiling for a fight and with the talent to win it. A few minutes in, Benny followed a thirty-yard strike to Oosterbaan with a twenty-five-yard dart to Louie Gilbert. With the Gophers' heads still spinning, Benny handed the ball to Bo Molenda, who coasted into the end zone behind a Michigan line that eviscerated the Minnesota forwards. Benny concluded the blitz by nailing the extra point.

More than the touchdown itself, it was the way Michigan scored it—with a sense of power and inevitability—that delivered the crushing message to the Gophers that they weren't playing Iowa anymore. The Wolverines displayed the full inventory of their talent the rest of the afternoon—Benny zinging the ball to Oosterbaan and Flora and Gregory; Molenda and Gilbert shedding tacklers and devouring yards on the ground; the Wolverine forwards taking out the big Gopher defenders with the ease of an assault on a blocking dummy; and the Michigan defense conveying with stark clarity the message to Herb Joesting and his running mates that there wasn't much running to be done. Supplemented by Friedman's spotless kicking—Benny boomed five points after touchdowns in five attempts—the performance was near-perfect, marred only by two uncharacteristic Oosterbaan drops that were compensated for by his two touchdown catches.

Yost led the revelry in the Wolverines' locker room following the 35–0 shellacking of Minnesota. Always at the forefront of any victory celebration, Yost was especially jubilant, making the rounds and expressing his endearment for his players with hearty slaps on the back. Benny's brilliance toward the end of the 1924 season had seduced the old coach and induced him to come back for one more hike up the mountain, and with the crushing victory he'd just witnessed on his beloved Ferry Field, Yost knew he'd reached the summit.

Friedman's demolition of the Gophers was a masterful brushstroke on his 1925 football canvas. The young Jewish lad had catapulted to the top of the nation's quarterback class, gaining recognition as the game's finest forward passer and as a field general without peer. Michigan's trouncing of Minnesota, combined with Illinois's defeat of Ohio State, left Michigan and Northwestern as the two teams in the conference with only one loss, and left the crowning of the Big Ten champion a matter of unfinished business.

• • •

Fielding Yost's 1925 team had compiled a 7–1 mark against some of the stiffest competition in training, outscoring opponents by 228 to 3 in the process. But Northwestern's shocking victory over Michigan in the Soldier Field swamp was delaying recognition of Yost's boys as sole Big Ten champions. A fair amount of sentiment abounded, particularly (and not surprisingly) in the Chicago press, that the Wildcats deserved a share of the title, if not the title outright.

On balance, the teams' records didn't support such sentiment. Michigan had played six conference games, winning five, while Northwestern had gone 3–1 in just four conference games. Michigan was the Wildcats' only conference foe with a winning record, while Indiana (a team that nearly defeated the Wildcats after Benny had manhandled them by a score of 63–0) was the Wolverines' only conference foe with a *losing* record. The 1925 Northwestern unit was a strong team—the best team in school history, declared the *Daily Northwestern*—but without the aberration at Soldier Field, there wouldn't have been an argument.

Tug Wilson, the Wildcats' athletic director who'd rebuffed Yost's attempts to call off that game, apparently realized just that. On November 24, in a rare gesture of sportsmanship, Wilson essentially conceded the Big Ten championship to Michigan. "We feel that due to Michigan's remarkable record, they are entitled to the honors of the conference, and we do not dispute them," Wilson said. "We, of course, are justly proud of our Wildcats who went out and licked them." Northwestern's president, Walter

Dill Scott, formalized the concession in a telegram to Michigan president Clarence Cook Little.

Wolverine boosters were thrilled at Northwestern's magnanimity, perhaps none more so than the University of Michigan Club of Detroit, a group of some five thousand Michigan alumni residing in the Detroit area. "Your timely and unselfish concession," the club's board of directors wrote in a letter to Scott, "will long be a matter of gratification to those of Michigan's alumni who seek for her, nothing but the best in intercollegiate athletics and relationships."

Yost welcomed the concession, but he must have found it strange that a team as relatively ordinary as Northwestern was even being mentioned in the same conversation as his Wolverines. Only days after his boys thrashed Minnesota, he praised them at the team's annual awards dinner: "You are members of the greatest football team I have ever coached; in fact you are the greatest football team I ever saw in action. I am making this statement cognizant of the wonderful record of the 1901 team and the point-a-minute teams that followed." Yost even replaced the gold 1901 football charm that had been attached to his watch for nearly twenty-five years with a 1925 football as a tribute to Benny and his teammates.

Yost's 1925 defense allowed fewer first downs than the number of *touchdowns* allowed by other teams. Bob Brown and Ray Baer anchored the center of the defensive front. Oosterbaan terrorized any ball carrier with notions of running wide. Benny patrolled the secondary and asserted himself as a tackling force all over the field. Collectively they humbled some of the country's best offenses.

On offense the 1925 Wolverines didn't have Willie Heston, but in Benny they did have, as heralded by the *New York Times,* "the modern Willie Heston." Of course, Heston never passed the ball like Benny did, and judging from descriptions of Benny's passing offered by writers who witnessed it, nobody else in football history up to that point had either. "He shoots passes with the same accuracy as a good shortstop throws out a runner at first base," stated the *Chicago Tribune.*

No less an authority than Knute Rockne declared that Benny's forward passing was the "sensation of the year," and while that was unquestionably the case, Friedman's open field running and precise and timely placekicking established him as college football's outstanding triple threat. The *New York Times*'s account of the way Benny immediately erased a fifteen-yard penalty in the Navy game colorfully capsulized the danger he presented to defenses as a runner: "Friedman peeled off those fifteen yards and four more in one mad dash that would have done credit to a whirling dervish," Richard Vidmer wrote, "as the Navy players were sliced off his hips like so many orange peels falling by the wayside."

Benny had no match as a field general. Though inside his emotions churned like those of any other man engaged in the maelstrom that is a football game, he played with a calm exterior that seemed to slow down the game and relax his teammates while unsettling his opponents. "He is the coolest man I ever saw on a football field," Yost said of Benny. "He is never ruffled. Regardless of how the play goes, he has never lost his poise. There is never a moment when your confidence in him wavers." As if that weren't praise enough, Yost would later call Benny the only quarterback "to never make a mistake."

Yost, the garrulous coach from the West Virginia hills, and Benny, his young, somewhat subdued quarterback from the Cleveland shtetl, were anything but cultural kindred spirits. But on the football field, it was a different story. There they were a perfect match: a coach and a quarterback who shared a liking for trick plays, lightning strikes, and outsmarting the opponent, and with the talent and willingness to work tirelessly in practice in order to pull it all off on game day.

Yost's three-prong football gospel—look over the defense, play for lateral position, and exploit the opponent's "disciples of Barnum"—had become Benny's mantra too. "[I] was [Yost's] fair-haired boy naturally because I took all the things that he always wanted to do and put them into action," Benny said later. Since the previous fall, Yost had been taking Benny on private strolls around Ferry Field, regaling his quarterback with tales of

Michigan's football glory as they walked. The coach, it seemed, could pick out precise spots on the turf where magic moments had occurred. "Right 'chere, right 'chere," Yost drawled, pawing at various patches of turf where Willie Heston had taken off on another startling run, where all-American lineman Germany Shultz had thrown blocks that knocked defenders halfway to East Lansing, and where Harry Kipke had launched sixty-yard punts that pinned opponents within inches of their goal line. Yost, charmer that he was, may have been playing fast and loose with Ferry Field geography, but it was heady stuff for a young quarterback.

Like Yost, Benny hardly ever yelled, and leadership flowed from him as it did from his coach. With a physical toughness second to none—Benny rarely missed a play even though the opposition routinely saved its most enthusiastic pounding for him—he earned the unequivocal respect and loyalty of his teammates. Friedman returned that respect with an unflagging appreciation of his mates' importance, notwithstanding a healthy regard for his own talents; Benny's standing policy was to avoid calling his own number when Michigan was inside the opponent's twenty-five-yard line so as to afford his teammates the satisfaction of scoring the touchdown. "He is a genius at handling a team, one of the inspired leaders that come but once in every two or three generations." Those words didn't come from Yost, although the coach wouldn't have quibbled with them. They came from Francis Powers, the man considered by famed sportswriter Grantland Rice to be the foremost authority on western football.

· · ·

The matchup between Michigan and Minnesota had attracted much attention that week, but the buildup to Red Grange's farewell to college football that weekend had been just as big a story. Illinois's battle with Ohio State in Columbus would be the redhead's last on a college football field, but there were other fields—littered with dollar signs—in Grange's not-too-distant future. Rumors were rampant that Red, in collaboration with a manager named C. C. Pyle, would turn professional immediately after the game—without waiting to graduate from Illinois. The NFL was showing signs of life but was still struggling mightily to convince the public that pro football was a product worth buying. The league, and particularly Chicago Bears owner George Halas, was virtually salivating at the prospect of the enormously popular Grange carrying the ball for pay, and Halas had been negotiating with Pyle for several weeks. Amidst all the reports and speculation surrounding Grange, Big Ten commissioner John L. Griffith announced on November 19 that any Big Ten player who signed a professional contract would immediately lose his amateur status and forfeit any remaining college football eligibility.

Red had tried that week to quell the frenzy with denials that he intended to turn pro, but he'd already shaken hands with Pyle to do exactly that. With the burst of the pistol ending Illinois's game with the Buckeyes (fittingly, Grange carried the ball on the last play), Red dashed to the locker room trailed by dozens of reporters giving better chase than the Buckeyes had in the game just completed. He managed to escape in a cab with Zuppke, where Red told his coach and mentor the news: he'd be leaving Illinois and turning professional immediately. Zuppke vainly attempted to dissuade Red from making what the coach considered a huge mistake. Red then boarded a train for Chicago, where he took a hotel room under an assumed name. The next morning, Grange revealed his plans to the press, surprising almost nobody. He would play the last two games of the NFL season with Halas's Bears and then join the Bears on a barnstorming trip of the East.

Yost disapproved of Grange's decision, hardly a surprise given his negative feelings toward pro ball. As the rumors swirled earlier in the week, Yost said he'd "be glad to see Grange do anything else except play professional football." And Red's decision to join the pros crushed Zuppke, especially since Grange didn't bother to wait to graduate. In fairness to Grange, the dollars dangling in front of his eyes would have been difficult for any young man to ignore, and he did complete his final season with the Illini. Zuppke, though, couldn't—or wouldn't—see the dollar signs. He saw only his greatest player ever, maybe anybody's greatest player ever, abusing the pure spirit of the game by prostituting himself. It was more than he could abide, and his anger spilled out at the Illini's annual football banquet. In his address to the team, the coach ripped into his onetime fair-haired boy, who was sitting at a table with his former teammates.

"The Grange we know and the Grange we have watched for three years is now a myth," Zuppke declared. "As time goes on, those runs will grow in length with the telling. Grange will pass on and be forgotten."

If those words didn't get Red's attention, Zuppke's closing shot did. "I tell you," Zuppke growled, addressing Grange directly, "that no other $100,000 player is going to be on one of my teams."

Red bolted from the room in tears.

• • •

One of the games scheduled for Grange's barnstorming tour was against a team of professionals in Coral Gables, Florida, on Christmas Day. The organizers of the game, looking to glamorize things and figuring that Grange's move to the pros would induce other college stars to follow, extended offers to several of the nation's top college stars. But Grange's leap into the NFL didn't produce the hoped-for copycat effect. Swede Oberlander, University of Chicago fullback Austin McCarty, and Iowa's Nick Kutsch all declined. McCarty and Oberlander were college seniors who'd just played their last games. They had no additional eligibility to protect, but they weren't offered "Red Grange money" or anything close to it. Kutsch, a junior, had another season of college ball ahead of him and wasn't about to challenge Big Ten commissioner Griffith's edict.

Benny also received a telegram offering him a contract to play in the Christmas Day game against Grange and the Bears. It's doubtful that even "Grange money" would have persuaded Friedman to take the leap. He'd just finished leading Michigan to perhaps its greatest season ever. He'd established himself as the finest quarterback in the land. He and Bennie Oosterbaan were on their way to becoming the most famous and greatest quarterback-receiver duo in football history, if they weren't there already.

He had another full season ahead of him to bring Michigan further glory and burnish his already glittering reputation. And he loved Fielding Yost. Benny also was pursuing his pre-law studies in Ann Arbor and still nurturing his dream of becoming a United States Supreme Court Justice. Arrayed against all this, the prospect of joining a vagabond professional outfit to play the foil to Red Grange had for Benny all the allure of playing for George Little. He responded to the telegram with one of his own that was as definitive as it was brief: "Not interested."

Benny was very interested, however, in being elected captain of the Wolverines for the 1926 season. There was no more prestigious honor for a player than to be elected captain by your teammates. The honor was an affirmation of your high quality as a player, your leadership abilities, and the respect held for you by your teammates. It gave you a special level of recognition and respect among fans, the media, and opposing players and coaches. The team became *your* team. Friedman's spectacular play and leadership during the '25 season pegged him as a natural for the honor for 1926.

The Wolverines traditionally elected their captain for the next season on the Monday immediately following the team's last game. On the afternoon of November 23, Benny strolled across campus to the student union for the election. It hadn't been that long ago that his only utility to the team was as a human tackling dummy, or that he was glued to the bench, or that he was one strong shove from transferring to Dartmouth. It wasn't even so terribly long ago that Sam Willaman had told Friedman he was too small to ever make much of a football player. Now Benny, widely acclaimed as the nation's premier quarterback and the Wolverines' undisputed leader, stood on the threshold of one of the most prized captaincies in college football.

But to some Michigan students who had spoken with Benny toward the end of the season, his election as captain was not a given.

"Will you play your senior season if you're not elected captain?" they asked Benny.

"Why?" he inquired.

"Well, because you're Jewish."

"Well," Friedman replied, "Bill Flora and I started together, he has every right to it as much as I. He didn't get any of the notice that I got, but he's a hell of a guy and a hell of a football player."

The conversation had troubled Benny. His experience with the Wolverines had been free of evidence of anti-Semitism (though he had his suspicions about George Little). He'd always considered himself a football player who happened to be a Jew. The exchange with the students confronted Benny with the unpleasant reality that at least to some people, he was a Jewish football player. And no Jewish football player had ever captained the Michigan Wolverines.

That afternoon of November 23, the team elected their next captain by unanimous vote. Religion was not the issue to the people who mattered most—Benny's fellow players. At the next Ohio State–Michigan game on November 12, 1926, when assistant Ohio State coach Sam Willaman would look at the kid who hadn't been good enough for East Tech High, he'd be looking at the captain of the Michigan Wolverines.

He'd also be looking at the 1925 All–Big Ten and all-American quarterback.

· · ·

A graph charting the development of Friedman's profile among America's Jews in 1925 would have shown a steadily rising line that, with his election as Michigan's captain, shot straight up and off the paper. On the night of his election as captain, Benny received seventy-eight telegrams from Jews around the country offering their congratulations. Thousands more poured into Ann Arbor over the next several days. More than any other Jewish athlete of the day, with the possible exception of lightweight boxing champ Benny Leonard, Friedman was—wittingly or not—the embodiment of the "tough Jew." There was Benny in a full-page photograph on the cover of a December issue of the *American Hebrew,* the most widely read general-interest Jewish weekly of the day. "Benny Friedman at Full Tilt," screamed the photo caption. The image is of anything but a nebbish: Benny is crouched low, on his toes, a football in the crook of his left arm, his right arm cocked, and his eyes glaring from beneath his helmet as if in warning to defenders to get out of his way.

The stereotype of the Jew as a physical weakling was held by both non-Jews and Jews, and the *American Jewish World* took note of how Benny's football stardom helped challenge the stereotype for both groups. In a piece entitled "The Five Big Jews of 1925," the writer reviewed the contributions of five Jews—one of whom was Friedman—who "have done the most for America within the last year." "[Benny] is causing the members of his race to revise the notions of their own physical competence . . . Hitherto, the Jew has stressed his intellectual capacity; he has derided, or perhaps has just been indifferent to, athletic achievements. This was due to a complex which had no justification in fact, as events now prove. The prevalence of so many Jewish names on many of our collegiate football teams is ample evidence of the changing of that complex. Benny Friedman is the crystallization of the new Jewish attitude toward athletics."

And Benny's singular gridiron feats, such as his demolition of the powerful Navy eleven and his conquering of the great Red Grange, made it increasingly difficult for Gentiles to cling to the narrow-minded belief that Jews were incapable of high athletic achievement. As the *American Jewish World* piece put it, "Friedman's prowess as a football star must inevitably reflect upon some Christians' attitudes toward Jews."

At a time when quotas limiting Jewish enrollment in universities were one stark manifestation of rising anti-Semitism, Benny's ascendancy in Ann Arbor offered the Jewish community some hope, if not assurance, that there was room for them after all. The *American Hebrew* remarked in a December 1925 issue: "This . . . Jewish prodigy of America's greatest collegiate sport is symbolic of more widespread tolerance in undergraduate life where youthful prepossessions and prejudices perhaps more often than in everyday life are prone to run away with fair judgments."

But even while trumpeting the gains Benny had brought his coreligionists, the *American Hebrew* observed that Jewish college students needed to meet a few conditions, as Benny had, before they could expect to be tolerated on campus: "[Friedman] symbolizes a tolerance based on recognition of character, intrinsic merit and pleasing deportment—qualities especially requisite of the Jew on campus."

The object of this ethnic hero worship was all of twenty years old. Never had Benny shied away from his Jewish identity, but neither had he courted such a pedestal among his people. He was just a young man working his way through school, studying hard to realize his dream of a spot on the Supreme Court, and playing the game he loved like no one before him had played it. He'd gained recognition as the greatest forward passer the game had seen. Week after week, he'd conquered defenses that some of the best coaching minds in America had designed just to stop him. He'd saddled the Navy with the most lopsided loss that proud program had ever suffered. He'd torched Wisconsin with a frenzied exhibition of passing and running comparable to the great Grange's exploits, and then outdueled the great Red. He'd been responsible for producing the finest season ever enjoyed by one of the finest college programs. And he'd reaped the rewards of his brilliance: election as Michigan's first Jewish captain and the fulfillment of his childhood dream of being named an all-American.

If all of this was somehow making the world a less hateful, more tolerant place, a better place for American Jews, that was fine with Benny.

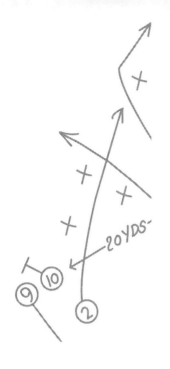

EIGHT

Senior Year

A few weeks after the season-ending game against the Gophers, Yost received a letter from a fan in Minnesota. It seems the fan's friends, perhaps tired of seeing their Gophers pasted by Yost's Wolverines, suggested that Yost was too old to coach any longer. "Stagg is sixty-four and is still going strong," the fifty-four-year-old Michigan mentor wrote back to the fan. "You tell my good Minnesota friends that if they are waiting for me to get 'too old' they will have to wait a long time yet."

Certainly, there was no way Yost was going to miss out on Benny's senior year, to say nothing of another year with the services of Molenda, Gilbert, and Flora. And then there was the gazelle Oosterbaan, already being hailed as the finest receiver ever to catch a football, returning a year wiser and stronger for his junior season. You don't strike oil and go home after filling your first barrel.

Still, the Wolverines' foundation would have some cracks. Friedman had received a lot of help from all-American forwards Bob Brown, Tom Edwards, and Harry Hawkins. All three of these standouts were lost to graduation. Red Grange's slow start in his senior year had in many circles been blamed on the depletion of Illinois's line. Could Yost re-engineer his line to allow Benny a reprise of 1925?

It wouldn't help matters, either, that Michigan would face a daunting schedule that would see every opponent bearing down just a bit harder on the defending Big Ten champion with the sensational quarterback. After two relatively mild games against Oklahoma A&M and Michigan State, the Wolverines would get, in succession, Minnesota, Illinois, the Navy, Wisconsin, Ohio State, and Minnesota again. Conquering this schedule would be a formidable chore even if each of these opponents didn't have a score to settle for the way Michigan had thumped them in '25. The Navy, battered by a Michigan performance Benny would call "as close to perfection as any ball club could get," would be particularly eager for their return engagement with the Wolverines, in Baltimore on October 30.

And as if preparing his team to defend its Big Ten title wasn't enough of a task, Yost would be burdened with another labor of love he hoped would dramatically alter the football landscape at the University of Michigan. Early in the decade Yost had started flirting with the idea of building a massive new stadium for the Wolverines, who were slowly but surely outgrowing Ferry Field. Even with the additional bleachers installed in 1921 that had increased capacity to 42,000, the old park didn't have nearly enough seating to accommodate the huge demand for the Wolverines' major home contests. Yost had seen Big Ten rivals Ohio State, Illinois, Northwestern, and Minnesota, buoyed by the unprecedented popularity of college football, build gleaming new stadiums in the past several years with seating capacity that dwarfed Ferry Field's. He'd seen the spectacle of Illinois homecoming in front of a crowd of more than 70,000 in 1924. The Horseshoe at Ohio State could accommodate more than 90,000 maniacal Buckeye fans (as Yost would soon discover firsthand). Such huge crowds provided an incalculable emotional lift for the home team, but more than that, Yost the athletic director and businessman understood the very calculable increase in revenue that 30,000 or 40,000 additional seats would produce for the university.

Yost's proposal for a new stadium was submitted to the university senate in the spring of 1925. Not unexpectedly, it was greeted with some skepticism. Academic types were concerned that the massive crowds would turn football games into spectacles inconsistent with the university's educational mission. Financial concerns abounded. The university tabled the proposal for months.

Then in October, Benny began to turn the Big Ten on its head. His astounding performance at the Wolverines' helm in 1925 gave Yost's proposal the shot of adrenaline it needed. He'd shown the doubters that, like it or not, Michigan football was every bit the spectacle that football was in Champaign and Columbus and Evanston and Minneapolis. In January 1926, the university approved plans for a stadium that would seat nearly 75,000, with foundation footings that could in the future accommodate seating for 100,000. The plan called for the stadium to be ready for Michigan's 1927 season, which meant that Yost could look forward to a very busy season of meetings with architects and engineers when he wasn't busy coaching his football team. But he, and Michigan, would have their stadium.

· · ·

Michigan's 1926 season opened with a 42–3 carnival against Oklahoma A&M on a summer-like day at Ferry Field. The overmatched Aggies, last-place finishers in the Missouri Valley Conference in 1925, had no answer for Friedman's "unerring passing," as the *New York Times* described it, or for Bo Molenda's line smashing, or for pretty much anything else the Maize and Blue wanted to do.

The following week, Bo and Benny treated the Ferry Field faithful to a 55–3 blitz of Michigan State. Benny supplemented his orchestration of Michigan's offensive explosion with two touchdown-saving tackles of Michigan State back Paul Smith. The Wolverines weren't the only Big Ten bully fattening up on an early-season weakling that day. Illinois, Iowa, and Northwestern also feasted against inferior non-conference opponents. And rival Ohio State, whose November 12 game with Michigan loomed on the calendar, rode captain Marty Karow's seventy-seven-yard touchdown run to a 47–0 pasting of Ohio Wesleyan.

Only Minnesota, the Wolverines' next opponent, had landed a tough game in the second week—against Knute Rockne and Notre Dame. The Gophers were no easy touch for Notre Dame, though, and the Irish strained to earn a 20–7 victory. Even in defeat, Minnesota perpetuated their reputation for bruising play, sending two of Rockne's starters to the sidelines with a broken jaw and a broken leg, respectively.

Minnesota's penchant for breaking opponents' bones was the reason they'd play Michigan twice in 1926. Big Ten rules required a team to play at least four conference games to be eligible for the conference title. As only the Wolverines, Wisconsin, and Iowa had agreed to play Minnesota—the rest of the Big Ten wanting no part of the tough Gophers—Yost enabled them to be eligible for the title by agreeing to a second game, which they would play on the season's last weekend on what was sure to be a cold late November afternoon in Minneapolis.

The two teams met at Ferry Field for their first encounter, and the first half of the game seemed like a continuation of Michigan's 35–0 romp over Minnesota in the 1925 finale. Benny's twenty-eight-yard reception was the prelude to a classic piece of Friedman deception—a Statue of Liberty play that found Louie Gilbert gamboling down the sideline and into the end zone, propelling Michigan toward a 20–0 halftime lead. Friedman shut down the offense in the second half, hoping to keep his more explosive plays from the prying eyes of future opponents' scouts. Herb Joesting and Mally Nydahl exploited Michigan's passivity with strong running, but only to a point—the Wolverines' defense stiffened each time the invaders from the north crept near the Michigan goal. The Wolverines escaped with a 20–0 victory and—despite jarring hits on Benny and Gilbert that were part of a bludgeoning one would expect from Minnesota—with their bones intact for their upcoming game against Illinois.

Michigan's preparation for this battle with the Illini would be more than a bit different from their work for the 1925 game. Red Grange was gone now, and the Wolverines didn't need to spend the week obsessing over a single player. But Illinois remained an imposing eleven, strong enough to have compiled a 3–0 record that included an impressive win over Iowa and "Cowboy" Nick Kutsch the week before. And while Grange was off making movies and running the football for pay, Bob Zuppke was still coaching the Illini, and Zuppke never needed much of a reason to have his teams at peak level for a battle with Fielding Yost. Grange or no Grange, the Wolverines had to be ready.

On a beautiful homecoming day at Ferry Field, an overflow crowd of fifty thousand watched through the smoke of the steam shovels busy at work on the new stadium as the Wolverines jousted with an intense, physical Illinois team through a scoreless first quarter and into the second. With his offense not in its usual flow, Benny resorted to his usual alternative for getting points on the board for the Maize and Blue—he nailed a field goal from thirty yards out and Michigan stuck its nose in front. The stalemate resumed after Benny's three-pointer. Illinois probed deep into Wolverine territory on several occasions, but into the fourth quarter they had no more to show for it than had the Grange-led Illini of a year earlier, which is to say zero.

Midway into the final quarter, Friedman blasted Michigan closer to victory with a twenty-seven-yard placement. Illinois still had time to surmount the 6–0 deficit, but they weren't able, and with only a few minutes remaining, Benny at last put them out of their misery. On the first play following Michigan's interception of an Illini pass, the Michigan captain hurled a perfect thirty-three-yard bomb to Oosterbaan, who was dragged down at the Illini 4. Illinois dug in bravely and turned back Molenda on three plunges, but they couldn't deny him the final foot across the goal line on the fourth. Benny then capped the scoring that day with the extra point. Michigan 13, Illinois 0. The Navy was next.

• • •

Michigan's trip to Baltimore to play the Navy would be the first time since 1917 that Fielding Yost had taken his Wolverines east. Yost had good reason to believe that his boys would return from this trip with a better result than the 16–0 spanking Pennsylvania had handed Michigan at Philadelphia's Franklin Field nine years earlier. The team was 4–0, they were healthy, and they had plenty of good memories from their encounter with the Midshipmen a year earlier.

Those same memories, however, also unsettled the coach. A 54–0 score tends to instill anger and focus in the loser and haughtiness in the winner the next time the teams play. "The will to win," Yost liked to say, "is not worth a nickel unless you have the will to prepare." Yost sensed the haughtiness infecting his players that week as they prepared for the Midshipmen. Their movement lacked zip. The focus Yost saw in practice before the season's first four games was missing. Meanwhile, in Annapolis, where the players had stomached the 54–0 massacre for a long hard year, anger and focus were in abundant supply. The Navy's scouting reports from Michigan's most recent games, together with the notes from the beating they took from the Wolverines the year before, formed a blueprint for their preparations. All aspects of Michigan's attack were accounted for, with the greatest attention focused on Friedman's passing attack. Frank Smith, the substitute quarterback who simulated Benny's moves in practice that week, wore a jersey emblazoned with the name "Friedman"—as if the Navy defenders needed to be reminded of their tormentor's name. The Middies toiled on both zone and man-to-man pass defense, hoping the different formations would keep Benny and the Wolverines off-balance.

Yost did his best during the week to fend off overconfidence. The coach's warnings not to take the Navy lightly were impactful enough for the *Chicago Tribune* to dub him the "Apostle of Grief." Benny's remarks to the Wolverine supporters who gathered at the Ann Arbor train station to see their team off to Baltimore indicated that he, too, had heard Yost's admonitions. "Last year's game is only a memory; it doesn't mean anything," Benny announced. "We know we've got a tough battle ahead and we aren't going down there with any illusions."

Friedman had said the right things, but Yost felt a queasiness as the train chugged out of Ann Arbor, and the ill feeling kept the old coach company all the way to Washington. By contrast, Yost's players were feeling just fine: hijinks on the trip east included a line-plunging exhibition down the aisle of the Pullman car, featuring Bo Molenda and a very friendly Bennie Oosterbaan making conversation with an attractive cigar counter attendant.

• • •

The nation's capital, not Baltimore, was the Wolverines' initial destination. They'd planned a sightseeing trip for the Friday before the game, centered around a visit with President Coolidge at the White House. Benny posed for photographs with Coolidge, who, football fan that he wasn't, had no idea who the star quarterback was. All in all it was an enjoyable field trip, but the frolic couldn't have done much to improve the Wolverines' focus on the game. Their cozy dinner that night at the Naval Academy—with the Navy players—couldn't have revved their competitive engines, either. A friendly meal with the enemy, punctuated by platitudes from Naval Academy and other government officials, wasn't the prescription for a Wolverines team already short on focus.

Eighty thousand fans and a perfect autumn Saturday greeted the teams as they barreled out of their locker rooms to take the field. Before the opening kickoff, Friedman was to receive an award as the greatest Jewish football player in the country from the Jewish Athletic Association. Baltimore mayor Howard Jackson presented Benny with a plaque from the association at midfield amid popping flashbulbs. Yost had to be hoping that his quarterback's play against the Navy in a few minutes would be worthy of the pregame pomp and circumstance.

Benny, as if buoyed by the recognition, came out firing passes all over the field. He was on the mark, too, but this time the Navy backs were ready. Alternating between a man-to-man defense and a zone featuring four defensive backs in a diamond and a fifth playing deep and keeping a keen eye on Oosterbaan, the Middies broke up nearly every pass, slamming into Bennie and the other Wolverine receivers just as they were about to pluck the ball out of the air. Friedman wasn't seeing the result of most of his throws, either; the quarterback was receiving an uncharacteristic pounding from the Navy's defensive front that frequently left him sprawled on the turf. The strongman training that had turned Benny's body into an iron pillar was helping him endure a physical beating the likes of which he'd never before absorbed. Even Brown and Hawkins and Edwards, the Wolverines' blocking stalwarts from 1925, might have been overwhelmed by the fury that the Navy forwards were bringing to their charge. "Those big Navy tackles, Wickhorst and Eddy, were murdering me," Benny would say later.

At one point Friedman thought he could blunt the Navy's pressure by changing things up a bit and giving Oosterbaan a chance to air out his powerful arm at quarterback. But the results were the same; the only difference was which man got slammed to the turf. It took only one play for Bennie to realize that things were much safer out at the end position. "Benny, if it's all the same to you," Oosterbaan said to Friedman, "I'd rather catch passes than throw them."

Despite the Navy's intense play, Benny managed two deep surges toward the Middies' goal in the second quarter. The first offered the Navy's Eddy the opportunity for some sweet revenge for playing Benny's sucker on the "Old 83" play in last year's game. The Navy lineman made the most of the chance, crashing through a seam in the Wolverines' line to block Benny's try for a field goal. The second Michigan incursion brought the ball to the Navy's ten-yard line with a first down. But Michigan could do no better than two futile line plunges, an incomplete pass, and a completed fourth-down pass that failed to gain the end zone.

Fortunately for Michigan, their defense was equally effective, if not quite as belligerent, as the Navy's, and the game remained scoreless at halftime. If the Wolverines could continue to stymie the Navy with their punting and defense until the Navy's brutal assault on Benny abated, they'd very happily accept a touchdown or two.

The Navy assault on Benny never did abate; the quarterback who had been hailed just a couple of hours earlier as the greatest Jewish footballer continued to taste the Baltimore Stadium turf, and the Middies kept on stifling Oosterbaan. Before the game began, most of the eighty thousand spectators would have accepted a Navy loss with a respectable score. But now it was 0–0 and it was deep into the third quarter, and the team that looked ready to crack wasn't the Navy. The Middies rooters weren't interested in a respectable loss anymore. Now they could see a victory in the making.

More important, so could the Navy players. With time in the third quarter dwindling, the Middies forced a fumble from the usually stout Molenda. Navy quarterback Tom Hamilton faked a kick and completed a twenty-five-yard pass to halfback Goudge, who rumbled eighteen yards on the next play to the Wolverines' 25. The Middies stalled on the next three plays, perhaps overcome by the tension of the moment created by their sterling play. But they'd already burrowed close enough for Tom Hamilton to try a dropkick. The Navy quarterback smashed the ball through from twenty-eight yards away, and incredibly, with barely more than a quarter left to play, the Navy was ahead of Michigan.

Could the Middies survive the perils of the fourth quarter with their slender three-point advantage? They halted a Michigan drive following a Louie Gilbert interception, then sailed down the field again with a mix of running and passing that might have had Yost thinking he was watching Benny instead of Tom Hamilton. Michigan had been flailing all afternoon, kept in the game only by their champion-like spirit, but that spirit was beginning to ebb. There is a moment in a football game when the teams' pregame hopes and expectations and bravado vanish, and the certainty of who will win and lose descends on the combatants. That moment arrived after the Middies halted a Michigan drive and sailed toward the Michigan goal line, and it became clear that Michigan could blockade the Navy no longer. Tom Caldwell unleashed pandemonium in Baltimore Stadium when he carried the ball into the end zone—the first breach of the Wolverines' goal line since Iowa's touchdown two years earlier. With the extra point, the score was 10–0. The game ended that way.

The regiment of Midshipmen catapulted out of their seats and onto the field, rolled to the goalposts and uprooted them. Then the sailors tore the posts to pieces and formed a human line. They snake-danced their way around the field, making sure to give Fielding Yost an unobstructed view as they pranced past the Michigan bench.

Other than against Northwestern in the typhoon in 1925, Benny and Michigan had never experienced such futility on offense, a situation Yost blamed on lax officiating. "I never saw one penalty called," Yost said years later. "They let everything go . . . Oosterbaan had been in front of at least five or six touchdown passes when some big Navy man would pile into him ahead of the ball. Friedman's throws were on target all afternoon and yet hardly a pass was completed."

The Navy might have received an assist from the officials, but one way or another, the "Old Man," as Yost's players affectionately called him, knew before the game began that his boys were going to lose. And Benny's recollections years later reveal that he too saw the beating coming: "We were quartered at the Naval Academy. The midshipmen looked at us in awe. 'There's the great Benny Friedman,' they would say. 'There's the great Bennie Oosterbaan.' Everybody got the treatment and we became muscle-bound from patting ourselves on the head."

• • •

The loss in Baltimore was a huge blow to Michigan's national championship dreams. Thankfully, though, it wouldn't directly affect the Big Ten race; victories over Wisconsin, Ohio State, and Minnesota would all but assure a championship. But those victories seemed a long way off on the train ride home to Ann Arbor. A Navy team that hadn't appeared as talented as any of Michigan's upcoming Big Ten rivals had just beaten up the Wolverines, and not just on the scoreboard. What's more, somewhere in the midst of the Baltimore battering, Benny's leg had been injured. There was some initial concern that the injury might force Friedman out of the lineup for the Wisconsin game, but Wisconsin always seemed to be the cure for what was ailing Michigan.

Poor Wisconsin. The schedule had served up the Badgers to Michigan in the week following Red Grange's massacre of the Wolverines in 1924.

Now the Badgers again found themselves on the Wolverines' chopping block following a rare Michigan loss. Making matters worse for Wisconsin was that Benny and Yost, who had a reserve of extra motivation where Wisconsin and George Little were concerned, would be playing and coaching their last home game for the Wolverines.

Yost got his boys' attention that week by mixing up his lineup in practice. Nobody except Benny seemed assured of a starting position against Wisconsin. The coach drove his boys relentlessly; the Wolverines would not be lacking "the will to prepare" for this game.

The hard work paid off. Michigan asserted itself after a tentative first few minutes as Benny tore gaping holes in the Badgers' secondary with several passes that gained more than forty yards. Oosterbaan again exhibited his peerless athleticism, snaring Benny's passes out of the air with a ballet dancer's grace and a bull's strength. This was Michigan's last home game of the season, and the Wolverine faithful were viewing the Benny-to-Bennie tandem, the greatest ever to play, for the last time, and it was a show to remember for the ages. Friedman even caught a touchdown pass himself, taking a toss from Gilbert and scampering into the end zone from seventeen yards out.

Nothing less than the 37–0 shellacking would have been suitable for the final home game for Benny and Yost, the last game that would ever be played at Ferry Field. Most everyone in attendance reveled in the joy and sentiment of the moment, but there was one small group of about forty who weren't there to soak up sentiment. Ohio State coach John Wilce and his squad of Buckeyes had taken the opportunity presented by the Buckeyes' week off to watch the Wolverines destroy Wisconsin. Notes on the Wolverines in hand, they made their way out of the stadium for the trip back to Columbus to prepare for Michigan.

· · ·

In the meantime, word had reached Benny that a Ben Friedman, the owner of a floral shop in Detroit, had been using the football star's name in the shop's advertising, urging football fans to buy their flowers from "Benny Friedman." This may have been good for the florist's business, but it did nothing good for Benny. "The boys seemed to have the idea that I was coming to Detroit before every game to sell flowers on the corner," Friedman said.

Benny decided to end the confusion and the florist's misappropriation of his name with a visit to Ben Friedman at his shop. None too delicately, Benny told the florist—whose shop was known as the Garrick Arbor Florist Shop before he figured out he shared a name with a nationally famous quarterback—to cut it out. When the florist refused, Benny proceeded immediately to the local Better Business Bureau, which referred the matter to a referee. By day's end the florist agreed to stop using the name "Benny Friedman" in his advertising, and Benny returned to Ann Arbor, pleased that he had protected his good name and ready to focus on the Ohio State Buckeyes.

NINE

"Benny Friedman Passed All Afternoon Like Only Benny Friedman Can"

Ohio State was in the midst of an interesting year in 1926. They were 6–0, but there was some question about the quality of the opponents they'd beaten. Other than a solid Columbia team, every one of the Buckeyes' foes would finish the season with a losing record. And even though Wilce had rested most of his regulars in their latest game against tiny Wilmington College, Ohio State barely survived, 13–7.

If the Buckeyes had focused one eye on the approaching battle with Michigan while scrapping with Wilmington, it was entirely understandable. The rivalry between these two schools dated back to 1898. By 1926 the Buckeyes and Wolverines had already played each other 26 times. The 1926 game would have been a feature, if not *the* feature, of the college football schedule that weekend even if the teams had entered the proceedings with losing records. The case was just the opposite: the antagonists were powerful squads with only one loss (a non-conference loss at that) between them, and each had emerged as the other's main impediment to the Big Ten championship.

The entire state of Ohio was enthralled at the Buckeyes' title run. The team hadn't won a conference championship since 1920, the last year they'd defeated Michigan. Mild-mannered John Wilce had hinted during preseason workouts that his unit might finally escape the conference wilderness, and his boys had borne out their coach's suspicion. One reporter called the Buckeyes "football material that coaches get only once in a decade." This might have been a bit overstated, but Fielding Yost was tickled at such praise for his opponent. The Old Man was just fine with the role of underdog for a change.

If the relative talent and records of the teams were too close to call, then the site of the game—Ohio stadium in Columbus, called the "Horseshoe" for its shape—figured to favor the Buckeyes. The frenzy over this game throughout Ohio promised to pack the mammoth stadium with a record number of scarlet and grey rooters. Stadium officials scrambled during the week to welcome an expected throng of more than ninety thousand. Chairs were placed in the aisles. Field boxes were expanded. Capacity in the bleachers was more than doubled. Areas to accommodate thousands of standing-room fans were readied.

Yost wanted his boys to get a feel for the Horseshoe and arranged a light workout there shortly after they arrived in Columbus on Friday. As the Wolverines limbered up in the chill of a late November afternoon, Friedman and Oosterbaan strolled off by themselves for their own private warm-up. Benny and Bennie were the greatest pass-and-catch team in football history, and they knew they'd need to play like it if the Wolverines were to win this game. In the shadows of the huge vacant stadium, whose every space would soon be filled, the two all-Americans tossed the ball back and forth, enriching the timing and coordination that had spellbound a nation of fans and writers and players and coaches for the past two seasons. They would be ready for their penultimate game together.

Ohio State may not have had a Red Grange threatening to wreck the Wolverines' title hopes by himself, but it did have a very talented group of players who collectively were good enough to beat Michigan. Marty Karow, Benny's old foe from Cleveland and captain of the Buckeyes, had already played five games against Friedman—three for West Tech High and two for Ohio State. An adept line plunger, Karow was 0–5 against Benny, but it appeared he finally had the supporting cast that could get him past Friedman. The Buckeyes' line, featuring all-American Ed Hess, was every bit as tough as Michigan's; Elmer Marek was a fine runner; and sophomore back Byron Eby's open-field speed reminded some of Grange. Coordinating it all for the Buckeyes was quarterback Meyers Clark. Clark was also the Buckeyes' reliable kicker, and in a game that looked to be a toss-up, a reliable kicker was a necessity, not a luxury, for the Buckeyes. "It is only natural to suppose that Capt. Benny will kick a few if he gets the chance, and it wouldn't be much of a surprise if his toe meant the difference between a tie and a Michigan win," Irving Vaughn wrote in the *Chicago Tribune* the day before the game.

. . .

The morning of the game, a mild chaos prevailed outside the stadium. With more than ninety thousand people cramming into the Horseshoe, it was the largest crowd ever to see a football game, anywhere. Still there were thousands of ticketless fans clamoring to get in. A riot nearly erupted as the police tried to calm the mob, resulting in a number of minor injuries. And inside the stadium, a pregame fireworks display arranged by Ohio State officials went terribly awry; one of the devices that should have exploded in the air high above the stadium fell into the stands, where it detonated and burned two girls, one badly enough to land her in the hospital for several weeks.

The next explosion in the stadium was the sound of Louis Gilbert's foot crashing into the ball on the opening kickoff. The game that one writer previewed as the "greatest sporting spectacle in Ohio history" was under way.

. . .

Just twelve minutes into the game, Michigan called a time-out, and Wolverines back Wally Weber breathlessly collared Oosterbaan as he strode toward the Michigan sideline.

"At this rate, they're going to drub us by forty points!" Weber bellowed.

The Buckeyes had leaped to a 10–0 advantage over Michigan—precisely the kind of opening the Wolverines had hoped to avoid. Instead of taking the massive crowd out of the game with a strong early performance, Michigan's uneven play spurred on the Buckeye throng. Trouble began almost immediately, when a booming punt from Ohio State's Fred Bell rode a gust of wind over Benny's head and landed near Michigan's ten-yard line. Instead of playing things safe and punting on first down, the Wolverines tried to run the ball out from the shadow of their goal. Gilbert fumbled and Bell recovered for State. The Wolverines stonewalled the Buckeyes on three straight plays, but they couldn't derail the dependable Meyers Clark, who calmly drilled a dropkick between the uprights to give State the first points of the game.

Then things got worse for Michigan, quickly. Ohio State had the ball again after stopping the Wolverines on downs near the Buckeyes' 40. Like a Yost team hunting for touchdowns instead of first downs, State needed only two plays to transport the ball to the Michigan one-foot line—an eighteen-yard dash by halfback Fred Grim and a spectacular diving forty-two-yard reception by Meyers Clark that the great Bennie Oosterbaan would gladly have added to his own highlight reel. Marty Karow took care of the final foot on the next play, barreling into the end zone behind Ed Hess. Clark, still breathing hard from his clutch catch, sent the ball through the uprights and sent Wally Weber into his panic as the Wolverines retreated to the sideline for their time-out.

A year earlier, Oosterbaan, in a near-panic of his own, had looked to Benny to calm him down before taking on Red Grange. Now it was the great receiver's turn to ease a teammate's distress, though neither his words for Weber nor his delivery of them were gentle.

"Dammit, Wally," Bennie barked, "we haven't even had the ball yet!"

Oosterbaan had made his point, even if he wasn't quite accurate (Michigan had already had one possession). Weber and the Wolverines settled down. Gilbert tossed a twenty-six-yard strike to Friedman that brought the ball close enough for Benny to try a placement from the 27.

Then Benny startled everyone—he missed, and Ohio State took possession with another chance to step on the Wolverines' throat.

But the frenetic pace of the game and the Buckeyes' strenuous effort appeared to be wearing on them; they again failed to move the ball and punted it back to Michigan. Benny made the Buckeyes pay for their missed opportunity. Employing his classic assortment of passing, receiving, and deception, Friedman had the Wolverines in the end zone in just a few plays. The touchdown came on a fake field goal executed perfectly by Louis and Benny. Gilbert knelt, took the snap, and placed the ball down. Then the quarterback picked up the ball and delivered a thirty-eight-yard beauty to Oosterbaan in the corner of the end zone. Friedman's extra point made the score 10–7.

Benny's touchdown pass to Oosterbaan was heard by one very interested listener lying in a bed in a Cleveland hospital. Benny's father, Lewis, had taken ill that morning and was in poor condition when he arrived at the hospital. He seemed to brighten a bit when Oosterbaan tucked away Benny's scoring pass.

Michigan still trailed as halftime approached. Though the Wolverines' deficit was only three points, the psychological edge that would propel Ohio State into the third quarter if they could hold the lead until the break would be difficult to overcome. Somehow, the Wolverines had to find a way to erase the lead.

The defense did its part following Michigan's kickoff, smothering the Buckeyes and forcing a quick punt. Benny-to-Bennie took over from there. Actually, this time it was Bennie-to-Benny—Oosterbaan passed and Friedman caught, and the twenty-yard play sent the ball to the Buckeyes' thirty-five-yard line, a few steps in from the left sideline.

Twenty-nine seconds remained in the half. There wasn't enough time to run the ball. Passing for a score against a defense laying for the pass would be a tall order, even for the best passer in the game. And a field goal—from forty-four yards away *and* at a forty-five-degree angle—seemed nearly impossible.

So when Benny called for a field goal try and Louis Gilbert retreated to the forty-four-yard line for the placement, everybody in Ohio Stadium knew the master of the fake field goal—who'd already duped the Buckeyes once in the game—was at it again. A fake seemed all the more assured when Oosterbaan dashed over to Gilbert, whispered in his ear, and then sprinted to his position on the line. The Ohio defenders, spotting Oosterbaan's brief conversation with Gilbert, bellowed out screams of "Fake!"

By all rights, it should have been a fake. Only once before had Benny booted a ball through the uprights from such a distance, and it wasn't from the extreme angle he now confronted.

None of that mattered to Friedman. What mattered was the moment. The moment found him, his teammates, his beloved coach, and their Big Ten title dreams dangling on the precipice.

Friedman dropped back and took his mark; the ball was so close to the sideline that he needed to be careful not to line up out of bounds. He stole a glance at the goalposts as Gilbert readied for the snap. Center Joe Truskowski sent the ball back to Louis perfectly. Gilbert snared the ball and placed it down without a bobble—and without much of a rush from the Ohio linemen, who stayed back to defend against the fake they were certain was coming. The absence of pressure allowed Benny an extra moment to gather himself for his approach. Then he jumped forward, drew back his leg, and snapped it goalward, launching his toe into the ball with a controlled violence that would meet this kick's contradictory requirements of extreme distance and extreme accuracy. The ball cleared the Ohio line easily and then continued to soar, and its path couldn't have been truer if Fielding Yost himself had been guiding it on a string. With plenty of room to spare, the ball cleared the crossbar, seemingly at its very midpoint.

Ohio State, flush with talent and buoyed by ninety thousand supporters, had played about as good a half of a football game as they could have dreamed of playing against a great team like Michigan. They'd fired their best shot and had nothing more than a 10–10 tie at halftime to show for it.

• • •

While the Wolverines and Buckeyes were doing battle at the Horseshoe, Northwestern was administering a 38–7 mauling to the University of Chicago in their annual Windy City tussle. Minnesota, the other team still alive in the Big Ten title chase, was having an even easier afternoon. The Gophers were turning their match with non-conference Butler into an 81–0 warm-up for their season-ending showdown against Michigan on November 20.

It's not clear whether the Wolverines knew how their rivals were doing, but scoreboard watching wasn't going to solve their predicament in Columbus. They'd tied the score, but at a tremendous cost in effort and with a minor miracle from Friedman.

Wilce, meanwhile, was trying to figure out how to get some production out of Elmer Marek. The star back was hampered by a hand injury and had been invisible so far. Wilce couldn't afford another half of dull football from Marek; he'd replace him with sophomore flash Byron Eby if the senior star didn't find his stride quickly.

Neither Marek nor anyone else on either side accomplished much in the third quarter. The Buckeyes were worn out from their dramatic opening, and Michigan had spent itself clawing back into the game. The teams' mutual exhaustion transformed the game into a punting contest, and with just enough time remaining in the quarter for one more play, Marek retreated deep into Ohio territory to receive Gilbert's boot.

The ball landed and bounced toward the Ohio goal, and Marek needed only to let the ball bound into the end zone for a touchback that would move the ball from the shadow of the Buckeyes' end zone to the twenty-yard line. Perhaps he thought he could surprise Michigan by fielding the ball and returning the kick, and in one dramatic moment atone for what had been a miserable performance. Or perhaps Marek just froze, the occasion getting the better of him, inducing him to forget just how close he was to his end zone when he reached for the ball. On the Ohio sideline, John Wilce had been ready to replace Marek with Byron Eby but for some reason hadn't pulled the trigger, and now the coach could only watch in horror as the ball caromed off Marek's hands and dropped to the turf. Michigan lineman Sid Dewey pounced on it. The third quarter, and Michigan's stupor, was over. The first play of the fourth quarter would find Michigan with the ball, first and goal at the Ohio 7.

Benny avoided the temptation of immediately trying to pass for a touchdown and instead called one run, then another, and then another, all stopped dead by an Ohio State defense that had also awakened from the stupor of the punting contest. The ninety-four thousand Ohio fans were fully alert as well, shrieking in support of the wall of Buckeyes that rejected the Wolverine smashes one after the other. Now fourth down was staring Benny squarely in the eye, and the quarterback knew this would likely be Michigan's last chance to score. He had to make it happen.

A field goal seemed to be the play. The Wolverines were inside the Buckeyes' ten-yard line; from that close, Benny was nearly certain to connect and give Michigan the lead. The wisdom of a field-goal try seemed all the more apparent in the wake of the Wolverines' uninspiring tries for the end zone on first, second, and third downs.

But under the most extreme pressure, Benny had the skill, and the nerve, to pull off big plays that others wouldn't even consider. He wasn't going to bypass the opportunity to score a fourth-down touchdown instead of a field goal. The last three plays showed that Michigan wasn't going to get that touchdown on the ground. It had to be a pass.

In the Michigan huddle, Friedman eyed his receivers, Flora and the great Oosterbaan, and figured they'd attract too much defensive attention. Wally Weber, the line-plunging specialist, hadn't yet been used as a receiver. The Buckeyes wouldn't be looking for the big fullback to catch a fourth-down pass in the end zone. Benny called for a pass to Weber over the center.

Then the ball was snapped, and Benny's play vaporized in the chaos that football often becomes. Friedman looked for Weber and saw him at the bottom of an avalanche of Ohio defenders. With a relaxed urgency, the quarterback scanned the field for an open teammate and found one. It wasn't Oosterbaan or Flora or Louis Gilbert. Iolas Hoffman, a little-used substitute halfback, was standing in the end zone, uncovered and with no bodies between himself and his quarterback. Benny knew he'd have this unencumbered path only for an instant. This pass could not be floated. "No soft ball here . . . "I threw the fastest pass I ever made," Benny would later write. The dart hit Hoffman in the gut. The force of the throw knocked Hoffman to the turf, but he held on to the ball.

Benny then calmly kicked the extra point to make the score 17–10.

Now it was Ohio State's turn to explore the depths of their resolve and try to salvage a game they had all but owned. The Buckeyes had the good fortune to have Byron Eby to lead the effort. The young back who'd wasted away on the bench in favor of hapless Elmer Marek passed and ran his team down the field with the skill and urgency the situation mandated. A diving Friedman grazed the ball on one of Eby's long throws, nearly knocking it down, but the reception brought the ball deep into Wolverine territory. Eby then finished off the remarkable drive with a nine-yard dash around left end. Now it was up to Meyers Clark to hammer home the game-tying extra point.

Clark had played a fine, even outstanding game. He'd boomed a field goal to stake Ohio to an early lead. He'd made a spectacular forty-two-yard catch to set up Ohio's first touchdown. Then he'd notched the extra point following Marty Karow's touchdown plunge. And playing opposite the greatest quarterback in football, he'd led the Buckeyes with poise and skill throughout the battle.

None of that mattered now. One point still separated Ohio from Michigan—one point to be produced with a simple dropkick by Clark, just like the one he'd booted in the first quarter. But dropkicks late in the fourth quarter to tie a game for the Big Ten championship aren't simple. The din of the crowd imploring you to come through, the fatigue you feel from four quarters of struggle, the dusk and chill settling over the stadium, and the consequences of a miss conspire to make you do exactly that—miss.

Wilce, watching Meyers line up for the kick, could do nothing beyond silently hope that he would remember not to reach for the ball so as to meet it too high and kick it too low. But kick it too low he did. The ball cleared the onrushing Wolverines and headed straight for the crossbar, passing underneath it by a few inches.

Clark hurled himself to the ground in tears. The four thousand or so Wolverine supporters in the stadium shook the Horseshoe with shrieks of stunned glee. Incredibly, though, victory was not yet theirs. A few minutes still remained in the game. Michigan couldn't make a first down and had to punt the ball away. Ohio again bolted down the field, and with under a minute to play, Buckeye back Robin Bell launched a pass intended for Clark near the Wolverines' thirty-six-yard line. Benny stepped in front of his counterpart for the interception that was, finally, the stake through the Buckeyes' heart.

Against Michigan's powerful archrival, before an overwhelmingly hostile crowd that was the largest ever to see a game, with the Big Ten title at stake, Benny had been the true virtuoso that Michigan needed him to be. No other player—not Grange, not Nevers, not Moon Baker at Northwestern—could have brought to bear the total package of running, receiving, kicking, and leadership that Benny displayed at the Horseshoe. And this is to say nothing of his passing, an area where his supremacy was already beyond debate. The *New York Times*'s story on the game would simply yet powerfully capture Benny's prowess. "Benny Friedman passed all afternoon," the *Times* reported, "like only Benny Friedman can."

Amid the buzz of an Ohio Stadium crowd still trying to absorb the last three hours of football, the jubilant Wolverines hoisted their captain onto their shoulders and rushed him to the locker room. Jerry Friedman was waiting there for his brother with word of their father's illness. It was more than the young quarterback, already flush with the emotions of his greatest victory, could bear. He burst into tears, and then buried his head in Fielding Yost's shoulder. Yost didn't know that Benny's father had been ill, and it took Friedman a few minutes to compose himself before he was able to tell his coach the news.

A short while later, Benny and Jerry jumped in a car and headed back to Cleveland to see their father.

• • •

Lewis Friedman had no use for football when his son Benny began playing in the Cleveland streets and schoolyards. Gradually he began to tolerate the game and Benny's love for it, and as his son's fame grew, that tolerance grew into mild interest. When he became ill on the day of Benny's game against the Buckeyes, though, football suddenly became more than a mild interest. It became his lifeline. Lewis's doctors were stunned to watch the seriously ill man improve before their eyes as he listened to the radio broadcast of his son's heroics in Columbus.

Benny didn't know he was helping his father at the same time he was beating the Buckeyes. He expected to see a very sick man; tears of relief poured from his eyes when instead Lewis greeted him with smiles and congratulations. At that moment Benny wasn't the imperturbable captain of the Michigan Wolverines. He was just a frightened twenty-one-year-old confronting his father's mortality.

"I'm better now," Lewis said to Benny, reaching for his hand. "Don't stay with me. Go to your studies."

Then the tailor from Russia added a few more words of encouragement for his famous son.

"And beat Minnesota."

TEN

King of the Big Ten

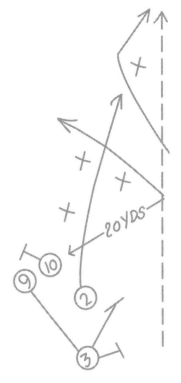

It seemed almost unfair that after the epic battle in Ohio, Michigan would have to play one last game before it could secure the Big Ten title. The game would be against fearsome Minnesota, and when Yost saw hay covering the Minnesota field the Friday before the game—to minimize ice formation—he had to think trouble was brewing for his Wolverines in Minneapolis. Ice and the expected freezing temperature at game time didn't bode well for the passing game. It did, on the other hand, play quite nicely into the hands of Minnesota's three-headed battering ram of Mally Nydahl, Bob Peplaw, and, especially, two-time all-American fullback Herb Joesting, popularly known in Minnesota as the Hammer of Thor. Joesting had earned the moniker at the expense of countless defenders he'd trampled during the last two seasons.

Minnesota had more than weather and field conditions in their favor. They'd be cheered by a feverish homecoming crowd—it seemed like Michigan was every Big Ten team's homecoming foil. And, maybe most important, they'd be rested, healthy, and confident following their 81–0 wipeout of Butler, while Michigan would be staggering into Minneapolis on fumes after their life-and-death struggle in Columbus.

One look at that hay on the field undoubtedly had Yost reevaluating his good nature in agreeing to play the Gophers twice. But the coach knew it was too late for that. He also knew the field would be wet when that hay was removed and that handling the ball during the game would be tricky business.

So, on the eve of the game, in the last practice he would ever run as head coach of the Michigan Wolverines, Fielding Yost had his boys practice fumble recoveries.

. . .

Sixty thousand fans braving frigid temperatures watched Joesting and Peplaw and Nydahl pound the Michigan line relentlessly from the start of the game. Minnesota had finally learned that the best way to halt Benny-to-Bennie and the rest of the Wolverines' arsenal was to keep the ball away from them. With the Gophers grinding out first downs, Friedman had few chances to pass. When Benny did have the ball, he had no one to throw to. Minnesota's line was so outplaying the Michigan forwards that the Gophers could afford to drop a lineman back into coverage of Flora. The double-team was so effective that Yost had to bench the normally sterling receiver in his final game. Oosterbaan was having almost as much difficulty finding space. The frozen tundra and frigid air weren't too friendly to Benny, either.

First downs, however, don't always translate into points, and into the fourth quarter Minnesota's lead was only 6–0 on the strength of a Joesting touchdown. A combination of stout Wolverine line play when it was most needed and several Friedman interceptions when the Gophers tried to surprise Michigan with passes had kept the score down. As the second half wore on, Minnesota throttled back a bit, perhaps sensing that six points was all it would need this day, though they would have felt a little better had Bob Peplaw not missed the extra-point attempt.

With only a few minutes separating the Gophers from their first victory over Michigan in eight tries, they embarked on yet another drive through the Wolverines' defense, which by this point had nearly exhausted its resolve. From Michigan's forty-yard line, Nydahl burst wide on a sweep play that had piled up yardage all afternoon and looked like it would again—until Nydahl fumbled the ball. Oosterbaan's eyes lit up as he watched the ball bounding loose on the field. Bennie swooped in from his left end position, scooped it up, and blasted off toward the end zone, sixty yards away, with Michigan's first and almost certainly its last chance to score against the belligerent Gophers. Bennie's teammates scrambled to give him an escort, but he wasn't waiting for one; he sprinted toward the goal line. The Gophers' Bob Peplaw churned after him, arms pumping like pistons. Peplaw was closing as Oosterbaan reached the ten-yard line. At the five, the Minnesota man was even closer to Bennie but still hadn't quite reached him. Desperately, Peplaw dove at Oosterbaan's feet, but Bennie sidestepped the Gopher and crossed the goal line.

For nearly sixty minutes, Minnesota had pulverized the Maize and Blue as if they were an inept freshman squad. Now, for a single moment of sloppiness, the Gophers had been made to pay dearly by one of Michigan's two great players, and the other one was about to collect the rest of the debt. Benny was lining up for the extra-point attempt.

This would surely be the last time Louie Gilbert would take a snap and place a ball down for Benny, and among all their crucial kicks, none would be as challenging. The cold had frozen the ball into a springless mass. Sixty thousand people were howling at Friedman as if the very existence of the state of Minnesota hinged on him missing. The quarterback was drained from the nearly sixty minutes of football he'd played against the Gophers and the lingering effects of the sixty brutal minutes he'd played against Ohio State. He'd weighed 183 pounds before the Ohio State game and was now down to 169.

Michigan broke their huddle and Benny retreated to his spot, and then turned to face the goalposts. He assumed his familiar pre-snap pose—head down, eyes on the spot he and Gilbert selected, legs braced, arms dangling limply to allow the tension to flow from his body. The end of his last college game was near, and he was about to boot a ball for Michigan for the last time. This kick would decide the winner of the Big Ten championship.

"Come on, Benny!" Fielding Yost roared from the Wolverines' sideline. "You can do it!" And then, in an instant, the ball was in Gilbert's hands, and he placed it down and Benny drove the ball, up and over Minnesota's surging line that had pushed Michigan's blockers nearly into Gilbert. The ball cleared the crossbar comfortably, and the hysterical crowd became gripped by silence.

Benny's teammates, ecstatic at having been rescued for a second straight week, mobbed their captain and savior. Friedman, usually stone-faced on the field, broke into a huge grin.

A couple of minutes later, the final whistle blew an end to Benny's college career and Fielding Yost's coaching career. Assured of no worse than a share of the Big Ten title (if Northwestern beat Iowa), the grand old man of Meeshagan football lit up his first cigar in years.

· · ·

With its stunning defeat of Minnesota, Michigan finished the 1926 campaign with a 7–1 record and a perfect 5–0 Big Ten mark, but as in 1925, Northwestern was there to complicate things. The Wildcats had defeated Iowa in their final game and also claimed a 5–0 conference record, and this time there was no concession forthcoming from Evanston. The only "concession" that seemed to be in the air was one reportedly demanded by Northwestern of Michigan. But given the vastly stronger competition the Wolverines faced, if either school was entitled to demand a concession, it was Michigan. Northwestern's conference opponents all had losing records, while Michigan's conference opponents all had winning records. The only high-quality team Northwestern met all season—non-conference Notre Dame—defeated them. In any case, Northwestern president Walter Scott denied demanding a concession, Michigan president Clarence Little accepted the denial, and the two presidents exchanged congratulations for the fine seasons their teams had enjoyed.

· · ·

In terms of individual Big Ten kudos, no honor was more prestigious than the *Chicago Tribune*'s annual Silver Football award, given to the conference's most valuable player, or in the parlance of the day, "the player of greatest value to his team."

In some ways, Benny had performed more spectacularly in 1925 than in 1926. Yet Northwestern's Tim Lowry snuck by Friedman for the 1925 Silver Football, probably on the strength of his "genius" call for the intentional safety in the Soldier Field typhoon. It didn't hurt Lowry, either, that he had been a senior and Northwestern's captain, while Benny had been a junior then.

Benny was a senior now, but he had some very worthy competition. Cowboy Kutsch at Iowa, Marty Karow at Ohio State, and Illinois's Frosty Peters all enjoyed excellent seasons. Herb Joesting gave Knute Rockne fits in Minnesota's game with Notre Dame and nearly brought Minnesota a Big Ten title. Moon Baker was a truly outstanding back who carried Northwestern most of the season.

In the end, though, the panel of voters—the Big Ten head coaches, game officials, and *Tribune* sports editor Harvey Woodruff—couldn't deny Friedman his due. In individual areas of the game—passing, kicking, field generalship, even, arguably, broken-field running—Benny was unequaled.

Grantland Rice didn't have a vote in the Big Ten MVP sweepstakes, but his comments about Friedman in selecting him as the 1926 all-American quarterback left little to the imagination as to whom Rice would have awarded the Silver Football. After offering due praise to the many fine quarterbacks throughout the nation, "Granny" turned his attention to Benny. "For all-around football smartness and football ability," Rice wrote, "it is impossible to find a better man than Benny Friedman . . . In addition to his generalship, passing and kicking he has been a good man carrying the ball and a fine defensive back . . . Friedman had a terrible schedule to face where he was a marked man and yet he continued his dazzling all-around display straight through." In this respect Benny had succeeded much as Grange had succeeded in the teeth of enormous attention from the enemy—except that Grange hadn't faced the grinding schedule that Benny had, and he hadn't led Illinois to any Big Ten championships, either.

Rice didn't hold Benny's performance in the Navy game against him; to the contrary, he marveled at Benny's ability to "pass as accurately as ever to ends and backs who were nearly always covered" even as he was repeatedly pounded by the relentless Navy forwards.

The *American Jewish World* selected Friedman unanimously as its Jewish all-American team's quarterback for 1926, observing that Benny was "the man whom Walter Eckersall, the Walter Camp of the Midwest, and a great quarterback himself, called the perfect triple-threat man." Benny's greatness on the gridiron also earned him a place in the *American Hebrew*'s 1926 "Who's Who Among American Jews" alongside the likes of Louis Marshall, a renowned attorney, and Julius Rosenwald, who would build Sears, Roebuck into one of the nation's great department stores.

• • •

Thanksgiving 1926 found Benny home in Cleveland with his family. While the two-time all-American quarterback was unwinding from the rigors of the just-completed season, it was reported that during the season, promoters had offered him substantial money—in the five-figure range—to leave Michigan and turn professional. Benny confirmed the offers but wouldn't say who'd made them. He also explained at least one of the reasons he rejected the offers. "Break faith with the Old Man and with Michigan?" Friedman said. "Never. Whatever I have accomplished as a football player, I owe to the Old Man."

Benny's rejection of the pro offers reflected his deep feelings for Yost but was undoubtedly motivated by other factors as well. Leaving Michigan before earning a degree would have compromised his chances for a career as a lawyer (even though law school was, at least in the short term, out of the question in light of Benny's father's poor health and the need for Benny to provide for his family). Unlike Grange, Benny was an accomplished student; leaving Michigan before graduating was not in his makeup. And he was far from sold on the uncertain life of a professional football vagabond.

Indeed, although college rosters had been liberally sprinkled with Jewish players for years, very few of them had made the leap to pro ball. There simply wasn't enough money in it. Most players for pay were lucky if they received a hundred bucks a game to risk life and limb before a few thousand fans in some drafty ballpark. For Benny, the situation was a bit different. The money he was offered was real money, maybe enough to induce him to put a legal or business career on hold for a while. But he wasn't leaving Michigan without a diploma, and he wasn't going to disappoint Fielding Yost.

Many college coaches and administrators worried that other talented college players wouldn't be so virtuous. Stanford's great all-American, Ernie Nevers, had already followed Grange's example. After Stanford's 1925 season, Nevers signed to play against Grange on Red's barnstorming tour that winter. The stewards of the college game feared a mass exodus of college stars to the pro ranks, and they took action to prevent it. "We wish to deal a death blow to professional football," said W. G. Manley, the University of Missouri's representative on the Missouri Valley Conference board, commenting on that conference's resolution barring any player or coach associated with pro ball from employment in member university athletic departments. Other conferences shared Manley's sentiment and enacted similar resolutions. The hue and cry from the campuses persuaded the NFL to adopt a rule in 1926 prohibiting the signing of a college player before his class graduated.

Grange, meanwhile, wasn't looking back at his college days. He was too busy playing football games and counting his money. The barnstorming deal that C. C. Pyle had negotiated with George Halas and the Chicago Bears for 1925 gave Grange, and Pyle, a guarantee and a percentage of the gate from each game. Pyle had figured, correctly, that the fans would flock to the stadiums to see the great runner barnstorm his way into the pro game. The biggest coup of the 1925 tour for Grange and Pyle, and for the future prospects of professional football, had been a game against the New York Giants at New York's Polo Grounds on December 6, 1925. More than seventy thousand fans (including Benny and a number of his fellow 1925 all-Americans who were in New York to be honored at a gala dinner sponsored by the *New York Sun*) jammed into the stadium to see the great runner that day. Grange didn't evoke memories of his five-touchdown performance against Michigan in 1924, but he was far from a disappointment. On the last play of the game, he intercepted a pass and scampered thirty-five yards for a touchdown to top off a 19–7 Bears' victory. Then Pyle topped off Red's day by handing him a check for $50,000.

The Polo Grounds spectacle was the high point of a hectic barnstorming campaign in 1925 that together with commercial endorsements and movie deals negotiated by Pyle yielded Grange income in the neighborhood of $200,000. George Halas and his Chicago Bears also made out handsomely that year; Halas and his partner, Dutch Sternaman, doubled their individual draws to $12,000 each and the team turned its first "worthwhile" profit, in Halas's words.

But the rest of the NFL continued to struggle, particularly after the fanfare accompanying Grange's 1925 appearances abated. Franchises like the Duluth Eskimos, the Frankford Yellowjackets, and the Providence Steam Roller bled money. Even the New York Giants, bought in 1925 for the princely sum of $500 by a New York bookmaker named Tim Mara, couldn't make any money. On game days throughout the 1926 season, the Polo Grounds, the Giants' home field, resembled a big grey tomb perched on the banks of the Harlem River. The Giants literally couldn't give tickets away; even the offer of free tickets couldn't bring in more than an average of four thousand fans a game. Only Mara's willingness to subsidize the Giants with funds from his other more successful business activities kept the Giants alive.

Grange didn't do the league any favors in 1926, either, when he and Pyle, angered first at Halas's refusal to grant them an ownership interest in the Bears, and then at the league's refusal to grant them their own franchise, formed their own league—the American Football League. But not even the magnetic redhead could sustain the venture; the league foundered after one season. The New York Yankees, the team Grange and Pyle had formed as the AFL's flagship eleven, was offered a slot in the NFL, thus giving Red and his manager the NFL franchise they had sought to begin with, but there was a catch: in order to protect Mara and his Giants, the Yankees were allowed only four games in New York City, all of which had to be scheduled on days when the Giants were on the road. Even Grange was subject to the considerable vagaries of the professional football world.

. . .

Meanwhile Benny was enjoying his campus celebrity and his last months in school. On January 24, amid appropriate pomp and circumstance, Benny was presented with the Silver Football trophy at halftime during a basketball game between Michigan and Minnesota in front of an adoring hometown crowd in Ann Arbor. In the spring of 1927, he teamed with Bennie Oosterbaan in a baseball variation of the famous Benny-to-Bennie combination. This time it was Benny Friedman, the Wolverines' varsity third baseman, throwing the baseball to Oosterbaan, the Wolverines' first baseman. Friedman was a solid ballplayer, but Oosterbaan's baseball ability was nearly equal to his gridiron skills. Major league scouts had their eyes firmly planted on Bennie, who in a year's time would have a difficult choice to make as to which sport to pursue professionally, assuming he opted to pursue a professional playing career at all.

Friedman's choice for his future would be coming up a lot sooner: in May, he graduated from the University of Michigan, and he had some encouraging words to take with him as he embarked on the next phase of his life:

To Benny Friedman
    You were a bulwark to Michigan. You were a great strategist, a thinker, a doer. You inspired, you calmed. Your brain functioned sixty seconds a minute. You were loyal, unselfish. To you, Michigan came first. In a tight place, you turned defeat into victory. I am for you; Michigan's for you; your opponents are for you. The game to come will be more wearing, more wearying. But as Michigan football teams fight in years to come, we all know you will be fighting too—calmly, coolly, collectedly, courageously.
                                                —Fielding H. Yost

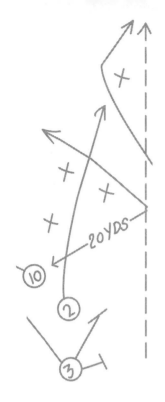

ELEVEN

The Pros Come Calling

On May 10, 1927, a member of the Philadelphia Athletics major league baseball team arrived in Detroit to the kind of hero's welcome that Julius Caesar used to receive upon his return to Rome from his latest battlefield conquest. The incongruity of such a grand greeting in Detroit for a baseball player not a member of the Detroit Tigers is easily explained: the player was the former Tiger Ty Cobb, the greatest Tigers player ever. For twenty-one seasons beginning in 1905, the year Benny was born, the Georgia-born Cobb had worn the Tigers uniform, exhibiting batting and base-running skills and a competitive ferocity so outstanding that most Tigers fans were willing to overlook his surly personality and none-too-subtle racism, to say nothing of game-fixing allegations against him that he denied and were never proven. Those allegations, surfacing in 1926, had hastened the aging Cobb's retirement from baseball. When baseball commissioner Kenesaw Landis dismissed the allegations, Cobb returned to baseball for one last hurrah in 1927 as a member of the Athletics, who were in Detroit that May week for a series with the Tigers.

The highlight of the "Ty Cobb Day" festivities was a huge testimonial luncheon given in Cobb's honor. Eleven hundred guests squeezed into Detroit's Masonic temple to hear tributes to Cobb from a number of luminaries that included speeches from the University of Michigan's two most prominent goodwill ambassadors, Fielding Yost and Benny Friedman.

The reception for Cobb reflected the enormous popularity enjoyed by professional baseball at that time. For professional football, that kind of popularity was nothing more than rank fantasy in the spring of 1927. Red Grange's spectacular entry into the pro football world in 1925 had given the pros an undeniable jolt, but the momentum from that jolt was now nearly gone. The NFL was learning a difficult lesson: as magnetic a personality and as great a football player as Red was, one man was not enough to establish a successful league—especially when that man and his agent, "Cash and Carry" Pyle, seemed more intent on building their personal fortunes than on league-building.

The backbone of the storied college teams, teams such as Michigan and Notre Dame, the Army and Pennsylvania, had always been the team itself, and not their individual stars, as phenomenal as they were. Identity with a team is what filled the eighty-thousand-seat stadiums at college campuses on Saturday afternoons. And a fan's identifying with a team would be needed to fill Yankee Stadium and Soldier Field and other pro parks on Sunday afternoons. In the first six years of the NFL's existence, the league had too many teams in too many small cities, teams whose loyal but small local following could not sustain them. The league needed stable franchises in big cities, cities with enough fans to supply a large and reliable base.

. . .

A month before speaking at Ty Cobb's testimonial luncheon, Friedman had traveled to New Orleans, ostensibly to visit friends. Actually, Benny met with Tulane University football officials about the head football coaching job there. The Tulane job wasn't the first coaching job to cross Benny's horizon; back in December 1926, he had reportedly been a candidate for the job at the University of Kentucky, though nothing had come of it. It would be difficult, indeed impossible, to imagine prospective college graduates

John Elway or Dan Marino or Peyton Manning, some sixty or seventy years later, inquiring about a coaching job rather than a position in the NFL. Such was the dim allure of the pro game in 1927.

But when things didn't work out with Tulane, Benny began listening more closely to the pro ball suitors trying to persuade him to play for pay. The most interesting proposal was coming from a friend from Cleveland named Sammy Deutsch, a jewelry dealer and local sports impresario. Deutsch had owned the NFL's Cleveland Bulldogs a couple of years earlier. The Bulldogs won the 1924 NFL championship, but not enough people seemed to care. Deutsch lost money and sold the team, which folded shortly thereafter. Nothing if not persistent, Deutsch reorganized the team in 1926 as the Kansas City Blues. As 1927 approached, Deutsch started thinking about bringing the Bulldogs back to Cleveland, and he knew just the right Cleveland native—a two-time all-American quarterback—around whom to build a new Bulldogs incarnation.

Deutsch figured the famous quarterback from the streets of Glenville would be a big hit in Cleveland, and he was willing to pay his prospective drawing card handsomely: a salary of about $18,000 for the 1927 season. Not even Grange received as much in straight salary, though his share of the gate vaulted him well above that amount. Deutsch was making Friedman a staggering offer, dwarfing the $150 or $200 game-by-game pay most players received.

Whatever the vagaries of the frontier that was the NFL, this offer was too good to ignore. An $18,000 salary would go a long way toward relieving Benny's family's financial burdens. Although Yost was no fan of the pro game, Benny wouldn't be leaving Michigan before he graduated and, at least in that respect, he'd be honoring the Old Man's wishes.

In April 1927, NFL owners, determined to strengthen the league, met in Cleveland and decided to eliminate some of the smaller struggling franchises. Such teams as the Columbus Tigers, the Akron Indians, and the Hammond Pros were either dismissed from the league, marginalized as one of the many vagabond independent pro teams of the day, or banished into nonexistence. When the bloodletting was complete, twelve franchises remained. One of them was Sam Deutsch's reconstituted Cleveland Bulldogs.

A few months later, it was announced that the Bulldogs' quarterback in 1927 would be Glenville boy Benny Friedman.

• • •

Of the twelve teams that survived the franchise purge at the meeting in Cleveland, the Chicago Bears, the Green Bay Packers, and the New York Giants were probably the teams most likely to lead the league's push for prosperity and acceptance. The Bears were a league original well versed in the travails of the fledgling NFL. They had the locale, if not yet the massive backing, of the great city of Chicago. Their roster boasted a contingent of excellent players such as outstanding halfbacks Paddy Driscoll, the former Northwestern all-American; Dutch Sternaman; rugged lineman Ed Healey; and tackle George Trafton, who never met a pileup of bodies on a football field that he didn't like. Another Bears lineman, Bill Fleckenstein, wasn't as talented as Healey or Trafton, but he had a well-earned reputation for physical, even dirty, play.

Most of all, the Bears had Halas, or, as some might have said, the Bears were Halas. Player, owner, coach, even ticket clerk—no task concerning the well-being of the Chicago Bears was too insignificant for George Halas.

The Packers didn't have the cache and huge fan potential of a city like Chicago, but in Curly Lambeau, they had a sort of Halas of their own. Lambeau was a shipping clerk for the Indian Packing Company in Green Bay when, in 1919, he formed the Packers with financial backing from his boss. Two years later the team joined the NFL. Beset by financial difficulty, the Packers became a community-owned team, with local businessmen and residents purchasing stock in the club. As coach and player, Lambeau was somewhat of an autocrat who wasn't terribly popular with the other players, but in general, he didn't seem to care much about that. He liked to win football games, and, with the help of such star players as Red Dunn, Verne Lewellen, and Marquette University star Lavie Dilweg, he was good at it. He liked women, a lot, and he was good at that too.

Unlike Lambeau and Halas, who seemed to be born to the game, New York Giants owner Tim Mara didn't know much about football when he ponied up five hundred bucks for a new NFL franchise in 1925. Mara's specialty was bookmaking—legal in those days—and boxing promotion. Both of those activities produced enough money to bankroll an unprofitable professional football team, which is what the Giants were as the 1925 season stumbled toward its conclusion.

Desperate to reverse his team's fortune, Mara had traveled to Chicago late in 1925 with the intention of signing Red Grange immediately following Grange's last college game for Illinois; even a football novice like Mara knew of Grange and his box office potential. Unfortunately for Mara, George Halas and the Bears had already cashed that ticket. Mara didn't return to New York completely empty-handed, though; he managed to secure a commitment from Halas for a game between the Bears, with Grange, and his Giants at the Polo Grounds in New York. The famous game, the one in which Grange capped a Bears' 19–7 victory with an interception return for a touchdown on the last play, rescued Mara from a serious pool of red ink and actually made the Giants profitable for the 1925 season.

However, 1926 presented no such life preserver. When Halas wouldn't succumb to C. C. Pyle's demand for a piece of the Bears, Pyle and Grange took their football and went home, or, actually, to their ill-fated American Football League. The season was an unmitigated financial disaster for all concerned—Grange, Pyle, Halas, Mara, and everyone else in the NFL. On the field, things were better for Mara. After losing three of their first four games, the Giants rallied to finish the season at 7–4–1. Harry March, the "football man" Mara had hired to cobble together a competitive team, had done just that. Huge lineman Steve Owen and Cal Hubbard anchored a physical and skillful defense. Backs Jack McBride, a speedster who'd starred at Syracuse University, former Penn State whiz Hinky Haines, and Jim Thorpe's old teammate at Carlisle Institute, the seasoned Joe Guyon, were stalwarts on offense.

Sammy Deutsch's new Cleveland Bulldogs had a few stalwarts of their own; the jewelry-dealer-turned-football-team-owner was intent on fielding a winner again. End Carl Bacchus had been a two-time all–Missouri Valley Conference player for the University of Missouri in 1926. Ossie Wiberg was another accomplished pass receiver. Tiny Feather, anything but tiny at six feet, 190 pounds, was a powerful inside runner. Al Bloodgood was a dangerous runner and a skilled punter and dropkicker. Of course, Benny could kick, too, but that's not what Sammy Deutsch pried him away from the pursuit of a white-collar life to do, at least not in the main. Friedman was expected to draw fellow Clevelanders out, by the thousands, to Luna Park to watch him throw passes, a lot of passes, as nobody before him had done.

. . .

Saint Louis University coach Eddie Cochem's forward pass experiment back in 1906 didn't change the game of college football overnight, but over the next two decades, more than a few college teams had implemented the pass as at least part of their offense. And for the occasional team with an unusually talented quarterback like Benny, or Dartmouth's Swede Oberlander, the forward pass became the offensive focal point.

But the passing game had been slow to catch on in professional football. The rules governing passing had eased somewhat since the century's first two decades, but they were still far from passing-friendly. Passers still had to be at least five yards behind the line of scrimmage when the ball was thrown. This rule severely restricted a quarterback's ability to throw on the run and create confusion in the defensive secondary by moving with the ball behind and up to the line of scrimmage. A pass thrown into the opponent's end zone that fell incomplete was still ruled a touchback, with possession going to the opponent. A team that threw more than one incomplete pass in a single series of downs incurred a five-yard penalty. And a passer daring enough, or crazy enough, to throw the ball from behind his own goal line would still cost his team two points with an incompletion.

These prohibitive rules were daunting enough on their own, but with the ridiculously difficult-to-throw "melon ball" in use at the time, they were nearly the equivalent of an outright ban on forward passing. Few players could throw the ball well enough to risk incurring the penalties awaiting them for a misfire.

Furthermore, pro football was trapped in the inertia of a mentality that the players, coaches, and the owners couldn't or wouldn't escape—the old grinding, plodding, blue-collar mentality that had ruled football since its creation. Maybe that had something to do with the blue-collar people who were playing the pro game. In 1927, most of the pros weren't fancy two-time all-Americans entering the league amidst media hoopla and great expectation. They were mostly coal miners or factory workers who'd earned their football stripes mucking around in scarred sandlots in front of a few dozen friends and family members. It was an unglamorous way of life suited to an unglamorous style of play—pound the ball up the middle, then do it again, and again, until you reach the end zone or have to punt. Some teams were a little more adventurous: Curly Lambeau liked to pass, and Ernie Nevers, the great Stanford all-American, began throwing the ball a fair amount when he signed with the Duluth Eskimos for the 1926 season.

If the NFL was going to attract the kind of fan base needed to make the game profitable, though, it was going to have to escape the doldrums of a game dominated by line plunging. Red Grange had provided a glimmer of hope that pro ball could sell, but the league needed to take another step. It needed to give the fans a taste of the excitement that only a long downfield pass could bring, the kind of excitement that fans in Big Ten stadiums had been lucky enough to witness over the last three seasons when the Michigan Wolverines were in action.

The league needed to open up the game. The Cleveland Bulldogs' twenty-two-year-old rookie quarterback—even without Bennie Oosterbaan running downfield for him—was ready to do just that.

• • •

Benny Friedman's professional football baptism began in the second week of September 1927 amidst the tranquility of Excelsior Springs, Missouri, a quiet resort town known more for the supposed curative powers of its natural sulphur springs than as a site for a football training camp. Bulldogs coach Leroy Andrews quickly made it clear, however, that his players weren't there to luxuriate. Andrews drove them through demanding two-a-day practices in a midwestern summer heat that was brutal compared to the Ann Arbor Septembers Benny had experienced. During the cooler nights, Andrews conducted "skull sessions," reviewing plays and formations.

For Benny, the comfortable cocoon of Ferry Field and Fielding Yost and his teammates at Michigan, most of whom hailed from Michigan or other eastern states, was now a memory. "I was the only chap east of the Mississippi on that ball club," Benny recalled. "The rest of them came from Nebraska, Oklahoma, Texas, and the like." Benny had been made captain of the Bulldogs by sheer dint of his celebrity, reputation, and the position he was playing, but he had to show his pro teammates that he deserved the honor. "I had to earn my spurs with my gang," Friedman said later.

Meanwhile, Benny's "old" gang at Michigan was adjusting to life without their great quarterback. Oosterbaan succeeded Benny as captain, but the larger concern in Ann Arbor that fall centered on who would succeed Friedman at quarterback. New coach Tad Weiman spent preseason workouts looking for the answer. With Benny no longer there to throw the ball to Oosterbaan, the coaching staff began training the big end to throw the ball himself. Louis Gilbert, Leo Hoffman, and Sammy Babcock also got a good look. Nobody expected anyone to equal Friedman's stunning success, but skepticism abounded as to whether this committee of throwers could present even a faint facsimile of it.

Many wondered whether Benny the pro would reach the level of greatness of Benny the collegian. More often than not in the NFL's young life, college heroes had failed to replicate their skills on the professional gridiron. One only had to examine the recent example of Red Grange as proof of that fact. Grange had enjoyed some spectacular moments thus far as a pro, but nobody was mistaking his current form for that of the Galloping Ghost of Illinois who had captivated the nation.

· · ·

Aside from the annual frenzy among the press and the fans that greeted the onset of every college football season, the two athletic happenings captivating the nation in September 1927 had nothing to do with football. As his New York Yankees, the famed "Murderer's Row," were laying waste to the American League, Babe Ruth, the great Sultan of Swat, was in hot pursuit of the single-season home-run record of fifty-nine, set in 1921. Of course, Ruth himself had set that record. Actually, no one but Ruth could have set that record. From the moment in 1919 when the Babe had yielded the pitcher's mound to hurlers less able than he—and that was just about every other pitcher except the great Walter Johnson—the Bambino began slugging home runs with a frequency so far in excess of his nearest pursuers that it seemed he was playing a different game. In this sense there was a strong parallel between Ruth and Friedman, for without yet playing a down in a pro game, Benny had already demonstrated a peerless ability to pass the football. Sportswriters' frequent references to Benny as "the Babe Ruth" of his sport were not accidental.

The other event that had the sporting public in a tizzy was the rematch for the heavyweight title upcoming on September 22 between challenger Jack Dempsey and champion Gene Tunney. Dempsey, nicknamed the "Manassa Mauler" for his Colorado hometown and his unambiguously physical style of fighting, had captured the heavyweight championship with his brutal beating of Jess Willard in 1919. Over the next seven years, Dempsey, whose rugged countenance suggested he'd caught a few too many blows in the ring, and maybe outside it, too, had intermittently defended his title and participated in the festivities and merriment of 1920s America that would ultimately earn the decade the label of the "Roaring Twenties." Dempsey was just the type for the times—he liked the ladies, he liked to party, and every so often he would attend to his business. It was a smooth arrangement until Gene Tunney came along.

Tunney was the anti-Dempsey. He had an unmarked, appealing face that belied the barbarism of his profession. He was a disciplined ex-Marine, educated, refined, understated, and—as his 1926 bout with Dempsey approached—underrated. He didn't brutalize opponents in the eye-catching manner of Dempsey, but his tactical, defensive style was just as effective. And to the utter shock of the American sporting public, he stole Dempsey's title with a typically brilliant display of defense and a fair share of annoying offense that thoroughly frustrated the slugger.

Before the 1926 fight, most "experts" had favored Dempsey to deposit Tunney into a ringside seat. After observing Tunney thoroughly confound the Mauler, many of those experts didn't see much sense in a rematch. Jack's advanced boxing age of thirty-two, three years older than his nemesis, didn't bolster his case for a rematch, either. But Dempsey wasn't inclined to disappear from the scene he'd dominated for so long. He refused to believe he couldn't dent Tunney's defenses. On reflection, Jack said he'd had Tunney in serious trouble but didn't realize it at the time because he didn't think he'd hit Tunney hard enough to have hurt him. Jack kept pushing for a rematch and finally got it.

More than 104,000 people squeezed into Soldier Field on September 22 to see if Dempsey could finally catch up with the cagey Tunney. Millions more tuned in on radio. Dempsey, never a big fan of training, had come to Chicago as prepared as he'd ever been for a fight following a disciplined and intense training camp. He practically sprinted out of his corner at the opening bell toward Tunney and launched a vicious assault against the former Marine. It was the kind of tactic that had worked for Dempsey against a bunch of fine fighters he'd knocked out in the first round in 1918 and 1919 on his way to taking Jess Willard's title. But this was 1927, not 1919, and he was fighting Gene Tunney, not Jack Moran or Kid Harris or Tony Drake. Tunney held his ground while suffering minimal damage, and the fight settled into a reprise of the first bout. It had to be maddening to Dempsey that he couldn't reach a guy whose favorite pastime outside the ring was reading the classics.

Then, in the seventh round, Tunney finally got careless for a moment. The two men had drifted toward a corner of the ring. Dempsey launched an overhand right over Tunney's dropped left hand. The punch connected and backed up Tunney. Dempsey himself was probably stunned that he'd finally landed a meaningful blow. But now, unlike in the first fight, he was sure he'd hurt Tunney, and he pounced. For the first time in seventeen rounds of parrying the Manassa Mauler's every thrust, Gene Tunney was in trouble, big trouble. The punches came quickly, four or five of them in a second or two, with a big left hook the most prominent blow, and then Tunney was down on his buttocks, his left arm dangling over the lower rope, a visitor in that same hazy place where Dempsey had sent nearly all his opponents.

Traditionally, a fighter who had knocked down an opponent was permitted to stand over him, waiting to resume the attack the moment his victim rose to his feet. That rule had recently been changed: the ten-second knockdown count was not to commence until the fighter scoring the knockdown had arrived in a neutral corner to await the count. Dempsey, either unaware of the new rule or too inflamed with his sudden good fortune to respect it, hovered over Tunney before moving to a neutral corner. Five seconds elapsed before the referee began counting to ten. After one or two seconds of the count, Gene sat more upright and his grip on the rope seemed to grow stronger. He sat motionless, staring to his right, but he seemed to be listening carefully as each second was counted. When the referee intoned "Nine," Tunney hoisted himself to his feet. Some fourteen seconds had passed since the moment he'd first hit the canvas—four more seconds than the wounded fighter should have had to clear his head had Dempsey gone immediately to the corner.

Tunney endured the rest of the seventh round, and by the eighth he'd fully regained both his senses and his control of Dempsey, even knocking Jack down for a quick count with a crisp right cross. Gene went on to claim another clear decision over Dempsey.

Even today, the famous "long count" is debated—did Tunney need those extra few seconds to avoid a knockout? Tunney always insisted he could have jumped up in time even if the count had commenced immediately. Whatever the speculation over the long count's effect, there was nothing speculative about the cool $1 million Tunney earned for the fight, the largest payday ever for a boxer. Dempsey, as the challenger, received about half that amount.

To the members of the Cleveland Bulldogs preparing for their season opener against the Packers in Green Bay on September 25, that kind of money must have seemed like some sort of fantasy. Most of Benny's teammates wouldn't clear more than a hundred bucks or so for the game. Of course, they weren't going to bring in more than a hundred thousand people and a radio audience of many millions more, as the Dempsey-Tunney battle had.

Though Benny's debut as a Bulldog wasn't a national story, regional and local press coverage was strong. At the July league meeting, the owners had figured that an appearance by Benny against the Packers in Wisconsin, where fans still had fresh recollections of his heroics against their Badgers, would draw a healthy amount of attention. The media wasted no time picking up on Benny's upcoming appearance in the Badger state. "BENNY FRIEDMAN TO PLAY IN GREEN BAY," trumpeted a local headline the very day following the announcement in July that Benny had turned pro. During the week of the game, a good number of stories reflected the anticipation of the great Michigan all-American's appearance. "Sunday is going to be 'Benny Friedman Day' at the city stadium," read one local piece, "and Michiganders for miles around are coming here to pay tribute to the Wolverine star . . . Everybody who can beg, borrow or steal a ride down from the 'Yukon' is planning to be here Sunday."

Anticipation wasn't a word associated with Benny's college football debut. "Anonymity" was a much better fit for that occasion, when Benny bolted off the pine to mop up the crumbs Red Grange had left in his wake. Now, three years later, Benny's greatness and fame were preceding him. "Football fans in all parts of the country," wrote one reporter, "will be anxiously waiting to hear how Fielding Yost's famous Wolverine made the grade in his initial appearance on the postgraduate gridiron."

As the Bulldogs broke camp and checked out of the Hotel Royal in Excelsior Springs that week, Benny was a little anxious. Physically, he was sharp and fit, but he wasn't about to face Ohio Wesleyan or the Michigan Aggies or even the Ohio State Buckeyes. He knew what he could do against those teams.

He didn't yet know what he could do against the Green Bay Packers.

. . .

Benny's pro debut took place in a steady rain on a wet, sloppy field decidedly ill-suited to an explosive forward passing exhibition. Once on the field it took Benny only a moment to realize that he was going to have more serious matters to cope with than the poor weather. The first-team Packer defenders appeared much bigger, stronger, and fiercer than the college lines Friedman had been accustomed to surveying. And they were. Benny allowed himself a glance at the Packer substitutes on the sideline, hoping to see a much softer-looking group, but he saw a bunch that mirrored the starters. "That doesn't make the outlook much brighter," the nervous young quarterback droned.

Benny was surprised to hear a Packer lineman respond.

"Keep your chin up, Benny. It's a nice, friendly game," the lineman said—in Yiddish.

Friedman hadn't expected to hear any opposing players speaking his parents' native tongue. He wasn't even sure which Packer had spoken until he saw a Green Bay end bust out in laughter.

"What's your name and where are you from?" Benny shouted at him.

"O'Donnell of Notre Dame," Packers end Dick O'Donnell replied.

Benny didn't have time for a follow-up question, such as where an Irish end from Notre Dame had learned his Yiddish. From the opening whistle, the game was anything but nice and friendly. Green Bay, maybe with a bit of motivation to stop the heralded rookie quarterback, was rather forcefully indoctrinating Benny to the rigors of pro ball. The Packers imposed their strength and size and willfulness on the young quarterback. Andrews benched his ineffective, jittery quarterback before the end of the first half to calm him down. Cleveland's strong defensive play allowed the team to retreat to the locker room at halftime in a scoreless tie.

As Benny stayed in his seat for the start of the third quarter, Green Bay took control. After a Packers' punt buried Cleveland deep in their own end, the Bulldogs tried to punt themselves out of trouble, but Lavie Dilweg blocked Al Bloodgood's kick in the Cleveland end zone. The Packers' six-foot-two-inch, 230-pound tackle, Tiny Cahoon, fell on the ball to give

Green Bay a 6–0 lead. The extra-point try failed. The Packers scored again in the quarter, smashing the ball over the goal line after an impressive drive. Again the Packers missed the extra-point try, and the score remained 12–0.

At the start of the fourth quarter, Andrews finally put Benny back in the fray, and Friedman seemed a bit more acclimated to his professional surroundings. As described by one reporter, Benny "immediately began shooting passes in the true 'Michigan' style." One of Friedman's connections with Al Bloodgood went for fifty yards and a touchdown. It wasn't quite "Benny-to-Bennie," but it was a start. Bloodgood dropkicked the extra point and the score was now 12–7. That, however, was as close as Benny was going to bring the Bulldogs in his introduction to the National Football League.

The attendance at the game, about 4,500, wasn't staggering, but considering the poor weather and the fact that many pro games in the past had been fortunate to draw half that many people, there was reason to be encouraged.

Years later, Benny commented on the education he'd received in his first professional game. "Precision, exactness, hard-hitting—those young men knew their business better than any varsity team I had ever opposed," Friedman wrote. "When they tackled, it was at your shoestrings; when they blocked, you went down and stayed down."

"I got through that game," Benny continued, "with a few rest spots to soothe battered bones. My team lost. My own performance had been fair but undistinguished; but I'd seen more fast football in that hour than in an entire schedule of varsity games."

The action didn't promise to get any slower in the Bulldogs' next game, their home opener at Luna Park. Tim Mara's New York Giants were coming to Cleveland.

TWELVE

"One Sweet Tough Racket"

If Benny was looking to recover from the Packers' beating in the comfort of his Glenville home, he was in for a disappointment. Apparently, Sammy Deutsch and Bulldogs president Herb Brandt had decided that a team that lives together plays together. The Bulldogs—every one of them—would be calling a Lake Erie shoreline mansion their home for the football season. Actually, the place more closely resembled a frat house than a mansion, and that was fine with Brandt, who wanted a little of the old college spirit in his team's approach to football.

All of the Bulldogs—Benny included—were going to need to play with more energy, and precision, than they'd produced against the Packers to confront the powerful New York Giants. With Jack McBride and Hinky Haines providing the speed, running, and passing, and Joe Alexander, Wilbur "Pete" Henry, Steve Owen, and monstrous Cal Hubbard controlling line play, Tim Mara's group was a serious force. Owen was a fireplug of a man whose 255 pounds were crammed into a five-foot-ten-inch frame, and he played with a meanness that matched his stoutness. Hubbard had been particularly imposing in the Giants' season-opening win against Providence, snuffing out the Steamrollers' running plays before they got started and, on the decisive play of the game, smashing his six-foot-four-inch, 250-pound frame through the Providence line to block a punt and set up the Giants' winning score.

The Bulldogs were hoping for a healthy hometown boost, anchored by the return of the boy from Glenville. But the game wasn't generating much media buzz as the week progressed. The *Plain Dealer* was all but silent on Benny's impending pro debut in Cleveland; the upcoming decimation of the Pittsburgh Pirates by Babe Ruth, Lou Gehrig, and the rest of the Yankees' Murderer's Row, and the looming kickoff of the college football campaign gobbled up the sports pages' premium space.

Friedman's homecoming did create some excitement in Cleveland's Jewish community. A lengthy tribute in the Cleveland *Jewish Review and Observer* lionized Benny as a beacon to Jews for his heroic performance against Ohio State in 1926 while his father lay ill in a local hospital. Never mind that the quarterback hadn't learned of his father's condition until after the game; undoubtedly, the *Review and Observer's* version lent more drama to the account.

That local ethnic pride was a prime reason Sammy Deutsch had clamored after Benny's services, but, by itself, it wasn't going to sell enough tickets. The Bulldogs' management appealed to the greater Cleveland community by placing ads such as one in the *Plain Dealer* urging fans to head to the Union Trust Arcade downtown for tickets to see "BENNY FRIEDMAN'S BULLDOGS vs. NEW YORK GIANTS."

The characterization of the Bulldogs as "Benny's" team elevated the twenty-two-year-old quarterback into the rarified air breathed by Grange and Ernie Nevers. Those two were established professional stars whose teams came to be referred to as *their* teams. This made perfect sense; in these nascent days of the NFL, these great stars *were* their teams in the public's eyes. Unlike Grange and Nevers, however, Friedman hadn't yet done much to merit such a lofty status. He'd played exactly one professional game and hadn't played too well. In essence, he'd received this status on the come, based on his legendary feats at Michigan. And, at least insofar as the *Plain Dealer* ad was concerned, it didn't hurt to trumpet the name of the local hero.

Could Friedman produce for "his" Bulldogs? The Packers had battered him, upsetting his equilibrium to the point where he questioned his ability to play with the pros. His passing hadn't been so erratic since his uneven performance against Ohio State in 1925. Following that game, Benny had Yost and Bo Molenda and Louie Gilbert and Bennie Oosterbaan, and the pride and comfort that came with being a Michigan Wolverine, to help him regroup. Now he had none of that; he had only a collection of strange teammates from strange places, a coach he barely knew, and an owner who was paying him a lot of money—a lot more than he was paying any other player—to win games and draw fans.

"This is one sweet tough racket, what I mean, and no kidding," Benny said shortly after the Packers game. "In college games you occasionally bump up against a boy who is hot stuff, but most of the time it's easy.

"But pro football—that's a horse from an entirely new stable."

Benny's owner didn't share his reservations about his pro prospects. "He will be the sensation of the league," Herb Brandt said after watching Benny recover in the fourth quarter against the Packers following his rough start. "His success in the pro game is assured from what he showed in this game."

• • •

Luna Park, on Cleveland's East Side, was just a few minutes on the trolley from Benny's Glenville boyhood home. The park opened in 1905, the year Benny was born, and it was more Coney Island than football venue—most Clevelanders visited the park for its amusement rides and carnival-like atmosphere. The twenty-thousand-seat stadium where the Bulldogs would play their games, sitting at the park's west end in the roller coaster's shadow, was almost an afterthought.

Despite slow advance sales for the Giants game, Deutsch and Brandt optimistically announced that the gates would open at noon for the 3:00 game and that twenty-four ticket windows would be available for what they hoped would be a large walk-up crowd. Their hopes might have been buoyed a bit on the morning of the game when they turned to the *Plain Dealer*'s sports section and saw, at last, that Cleveland's largest newspaper had written about the game, a nice lead story that highlighted Friedman's homecoming.

As game time approached on Sunday, it became apparent that the Bulldogs management could have done without about twenty of the twenty-four ticket windows. Barely three thousand fans dotted the stadium's concrete bleachers. The last time Benny played a football game in Cleveland, in 1922, fifteen thousand fans jammed Dunn Field to see two *high school* teams battle for the city Senate championship. The sparse turnout had to be a huge disappointment to Giants' owner Tim Mara and NFL president Joe Carr, who had made the trip. Friedman as a pro drawing card was thus far unimpressive.

Benny and his Bulldogs spent the first quarter mired in neutral, unable to budge big Cal Hubbard and the other Giants defenders. Jack McBride didn't do any better on offense for the Giants, and the slow first quarter probably had the few fans who *had* shown up for the game wondering why they bothered.

Then Friedman came to life. He followed a twenty-yard bolt to Bloodgood with another to Proc Randels. He then changed things up, catching the Giants off-balance as he called his own number as a receiver and caught a pass from Tiny Feather for another twenty yards. For the first time as a pro, Friedman was beginning to feel it now—that flow, that surge of confidence that told him a touchdown might come on the next play, or the play after that, or the play after that, but that it was surely coming. It nearly always did when he was at the Wolverines' helm, partly because the opponent knew it was coming just as well as Benny did.

Today, though, the opponent was the New York Giants. Aware though they were of Benny's reputation, they'd never played against him. They weren't consumed by any sense of negative inevitability. Just as quickly as they'd yielded ground to the rookie, they smothered him and the Bulldogs on three straight downs, forcing them to try a dropkick for three points just before halftime. The Giants crashed through the Bulldogs' interference and blocked Bloodgood's boot, and the half ended in a scoreless tie.

Things didn't get much more interesting in the second quarter. The most exciting play was when Benny prevented a possible game-winning New York touchdown by recovering a blocked Bulldogs' punt near the Cleveland goal line. At game's end, there was no score but rather a 0–0 tie.

Diving into a pile of bodies to recover wayward kicks wasn't generally Benny's way of making his mark on a football game. He'd have a chance to do better on the field, and at the gate, when the Bulldogs visited the Giants in New York in two weeks.

First, however, the Bulldogs headed to Detroit to meet Red Grange and his New York Yankees. The game in Ann Arbor's backyard was another homecoming of sorts for Friedman, and his first professional tussle against his great collegiate rival.

Twenty thousand fans showed up at Detroit's Navin Field on October 9 for the game. The crowd wasn't even a third the size of the audience that saw Grange torch Michigan for four touchdowns in twelve minutes in 1924. But it was still the NFL's largest crowd of the young season by a huge margin, and it was a safe bet that just about everyone had come to see Red and Benny reprise their collegiate magic.

One young fan who may have been at the game had a unique rooting interest. He was a high-school junior from Detroit, a quarterback, and Jewish. As Benny had done in Cleveland a few years earlier, the boy was making quite a name for himself in Detroit, flashing all-around skills eerily similar to Friedman's if not quite as developed—he was a standout runner and place kicker and a natural leader and field general. He also could have been mistaken for Friedman by his stocky build and height—but not by his passing game, a deficiency he'd begun to address at a football camp during the past summer under the tutelage of none other than Friedman himself. Benny worked hard with the boy, teaching him his peculiar technique for passing a football. The boy's name was Harry Newman.

If Newman was at the game, he must have been disappointed with what he saw. Neither his mentor nor Grange generated any offense. Bo Molenda, Benny's outstanding fullback at Michigan and now Grange's Yankee teammate, outplayed both of them. The Yankees scratched out two second-quarter touchdowns, one on a fumble recovery in the Cleveland end zone, and led at halftime by 13–0.

In the third quarter, from his defensive safety position, Friedman swooped in front of an intended New York receiver and intercepted a long pass. The play seemed to energize the rookie quarterback. He took the snap on the first play following his interception and drilled Bulldogs end Hal Cunningham with a perfect throw for a twenty-yard gain. Several plays later, Benny had the Bulldogs in the end zone. They closed to within six points when Benny kicked the extra point.

But they got no closer. Friedman kept connecting on passes and moving the ball down the field but the winning recipe eluded him. Yankees 13, Bulldogs 7.

The Bulldogs limped out of Detroit with a 0–2–1 record. In three games they'd scored a total of fourteen points—a decent *quarter's* worth of work for Friedman at Michigan. There was a certain physicality and mercenary mentality to pro ball that would take some getting used to, and the adjustment was proving much more difficult than Benny had anticipated.

Next up for the Bulldogs was a visit to the Polo Grounds to battle the New York Giants in their home opener on the fifteenth. This would be Friedman's first game in New York City, and again team and league officials were anxiously waiting to see what kind of gate the young star would attract. If the pregame attention showered on Benny was any indication, it would be a strong one. "One of the greatest Jewish stars known to intercollegiate football," as the *New York Times* described Benny that week, was honored at a number of gala dinners, including an affair at the Hotel Majestic sponsored by the Young Men's Philanthropic League, a Jewish charitable organization.

In the midst of shuttling that week between workouts at the Polo Grounds and functions at midtown hotels, Benny happened upon another

1926 college football star, Dartmouth quarterback Eddie Dooley. They'd first met a couple of years earlier in New York at a dinner honoring football all-Americans. As they clasped hands and renewed their acquaintance, it wasn't long before the two quarterbacks launched into an animated discussion of the finer points of the art of throwing a football. After some back-and-forth, the two men bolted out of their chairs and headed off to the Polo Grounds. They made their way uptown alone—no fans, no gaggle of media. Then two of the greatest passers ever to handle a football strode into an empty stadium for a gentlemanly contest to be witnessed by a stadium caretaker and three other people. It was as if Babe Ruth and Lou Gehrig had sneaked off to Yankee Stadium for a private impromptu home-run contest.

Benny and Dooley each made a series of throws on the run, aiming for a designated spot, in a contest to determine the more accurate passer. The four witnesses adjudged Benny the clear winner.

Dooley, not inclined to surrender, proposed to see which of the two could throw the longest ball. The two men strode to the center of the field. From the fifty-yard line, Dooley, with hands that rivaled the size and strength of Benny's, grabbed a ball and flung it ferociously downfield, toward the goalposts. The ball sailed over the crossbar and landed in the end zone—a heave of some sixty yards. The Dartmouth man, with the confidence of a long jumper who knows his first jump in a competition is all he'll need to win, then watched as Benny tried mightily, but futilely, to match him.

They strode off the field, leaving a vacant stadium that Benny hoped would be at least partially filled on Sunday.

"I was all set to go to your school myself," Benny said to the former Dartmouth star. "A week before I was to go east, I went up to Ann Arbor and liked the place so well I stayed."

"Lucky for me," Dooley replied, obviously pleased at Benny's choice of schools. "They'd have had to make a center or something out of me if you had come to Hanover."

. . .

On Sunday, October 15, fifteen thousand to twenty-five thousand fans, depending on which of several estimates was accurate, gathered in the Polo Grounds to watch the Bulldogs-Giants rematch. This gathering was no match for the sixty thousand fans that one week earlier had flooded Yankee Stadium, a couple of miles away across the Harlem River, to watch Babe Ruth and his teammates finish off the Pittsburgh Pirates in a four-game World Series sweep. Still, even at the low end of the estimated fan count, NFL officials had to be pleased.

A sizable number of the fans were Jewish, many affiliated with the Young Men's Philanthropic League, who had gathered to cheer on Benny. From the start of the game, Friedman whipped the ball around the Polo Grounds like he owned it. His forwards were neutralizing Hubbard and Owen and Pete Henry, giving him time to throw. Occasionally the Giants linemen did bust through to harass or even tackle the quarterback, but Benny was often able to sprint away from the pressure and throw on the run. The piercing blow was a thirty-five-yard dart to Tiny Feather early in the third quarter that instigated a touchdown-scoring drive capped by fullback Jim Simmons's one-yard plunge.

Benny's missed extra point left Cleveland with a precarious six-point lead, but on this day, that proved good enough. Hinky Haines and Jack McBride didn't fire, and the Giants never seriously threatened to score, their most ominous foray being a badly missed McBride field-goal try. Cleveland's margin of victory would have been larger had Carl Bacchus not dropped Benny's perfectly thrown fourth-quarter pass in the end zone, but the Bulldogs were more than happy with a 6–0 victory.

Thousands of fans, no doubt many of them Jewish, lined the streets outside the stadium following the game, waiting for an up close glimpse of the sensational passer. Such gatherings had been standard in Ann Arbor— there was always a throng of Michigan fans at the train station to send off the Wolverines to an away game and greet them when they returned—but in the pro game, Red Grange was, until now, the only player to inspire such hero worship.

The game with the Giants was an important one in several respects. It gave Cleveland its much-needed first victory. It marked Benny's first commanding performance. It showed the potential of one of the league's marquee franchises, and one of the league's marquee players, to draw a respectable gate. And, generally speaking, it was a moment for the league and its players and owners to feel good about their enterprise. But in the words of New York columnist Walter Trumbull, it was an enterprise whose viability was still very much an uncertainty.

> Professional football drew only about 18,000 spectators to the Polo Grounds yesterday, and how many of these actually paid to get in we don't know . . . Now a crowd of 18,000 at the Polo Grounds makes the place look pretty empty. Yet on those two elevens were some of the greatest players the game has known.
>
> . . . Most of these men had played before frenzied throngs of 70,000 rooters. They tell us that they were none too inspired. It is small wonder.
>
> But if those had been two college teams, with those men in the lineup, if that had been a college game, the customers would have battled bitterly to secure tickets and the speculators would have been busy. It is not the players who make football. It is the loyalty of men to their colleges and the traditions which only time can grow.

Even worse for pro ball's prospects than pessimistic media may have been the fallout from a crunching tackle in the Bears-Yankees game that weekend. Red Grange had snared a pass coming out of the backfield, and as he turned to head upfield, Bears' tackle George Trafton, pursuing the play from Grange's right side, crashed into the Ghost's right knee. Grange went sprawling to the turf with a severely torn ligament. He spent the afternoon in a Chicago hospital, and it was clear right away that he'd be missing games. The only question was how many. Ironically it was the Bears, the team that had given Red his first professional windfall, that had delivered the career-threatening blow.

. . .

George Trafton probably wasn't trying to hurt Grange, but it's a pretty safe bet that as the big Bears lineman thundered toward Red, he wasn't overly concerned about the consequences of his impending hit on his former teammate. The Chicago Bears played the physical game of football very physically, with Trafton and fellow linemen Link Lyman and Ed Healey sometimes more inclined to throw a punch than a block. And then there was Bill Fleckenstein. The marginally talented six-foot-two-inch, 210-pound brute couldn't match the football skills of Trafton, Lyman, and Healy, but they had nothing on "Wild Bill" when it came to instigating extracurricular mayhem.

Tough as the Bears were, they were just as likely to beat opponents on the scoreboard as they were to beat them up. They were, in a word, good. Healy, Lyman, and Trafton were future Hall of Famers—as were halfback Paddy Driscoll, the great Northwestern all-American, and George Halas, who, in addition to owning and coaching the team, was a pretty fair end. This combination of talent and toughness had carried the Bears to the NFL championship in 1926, and they were off to a flying start in defense of the crown, standing at 3–0, with the Bulldogs up next.

The day before the Bears' game, Benny was in Ann Arbor for homecoming weekend and the dedication of the new Michigan Stadium. On a perfect day for football, Benny joined in the celebration with former teammates, current Michigan players, and eighty-five thousand Wolverines fans. The happy occasion was made even happier by the 21–0 spanking the Wolverines gave to Ohio State, a victory that raised Michigan's record to a spotless 4–0.

Friedman had to hustle to Chicago after the game for the Bulldogs' game the next day against the Bears. On the ride there, Benny had time to reflect on the glorious day in Ann Arbor. Beating Ohio State—and Benny had done it three times in three tries—never got old for a Wolverine. But there had to be some wistfulness mixed in with whatever giddiness Benny was feeling. His heroics at Ferry Field had helped create the demand for the massive new stadium, and yet, by just one year, he had missed out on the joy of playing there.

. . .

Friedman's only previous game in Chicago had been the infamous 3–2 Michigan loss to Northwestern during the Soldier Field monsoon in 1925. The dry, chilly weather that greeted the Bears and Giants this Sunday was far more fan-friendly, and passing-friendly, and Benny thrilled the twenty thousand fans in Wrigley Field right from the start. He hit Hal Cunningham for a sixteen-yard gain on the first play from scrimmage and then, on the next play, found Ossie Wiberg for fourteen more yards. Just two plays into the game, the powerful Bears' defense was off-balance. They'd expected Benny to come out throwing and had prepared a special pass-rushing scheme to confuse him—on one down, the defensive ends would rush Benny, and on the next down, the rush would come from the tackles. It wasn't working. Like so many other defenses lying in wait for Friedman, the Bears weren't quite ready for the reality of Friedman's attack.

Benny mixed in a few runs on the Bulldogs' march toward the goal line. It was a seamless blend of play-calling—"perfect football," as one writer later described it—that confounded the Bears, whose fearsome linemen hadn't yet laid a hand on their young tormentor. Benny finished off the drive with a three-yard touchdown pass to Carl Bacchus. Friedman missed the extra-point try, but still, almost effortlessly, he and his Bulldogs jumped out on top of George Halas and his defending champion Bears, 6–0.

That first drive might have been too easy for Benny's own good. Halas's star linemen set out after the upstart quarterback with a fury that was actually the second component of their pregame preparations for Friedman—hit him hard on every play, whether or not he has the ball. Trafton and Healy and Lyman left Benny's blockers grasping at air and Benny lambasting referee Jim Durfee for his blind eye toward the Bears' blatant rough stuff. That Durfee was allowing Chicago's linemen to have their way with Friedman wasn't a total surprise. Referees were typically handpicked by the home club, and impartiality wasn't high on the list of selection criteria. As if the mauling wasn't bad enough for Benny, Durfee drove the quarterback crazy with constant chatter about Fielding Yost.

"Mr. Durfee," a glaring Friedman said to the ref, "I'm not interested in Fielding Yost today, but I am interested in what's going on in this game and apparently you're not. Why don't you stop talking about Fielding Yost and pay attention to what's going on."

Durfee was apparently unmoved, because the physical onslaught continued throughout the second quarter. Benny then tried appealing to George Trafton's gentler side.

"George, this isn't football," Friedman said to the ferocious Bears lineman. "What are they trying to do, kill me?" Trafton appeared sympathetic and told Benny he'd have the Bears cut it out.

"Friedman said that if you don't lay off him," Trafton reported back to his teammates, "he's going to kick your teeth out."

Trafton's report insured an even more vigorous assault on Benny. Midway through the third quarter, Friedman had had enough. He ripped off his helmet, threw it to the turf, and walked to the sideline, done for the afternoon.

The Bulldogs were now trailing, thanks to a safety on a botched punt from their own end zone and two sweet touchdown drives engineered by Chicago halfback Paddy Driscoll. The former Northwestern all-American was into his ninth season of the pro football wars, but he was still a player to be reckoned with. Al Bloodgood, who had replaced Benny at quarter, retrieved one of those two Bears' scores with some pretty passing, and the Bulldogs snuck closer. But 14–12 was a close as they'd get—a respectable score against the defending league champs, but a loss nonetheless.

His early exit from the game notwithstanding, Friedman was a hit with the Wrigley Field crowd and, as usual, with the press. "BENNY'S PASSES THRILL," the *Chicago Tribune* declared.

But it was a mere blurb that best summed up that this rookie was showing the NFL something entirely new. "The Bulldogs' touchdowns were gained from passes, generally thrown by Benny Friedman, former Michigan star," wrote the Associated Press, "while the Bears, with minor exceptions, played straight football."

• • •

Ernie Nevers was a reserved man who was uncomfortable talking about his talents. He left that job to others, and there were plenty of players and coaches willing to do it. Ernie's Stanford coach, the famed Pop Warner, may have been his most loquacious booster. Warner believed Nevers was the best player he'd ever coached in his nearly forty years at coaching's highest level—better even than the marvelous Jim Thorpe, whom Warner had coached at Carlisle a decade earlier.

Thorpe was the greatest player ever in the view of many experts, but in the view of Warner, the expert who knew Thorpe best, Nevers's superior discipline and fighting spirit gave him the edge over the great Sac-and-Fox native American.

Any favorable comparison to Thorpe made by the coach was high praise, but, if any player was worthy of it, Nevers looked the part. The six-foot-one-inch, 205-pounder was a blonde-haired block of granite, with great strength, speed, and agility. He was an irrepressible runner, especially when it came to line plunging; an accomplished passer, one of a very few other than Friedman who viewed the pass as a weapon of choice and not of last resort; a marvelous dropkicker and punter; and a standout on defense. His competitive thirst and appetite for winning spurred him to play with utter disregard for his safety. No injury kept Nevers from a game, not even the two broken ankles on which he played against Knute Rockne and Notre Dame in the 1925 Rose Bowl. Stanford didn't win that day, but not for lack of effort from Ernie. "He tore our line to shreds," an admiring Rockne remarked following the game.

C. C. Pyle was another Nevers admirer. In the summer of 1926, Pyle began wooing Nevers to join Grange in the upstart AFL. The promoter offered Nevers a $15,000 salary plus a cut from some of the larger gates he would draw. But Ernie decided to play for the NFL's Duluth Eskimos and their owner, Ole Hausgrud, Nevers's high-school classmate, on the same terms offered by Pyle.

The Duluth Eskimos epitomized the vagabond nature of professional football in the 1920s. With no home stadium, they were a perpetual travel-ing road show. In 1926 they played a fourteen-game NFL schedule—and supplemented that with fifteen exhibition games. Nevers was on the field for nearly every play in every one of those twenty-nine games. And there was little rest for him even when the long season ended in the spring of '27. The talented athlete changed football cleats for baseball spikes and pitched for the major league St. Louis Browns. Nevers had a lively fastball, but it wasn't quite snappy enough to sneak past Babe Ruth, who touched Ernie for two of his record-making sixty homers that year.

Benny hadn't yet crossed paths with Nevers on a football field; Michigan and Stanford hadn't played each other during their college days. The two stars had met at a couple of football dinners, and Friedman came away impressed with the blonde bulldozer.

The Pottsville Maroons were also pretty impressed with Nevers after Ernie and the Eskimos handed them a 27–0 thrashing on their own field on October 23. In a performance that Benny himself would be pleased to match, Nevers connected on seventeen out of twenty passes—four for touchdowns. He also nailed three out of four extra-point attempts. Ernie's spectacular game against Pottsville added some spice to an already hotly anticipated showdown with Friedman.

Twelve thousand giddy fans—four times the number at Cleveland's home opener against Green Bay—were in Luna Park on October 30 to watch Pop Warner's "player without fault" battle Fielding Yost's footballer who "never makes a mistake." The two stars hoisted their respective teams on their backs and grabbed hold of the game from the outset. Benny's throws dissected the Eskimos, eating up huge chunks of yardage and creating opportunities for him to do what no other quarterback had ever really done—use the forward pass to set up the run. "Until Friedman came along," George Halas would later write, "the pass had been used as a desperation weapon in long-yardage situations on third down—or when your team was hopelessly behind. Benny demonstrated that the pass could be mixed with running plays as an integral part of the offense." Several times Friedman smashed and dashed downfield against a surprised Duluth defense that expected him to throw the ball. Nevers, meanwhile, was nearly as sharp, penetrating Cleveland's defense with passes, bucking the line, and booming punts. But through three quarters, Benny had registered the more telling blows, and the scoreboard showed his Bulldogs ahead by 21–7.

Even with this late two-touchdown lead, Benny knew the game was far from safe. Anything was possible with Nevers on the field. This was a man who single-handedly drove Knute Rockne crazy—on two broken ankles. And sure enough, Ernie stormed back, leading the Eskimos to two late touchdowns. Unfortunately for the league's nomads, one of Ernie's two extra-point attempts was blocked, and the dramatic comeback ended one point short. Cleveland 21, Duluth 20.

Friedman had won the heralded matchup with Nevers, but Benny came away forever impressed by Ernie's talent and even more impressed by his refusal to succumb. "I used to think of him . . . as a crusader with a flaming sword," Friedman later said of his great opponent. "I never saw anyone who epitomized the idea of a will to win more so than Ernie."

• • •

Slick public relations operations with full-time employees and hefty budgets are commonplace for today's National Football League teams. The 1927 Bulldogs did things much more simply. Benny ran the PR "operation" with the club's "publicity man," *Cleveland News* sports editor Ed Bang. "[Ed] and I used to travel a day or two ahead of time to the city we were going to play in," Friedman said later. "Ed would buy two bottles of whiskey and we'd walk into a newspaper office. He'd hand one bottle to the sports editor and the other to the sports columnist, he'd introduce me, and then we'd kibitz. That was the way we got our publicity."

Despite the promotional efforts of Benny and Bang, just 2,500 fans showed up for Cleveland's next game against Grange's Yankees at Luna Park. Maybe Bang and Benny needed to upgrade their whiskey. Or maybe Grange's knee injury kept the fans away, or maybe the culprit was the cold, rainy, snowy November weather that turned the turf into a bog. The muck moved one writer to invoke the name of the day's celebrated long-distance swimmer. "Gertrude Ederle herself would have had great difficulty making it across one spot near the west goal where the tide seemed particularly tricky," the *Plain Dealer*'s Al Sommer wrote. "Realizing this and knowing that he is no Ederle, Benjamin Friedman did what a Friedman would do. He passed." And the Bulldogs won, 15–0.

The Yankees game was the first of three games the Bulldogs were to play over seven days. *Three games in seven days,* including two games against the Frankford Yellow Jackets: on November 12 in Frankford and on November 13 in Cleveland. In today's era of the pampered NFL player, one can barely imagine a team *practicing* three times in seven days.

Benny played poorly in Philadelphia as the Bulldogs lost their first game with Frankford. He picked things up the next day in Cleveland, propelling the Bulldogs to a 37–0 romp over the Yellow Jackets in the rematch. Two weeks later, on November 27, the "post graduate master of the forward pass," as one writer described Friedman, "gave 5,000 pro gridiron fans and the Chicago Cardinals lesson number two from his textbook, 'How to Throw Touchdowns.'" The lesson included touchdown passes of 65, 50, and 52 yards and resulted in a 32–7 Bulldogs' triumph. The Cardinals "had a million ideas about winning the game, but not a darn man to stop Friedman's passes," George Strickler wrote in the *Chicago Herald Examiner.* "In this, however, they are just like the other teams of their league and a lot of college teams Friedman has played against."

Benny had plenty left for a rematch with Nevers at Luna Park on December 3, and once again he bested the greatest football player ever coached by Pop Warner. This time the score wasn't that close—a 20–0 whitewash made possible by Benny's two long touchdown strikes and a strong effort from the Bulldogs. The game turned out to be Cleveland's last of the league season. They were scheduled for a Windy City rematch with the Bears the following week, but an arctic blast that lowered the game-time temperature to five degrees and winds that made it seem far colder than that forced a rare cancellation minutes before the scheduled kickoff.

Benny's performance in his rookie season was not without its warts. He had been badly overmatched, even intimidated, by the Packers, pounded by the Bears, and ineffective in his first of two games against Frankford. Yet these demerits couldn't obscure the fact that Friedman was a sensation the likes of which the league hadn't yet seen—Grange included. Benny had taken that homemade throwing motion and all-around ability from the fields of the Big Ten to the fields of the professional league and hadn't missed a beat. The pros were as defenseless against his passes as were the collegians, and he didn't even have the great Oosterbaan loping under his feathery tosses anymore. His nearly seventeen hundred passing yards and eleven touchdown passes led the league by a wide margin, though not at the expense of his outstanding running ability. He beat Ernie Nevers twice and Red Grange twice, and the Bulldogs finished fourth in the league with a fine 8–4–1 mark, trailing only the mighty league triumvirate of the Bears, Packers, and Giants, who, although champions with an 11–1–1 record, didn't escape from the rookie passer unscathed. That one loss and one tie were courtesy of Benny's Bulldogs. Every panel of writers and coaches made Friedman their runaway pick as first team All-Pro quarterback.

Yet aside from the crowds at the Giants' game in New York, the first game against Grange in Detroit, and one or two other contests, Benny's presence hadn't dramatically increased attendance, not even in his hometown. The Jewish press's coverage of Benny had fallen off somewhat from his college days. Reduced Jewish media interest mirrored the nation's disinterest in pro ball relative to the college game. It also likely reflected a Jewish cultural indifference, if not a disinclination, toward football as a career rather than as a healthy adjunct to a boy's collegiate experience that showed Jews could excel beyond the classroom. In any case, Cleveland Jews did not flock to Luna Park to see their Glenville hero, and at season's end, the Bulldogs' owners found their football operation in a familiar position— wallowing in red ink.

Benny's $18,000 salary in 1927—the highest in the league—didn't help the Bulldogs' balance sheet. Not that he was making any apologies. He figured he was worth every penny and then some. So when it came time to plan a five-game West Coast barnstorming tour for January 1928, he had no qualms about demanding $750 per game, while most other players would receive $50. He got it, too.

Michigan quarterback Benny Friedman. *Rentschler's Studio (Ann Arbor, Mich.), Box 6, Bentley Historical Library, University of Michigan*

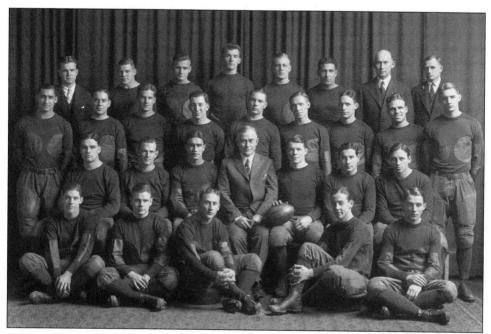

Fielding Yost's greatest team—the 1925 Michigan Wolverines. Benny is seated in second row, third from left, next to Yost. Bennie Oosterbaan is in second row from top, far right. *Rentschler's Studio (Ann Arbor, Mich.), Box 2, Bentley Historical Library, University of Michigan*

Placekicking practice at Michigan, November 3, 1925. Louis Gilbert is the holder. *Bettman/Corbis*

Benny soars to intercept a pass against the University of Minnesota. *University of Michigan Athletic Department, Box 8, Bentley Historical Library, University of Michigan*

Fielding Yost *AP Images*   Knute Rockne *Notre Dame Archives*

Benny and Bennie Oosterbaan and a Packard convertible, 1927. *Courtesy of the Detroit Public Library, National Automotive History Collection*

Benny and Bennie at the 50th reunion of the 1925 Wolverines at Michigan Stadium, 1975. *News and Information Services, Bentley Historical Library, University of Michigan*

Benny and Red Grange at the Polo Grounds, November 16, 1930. *Getty Images*

Benny's Brandeis players carrying their coach from the field following a victory. *Robert D. Farber University Archives & Special Collections, Brandeis University*

Lieutenant Commander
Benjamin Friedman, USN.
Author collection

Benny and wife, Shirley. *Author collection*

"King" Benny holding court amidst a throng of starstruck youngsters, Chicago, Illinois, 1927. *Chicago History Museum*

Williams Shaving Cream ad, 1937.

"You never knew when he was going to pass." Benny, with the Brooklyn Dodgers, loosening up, 1933.
AP Images

The barnstorming tour would be much like a tour Nevers and Grange led the previous winter. Benny's Bulldogs and three other teams, captained by Ernie, Red, and former University of Washington all-American back George Wilson, would play a five-game round-robin in San Francisco and Los Angeles—a treat for West Coast football fans who rarely got to see top-shelf pro footballers.

The Bulldogs' first game, against Nevers's team in San Francisco, was scheduled for January 6. Benny and his boys arrived there on January 5 and promptly headed for a public workout at Ewing Field, the former home to baseball's San Francisco Seals that had been reconfigured into a football stadium. Most of the fans' attention was on Friedman, and Benny didn't disappoint. According to one report, the quarterback "unleashed his throwing arm and astonished the spectators with his all-American passing."

The next day, Benny extended his winning streak to three over Ernie Nevers. Ten days later, the Bulldogs were back at Ewing Field and again they prevailed, whipping George Wilson's unit by 12–6, with Benny breaking off a sixty-seven-yard touchdown run. After the game the Bulldogs packed their gear and headed down the coast to Los Angeles for the last three games of the tour.

Benny's arrival in Los Angeles caused a stir among football fans and the sporting press, including the *Los Angeles Times,* which couldn't help but note Benny's religion in its lead: "Benny Friedman, the greatest Jewish player in football, arrived in Los Angeles last night with his Cleveland Bulldogs, one of the outstanding teams in the professional grid racket."

The *Times's* reference to Benny's religion drew precisely the kind of distinction Friedman disdained. In his mind he was a football player who happened to be a Jew, not a Jew who happened to be a football player. But the press, and most of its constituents, apparently didn't see it that way. The culture of anti-Semitism wouldn't allow them to see it that way. It wasn't violent anti-Semitism like that brewing in Germany and elsewhere in Europe. Its tone was far more subtle, intended not to inflict physical harm but to remind that there were Jews and there were Gentiles, and they were not the same.

• • •

Red Grange was next up for Benny and his Bulldogs on January 22. Though his injury had curtailed his playing time and compromised his playing quality during the 1927 NFL season, and though he wasn't drawing the enormous crowds that flocked to see him as a rookie in 1925, Grange was still the most popular attraction in the pro game. Back in 1925, Harry Conzel, whose sports column was syndicated in Jewish newspapers throughout the country, had questioned why Friedman, whose all-around talents were superior to Grange's, could not match the fan appeal of Red, "the greatest of all sports box-office magnets, with the possible exception of Jack Dempsey." Conzel's answer was that Red's individualistic style of play was more fan-friendly than Benny's more clinical, team-oriented style. On its merits, that explanation is debatable, as Benny's spectacular passes could appear as "individualistic" as any Grange run, but it is also possible that Conzel was implicitly suggesting anti-Semitism as the explanation.

Red wouldn't have known if that was Conzel's point, but he was in agreement with the columnist as to Benny's ability. "He's a truly great football player," Red said that week as he and Friedman prepared for their barnstorming battle. "Not only that, but he's smart. They talk about Benny being a good passer, but that's only half the story. He can carry the ball as well as anybody on his team. In addition he's a great field-goal kicker, as he proved against us back in 1925."

On January 22, about ten thousand fans showed up at Los Angeles's Wrigley Field, home to baseball's minor league Los Angeles Angels and a popular Hollywood movie-filming site, to see Grange and Benny put on a show. Friedman began the game by completing eight of his first nine passes, showing off the accuracy that West Coast fans had read so much about. Benny would have had nine straight completions had Carl Bacchus not muffed a perfect pass. "There were long shots and short ones, but regardless of length the ball always sailed straight and true into the arms of Friedman's receivers," wrote one reporter.

The Yankees managed to keep Benny's passes from piercing the goal line. And Friedman gave his foes a little help, fumbling a punt deep in

Cleveland's territory. Benny didn't make many errors on a football field, but he seemed to be prone to the occasional bobbled punt, and this miscue lead to a Yankees touchdown. That score and just enough solid play from Red, Bo Molenda, and Ray Flaherty managed to best the Bulldogs, 9–7. Benny's team didn't fare much better in the next two games in L.A., a scoreless tie with Wildcat Wilson's group and another, tour-ending loss to Grange's Yankees, in which Ernie Nevers played with Friedman and the Bulldogs.

Though the tour didn't go well for Friedman on the scoreboard, he had lived up to his billing. Attendance at the games had been decent. But in the view of at least one writer, it was far from decent enough to indicate that professional football was catching on—or ever would. "Commercialized football has endured long enough now to enable observers to place it pretty definitely," the *Oakland Tribune* declared near the end of the tour. "Even at its best—which last fall appeared to be in the east, it was not at all a big earner, was but moderately successful and attracted little public attention . . . In other words football as a distinctive college game continues to stand supreme and the mercenary game will never be a serious rival." As Benny and his Bulldogs headed home, they realized that their last game on the coast might have been the last game the Cleveland Bulldogs would ever play.

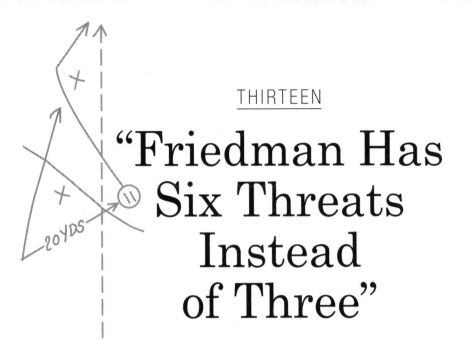

THIRTEEN

"Friedman Has Six Threats Instead of Three"

When the 235 pounds of reckless abandon that was George Trafton crashed into Red Grange's right knee, Red was probably thankful that C. C. Pyle had had the foresight to introduce him to acting as an alternative career. Although Grange was no threat to Clark Gable in the looks department or to Lionel Barrymore's dramatic range, he had just enough of both, combined with his football cache, to enable him to earn a tidy sum on the silver screen.

Red's Hollywood adventure might have inspired Friedman, who, like most pro footballers, needed to work in the off-season. Benny took some screen tests in February and learned that he had the build and the face for a camera but not the acting skills. So Benny sold insurance in Cleveland during the summer of 1928.

As the summer wore on, it became apparent that Herb Brandt and Sammy Deutsch were finished subsidizing their financially strapped football team. Friedman stepped in. He helped assemble a group of twenty Detroit businessmen looking to move the Bulldogs from Cleveland to the Motor City. Each of the twenty men contributed $500. They handed over

$2,500 of the $10,000 nest egg to league president Joe Carr, and, just like that, the Cleveland Bulldogs became the Detroit Wolverines.

There wasn't much other change in the league's teams. No other new franchises were added, and only the league's two bottom dwellers, the Buffalo Bisons and the Duluth Eskimos, folded. Duluth's demise gave Ernie Nevers a chance to return to Stanford to help Pop Warner coach at his alma mater. And Red Grange was taking a sabbatical. The winter barnstorming tour had been hard on his damaged knee, and he needed to rest.

With Grange and Nevers out of the picture, Benny would be the league's main attraction in 1928. But the fans would have to wait a while to see him; though league play began in late September, the Wolverines' first game was not until October 14 against the Grange-less Yankees. In the interim, the Wolverines warmed up with 52–0 and 47–0 exhibition thrashings of semi-pro teams from Pontiac, Michigan, and Sandusky, Georgia.

Then, before ten thousand fans at Yankee Stadium, Benny piloted a 35–12 demolition of the Yankees. "He was the same old Benny, reinforced with the wisdom and skill of a postgraduate course among the pros," the *Herald Tribune*'s Rud Rennie gushed. "Some passes were short and some were long but all were beautiful." Benny's twelve completions were good for 217 yards and three touchdowns and served loud and clear notice to the league that his sensational passing in 1927 was no fluke.

An even more ominous notice for the rest of the league might have been delivered when Benny tore through the Yankees' line and romped through their secondary for 124 yards on only sixteen carries. Maybe he wanted to let Detroit's future opponents know they'd have more to worry about than his throwing. He also connected on five of six extra-point tries, rounding out what the *New York Times* called "as splendid an individual performance as has been seen on a local gridiron in years."

What a difference a year makes! The skittish rookie whom the Green Bay Packers had battered in the 1927 season opener was now long gone—

not good news for Tim Mara's New York Giants, who were heading to Detroit to battle the Wolverines in their home opener.

Nearly all of the Giants' stars from the 1927 league championship team were back, and they had a lot of new help: quarterback Bruce Caldwell from Yale; tailback Tony Plansky from Georgetown, a muscleman with world-class trackman's speed; outstanding end Ray Flaherty, a future pro football Hall of Famer; and the versatile Al Bloodgood, the best player from the Cleveland Bulldogs that Benny lost in the transition to Detroit.

The Wolverines' pedigree was not so royal. Detroit boasted no former all-Americans other than Friedman. But they played with discipline and skill and teamwork, and they competed without a hint of quit in them. "They all came from the cow country, the oilfields, the wheat fields and so forth," Benny said later about his teammates, "and they all chewed Beechnut tobacco except one guy, he chewed snuff, he was a Swede. And they were wonderful . . . and I of course was something different, but we turned out to be really a team with a great deal of rapport and a great deal of team spirit."

· · ·

By the fall of 1928, Benny's revolutionary passing skills had opposing coaches scrambling to come up with defenses to deflate his aerial attack. Teams would usually stack the line of scrimmage with eight or even nine defenders to smother the running game, knowing they couldn't be hurt by the pass. Against Benny, however, that was a formula for disaster. To combat the brilliant passer, teams were forced to drop three or four backs into pass coverage and have some of their linemen drop back off the line and rove—an early incarnation of what is now known as the linebacker position. Years later, George Halas would describe Friedman's transformative effect on football bluntly and powerfully: "Benny revolutionized football. He brought defenses out of the dark ages."

On October 21, Tim Mara, sitting amongst the largest crowd ever to see a football game at Detroit Stadium, wondered whether his Giants' defense could solve Friedman. He didn't have to wait long for the answer. Benny trampled Mara's collection of stars right out of the chute. By the end of the first quarter, Detroit had amassed a 14–0 lead. The Giants' defense dug in after that, but their offense couldn't get them back in the game. The anticipated duel between Benny and Giants' rookie Bruce Caldwell, the Yale hero, turned out to be a promoter's fantasy. Caldwell was totally flummoxed by the rigors of playing against professional defenders. With the score still 14–0 at halftime, Benny rested through a scoreless third quarter.

Then he returned to put the Giants away. On Detroit's second play from scrimmage in the final quarter, from their forty-two-yard line, Benny called his own number on a straight off-tackle run. He faked a pass, darted through a hole in the Giants' line, and was off, dodging defenders and breaking tackles until it was a race to the goal line between Friedman and Jack McBride. Jack was an outstanding player, selected as the league's most valuable player in 1927, and the fleet Giant had tracked Friedman almost from the moment he'd taken the snap from center. But McBride couldn't catch him.

Friedman's spectacular fifty-eight-yard touchdown dash shredded whatever was left of the Giants' psyche. New York simply didn't know what to do about him. The image of the afternoon was one of a Detroit Wolverine standing in the Giants end zone with the football—four different times, each precipitated either by Friedman's passing or running.

But the Wolverines' 28–0 dissection of the defending league champs was no one-man affair. For Benny, playing with his pro mates wasn't quite like working with Molenda and Baer and Louie Gilbert and Bennie Oosterbaan, but there was a bonding in progress and, former all-Americans or not, these Wolverines could play. Carl Bacchus, in particular, was fast impressing Friedman, who was starting to mention the end nearly in the same breath with Oosterbaan.

Bennie Oosterbaan himself had come out to the Wolverines-Giants game to check out his old quarterback. It was an easy trip to Detroit for Bennie, coming from Ann Arbor. Upon graduation from Michigan in the spring of 1928, he had rejected a slew of offers to turn pro and instead became an assistant football coach for his alma mater. The NFL's loss was surely Michigan's gain. Oosterbaan was more than maybe the greatest ever all-around athlete at Michigan; he was also respected like few others and seemed a can't-miss prospect as a coach. As Friedman sat on the Detroit bench with Bennie during halftime of the Giants' game, talking about old times and, perhaps, of times to come, was he second-guessing his decision to turn pro? Did he envy Bennie's position at their beloved alma mater? Ultimately, Benny and Bennie would both become college head football coaches. But they would come to their coaching positions, very different positions, in very different ways.

Oosterbaan would get the job Benny wanted most. Benny would get the job that wanted him most.

· · ·

With the Wolverines preparing for a trip to Wrigley Field to face the Bears on October 28, Benny recalled his 1927 trip to Wrigley, when Chicago's handpicked referee had blithely stood by rambling about Fielding Yost while the Bears mugged him. Benny wasn't about to stand for a repeat performance. He insisted on a neutral referee for this game, and no-nonsense Tommy Huglit got the assignment.

Meanwhile, George Halas drilled his charges hard that week on pass defense. Halas's preparation paid dividends, as Detroit's passing attack was uneventful early in the game. But Benny could see that Halas had picked his poison, so in front of twenty thousand fans, he pounded the physical Bears on the ground. He banged out 164 yards on thirty-one carries and kept the ball away from the Bears' offense for most of the game. They weren't just end runs, either; there were plenty of line plunges between the tackles, where Friedman threw himself into the meat grinder operated by Trafton and Link Lyman and Wild Bill Fleckenstein. Most of the time, Benny got the best of these brutes with a major assist from his Detroit forwards who blocked superbly. Benny also received an assist from referee

Huglit, who early in the game made clear he would not tolerate target practice on Friedman by ejecting the first Bear that took a cheap shot at him. Friedman mixed in the occasional pass just to keep the Bears honest, and Halas's men never found their balance. Somehow, they managed to keep the Detroiters out of the end zone, but when Detroit's Pete Jackson smashed over the goal line in the fourth quarter, finishing off a drive that Benny engineered expertly, the Wolverines finally had their touchdown. Benny missed the extra point and the score stood at 6–0.

After the Bears received the ensuing kickoff, they drove nearly the length of the field, powered by the great Paddy Driscoll. But the drive stalled at the Detroit four-yard line, where the Wolverines took possession on downs with about seven minutes remaining. Detroit had the ball, but they also had trouble. Pinned deep in their own territory, trying to do too much with the ball was risky. The smartest play for the Wolverines was a punt that would hopefully push the Bears too far back down the field for them to score before time ran out.

Detroit lined up in punt formation on first down—but faked a kick and ran the ball. They did the same thing on second down. The two runs netted just five yards. Again, on third down, the Wolverines lined up to punt. This time, with only one down remaining to them and the ball perched in the shadow of their end zone, they surely would kick it away.

Friedman had something else in mind. "We fooled them by calling for a double pass from the fullback to myself, with the right end going straight down and the right half out flat to the right and the left over center," Benny wrote later. Benny took the pass back from Wiberg and delivered the ball downfield perfectly to right end Lyle Munn, who was uncovered by the startled Bears. The bold play was good for thirty yards—a prime example of Benny's willingness to throw on any down, from anywhere, at any time. It was just such a play that George Halas undoubtedly had in mind when he wrote in his autobiography years later: "Benny was specially dangerous because you never knew when he was going to pass." This unique unpredictability was born of Benny's quirky boyhood exercises, his years of diligent practice, natural talent, and, maybe most of all, a healthy ego. "He had the balls for it," Benny's friend Herman Maisin said years later in describing Benny's daring. "You could see it on him."

Benny's fourth-quarter aerial gamble against the Bears effectively clinched the game, as it enabled the Giants to run out the clock. But it was his stunning exhibition of power football throughout the contest—an exhibition that Halas and the Bears never saw coming—that brought victory to Detroit. "Benny as a forward passer and perfect field general is well known," the *Tribune's* Wilfred Smith wrote. "But yesterday it was Benny the line plunger and open field runner who won the plaudits of the crowd. In sixty minutes Friedman carried the ball 164 yards from the line of scrimmage . . . Twisting, shifting out of tacklers arms, dodging, he carried on. Buried under a mass of tacklers at the end of each sprint, yet he was unstoppable . . . [The Bears] could not cope with this new Friedman who outran them and drove over them."

Though this wouldn't be the last time the press would tout his rushing skills, years later, Benny seemed to feel his outstanding running talents hadn't received due credit, at least not when compared to how the modern-era press and fans fawned over backs who rushed for more than a hundred yards in a game.

"I did that lots of times," Benny remarked, "and hardly anyone ever noticed."

. . .

"Friedman remains today the best player in football, college or professional," Benny's friend Harry Salsinger wrote in one of his *Detroit News* columns. "His generalship, his forward passing, place-kicking, ball carrying, blocking and tackling set him apart from the remainder of the field. He is the one player in professional football worthy of an afternoon of your time whatever the admission price happens to be."

More than 40,000 people paid that price of admission to see Detroit's first three games in 1928. That total was a little less than half the size of many single-game crowds that witnessed Friedman's games during his college years. Still, it was a positive sign, and the numbers pointed to Benny as the primary drawing card. Detroit's game against the Bears drew 20,000, while one week earlier a visit to Wrigley Field by the rival Packers attracted 5,000 fewer fans. The week before that, the defending champion, star-studded Giants also drew 5,000 fewer fans.

Things on the field had also started much better for Benny than they had in his rookie season. The Bears, Packers, and Giants were all struggling, while Friedman's Cleveland transplants were soaring with three impressive wins.

The Frankford Yellow Jackets were next for the Wolverines, and they reprised their rude treatment of Friedman a year earlier and thumped Detroit, 25–7. The Wolverines' reward for their dull showing was a train ride to Providence for a game with the Steam Roller at the Cycledrome the following day.

The Cycledrome came by its name honestly. It wasn't really a football stadium; it was a cycle track, with bleachers surrounding the track, and a football field crammed inside it. There was room for about ten thousand spectators, though more could squeeze in, and, as the saying goes, there wasn't a bad seat in the house. The bleachers were so close to the field that fans in the first few rows occasionally found themselves shaking hands with players who were tackled out of bounds.

About 8,500 fans, the largest Providence crowd to that point in the season, showed up to watch their star, George "Wildcat" Wilson, battle Benny. During the West Coast tour, Wilson had acquired a pretty good idea about how to defend Benny, and his team had shut out the great passer in Los Angeles in their second meeting there. In the Cycledrome's cozy environs, the Wildcat did it again, leading Providence to a 7–0 win, with some help from a field full of muck. For the second time in less than twenty-four hours, Friedman was thoroughly ineffective. He was also thoroughly frustrated, pitching a temper tantrum on the game's deciding play, a late Providence touchdown pass on which Benny claimed the receiver had interfered with him.

Just forty-eight hours earlier, the Wolverines had been in first place with three straight wins to open the season, two of them coming against the vaunted Bears and Giants. But Benny couldn't handle two teams with a history of mediocrity. Detroit's lost weekend landed them in the middle of the league's pack, with the New York Giants up next for them.

For the Giants, the rematch with the Wolverines would be a chance at redemption following the embarrassment they'd suffered in Detroit a couple of weeks earlier. For Benny—and for the National Football League—it would be a life-changing event.

. . .

Tim Mara was a gregarious sort of guy, but he was also a bookmaker, and bookmakers don't like to lose. Thus far in 1928, Mara's Giants were losing, both on the field and in the pocketbook. His collection of all-stars seemed to be getting old or hurt, or both, all at once. Cal Hubbard was making noises about leaving for Green Bay. Jack McBride suddenly seemed to have lost a step. Bruce Caldwell, the rookie from Yale, was enduring a rude welcome to pro ball. And not nearly enough fans were showing up at the Polo Grounds on Sunday afternoons. A year or two earlier, Mara, then ambivalent about football, probably would have shrugged off these woes. But football, and his Giants, had grown on the good-natured Irishman. He'd developed an understanding of and a fondness for the game. He liked the idea of owning the league's entry from the nation's biggest city. He didn't like invading the surpluses of his other, profitable businesses to keep the team afloat.

Mara had gotten an eyeful of Benny when the quarterback demolished his Giants in Detroit back on October 21. He hadn't forgotten Benny's display that day. It was the kind of display that could start a forward-thinking mind like Mara's thinking—thinking about what a stunning Jewish quarterback could do for a team and the team owner's bank account in a city like New York, with its large Jewish population. Nor had Mara forgotten Friedman's 1927 visit to the Polo Grounds, when thousands of fans had waited outside the stadium after the game hoping for a glimpse of the sensational quarterback.

The nearly thirty thousand fans who clambered into the Polo Grounds for the Giants-Wolverines rematch on November 11 were another sign of Friedman's New York appeal. But it was the Giants' Hinky Haines, not Benny, who supplied the game's early excitement. Just a couple of minutes after the opening whistle, Haines received a Detroit punt and tore through the late autumn chill and the Wolverines on a seventy-yard touchdown jaunt. Just like that, Tim Mara's team had sent a message: there would be no repeat of the 28–0 fiasco in Detroit.

In the second quarter, the Giants hit another big play when a twenty-seven-year-old rookie back named Oscar Eckhardt rumbled fifty yards from scrimmage for a touchdown. "Ox" Eckhardt, a three-sport star at the University of Texas, would one day compile the highest batting average in Triple A minor league baseball history. The 1928 campaign as a pro football player would be his first and last, and he'd spend most of it firmly rooted to the bench. But this day against Detroit, he was playing, and his long touchdown burst had hurt the Wolverines badly.

When McBride scored another touchdown in the third quarter and added the extra point, the score was 19–7. It stayed that way into the fourth quarter. Benny had been playing well, but the Giants had so far prevented a Friedman explosion. They needed to hold the great quarterback for only one more quarter to defeat him for the first time in three tries.

Calmly, Friedman went to work, chipping away at a New York defense that had played nearly flawlessly most of the day. Mixing the run and the pass, Benny drove the Wolverines to the Giants' 36. Then Len Sedbrook turned the corner on an end run and scampered all the way to the end zone. Now it was 19–13—Benny missed the extra-point attempt—and time was distinctly on the Giants' side. The Detroit defense needed to hold and get the ball back quickly.

Hinky Haines, who'd stuck a dagger in the Wolverines' back with his punt return in the first quarter, then did Detroit a big favor. From deep in the Giants' end of the field, he tried to surprise Detroit with a pass downfield, looking for the completion that would have salted away the game for

New York. Tiny Feather intercepted the risky throw, and Benny had one more shot to pull out the game.

After several plays, Detroit worked the ball to the New York 30. It was fourth down. Mere seconds remained on the clock. The Giants, Tim Mara, and every one of the thirty thousand spellbound fans at the Polo Grounds knew that Benny Friedman was going to try to break the Giants' hearts with one of his patented passes.

Cal Hubbard and the rest of the Giants' line practically launched themselves into the Detroit backfield on the snap, desperate to get to Friedman before he could let loose. The incursion forced Benny way back behind the scrimmage line in a search for time to find a receiver and space to throw the ball. It didn't look like he was going to get either—the entire New York forward wall had crashed in on the quarterback and sealed him off. Or so it seemed. Benny spied just a sliver of an opening in the ring of defenders. At about the same instant, he also spied Carl Bacchus breaking free in the end zone, some thirty-five yards downfield. In the stands, Tim Mara watched Benny coolly step through the opening and out of the maelstrom, draw back the ball, and fire a missile that bisected Bacchus's midsection.

The last-second touchdown tied the score at 19. Then, shockingly, Friedman's normally reliable toe failed to convert the extra point that would have won the game.

The fans barely seemed to notice the missed kick; they were still in a tizzy following Benny's lightning bolt to Bacchus. "After it was all over, old time football men said they never saw anything like it," Rud Rennie wrote in the *Herald Tribune*. To Tim Mara, also, the missed kick was beside the point. Earlier in the season, he'd seen Friedman's passes wreck his defending champions as if they were a second-rate sandlot club. Now he'd just witnessed Benny complete a miraculous fourth-quarter comeback by making a play he was sure no other player could make.

Right then and there, Tim Mara knew that at some point, somehow, he was going to get Benny Friedman into a New York Giants uniform.

• • •

The field turned up heavy and slick for Detroit's November 18 tilt with the Yankees. Some of Benny's poorest showings, like the back-to-back losses to Frankford and Providence, had come on "off-tracks." This time Benny handled the muck pretty well. Right from the beginning he and Len Sedbrook established a nice rhythm, and their game of pitch and catch quickly resulted in a thirty-five-yard touchdown on a play set up by Benny as a fake punt, a play he would later describe as one of the strangest he ever took part in. "We were in punt formation . . . the ball was snapped back to me," Benny said, "and as I stood there, looking for a free receiver, two giant tackles charged in upon me. I could not find a receiver. I was cornered . . . Motioning as if to pass and using a follow through, I ducked slightly, hanging on to the ball at the same time. The two linemen lunged for me but grasped each other instead and crashed to the ground locked in each other's arms. As Fielding H. Yost . . . used to say: 'They had arrived at the crossroads a bit too late.' With the two tackles deadlocked and on the ground behind me . . . I completed the pass and we scored a touchdown."

After the touchdown, Benny kept the Yankees defenders guessing all day with a blend of running and passing. The New Yorkers didn't know whether to lay off the line or stack it. In the third quarter, the Yankees guessed wrong, flooding the line with defenders while Benny hit Sedbrook with another long gainer downfield. A few plays later, Tiny Feather bulled into the end zone for Detroit's second score. The final tally was Detroit 13, New York 0.

At least on paper, the New York Giants, the Green Bay Packers, and the Chicago Bears were supposed to dominate in 1928. But with only a few games left in the season, it was clear there had been a divergence between theory and fact. Sitting atop the league were Providence, Frankford, and Detroit, in that order, while the teams of Halas, Lambeau, and Mara were mired in the middle of the pack. Providence and Frankford had lost only one game each, a fact that made Detroit's losses to those teams—their only two losses—look a little better. The Wolverines had come through the bulk of the season in good shape, but they still had to navigate through three more games—against the Bears, the Dayton Triangles, and, one more time, the Grange-less Yankees.

Friedman's 164 rushing yards against the Bears a couple of weeks earlier had taught George Halas a lesson. This time the Bears didn't overdo their pass defense preparation, and their balanced approach was evident in the first half as they squelched Detroit's running and passing forays. Chicago ran to the locker room with a 7–0 lead, and they were convinced they had Benny beaten. Unfortunately for Halas, Benny passed, he kept banging at George Trafton and Link Lyman on the ground, and he scraped together two long drives that ended in two Detroit touchdowns and a 14–7 Wolverines victory. Friedman himself scored the two touchdowns on short runs, the second one coming in the game's final seconds. The Bears were fierce opponents, and Benny took the highly unusual step—twice—of calling his own number near the goal line.

The Dayton Triangles and their tough fullback, former Illinois star Earl Britton, visited the Wolverines in Detroit on Thanksgiving Day 1928. Four years earlier, Benny had watched Britton help clear Red Grange's path to four touchdowns in twelve minutes against Michigan. Britton didn't have Grange or any runner remotely resembling him to block for on the lowly Triangles. Like the Duluth Eskimos, Dayton was a football nomad, a team with no home stadium, perpetually assigned to the visitor's locker room. They trudged into the University of Detroit Stadium that day with a perfect record of futility—no wins and six losses, though they'd come close a few times, including narrow losses to the league's top two teams, Providence and Frankford.

This day, against Benny and a Detroit team looking to finish the season convincingly, Dayton didn't come close. Friedman electrified the home fans with an early barrage, hitting nine of eleven passes. He threw for two touchdowns, including a forty-yarder to Rex Thomas, and ran for another in a 33–0 rout.

Detroit was now 6–2–1 and looking good to finish the season in a week with a win over the Yankees. But 7–2–1 wasn't going to get them first place this year. While Benny was blitzing the Triangles, Providence was clinching the 1928 league championship with a 7–0 victory over the Pottsville Maroons at tiny Minersville Park in Pottsville, Pennsylvania. Benny and the Wolverines poured it on the Yankees just the same, beating them 34–6 on a snowy, frigid day in front of just 2,500 souls at Yankee Stadium who were either brave or crazy, or maybe a little of both.

No one could dispute that after two sensational years in the laboratory of pro football, Benny had been a very quick study. His eleven touchdown passes as a rookie in 1927 set the league record for touchdown passes in a season. In 1928 he'd nearly broken it, throwing ten more. He had thrown for more than three thousand yards over the '27 and '28 campaigns, leading his nearest pursuers by almost too many yards to count. His spectacular passing tended to obscure his brilliance as a runner, but by the end of the '28 season, after he had taken control of several games with his blend of power and deceptive speed, that had changed.

Remarkably, in 1928, Benny led the league in both passing *and* rushing touchdowns. Nobody had ever done that before. No player has done it since.

Benny's fellow pros knew they had a special player in their midst. The rare player who could pass, run, and kick, all with a high degree of skill, was considered a "triple threat." About Benny, one player gushed: "Friedman has six threats instead of three. He can pass, also receive, he can run through a broken field, he can carry the ball, he can kick, and how that baby can think." The great Paddy Driscoll, an all-American at Northwestern, one of the NFL's great backs, and a future pro football Hall of Famer, had come across everything and everyone at the highest level of college and professional football. Paddy declared, simply, that Benny was the greatest football player he'd ever seen.

All of this was high praise for a young man, just twenty-three years of age, who had played only two professional seasons. And to be sure, there were a number of things the sensational quarterback hadn't yet done. Like beating the Green Bay Packers, for one.

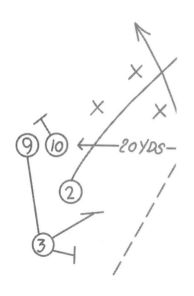

FOURTEEN

New York

The year 1928 was nothing short of a disaster for the New York Giants. The fearsome outfit of 1927 that compiled an 11–1–1 mark had plummeted to the league's midsection, posting a 4–7–2 record. The team's bottom line plummeted, also, to the tune of forty thousand dollars' worth of red ink.

Tim Mara hadn't seen this debacle coming, and he quickly resolved to prevent a repeat performance. He needed a new coach. He needed to overhaul the roster. And, more than anything else, Tim Mara needed to acquire Benny Friedman. But Mara discovered during the off-season that wanting Friedman and actually getting him weren't necessarily the same thing. Detroit's ownership knew Mara's desperation. All through the spring and into the summer of 1929, they made the bookmaker sweat, rejecting one trade proposal after another.

Four years earlier, Mara had been an eyelash too slow in getting after Red Grange, and George Halas had beaten him to the most spectacular drawing card the young league had seen. Mara was a rookie then, having just bought the Giants. He wasn't yet attuned to football and the vagaries of life in the fledgling NFL. But he'd learned since then. Grange had gotten away, but Mara was prepared to move heaven and earth to make sure Benny didn't. He continued to pound away at the Wolverines and, finally, found the solution to their intransigence. If he couldn't trade for Friedman—and, as the league's annual July meeting loomed, it appeared he couldn't—then he'd simply buy the entire Wolverines' team.

Finally, Detroit's ownership had an offer they couldn't refuse. The Wolverines had done better financially than most teams had in 1928, with each of the twenty investors nearly breaking even. But without an encouraging forecast of profitability on the horizon, they took Tim Mara's money—$3,500.

The acquisition of the Wolverines did more than bring Mara his cherished Jewish quarterback. Now the owner had another entire roster of players—good players—to mix and match with his Giants to form a powerful unit. Of the twenty-six players on the 1928 Giants roster, Mara kept only six: Tony Plansky, Hap Moran, Steve Owen, Ray Flaherty, Jack Hagerty, and Mickey Murtaugh. Joining these holdovers were Benny and seven of his Detroit teammates, including backfield bruiser Tiny Feather and outstanding receivers Len Sedbrook and Lyle Munn.

Teaming with this amalgam of Giants and erstwhile Wolverines were eight rookies, including Saul Mielziner, Benny's close friend and teammate at Glenville High, who'd just finished an outstanding college career at Carnegie Tech. Mielziner and his fellow rookies brought the number of Giants to twenty-two—a leaner and, Tim Mara hoped, meaner Giants squad for 1929.

Friedman was named captain of the squad immediately, as he had been for Michigan and the Bulldogs and Detroit. "He made us believers," "Stout" Steve Owen said later. "He was a natural leader who came to us with a great reputation, someone we were able to respect right away because he had already proven himself."

While gaining Friedman, however, Mara had also lost a player he wanted to lose about as much as the bookmaker liked to waive the vigorish on a bet. Cal Hubbard wasn't comfortable in New York's big-city atmosphere. He wanted to play in Green Bay. He had threatened to retire if Mara refused to trade him to the Packers, so Mara accommodated the giant lineman. Hubbard's move wasn't going to make Benny's future encounters with the Packers any easier.

The league itself underwent a makeover that was perhaps even more comprehensive than the Giants'. The Pottsville Maroons moved to Boston and became the Bulldogs. The Buffalo Bisons, inactive in 1928, returned for the '29 season. Ernie Nevers's old team, the Duluth Eskimos, was sold and reincarnated as the Orange Tornadoes. Nevers came back to the league with the Chicago Cardinals, who had been sold but remained in the Windy City. Staten Island joined the fray with a new team called the Stapletons, who boasted the services of a very promising rookie from New York University named Ken Strong. The daring gambit of C. C. Pyle and Red Grange, otherwise known as the New York Yankees, finally succumbed to massive financial losses and disappeared forever, with Grange landing back with the Chicago Bears and his new old friend, George Halas.

The city of Detroit had lost its Wolverines and, with them, its great Jewish athletic star. Most Detroiters probably didn't know that a new Jewish athletic star, a young man grooming himself in baseball's minor leagues, would launch his own phenomenal career in the Motor City just one year later. The young man's name was Hank Greenberg.

A mere two years had passed since Benny had graduated from the University of Michigan, but as the summer of '29 faded and another football season loomed, he was readying himself to play in his third city. The non-stop carousel that was the NFL was sweeping Benny along, and he was headed to its biggest stop.

Meanwhile, the country was engulfed in a tide of unprecedented mirth and revelry, a social and cultural revolution of sorts that history would come to identify as the Roaring Twenties. Following the horror of World War I, America was in a partying mood. For the better part of the decade, the party was fueled by a strong economy and Prohibition-dodging speakeasies and stills, dance clubs and jazz clubs and theaters, and a love of sport. New York City was the epicenter of the merriment, with all the necessary accoutrements: ballrooms; Broadway theaters; and jazz clubs, from the Cotton Club in Harlem to the white-owned establishments of Fifty-second Street, where the horns of Louis Armstrong and Charlie Parker and Coleman Hawkins blared and the ivories of Art Tatum and Duke Ellington tickled.

And there was the New York sports scene. Big boxing matches were commonplace in the Big Apple. The champion lightweight Benny Leonard, probably the greatest in a long line of great Jewish fighters of the day, was seemingly putting his title on the line in a New York ring every month. In the spring and summer, New York was a baseball town. Babe Ruth and Lou Gehrig and the New York Yankees—the *baseball* Yankees—packed Yankee Stadium. Across the Harlem River at the Polo Grounds, John McGraw, whose acumen as a manager of baseball's New York Giants was matched by his petulant manner, was winning National League pennants and World Series championships with monotonous regularity.

And as late summer turned to autumn, attention would shift to the dawn of another football season—another college football season. Local teams such as Columbia, New York University, and Fordham attracted huge crowds. Interest wasn't limited to the city schools; eastern football generally, especially Ivy League football, gobbled up massive space in the city's many sports sections. During the week of a leading Ivy League contest, detailed stories about the teams' star players and their game preparations would run daily. Meanwhile, the Giants would be lucky to claim a tucked-away quarter of a column the day before and after a game, both of which a reader could miss if he blinked.

It wasn't surprising, then, that the press barely noticed Tim Mara's announcement on July 18, 1929, that he had signed Benny Friedman to play for the Giants that fall. One New York writer did remark that the "acquisition of Friedman is a ten strike for Mara, both from the playing and box-office points of view."

That remained to be seen, but if it turned out to be true, Mara would be shelling out a grand to Benny for each strike. He'd agreed to pay his new star and hoped-for savior a league-high salary of $10,000.

• • •

Benny and the Giants marched into the Knights of Columbus Stadium in Orange, New Jersey, on September 29 for their season opener against the Orange Tornadoes. The teams promptly plunged into a hard-hitting, grind-it-out affair nearly devoid of passing. So much for the Giants' new quarterback making use of his fleet corps of receivers, at least in this game. The best thing about the ugly 0–0 tie for the Giants was that all their players emerged from the fracas reasonably healthy, ready to play the following week in Providence.

More than fourteen thousand fans crammed into the ten-thousand-seat Cycledrome on Sunday, October 6, to see Friedman and the Giants battle the defending league champion Steam Roller. It's not known how many of those fans were Jewish, but it's safe to assume that most Jewish fans in Providence, and everywhere else, for that matter, were praying in synagogue or resting at home in observance of the first day of Rosh Hashanah. Maybe Benny found a temple in Providence that morning before the game. Probably he didn't. And, most definitely, he was not resting that afternoon. He led the Giants to a bitterly contested 7–0 win over Providence, hitting Len Sedbrook with a ten-yard scoring pass.

On September 10, 1934, nearly five years after Benny led the Giants to victory in Providence on that Rosh Hashanah afternoon, the great baseball slugger Hank Greenberg would sit in the Detroit Tigers locker room, staring at his uniform, wondering if he should put it on. Normally, Greenberg would have already been on the field with his teammates who were taking batting practice, getting ready for a crucial late-season game against Boston in the midst of the pennant race. But this was not a "normal" day, at least not for Hank. It was Rosh Hashanah, and Greenberg sat on his stool, his desire to help his teammates in the hugely important game dueling with his sense of obligation as a Jew to refrain from working on the High Holidays. His teammates, naturally, pressed him to play.

"The newspapers had gone to the top rabbi in Detroit and asked him if it would be socially acceptable for me to play on that day," Greenberg would later write in his autobiography. "The rabbi was supposed to have looked in the Talmud and came up with the theory that since it was the start of a new year, and it was supposed to be a happy day, he found that Jews in history had played games on that day, and he felt it would be perfectly all right for me to play baseball. That momentous decision made it possible for me to stay in the lineup on Rosh Hashanah, and lo and behold I hit two home runs—the second in the ninth inning—and we beat Boston 2–1."

There is a misperception that has spread over time that Greenberg did not play on that Rosh Hashanah afternoon. In fact, it was ten days later, on Yom Kippur, the holiest day for Jews, that Greenberg sat out a game. But Greenberg's very public, and publicized, struggle of conscience on that Rosh Hashanah, followed by his withdrawal from the Tigers' lineup on Yom Kippur, created a legacy for him of religious consciousness that, at least among many Jews, outstrips his superlative Hall of Fame playing career.

Friedman's participation in the game against the Steam Roller on Rosh Hashanah in 1929 was not preceded by the kind of "will he play or won't he?" publicity that framed Greenberg's actions in 1934. Baseball was the national pastime, while pro football was still lost in the wilderness of American sporting culture. The moral and religious dilemma faced by of one of the greatest players in the nation's most popular game—occurring in the stretch drive of a pennant race, no less—was a far more attractive story than any reservations Friedman might have had about playing in a professional football game at a cycle track in Providence.

If Benny had sought an opinion from a rabbi or was plagued by indecision over whether to play against Providence that day, he kept it to himself. He disdained religious distinction among athletes. As Benny had said back in 1925, when his heroics for Michigan began captivating the sporting public on a grand scale, "We are not a people apart. Physically and in general mental attitudes, there is nothing that distinguishes the Jewish athlete from any other. In the locker room, everyone is stripped clean of all sham and pretense. You're either a man or you're not."

Greenberg was similarly scornful, at least during his playing days, of his identity as a Jewish ballplayer. Ultimately, however, Hank grew more comfortable with, even desirous of, the religious identity that accompanied his baseball exploits. "I find myself wanting to be remembered not only as a great ballplayer, but even more as a great *Jewish* ballplayer," Greenberg wrote in his autobiography.

Benny never seemed to reach that level of religious sensibility, at least not in the context of his football-based celebrity. "I don't know whether there would have been any difference if I was not a Jew," Benny said years after his playing days. "I might have gotten more being a Jew, more attention, but I think the deeds speak for themselves, whether you are or you aren't, you know? . . . If I run forty yards for a touchdown or if I throw four touchdown passes against the Bears, what the hell's the difference whether I'm a Jew or a non-Jew, you know?"

Had Friedman been a boxer (the great boxing champion Benny Leonard reportedly said that Friedman was the only footballer he ever saw who would make a good boxer), it's safe to assume that his trunks would not have been adorned with a Star of David, as was the case with many Jewish boxers of Benny's day (though the symbol was often worn as a ticket-selling gimmick to attract Jewish fans rather than as a genuine statement of religious pride). But Friedman was proud of his heritage and never sought to obscure it.

• • •

Ken Strong was a six-foot-one-inch, 205-pound stick of football dynamite. A runner of great power and speed, a skilled passer, and an outstanding punter and kicker, the aptly named Strong had such writers as Grantland Rice gushing with favorable comparisons of him to players like Ernie Nevers and Jim Thorpe. In 1928, Strong enjoyed a spectacular all-American season at New York University, a mere A-train subway ride from the Polo Grounds. With matinee idol looks and a Manhattan fan base established from his collegiate heroics, Strong was a natural fit for the New York Giants.

Except that as Strong loosened up in the Polo Grounds in warm autumn sunshine for the Giants' 1929 home opener on October 13 against the Staten Island Stapletons, he was wearing a Stapes, not a Giants, uniform. It seems that Giants coach Leroy Andrews, whom Tim Mara had dispatched to sign Strong upon his graduation from NYU, offered Strong only half the salary Mara had authorized. It's unclear whether Andrews was trying to protect Mara's pocketbook or enlarge his own by pocketing the difference. What is clear is that instead of the glitz and glamour of Manhattan—such as it was for professional football players in those days—Strong had opted for the relative obscurity of Staten Island.

And on that warm October afternoon, the NYU all-American lit into the Giants, letting Mara know what he'd missed out on. In the first half, Strong stormed into the Giants' end zone from six yards out and launched a seventy-yard missile of a punt that pinned down the Giants and helped the Stapes to a 9–6 halftime lead. But that, unfortunately for Strong, was as good as it was going to get for the Stapes. Giants backs Jack Hagerty and Hap Moran did some brilliant running and pass receiving in the second half, orchestrated by Benny.

"The passing of Friedman had the crowd tingling with excitement every moment of the time he was on the field," the *New York Herald-Tribune* blared. "It was his uncanny ability to dodge would-be tacklers and toss long-delayed passes which gave Hagerty a chance to get free for many long gains, and without Friedman the home team would have been badly outclassed—even with Hagerty and Moran working at their best." Benny sent thirty-thousand Giants fans home happy and sent Ken Strong back to Staten Island on the short end of a 19–9 score and with images of his first view of Friedman in action, images that would later elicit six words from Strong that captured Benny's transformative influence on football: "Benny really started the passing game."

Another crowd of thirty thousand flocked to the Polo Grounds a week later to watch the Giants take revenge against Frankford. In 1928 the Yellow Jackets had shut out the Giants—twice. Now, the new-look Giants and their new quarterback torched the team from suburban Philadelphia with touchdown passes of 43, 25, and 18 yards. Mule Wilson escaped on a fifty-five-yard touchdown run from scrimmage, and George Murtaugh topped off a 32–0 massacre with a thirty-three-yard scoring run.

Murtaugh was just one of the many fine players comprising Benny's talented supporting cast. But perhaps no Giants teammate was blessed with an ability equal to that of the whiz from Georgetown, Tony Plansky.

"He was the decathlon champion of the United States . . . He was always the fastest man on the field, a great ball-carrier and a tremendous pass receiver," Benny said of Plansky.

Plansky was also, it seemed, injury-prone. As a rookie in 1928, he broke his leg in the Giants' second game of the season, against Green Bay. Then in training camp before the 1929 season, he was injured again.

Friedman always prided himself on his durability, his ability to take severe punishment yet rarely miss a play. To Benny, this was no accident. It was the predictable result of his devotion to Fielding Yost's teachings about absorbing hits and falling in such a way to avoid injury. Friedman had mastered the technique, and he couldn't understand why others didn't follow suit. It wasn't that complicated: run low, keep the neck up, and fall in a compact ball with arms and legs drawn in. Benny spent some time with Plansky one afternoon in practice working on these fundamentals, and, after overcoming his training-camp injury, Plansky stayed healthy.

Tony hadn't figured prominently in the Giants' attack in the first three games, but coming off Friedman's three-touchdown pass exhibition against Frankford, Coach Andrews and Friedman felt they could surprise their next opponent, Providence, by running the ball with Plansky. So during practice that week at their uptown Manhattan ballpark, the Giants—amidst ominous stock market rumblings on Wall Street in downtown Manhattan—featured Plansky and Benny in extra running drills.

Sure enough, Providence wasn't ready for the Giants' sleight of hand. Tony had a big day, ripping off several long gainers and scoring two touchdowns. Friedman passed often enough to remind Providence's Wildcat Wilson, Jimmy Conzelman, and Jack McBride of the harm that awaited them should they focus too much on stopping the run.

The final was Giants 19, Steam Roller 0. It was New York's third shutout in its four games. The squad that Tim Mara had retooled after the collapse of 1928 was really starting to cruise.

· · ·

"A tidal wave of hysterical mob selling battered stock and convertible bond prices down to new lows yesterday under an unprecedented turnover of 16,410,030 shares on the New York Stock Exchange," the *New York Herald-Tribune* reported on Tuesday, October 28, 1929, with news of the first day of the two-day stock market crash. A small piece of the billions of dollars in losses had belonged to Tim Mara. Like many men of means, Mara had seen the bulk of his fortune evaporate on what would come to be known as Black Monday and Black Tuesday.

Throughout its brief existence, the National Football League had been struggling to attain a semblance of financial stability, even while the country at large had been enjoying unprecedented prosperity. The stock market crash signaled an impending financial crisis of long duration that would severely test the mettle of Tim Mara, George Halas, Curly Lambeau, and the other intrepid men who had cobbled together the league at the start of the decade.

For the present, however, it was business as usual, and for the Giants that meant getting ready for a date in Chicago with Halas and Red Grange and the Bears. Friedman's drawing power, which had lured ninety thousand fans to the three Giants' home games, followed him to the shores of Lake Michigan, where twenty-six thousand fans, the season's largest crowd at Wrigley Field, braved the late autumn chill. Benny gave the locals something to cheer about early in the game when he fumbled in the Giants' half of the field, leading to a Bears' touchdown a few minutes later with Red Grange doing the honors. The Bears happily took Benny's gift and a 7–6 halftime lead to the locker room.

They would have been better off staying there. Friedman figured out whatever the Bears had been doing on defense, and the Giants rang up twenty unanswered points in the third quarter. Three times Benny hit the Bears for runs of more than thirty yards, and one other of twenty-eight. In between he connected with Ray Flaherty on a thirty-five-yard touchdown throw. As usual, Halas and the frustrated Bears had no answer for Benny's two-pronged attack.

Wild Bill Fleckenstein may have been the most frustrated Bear of all. In the midst of the second-half pounding from the Giants, Fleck was a little less discreet than usual with his roughneck routine, slugging various Giants and being tossed from the game for his trouble. He didn't leave quietly, either, doubling back to take an exit swing at Ray Flaherty. Fleck's histrionics couldn't change the outcome of the game, which ended with the respectable score of 26–14—only because Benny and many other Giants regulars sat out most of the fourth quarter.

Flush with a 5–0–1 record, Benny and his Giants bussed from Wrigley Field to Union Station for a train ride to Buffalo, where they'd face the Bisons two days later on election day, November 5. As the Giants' train chugged past Benny's Cleveland hometown, along Lake Erie on its way into New York and up to Buffalo, Tim Mara's outfit was humming. Friedman had been everything Mara had hoped for, both on the field and at the box office. Benny's supporting cast—from ball handlers such as Hagerty, Plansky, and Sedbrook, to linemen such as Stout Steve Owen, Mickey Murtaugh, and Joe Westoupol—was made up of all-star caliber players. Their offense was piling up points and their defense had yielded just twenty-five points while pitching shutouts in four of their six outings. They were undefeated, with only that odd opening-game tie with Orange marring their record.

And all of that was good for *second* place in the league standings. Curly Lambeau had his finely-tuned Packers residing atop the league with a perfect 7–0 mark. The two teams had separated themselves from the pack and were eyeing each other from afar, awaiting their November 24 Polo Grounds showdown that likely would decide the league championship—if they could avoid a few potholes along the way.

It wasn't unusual for local papers to trumpet Benny's impending arrival, especially in the smaller cities the Giants rarely visited. A Buffalo daily ran this ad for the upcoming Giants-Bisons contest:

FOOTBALL
NEW YORK vs. BUFFALO
"GIANTS" "BISONS"
For the convenience of the thousands who will want
to see this extraordinary game, featuring the only appearance in

Buffalo of Bennie Friedman's Champion
NEW YORK GIANTS, tickets are on sale every day from
9 A.M. to 7 P.M. at the Bison Stadium. Regular prices.

The Buffalo franchise had been walking an existential tightrope since joining the NFL in 1924. In 1927, things had gotten so bad that they stopped playing in midseason. They remained inactive for the entire 1928 campaign. At the NFL's July meeting before the start of the '29 season, the league's impatient powers-that-be were a whisker away from throwing the Bisons out for good. They survived only on the strength of a threatened lawsuit and a payment to the league of what amounted to a security deposit of $2,500.

The Bisons survived, but they weren't very good. Loaded with rookies and aging veterans who were at best fair players in their youth, Buffalo's high-water mark up to that point in 1929—excluding their 16–0 victory the previous Saturday over a local non-league outfit called the Cazenovia Cazzies—was a 7–7 tie they scraped out against Providence. They'd lost their other four league games.

Fourteen first-quarter points by the Giants quickly eliminated any notions of an upset, and in racking up twenty-five more points in the second quarter, the Giants showed what a strong group of footballers at the top of their game could do to a less talented bunch. When the final whistle mercifully blew, the scoreboard read Giants 45, Bisons 6. "Despite the one-sided aspect of the score," wrote the *Buffalo Courier Express,* "the game was not lacking in interest to the spectators, as they were afforded enough thrills to last a lifetime. Just to watch the one and only Brilliant Benny propel passes through the air with uncanny accuracy was a treat in itself, while his educated toe added three extra points in as many attempts."

The Giants next avenged the season-opening tie with Orange by spanking the Tornadoes 22–0, with Friedman preserving the shutout with a touchdown-saving tackle on a return of a Giants' punt. Then, in removing their last obstacle before their summit meeting with the Packers, the Giants obliterated the Bears, 34–0. Benny barraged the Bears with four touchdown passes, and Hap Moran added one of his own. The Bears threatened to score only once, when a few stylish receptions by Red Grange early in the game brought the ball to the New York two-yard line. The threat vanished, however, when Red, playing with a badly injured shoulder, fumbled and the Giants recovered.

Red's pro career had not gone quite according to plan. The knee injury he suffered in 1927 had robbed him of his unique shiftiness. He was noticeably thicker now, no longer the lithe antelope ready to rip off a long gainer at a moment's notice. He was still good, still better than most. But the player who'd burned Michigan for four long touchdown runs in twelve minutes a little more than five years earlier was, sadly, a memory.

Friedman, on the other hand, was fast being acknowledged as the outstanding star in a brand of football that Benny considered far superior to the college game. "In the first place," Benny had said in Buffalo before he massacred the Bisons, "all a professional player has to think about is football, no studies to worry about and no examinations to meet. Then again, we practice twice as long as the average college team, a session in the morning and one in the afternoon. Three times a week we attend blackboard drill in the clubhouse."

It wasn't just the increased focus that made the pros better, according to Friedman. "When I played at the University of Michigan," he observed, "we hardly ever had more than three outstanding men on our eleven, while on the Giant team today we have at least two stars for each position, with no sacrifice to teamwork."

That seemed especially true about the Packers. At quarterback Green Bay had a two-headed monster: Red Dunn, a former all-American at Marquette University who, with Nevers, was probably the best passer in the league before Friedman arrived; and Verne Lewellen, a Green Bay–area district attorney in his spare time who was nearly Dunn's equal. They were the perfect quarterbacks for coach Curly Lambeau, who favored the pass almost as much as Friedman and the Giants. Dunn and Lewellen had outstanding receivers to throw to—Lavie Dilweg, another Marquette all-American (and, like Lewellen, a Green Bay–area lawyer) as dangerous in the defensive

backfield as he was as a receiver; Eddie Kotal; and Johnny "Blood" Mc-
Nally, who, when he wasn't too hung over or too worn out from an evening
with the ladies, was maybe the best pass receiver the young league had yet
seen. Johnny Blood could run with the ball, too, as could Lewellen and Bo
Molenda and big Cully Lidberg, a former University of Minnesota Gopher.
When the Packers offense stalled or they were simply playing for field position, Verne Lewellen was every bit the punter that Ken Strong was, maybe
even better; and, from time to time, the Pack also counted on McNally to
boom punts at an average of just under forty yards.

As stacked as the Packers were at the ball-handling positions, they may
have been even stronger on the line. Guard Jim Bowdoin was in the midst
of an all-pro season. A 240-pound mass named Francis "Jug" Earpe, who
had been in the league since its inception, and who was, like Bowdoin, enjoying an all-pro campaign, clogged up the middle.

And then there were Cal Hubbard and Mike Michalske. The towering,
massive Hubbard was a quarterback's nightmare, and not just because he was
bigger and stronger than everyone else on the field and could give a speed
merchant like Tony Plansky a run for his money in the hundred-yard dash.
What was really scary for quarterbacks and blockers was that on any given
play, they couldn't be sure where Cal would line up. Sometimes he'd play up
on the line, but just as often he'd back off the line and freelance—in essence,
Cal was playing a linebacker position, years before they called it that. He was
free either to greet any back who managed to breach the center of the line, or
to roam toward the sideline and chase down a ball carrier trying to go wide.
And when he reached the ball carrier, it wasn't for a social visit. Hubbard once
explained to a Packers rookie the fine art of using an opponent's helmet ear
holes to improve your grip in preparation for smashing the opponent's head
on your knee.

Mike Michalske wasn't as big as Hubbard, or as fast, but if you asked
Benny, there was no lineman as good—he was a taut 215-pound package
of speed, agility, aggression, and football smarts with a tendency to stick his
nose into just about every play.

The Packers looked formidable, but the Giants were playing at a very high level now. High-scoring games were unusual in the NFL, yet the Giants had erupted for eighty points in their last two contests and had barely broken a sweat doing it. Despite the Packers' untarnished record, there was some skepticism about their quality, at least in the East—just as eastern college football fans questioned the quality of football at midwestern schools.

At the same time, the Giants hadn't yet faced a unit of Green Bay's class. For these two talent-rich, undefeated squads, there would be no second chances—they weren't scheduled to play each other again and there were no playoffs at that time. The winner of this game was virtually assured of the 1929 league championship.

In the brief history of the league, there had never been a game as glamorous as the upcoming collision of these two titans.

• • •

Game day was also Benny Friedman Day—so designated by the Young Men's Philanthropic League, which was sponsoring the game. Twenty-five thousand football enthusiasts filed into the Polo Grounds and watched the Giants and Packers take the field under a steady gray drizzle. It was a respectable crowd, even if much smaller than the one that had witnessed Red Grange's historic New York appearance in 1925.

The Packers typically played a seven-man front on defense, but Curly Lambeau had prepared a little something special for Benny. He directed six of his linemen to all but disregard the run and storm after Friedman. He directed the seventh lineman—Cal Hubbard—to disregard the pass and focus solely on snuffing out any Giants running plays. Leaving run defense up to just one lineman was risky, but Lambeau figured the strategy would take away Benny's passing game, and besides, the one lineman left to handle the run was Cal Hubbard.

The Giants realized right away that they weren't playing the Buffalo Bisons anymore. Lambeau's defensive scheme had the Packers swarming all over Benny. Verne Lewellen's penetrating punts repeatedly presented Friedman with a long field to negotiate. The Giants were holding their own on defense, but as the first quarter progressed, the Packers were gradually winning the field position battle. After some hard running by Blood advanced the ball to the shadow of the Giants end zone, Lewellen pitched a short scoring pass to fullback Hurdis McCrary. Bo Molenda added the extra point, and the Midwest invaders had a 7–0 advantage.

The Packers' touchdown seemed to awaken the Giants. On their next possession, Benny finally found some time to throw downfield and hooked up with Ray Flaherty for a sixty-five-yard pass and run. Finally the Giants had infiltrated Packer territory. The excited home crowd started to find its voice as the Giants lined up a few yards from the Packers' goal line.

And then Cal Hubbard, in his grand return to New York, stepped in front of a New York receiver at the Packer one-yard line and intercepted a Friedman pass, crushing the scoring threat. A few plays later, Lewellen punted the Packers out of trouble, and the first quarter came to an end. The Giants' giddiness prompted by Flaherty's big play a few minutes earlier had changed to frustration as the New Yorkers realized they might not get another chance against this strong Packers outfit. At the half it was Green Bay 7, Giants 0, and, except for his big play with Flaherty, Benny was having trouble igniting his passing game.

In a sense, the Giants were in a pretty good spot when they came out for the second half. The Maramen had blown a huge scoring chance, had been beaten up physically, and had played nearly the entire first half in their own end of the field, but they were only a touchdown and extra point behind. Early in the third quarter, Friedman suddenly began to drive the Giants down the field. He connected on passes to Flaherty and Plansky. He himself took to the ground, bursting through the Packers' line and chewing up chunks of yardage that delivered the ball to the Green Bay 15.

The Packers and Lambeau's special defense were, finally, reeling.

Benny couldn't afford another mistake so close to the Packers' goal line. He sent Plansky on a diagonal route toward the end zone. The quarterback stepped toward Tony and a classic Friedman feather pass rolled off his fingertips toward the end zone's back corner. Plansky was behind the Green Bay defender now, staring down the ball through the raindrops as it arced over the Packer safety. The Polo Grounds erupted as Plansky, his back turned to the ball, reached up over his shoulder and, never breaking stride, plucked it out of the dusky sky.

The play was a gorgeous end to a gorgeous drive that seemingly had come out of nowhere. The Packers had been whacking the Giants around pretty well, and Benny showed his grit in leading his team back from the brink. Unfortunately for New York, Friedman missed the extra-point attempt, leaving the Giants trailing by a point in a game where points had been very hard to come by.

Early in the fourth quarter, on a third-and-nine from the Green Bay thirty-one-yard line, Lewellen dropped back to punt the Packers out of trouble yet again. Except this time he didn't punt. He allowed the New York linemen to come crashing in and then lofted a pass over them to Johnny Blood, who had slipped into the open. Blood snared the pass and started running, and by the time the Giants brought him to the ground, he'd gained twenty-six yards to the New York 43.

The fake punt energized the Packers. Behind Hubbard and Michalske and Jim Bowdoin and Jug Earpe, Molenda and Johnny Blood McNally pounded away at the Giants and didn't stop pounding until Molenda bulled into the end zone. Bo added the extra point.

It was now 14–6, and a difficult situation for the Giants had become a desperate one. Following the Packers' kickoff, Benny threw his second interception of the day, this one snared by Earpe. Then Johnny Blood crammed the ball down the Giants' throats on plunge after plunge. On the last one, the Packer back found himself in the Giants end zone for Green Bay's third touchdown. It hardly mattered when Molenda missed the extra-point try: 20–6 was plenty good enough.

"Wisconsinites Drub New York Eleven At Own Game" was a *New York Daily News* tag line the following day. Playing the entire game with just twelve men—only Jim Bowdoin was substituted due to injury near the end of the game—the Packers had put on a clinic for an opponent that, going in, looked at least as strong as they. What's more, they did it without the injured Red Dunn and Ed Kotal. The Packers never missed either player—Lewellen outpassed and outplayed Friedman, and Molenda and Johnny Blood ran the football with authority. Friedman's two-year wait for another shot at the team that had tormented him in his first pro game had ended miserably.

And barring some unexpected results in the season's last few games, it looked like the team Tim Mara had crafted to win a championship was going to have to settle for second place.

. . .

Three days later, on a Thanksgiving Day intra-city affair between the Bears and the Cardinals, the great Ernie Nevers set the record for points scored by a player in a game. Ernie scored six touchdowns and kicked four extra points to account for every one of the Cardinals' forty points in their 40–6 rout of George Halas's men. Nearly eighty years later, no player has yet to match the great Nevers's feat.

On that Thanksgiving Day, while the Giants were handling Ken Strong's Stapletons in Staten Island, Green Bay was all out to manage a scoreless tie with the Yellow Jackets. Only a Green Bay goal-line stand in the first quarter spared them their first loss of the season. The tie did wreck the Packers' perfect record, but it didn't really help the Giants. They needed Green Bay to lose a game.

As things developed, the scare against Frankford was the closest the Packers would come to losing. They shut out Providence and the Bears in their last two games of the season on December 1 and December 8 by identical 25–0 scores. In that same week, Benny and the Giants beat Ernie Nevers again and blanked Frankford twice to boost their record to 12–1–1. But by the time the Giants reached Chicago for their finale on December 15, even a thirteenth victory wouldn't be enough to catch Green Bay. With the Packers' win over the Bears on December 8, they finished the season unbeaten, clinching the league's top winning percentage and, with it, the championship.

The Giants beat the Bears anyway, winning 14–9 in a hard-hitting contest on a snow-covered field. As the teams headed toward their locker rooms, the thought of a long off-season with no opposing players to slug was apparently too much for Wild Bill Fleckenstein to bear. Fleckenstein sidled up to Giants guard Cliff Ashburn, who was strolling off the field, and smashed Ashburn in the face. Then, like a bomber bolting from his handiwork after lighting a short fuse, Fleck sprinted toward the dugout leading to the Bears' locker room. Every Giant on the field except the dazed Ashburn tore after him. Fleckenstein reached the dugout and scooted down the steps. The Giants were about to head in after the Chicago bully when a group of Chicago police officers cordoned off the dugout.

• • •

When it is considered that Tom Brady threw 50 touchdown passes in 2007 and that Peyton Manning had 48 scoring tosses just two years earlier, Benny's 1929 league-leading total of 20 seems puny—until you consider that Ernie Nevers, who finished second to Friedman in touchdown passes, had 6. It is no exaggeration to say that Benny's 20 touchdown passes in 1929 were every bit as astounding and groundbreaking an achievement as was Babe Ruth's 60 home runs hit two years earlier.

Benny's passing genius didn't come at the expense of the rest of his game. He rushed for more than 400 yards, averaging more than 5 yards a carry; he intercepted 4 passes while anchoring the Giants' secondary on defense; and he led the league with 20 extra points while hitting 65 percent of his tries, the highest percentage among players with a meaningful number of attempts. For the third straight season, Friedman was named as the quarterback on every all-pro team, including that of the *Chicago Tribune*, which wrote of him: "Benny Friedman is the quarterback and captain. There can be no other choice."

Friedman's transfer of his skills from the college gridiron to the pro game, when measured against how his fellow all-Americans had fared, was a phenomenon. As one writer observed at the time:

Usually the campus hero—the lad who set the world agog with his deeds for dear old alma mater—turns out to be just another football player once he finds himself in the unromantic atmosphere of the professional game.

Red Grange, most publicized of all college stars, is one of the outstanding examples. Red after a poor start has developed into a good pro player but has never played for money as he did at Illinois. He is regarded as a good journeyman halfback, but at Illinois he was a superman.

Ernie Nevers was so good as a Stanford fullback that Coach Glenn Warner hailed him as the greatest of all time. As a professional Ernie has done nothing out of the ordinary.

Bruce Caldwell, Yale star, was an absolute flop while Ken Strong of N.Y.U., Wildcat Wilson of Washington and others who ran wild in college became just average ground gainers in the money game.

Benny Friedman, former Michigan star and now captain of the New York Giants, is one of the few exceptions to the rule. The forward passing star who was good enough to win All-America honors two years in a row is even greater as a pro. With Detroit in 1928 and the Giants this year Friedman has played more sensationally than he ever did in college.

The writer may have shortchanged those other stars, particularly Nevers and Grange, who had been hampered by injury and certainly was no "journeyman." But Friedman was the NFL's big sensation.

What he wasn't yet was a champion, at least not a league champion. The failure against the Packers was a bitter disappointment for Benny, and for Tim Mara, but for a welcome change, the season-ending ink at the bottom line of the Giants' books was black, not red. The 1928 Giants had lost $54,000. Those steady 1929 crowds of 25,000 to 30,000 that had come to watch Friedman had produced a profit of $8,500. The New York Giants were now an enterprise capable of sustaining itself, no longer dependent on an infusion of dollars from Tim Mara's other assets. And with Mara still on his knees in the wake of the stock market crash and with the country's financial crisis deepening, he didn't really have many other assets.

It is no stretch to say that in 1929, the sensation that was Benny Friedman very likely saved the New York Giants from extinction.

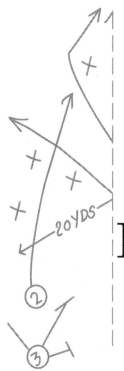

"That Redoubtable Descendant of Palestine"

New York City was a good fit for Benny and not merely because its large Jewish population helped make him a major star. Benny liked the excitement and culture of the big city, particularly its musical offerings. He was something of a musician himself, a talented percussionist who had played with symphonic orchestras in Detroit and Cleveland. Benny took in some of the best live classical music to be heard anywhere in the world at the Metropolitan Opera House and Carnegie Hall, both just blocks from the Central Park West apartment he shared with his old Glenville Tarblooders and current Giants teammate, Saul Mielziner.

Of course, Manhattan had no shortage of fine restaurants and speakeasies to accommodate the athletes, actors, musicians, and politicians who were so much a part of the city's lively pulse. Benny, dressed in a dinner coat and dining on steak at Gallagher's or some other hot spot, was right at home in that scene.

Feeling less at home in New York was Benny's mother, who still followed orthodox kosher dietary laws. Benny had long ago abandoned those laws, and on at least one occasion when his mother visited him, he was determined that she abandon them too. Benny took her to a speakeasy famous for its juicy double lamb chops, and he ordered them for her, with all the trimmings. When the waiter delivered the meal to their table—lamb chops dripping with blood instead of dried-out, oversalted kosher meat, accompanied by a potato with butter, which a kashrut observer is prohibited from mixing with meat, she recoiled. "Now, Mother, nothing vile is going to happen," Benny said. "You go ahead. I've been eating like this." And the former Mayme Atlavonik, from the old country in Russia, picked up her knife and fork and enjoyed the juicy double lamb chops and the potato smeared in butter.

. . .

Today's NFL stars spend their off-seasons spending a chunk of their hefty football salaries. The stars of Benny's day spent their off-seasons working. In January 1930, Friedman took a job as a customer's man with Wall Street brokerage house Sutro & Company. A couple of months later, Yale head football coach Mal Stevens, looking to improve an already solid team that had been 5–2–1 in 1929, asked Benny to come to New Haven for a few days of spring practice to help Yale's backs with their forward passing. Apparently Stevens was not bothered by Benny's Jewishness, despite the fact that Yale was perhaps the leading practitioner among colleges and universities of quotas limiting Jewish student enrollment.

Stevens had tapped into Benny's inner coach. When Benny had played in Detroit in 1928, it wasn't unusual to see him at Ferry Field in Ann Arbor working with Michigan's backs in practice. He enjoyed teaching younger players, and though he was in the midst of his playing prime, he knew that wouldn't last forever. He had a coaching position in a major program in his sights. Helping out Mal Stevens at Yale certainly wasn't going to hurt his long-term coaching prospects.

Friedman's main pupil at Yale that spring was a halfback named Albie Booth. Football players of Booth's era were nowhere near the size of modern-day players, but even for his time, Booth, at five foot six and a mere 145 pounds, was tiny. He looked like a better fit as part of a marching band than on a football field—except to annoyed tacklers who often grabbed for the elusive Booth and came up with nothing but air. The Army's would-be tacklers experienced that futility in their 1929 contest with Yale when Booth danced and darted through the entire Cadet team on a seventy-yard punt return for a score that won the game and elevated the diminutive sophomore to instant-legend status around New Haven. Now Mal Stevens wanted the instant legend to learn how to pass.

• • •

"The greatest football brain that ever called signals. Master of strategy, forward-pass wizard, Friedman also ranked with the top flight of ball carriers and safety men."

These words were spoken in September 1930 by "Big Bill" Edwards, a former Princeton all-American and a highly regarded football expert, when he named Friedman as his quarterback on his widely published, all-time all-American team. The honor was special considering a few pretty decent backs who didn't make Edwards's cut: the University of Chicago's great quarterback Walter Eckersall; George Gipp of Notre Dame, whom Rockne considered his best player ever; Ernie Nevers; and Jim Thorpe.

There was another all-American who didn't make that team, a man from Minnesota's north woods who had just finished his college career at the University of Minnesota. For three seasons as a fullback and a lineman, this man had run roughshod over the best the Big Ten had to offer. His name was Bronko Nagurski, and in the fall of 1930, he'd be playing for George Halas and the Bears, who were desperate to rebound from a very poor performance in '29.

Meanwhile, the Giants were determined to make up that one game that separated them from the '29 championship. They were going to have to do it without valuable end Ray Flaherty, who decided to take the year off to coach at Gonzaga, his alma mater. To make up for Flaherty, Tim Mara brought in Ossie Wiberg, Benny's reliable pass catcher from the

Cleveland Bulldogs. Mara also signed rookies Red Badgro, a star end at Southern California, and a Kansan named Dale Burnett.

Another change of note for the Giants was in their ownership. The stock market crash and ensuing Great Depression was threatening to ruin Tim Mara financially. Mara was determined that whatever losses he might suffer, the Giants would not be one of them. So he transferred ownership of the team to his sons, Jack and Wellington, and thus shielded the Giants from potential creditors. Tim, however, remained the de facto owner and operator of the team; Jack was twenty-six and Wellington still just a boy at fourteen.

The league's roster of teams changed as the Depression put marginal franchises Dayton and Boston, both of which had barely played half a schedule in 1929, out of their misery. The Bisons finally succumbed as well. The league gained two new squads: the Brooklyn Dodgers, who, like their baseball namesake, would play home games at Ebbets Field; and the Portsmouth Spartans, whose management wasted no time trumpeting Benny's upcoming appearance in Portsmouth, Ohio, that season. The league's one other change had to do with venue, as the Orange Tornadoes moved a couple of miles to Newark.

That's where the Giants found themselves for their 1930 season opener, an engagement that went considerably better for the Maramen than their scoreless tie in the '29 opener. This time the Giants swamped the Tornadoes, 32–0. They disposed of Providence the following week in more or less the same manner, winning 27–7 at the Cycledrome.

Green Bay was next. And once again, Curly Lambeau's boys flummoxed the Giants. This time, Johnny Blood got loose in the fourth quarter for a seventy-yard touchdown reception that propelled the Packers to a 14–7 victory. The Giants were getting a bit closer, but they still couldn't solve Green Bay. "We had no problem with anyone else, but the Packers were special," Benny said later. "They were so big, and yet they were so fast, that they almost won their games before they took the field."

The Giants left the field in Green Bay with some consolation: they would get another shot at Green Bay in New York on November 23.

Benny's cameo springtime role at Yale had gone well enough for Mal Stevens to ask him to continue with the Elis during the football season. "I was living in Brooklyn that year," Benny said later. "I'd get up at dawn, rush to the Polo Grounds for practice with the Giants, catch the noon train to New Haven, coach at Yale in the afternoon and get home late at night." It was a hectic schedule, but Benny enjoyed the coaching. George Joel wrote in the *Jewish Advocate:* "I don't know how many, if any, Jewish players will be on the Yale team this year, but I do know that if the Yale forward pass attack works successfully, a lot of the credit will be due to Benny Friedman, former Michigan star quarterback."

Benny also enjoyed the supplemental income, somewhere in the neighborhood of $5,000. With the league-high salary of $10,000 the Giants were paying him, Benny was in far better shape than most people wrestling with the financial crisis gripping the country. But he'd been supporting his family back in Cleveland ever since turning pro, and with his father's health deteriorating as rapidly as the economy, the extra money certainly didn't hurt.

Back in Michigan, another Jewish quarterback was generating quite a buzz, even in the East. The *New York Evening Post* wrote: "Take it from any angle, the talk of the Western Conference, familiarly known as the Big Ten, just now centers on a little Jewish lad who almost single handed is 'pitching' a mediocre team into a championship, or at least, a tie for the title."

The sophomore quarterback reminded many Michigan rooters of Benny. He could throw long or short, soft or hard, depending on what a given throw required—"exceptionally accurate and able to throw farther than any other passer in the Big Ten," according to Bob Zuppke. The boy had a strong all-around game, and he commanded the field with an assurance that hadn't been seen in Ann Arbor since Benny's time there. This brilliant young quarterback bore no facial resemblance to Friedman, but their builds were nearly identical. And the boy's throwing motion—the lining up of the feet to the target, the cocking of the wrist, the exaggerated follow-through—was eerily similar to Benny's.

This last similarity was no coincidence. The name of the "little Jewish lad" was Harry Newman, the boy Benny had tutored a couple of summers back. Harry's game was no longer limited to running the ball. He had learned his passing lessons from Friedman well, and now he was thrilling Wolverines rooters by presenting Michigan with a very reasonable Friedman facsimile.

After their loss to the Packers, the Giants resumed their practice of beating everyone else, beginning with a workmanlike 12–0 shutout of the Bears in Chicago and continuing with four straight triumphs in the friendly confines of the Polo Grounds. In two of those, a 53–0 shellacking of Frankford and a 25–0 beating of Providence, Benny threw a total of seven touchdown passes. His level of play remained as high as it had been in 1929. There was still no quarterback in the league who came close.

On November 2, three days before the Giants would head to Portsmouth for a night game against the league's new entry, Ken Strong and the Stapes were smothering Friedman and everything else the Giants tried. With about thirty seconds remaining in the bitterly fought contest, and Staten Island clinging to a 7–6 advantage, the Giants had the ball at the Stapes' 32. Benny knew that, on this day, the possibility of scoring a touchdown from that point with so little time left was remote. A field goal was the only realistic option.

Or was it? Benny hadn't yet kicked a field goal in the NFL. In fact, he'd barely even tried. Field goals were infrequent in the NFL, mainly because the goalposts weren't on the goal line as they were in college ball but were ten yards further back, at the back of the end zone. In 1929 the Giants had only two field goals, both by the ambidextrous Tony Plansky. And now, from forty-two yards out and with the game hanging in the balance, Friedman calmly stepped back, swung his leg, and broke Ken Strong's heart. Giants 9, Staten Island 7.

Next up for the Giants was the rare night game against the Spartans in Portsmouth's Universal Stadium. Friedman's impending arrival galvanized the local press all during the week preceding the game. "Friedman is

Coming" and "Benny Friedman Performs Tonight" were some of the headlines that gave the breathless fans in this hardscrabble Ohio area something
to distract them, if only for a few days, from the Depression's oppressive grip.

"Tonight is home coming night and the largest crowd of the season is
predicted," the *Portsmouth Daily Times* wrote on the day of the game.
"Benny Friedman is considered one of the best drawing cards on the grid
today. His reputation for throwing the pigskin has traveled far and wide
and people travel many miles to see him in action."

Benny didn't disappoint. Before the game even started, he captured the
fans with a long-passing exhibition in warm-ups. Then he guided the Giants
to a 19–6 win over a game Spartans club. Portsmouth's noble effort inspired one writer to biblical heights: "David with his little slingshot, battling Goliath in the old Hebrew days, didn't work any more diligently to
conquer the huge gladiator of the Philistines than did the Spartans in trying to lay low that redoubtable descendant of Palestine, Benny Friedman,
not so much a giant in physique as in football ability, mentality and
agility."

• • •

In the dwindling days of 1930, unemployment figures in New York City
were staggering: roughly 25 percent of the city's workforce was out of
work. Central Park became a shantytown as thousands who lost their
homes crammed into decrepit shacks surrounded by grand high-rise apartment buildings outside the park's perimeter that reminded one of better
times. Infamous "Hoovervilles" swallowed up the riverfront along the
Hudson. Thousands of jobless men spent their days waiting in breadlines
hoping to get food they no longer could afford to buy.

The football world was doing its part to help ease the misery by providing both the diversion of sport and, more tangibly, by staging exhibition
games to raise money for the unemployed.

New York's flamboyant mayor Jimmy Walker had his city's unemployed on his mind when he rode down to Philadelphia on November 8 to

watch his good friend Knute Rockne and his University of Notre Dame football team play the University of Pennsylvania. Notre Dame was undefeated, steaming toward a second consecutive national title under its legendary coach.

Penn was a strong unit, but the contest in Franklin Field that day wasn't a fair fight. The Irish trampled the Quakers, 60–20, and it wouldn't have been that close had Rockne not pulled his regulars near the end of the first half.

Walker was happy for his good friend, but that day the game was secondary to the mayor. He'd gone to Philadelphia to pitch to Rockne an exhibition game to be played in New York between a team of Notre Dame All-Stars and Benny Friedman's New York Giants, with proceeds of the game to be donated to the New York City Unemployment Relief Fund. Tim Mara had suggested the game to Walker a week or so earlier.

The idea was a natural for the public relations–minded Walker. Rockne was the most famous football coach in the world, maybe the most famous sports figure, period. His teams were hugely popular with New York's many Notre Dame alumni and always drew huge crowds when they played there. And the Irish's magnetism was even stronger than usual as the 1930 season drew to a close with a second straight national title on the horizon. No team had ever won consecutive national championships.

Maybe most compelling was the prospect of seeing how the pros would fare against the college players. Here was a chance for the pros to remove the yoke of inferiority that continued to choke them. And here was a chance for Benny to put Frank Carideo, Notre Dame's all-American quarterback and national media darling, in his place.

But Rockne reacted coolly to Walker's proposal. The coach was busy preparing his current team to complete the toughest schedule in the country. He wouldn't have time to assemble and drill a team of all-star players who might not even be in condition to play. And Rockne was sick, burdened with painful, at times incapacitating phlebitis. As it was, he had been ignoring doctors' warnings that the condition could kill him if he didn't stop coaching.

Besides, Knute Rockne didn't have much use for pro football. To Rockne, pro ball was an inferior brand of football played by generally inferior players. The pros' plays were too predictable. They didn't practice enough. They were spiritless mercenaries playing the glorious game of football for the wrong reasons. Like many coaches, Rockne discouraged his Notre Dame boys from playing professionally, and few of his players bucked his advice.

Still, there were a few things about the pro game that escaped Rockne's contempt. Benny was one of them.

Rockne had recently seen Benny and the Giants play the Bears at Wrigley Field. The Rock hadn't seen Benny play before; Notre Dame and Michigan, today one of college football's most compelling rivalries, did not schedule each other then. But Rockne had heard and read of Friedman's trailblazing play at Michigan and as a pro. He figured it was finally time to see what the fuss was about.

The coach watched in amazement as Benny single-handedly conquered the Bears. He'd never seen such all-around brilliance. Not from Carideo. Not from Harry Stuhldreher, the quarterback of his famed 1924 "Four Horsemen" backfield. Not even from his beloved George Gipp. "It was an afternoon of thrills at the miraculous dexterity of his passing," Rockne wrote of Benny's performance. "Four yards, 10 yards, 40 yards—harassed and pounded—he threw the ball from all angles, standing or running at terrific speed, hitting his target right on the button—never a miss."

Rockne's memory of Benny turning Wrigley Field into his own personal playground against the Bears was fresh as Jimmy Walker pitched the idea of the exhibition game. Rockne wasn't anxious for Notre Dame specifically and college football generally to receive that kind of a beating from a pro team.

Logically, everything was telling Rockne that Walker's exhibition game was out of the question. Except that with Knute Rockne, nothing was out of the question when a friend needed a favor. And Rockne and Jimmy Walker were more than friends. They were kindred spirits. They loved the spotlight of New York City. They loved the city's restaurants and theaters and social scene and often enjoyed them together. The game would be a huge boost for the city's unemployed and for the mayor. Rockne was wavering as Walter pitched the game as a chance for Rockne to demonstrate college football's superiority over the pro game.

That clinched it. The coach famous for tackling the toughest schedules in college football year after year had never ducked a challenge, and he wasn't about to start ducking now. The Fighting Irish All-Stars would come to New York and play the Giants at the Polo Grounds on December 14.

But the game's greatest quarterback and its greatest coach had some unfinished business to attend to in their separate football worlds before they would finally cross paths.

Things weren't so easy for the Irish following their rout of Penn. Drake, Northwestern, and the Army, the Irish's next three opponents, were talented teams that desperately wanted to deny Notre Dame a second straight national championship. But they failed to derail the Irish, though defeat for Rockne's boys grew nearer with each successive game. In the Army game, 110,000 near-berserk fans who braved a freezing, rain-swept day at Chicago's Soldier Field saw the Cadets score a fourth-quarter touchdown to pull within an extra point of upending Rockne's dream season. With his phlebitis-wracked legs screaming, Rockne watched an avalanche of Notre Dame players smother the Army's tying extra-point attempt to preserve a 7–6 victory.

While Rockne was guiding his team down the stretch, he had Adam Walsh, his 1924 all-American center, assemble the All-Stars in South Bend to prepare for the Giants. Walsh also happened to be the current Yale line coach, and, with Benny up in New Haven coaching the Yale backs, the great Rockne disciple needed to be careful about leaking any inside information on the All-Stars.

Walsh didn't have much trouble reeling in the players. When Knute Rockne put out the call, stars from most of the Rock's teams from the 1920s flocked to South Bend. The largest group was from the undefeated national champions of 1929, still only one year removed from the battle and itching to resume it.

Still undefeated and untied after the game-ending heroics against the Army, the Irish's last and biggest challenge awaited them. Far from the freezing rain and muck of Soldier Field, the Southern California Trojans were preparing a special greeting for the Irish amidst the palm trees and sunshine of Los Angeles.

The Irish might have felt less than confident on their cross-country train ride. The nation's toughest schedule had worn on them. Southern Cal was an offensive powerhouse, healthy, and would have ninety thousand of their best friends rooting them on. Defeat in Los Angeles would bring no shame for Notre Dame.

But for Rockne, defeat was a phantom that appeared so rarely it was unrecognizable. Carideo, Bucky O'Connor, and Marchmont Schwartz propelled the Irish to a 27–0 disassembling of the Trojans. The contest might have been mistaken for a spanking administered by a varsity unit to a freshman squad in a spring scrimmage if not for the vibrant game uniforms and packed stadium.

Rockne had done it. Unprecedented consecutive national championships were his. Headlines throughout the country hailed the 1930 Irish team as the greatest team of all time.

While Rockne was driving Notre Dame toward a championship, Benny was trying to do the same thing for the Giants. Four days after Benny's celebrity turn in Portsmouth, the Giants squeezed by Ernie Nevers and the Cardinals in Chicago, 13–7. But a week later, in New York, with the help of an icy drizzle that transformed the field into a mud bath, George Halas and Red Grange at long last beat the Giants. The rain and muck grounded Benny's aerial game and perfectly suited Bronko Nagurski's powerful running. The rookie sensation from Minnesota brutalized Giant tacklers all day long and scored the Bears' two touchdowns in their 12–0 victory.

Now the Giants would have to meet Green Bay on November 23 with the bitter taste of their first league loss to a team other than the Packers in nearly two seasons fresh in their mouths. Benny remained undaunted, predicting the Giants would defeat the Packers. Benny's unusual pregame boast was fueled by the Giants' signing that week of Chris Cagle, a three-time all-American for the Army. Cagle was a talented runner and passer who had given Knute Rockne and Notre Dame fits in the Irish's great battles with the Army.

"Cagle has greatly strengthened our team," Friedman said, "and the boys are all set to revenge some old accounts with the Packers. It should be one of the most sensational games ever seen in New York."

Forty-five thousand screaming Giants fans, easily the largest crowd of the year, packed the Polo Grounds to see if Benny could drive Cal Hubbard, Johnny Blood, and the rest of the Packers out of first place.

After a first quarter stalemate, Benny began to move the Giants. From the Packers twenty-three-yard line, Friedman struck the game's first telling blow, hitting a streaking Red Badgro in perfect stride down the sideline for a touchdown pass. Jewish fans in the Polo Grounds exploded with their trademark chorus of "Ya Ya Bennah!" as Badgro crossed the goal line. Benny added the extra point and the Giants had a 7–0 lead.

Friedman tried to get Chris Cagle involved in the action. But the first time Cagle touched the ball he ended up in a violent head-on-head collision with Packers lineman Tom Nash. When the dust cleared, both players were on the sideline, Cagle with a huge gash to the head and Nash with a broken nose. Cagle toughed out his rude welcome to the pro game, returning to the game to absorb more punishment.

In the third quarter, Hap Moran turned a fake punt from deep in the Giants' end into a ninety-one-yard romp. Lavie Dilweg saved the touchdown, yanking Moran to the ground at the Packers' one-yard line. Friedman called Hap's number for the scoring plunge, but the Packers rejected him, twice. When Cal Hubbard and his friends turned away Wiberg on third down, Benny departed from his usual inside-the-20-yard-line benevolence toward his teammates and called his own number on fourth down. He took the snap and smashed the ball over the line, increasing the Giants' lead to 13–0. The Packers managed a touchdown late in the third quarter, but the clock ran out on their game-ending drive with the ball on the Giants' one-yard line. Giants 13, Packers 6.

Three weeks before his showdown with Knute Rockne, Benny had at last overcome the Green Bay Packers. If the Giants could win their final four games, all against weak teams, they'd win the championship no matter how the Packers finished.

But the Maramen floundered against their next opponent, Staten Island. While Green Bay was handling Frankford, Ken Strong and the Stapes ruined the Giants' Thanksgiving dinner with a 7–6 upset. Three days later things got worse for New York. With Friedman on the sidelines nursing a knee injured during the Staten Island game—the first game Benny ever missed due to injury—the woeful Dodgers beat the Giants by the same 7–6 score.

The Giants had frittered away their advantage over Green Bay. Benny returned from injury to guide the team to victory over Frankford, but the win had come a little too late for Coach Leroy Andrews. The ill-timed losing streak had caused the coach to lose his grip on the team and on himself. He berated the players and even threatened to bench Friedman. President Herbert Hoover, besieged for his inability to reverse the Depression's devastation, would have been canonized on the steps of the New York Stock Exchange before Benny would ever ride the pine on Tim Mara's team. A furious Mara dumped Andrews and installed Benny as player-coach for the last game against Brooklyn. The Giants handled the Dodgers, but the Packers held the cards. Green Bay needed only a tie against Portsmouth in their last game on December 14 to clinch the title. There was nothing more Benny could do about the Green Bay Packers.

But he had a juicy consolation on the way. Knute Rockne and Frank Carideo and the rest of the Notre Dame All-Stars were coming to town.

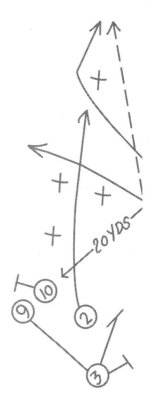

SIXTEEN

Benny and Rockne

Benny wasn't the only prominent New Yorker anxiously waiting for Rockne. The coach's arrival couldn't come too soon for Jimmy Walker.

"Beau James" Walker's flamboyant personality had been a sublime antidote for the Depression's gloom that had enveloped New York City. If the sharply dressed Walker wasn't at a Broadway opening or a boxing match, he could usually be found in a casino or a speakeasy. A Broadway chorus girl named Betty Compton saw far more of the mayor than his wife did.

And Walker enjoyed all the privileges and immunities of membership in the uncompromising political machine that was Tammany Hall.

For most of his term in office, Walker's popularity had protected him from allegations of Tammany corruption. But Beau James Walker's Teflon shield began to disintegrate as the Depression's stranglehold on New York tightened. New York governor Franklin Roosevelt had appointed a former judge named Samuel Seabury to investigate corruption in New York City government. Seabury took to the job like Knute Rockne took to a halftime speech. He was obsessed with breaking up Tammany Hall, and he wasn't beguiled by Beau James Walker.

So as Jimmy Walker's personal storm clouds were gathering, he did what he did best. He turned on his public relations charm and focused on Knute Rockne's impending collision with Benny Friedman.

Walker assembled a breathless press corps in his office on December 9 to hear him announce the All-Stars' lineup. Speculation about the lineup had been rampant. Would the team be a collective out-of-shape relic? Or would Rockne produce his biggest stars from years past and present, ready to play for real?

The first four names Walker announced provided the answer. "Harry Stuhldreher, Don Miller, and Elmer Layden, and Jim Crowley," the mayor thundered. The names rang out of Jimmy Walker's mouth with the force of a public relations earthquake. They were the fabled backfield of Rockne's 1924 national championship team, immortalized by Grantland Rice as the "Four Horsemen."

Then Jimmy Walker announced more big names: five of the famous "Seven Mules" line that had blocked for the Four Horsemen, led by all-American center Adam Walsh; John Voedisch and John Chevigney, standouts on the 1927 and 1928 teams; and Jack Cannon, an all-American only a year earlier on the 1929 national champions. Five other members from that 1929 team would also be playing.

The game got another boost a couple of days later when Rockne called Walker and confirmed that Frank Carideo and Bucky O'Connor, ripe from their victory over Southern Cal, would play. So would all-Americans Marty Brill and the feisty undersized guard Bert Metzger, if they could overcome nagging injuries. The All-Star team would include eleven current or former all-Americans and a host of other stars.

"Our team will be one of the strongest ever assembled," Rockne told Walker. "It will be fully equipped to carry out the best Notre Dame traditions. We don't expect to have our season's winning record broken by your team of Giants."

Benny liked his Giants' chances, but he wasn't ignoring Rockne's bravado. He'd learned from Fielding Yost that a team's performance at game time was an exhibition of habits learned in practice. Benny, now coaching as well as playing, put the Giants through tough practices on Thursday and Friday.

Despite Red Grange's spectacular pro debut in 1925 and the crowds Benny had drawn as a pro, professional football was still college football's poor stepchild, plain and simple. But now the country's economic misfortune had given Friedman and his pro mates a shot at the most storied coach and program in college football history.

. . .

The train from South Bend carrying the team the *Daily News* called "the greatest array of gridiron talent ever assembled" chugged into Grand Central Terminal at 8:30 A.M. Saturday, December 13. New York City welfare commissioner Frank Taylor and other members of Jimmy Walker's official reception committee greeted the bleary-eyed Irish All-Stars inside the station. Tim Mara was also in the welcoming party, representing his Giants.

The Irish stars and their coach piled into a fleet of cars and, escorted by fifty police motorcycles with sirens wailing, headed downtown to city hall for an official reception to be hosted by Walker. Not far from the motorcade's path, three thousand jobless New Yorkers standing on a breadline outside the Church of St. Francis of Assisi reminded everyone why the game was being played.

At city hall, Rockne and the team waited restlessly for Walker. Beau James Walker wasn't a morning person. After about an hour, the mayor still hadn't arrived, so the coach sent his boys up to the Polo Grounds for one last practice.

The mayor showed up a few minutes later. Dozens of men emerged from city hall's doors and inched their way down the steps toward the plaza. Walker stopped near the bottom of the steps behind a battery of radio microphones. Rockne settled in directly behind the mayor. Behind them and to their side stood various commissioners, other government officials, and police officers. Hundreds of reporters, photographers, and spectators crammed the plaza below the steps. An excited buzz permeated the air as the crowd waited for the ceremony to begin.

This was the kind of moment Beau James Walker lived for. The crowd hushed as he squared up to the microphones, dapper as ever in a perfectly tailored fur-collared overcoat. Sam Seabury couldn't touch him now.

"There has been no occasion which gives me greater pleasure than to welcome Knute Rockne and the Notre Dame team," Walker intoned from beneath the brim of his hat. "They have come here understanding well that there are fifty thousand families in need due to the economic depression and who are dependent upon this city and this administration for aid. New York is not only happy but proud to welcome you and the team." His hands clasped and his head rocking side to side with his every theatrical change of inflection, Walker praised Rockne's high ideals and sportsmanship. "You'll never live to know the day," he told Rockne, "that New York can forget the splendid things that you're doing by your presence and with the team in New York City."

"New York has always been very kind to Notre Dame," the coach said in a reserved tone as he took his turn at the podium.

Then Rockne's humility yielded to the performer in him as he spoke of how he'd been relieved of concern that his players wouldn't be up to the task awaiting them. "I was delightfully surprised Wednesday afternoon and Thursday afternoon as they worked out and to see them running around the same way they did when they were undergraduates," Rockne said. As he continued, his sense of reserve yielded to his sense of humor, and the reverent crowd greeted the Rock's jokes with robust laughter.

"If Benny Friedman's boys think they're going to have a lot of fun with us tomorrow, they're in for one unpleasant surprise," the coach declared, his voice sober now. "We didn't come here to lose."

Then the great coach headed up to the Polo Grounds to watch the All-Stars practice one more time. At the stadium, he politely but firmly threw Tim Mara and his prying eyes off the field. The Giants' owner and designated spy laughed as he walked off.

. . .

When the two teams arrived at the Polo Grounds the next day, the weather was cold and raw, the sky was gloomy and grey, and there was a chance of snow in the damp December air.

A slightly rotund man with a bald pate hobbled into the Giants' locker room with the help of a cane. He made his way through the room, joking with some of the players.

Then, having made his rounds, Knute Rockne shuffled over to a training table where Benny was being taped up.

At least outwardly, there were scarcely two more different people than the old Norseman and the Hebrew quarterback. Rockne was the fair-skinned Nordic immigrant; Benny had dark, Semitic features. The Rock was bombastic and lived life with a flourish. Benny was reserved and rarely raised his voice. Yet there were similarities. Both men commanded great respect from their players. Both lived the immigrant experience of the late nineteenth and early twentieth centuries (though Rockne was born in Norway while Benny was first-generation). Both experienced the tribulations of being a minority—Benny a Jew, Rockne a Protestant in Notre Dame's insular Catholic world (though he had converted to Catholicism in 1925).

But their truest common denominator was their approach to football. Both believed in disciplined practice as a prerequisite for success on game day. Both believed that a quarterback's field generalship was as important if not more important than premier physical skills. And though the forward pass didn't figure prominently with Rockne the coach, it had brought Rockne the player his proudest moment. The day in 1913 when he and Notre Dame quarterback Gus Dorais blitzed the Army with their passing attack was an early hint of the promise and excitement of the aerial game. Now Rockne asked the game's greatest passer how he was feeling.

"Fine," Benny replied. Benny's injured knee was still sore but he wasn't about to share that information.

Rockne's eyes were twinkling, his mind flashing back to the day he had seen Benny dismantle the Chicago Bears.

"That's too bad," the Rock said.

Then the coach hobbled over to the Notre Dame locker room to deliver a patented Knute Rockne pregame homily to his boys.

"Fellows, these Giants are heavy but slow," he barked in the unmistakable cadence his players had heard so many times before. "Go out there, score two or three touchdowns on passes in the first quarter and then defend—and don't get hurt."

Friedman might have thought he was back at Ann Arbor or Columbus when he led the Giants from the locker room. More than fifty thousand fans packed the Polo Grounds. Music blared from the New York City Police Department and New York University marching bands. The goal posts were adorned in the teams' colors. Bunting in Giants red and blue was draped on the railings and facades around half the stadium. Bunting in Notre Dame blue and gold covered the other half. Tim Mara outfitted his men with new uniforms and, for the first time that year, bright red helmets. The Giants, unaccustomed to such pageantry, soaked it all in for a few minutes.

With Rockne wrapped in blankets on the sideline and a stiff wind blowing from the stadium's north end, the Irish kicked off to the Giants. The All-Stars' defense took the field following the return and waited for Benny Friedman's first thrust. To the Notre Dame fans' delight, the Irish defense was firm. The Giants failed to make a first down and had to punt.

The change of possession brought the Four Horsemen onto the field to an eruption of cheers. But Stuhldreher and his friends weren't out there for long. The quartet's first foray went nowhere, and the Irish punted the ball back to the Giants.

Now Friedman started to roll. First he smashed through the All-Stars' line for eleven yards. Then he hit the fleet Len Sedbrook with a twenty-five-yard strike and followed that with another bullet to Sedbrook for a sixteen-yard gain.

At the All-Stars' eleven-yard line, though, Rockne's defense rose up again. The Irish got the ball back when Benny's fourth-down pass into the end zone fell harmlessly to the ground.

For a second straight possession, the All-Stars couldn't move the ball. The failure on their first possession had been innocent enough, an offense feeling out the defense. But their second try was foreboding. This time the Giants' line pushed around the Seven Mules like a bunch of tackling dummies. Over the years, Rockne's famed shift offense, with backs moving from one side of the ball to the other before the snap, had confused the greatest college teams. But the Giants were smothering the vaunted shift. On third down, Red Badgro stormed into the Irish backfield and slammed Sleepy Jim Crowley to the ground for a big loss, forcing the All-Stars to punt and forcing Crowley out of the game.

"How many people are here today, and why are they all wearing Giant uniforms?" a dazed Crowley asked referee Tom Thorp as he limped off the field.

Fortunately for the Irish, their defenders didn't seem as overwhelmed as Crowley. They forced another Giants punt, but the kick buried Notre Dame deep at their own eight-yard line. With Notre Dame's first two possessions having fizzled and the Irish parked in the shadow of their own end zone, Stuhldreher knew they needed a shot of adrenaline, quickly.

Harry thought the Giants would expect him to be careful with the ball so close to his end zone, and he tried to catch them napping with a surprise pass. But Badgro and Bill Owen were ready. They overran Adam Walsh and his linemates and squashed Harry in the end zone for a safety.

The first quarter wasn't over yet and already the thousands of Irish loyalists in the Polo Grounds had seen Jim Crowley knocked out of the game and Harry Stuhldreher belted to the ground in his own end zone. Never before had the Four Horsemen been so battered.

Following the safety, the Giants received the Irish's free kick and marched down the field again. By now, Benny had deciphered the Irish defenders. He could tell by their movements whether they were expecting a pass or a run, and he adjusted accordingly, mixing the plays beautifully and confounding the All-Stars with his matchless ball faking and generalship. Rip Miller, the great Notre Dame lineman, couldn't contain his frustration after Benny exploited him on two consecutive plays.

Miller yelled at Benny for making him look bad and implored Friedman to run the ball to the other side of the field. Benny obliged Miller and on the next play ran the ball away from Miller's side for a first down.

Benny then moved the Giants to the All-Stars' fifteen-yard line with a gorgeous pass to Badgro in the middle of the field that he flipped right over the top of a straining Irish line. Then, mercifully for the Irish, the first quarter ended.

Rockne had always prized quarterbacks who were skilled enough and smart enough to control the game, to run it themselves without the safety net of the coaches. Stuhldreher and Carideo had done that for him. Now the Norseman was watching Benny do that *to* him. Rockne needed to give Benny something to think about. It was time for the shock troops.

One of Rockne's innovations was to replace most or all of his players with a fresh unit—"shock troops," as they came to be known—that often would outplay a tired opponent. Now, from beneath his blankets, Rockne beckoned a new troupe of players into the fray to begin the second quarter. Frank Carideo, Bucky O'Connor, Jack Cannon, and John Chevigney led the new unit onto the field, and, on the first play of the second quarter, Benny greeted them with an eleven-yard run that brought the ball to the four-yard line. First and goal, Giants. Then Rockne's new unit dug in and slammed Len Sedbrook backward on the next two plays.

Benny gave the ball to Sedbrook in keeping with the standing rule he'd had since his days at Michigan: not to call his own number inside the opponent's twenty-five-yard line. But with Rockne's new lineup warming to the task, Benny wasn't going to give Sedbrook a third chance. On third down, Benny kept the ball and smashed into the end zone through the wall of blue and gold shirts that had again bested the Giants' blockers.

The Giants missed the extra-point attempt. But the score was 8–0, and the All-Stars hadn't yet made a single first down, much less threatened to score. If the Irish were to get in the game, it was time for Carideo and Bucky O'Connor to reprise some of their magical play from the week before against Southern Cal.

Except they just couldn't do it. O'Connor got loose around right end for a nice ten-yard run, but otherwise, with the Giants controlling the line, he went nowhere. The New Yorkers surrounded Carideo at the nimble quarterback's every turn. No team had ever stifled the heady two-time all-American quarterback like this. The Irish had to punt again. Like a dazed boxer hanging on for the end of the round, the Irish were praying for halftime.

Carideo punted the ball to midfield, but Benny ran the ball back down the Irish's throat to the thirty-four-yard line. A thirteen-yard completion later and the Giants were at the 21.

The situation called for a pass. Notre Dame's great lineman, Hunk Anderson, anxiously eyed Benny as the quarterback stepped to the line of scrimmage poised to strike the decisive blow.

"I'm dropping back," Anderson whispered to linemate Rip Miller, loudly enough to be heard on the subway platform behind the grandstand. All game long, Benny had spotted the Irish linemen dropping back in apparent passing situations and had fooled them with running plays. Now Benny thought Hunk, with his stage whisper, was trying to trick Benny into thinking he'd stay on the line, thereby inducing Friedman to throw into a defense laying for a pass.

Anderson should have known better. Friedman took the snap, faked a pass, and then followed his blocking backs through the hole created when Anderson stepped back off the line. Benny saw nothing but daylight.

The Irish closed quickly, though, and looked to have Friedman sealed off for only a short gain. Then Benny burst through one tackler, then a second, and then, astonishingly, a third All-Star who had dead aim on him. The field was littered with prostrate Irish defenders as Benny dragged a fourth would-be tackler into the end zone. Friedman dusted himself off and kicked the extra point to make the score 15–0. The gun ending the half sounded a couple of minutes later, not a moment too soon for the reeling All-Stars.

Rockne was in unfamiliar territory during the break. His team hadn't been in such trouble at the half since the 1928 Army game in Yankee

Stadium. On that day, the Rock called upon the memory of maybe his greatest player ever, George Gipp, to rally his team. Gipp, who had starred for the Irish in the early 1920s, had passed away at the age of twenty-five, shortly after contracting a respiratory infection. Legend has it that on his deathbed, Gipp told Rockne to tell his boys to "win just one for the Gipper" if they ever found themselves in a tough spot. Rockne had made that emotional plea to the Irish at halftime against the Army in 1928, and Notre Dame went on to defeat the Cadets. This day, however, the first-half drubbing the Giants had administered to Notre Dame suggested that neither George Gipp nor anything else would make much difference. Rockne tried anyway, exhorting his boys with his legendary brand of halftime oratory, hoping to raise a pulse in his overmatched stars.

On Notre Dame's return of the second-half kickoff, it looked like Rockne had found that pulse. Stuhldreher broke clear and was on his way to cutting the Giants' lead in half on one play. But Harry slipped on the moist turf as he was sidestepping the last Giant tackler.

Rockne kept Harry in at quarterback to give the leader of the Four Horsemen one last chance to move the Irish. They did move—backward. Against the Giants substitutes—Benny, sensing that the game was in hand, had pulled the regulars at halftime (perhaps of Rockne's request)—the Irish were thrown for losses on three straight plays. The Giants' defenders were cavorting in the Irish backfield as if they owned it. The All-Stars were forced to punt yet again from the shadow of their own goal line.

After the punt, the Giants finished off a steady drive with a touchdown pass from Hap Moran to Campbell. The extra point made it 22–0.

Late in the game, the All-Stars got the ball for one last chance to crack the Giants' wall. Bucky O'Connor launched a long pass downfield, but the ball came down into the wrong hands. Cris Cagle's interception was the exclamation point to an utterly dominant performance by the professionals.

The final score of 22–0 didn't fully reflect the iron grip the Giants had on the game from start to finish. The Irish offense had managed just one first down the entire game. On defense, except for their opening goal line stand, the All-Stars were willing, determined, hard-hitting—and almost completely ineffective. "Friedman played one of the greatest games witnessed on any gridiron," wrote the *New York Evening Journal.* Had Benny played in the second half, the final score likely would have resembled the routs he engineered back in Ann Arbor. To Adam Walsh, it was as if Benny had been in the Irish defensive huddle all afternoon. At the end of the game, Walsh grabbed Benny, looking for some answers.

"Who gave you the signals for our defense?" Walsh demanded.

Benny looked into the eyes of the great Notre Dame lineman and laughed.

"Adam, you should know better than to play percentages against me."

The afternoon's only negative for the Giants was that while they were manhandling the Irish, the Packers were scrounging out a championship-clinching tie with Portsmouth.

• • •

If the Rock was disappointed, he kept it to himself. During the buildup to the game, some had wondered if the All-Stars could challenge the Giants. Some of the Notre Dame stars hadn't played for several years, and they'd practiced together for only a couple of weeks. Rockne's brazen predictions of victory had quieted much of that speculation by game time. Had he merely been trying to sell tickets? Or was his contempt for pro ball so strong that he truly believed his players would win? After the game he told his players—"one team in a thousand," he called them that night at a gala dinner given in their honor—to hold up their heads and said of the Giants: "That was the greatest football machine I ever saw."

Not to be outdone at the dinner was Jimmy Walker, who said: "Today we saw the greatest football game ever played in town . . . In behalf of the city of New York, we salute you, Rock, the team, and the Notre Dame alumni."

A few days later, Benny and Tim Mara went to city hall and presented Walker with a $115,183 check for the Unemployment Fund.

In addition to giving the city an opportunity to help its unemployed, Rockne had also given pro football something: the opportunity to trump college football. The coach had feared this from the moment Jimmy Walker pitched the game to him. Now the game had been played, and Rockne had watched Benny take full advantage of the high-profile chance to boost professional football. It didn't matter that the game was for charity. It didn't matter that the All-Stars may have been in less than perfect shape. They were still Frank Carideo and Adam Walsh and Jack Cannon and the Four Horsemen. They were still Knute Rockne and Notre Dame.

If Benny and the Giants hadn't completely shattered the myth that the pros couldn't compete with the college boys, they'd at least cracked it wide open.

SEVENTEEN

"The Greatest Football Player in the World"

The spectacle that was the Giants–Notre Dame charity game was vivid proof that even with the country locked in the throes of the Depression, Americans—more than ever—needed their sports and their sports heroes. Some very special heroes had stepped forward in 1930. With the masterful jockey Earle Sande along for the ride, Gallant Fox riveted the nation as he romped home in the Kentucky Derby, the Preakness, and the Belmont Stakes to capture thoroughbred racing's Triple Crown. Bobby Jones, already a golf legend several times over, achieved what until then many believed was unachievable by winning the United States Open, the United States Amateur, the British Open, and the British Amateur—golf's Grand Slam. Baseball was again the domain of the great slugger Babe Ruth, as much the coarse rogue as Jones was the refined gentleman.

And of Benny Friedman, the famous sportswriter Paul Gallico had this to say:

> As a professional Friedman is fifty per cent better than he was in school. Better than Red Grange? Certainly! Grange has only learned to play football since he became a professional. He is a great player today,

but he cannot touch Friedman. Right off the bat, Benny would out-think him six to one. Professional football has not yet been as highly publicized as other sports. It has been slow to catch on with the public. But in his own game, Friedman is in a class with Babe Ruth and Bobby Jones and Earle Sande and Gallant Fox. He is a champion.

The things that a perfect football player must do are kick, pass, run the ends, plunge the line, block, tackle, weave his way through broken fields, drop and place kick, interfere, diagnose plays, spot enemy weaknesses, direct an offense, and not get hurt. I have been describing Friedman's repertoire to you.

Gallico was the sports editor and a columnist for the *New York Daily News*. He often watched the Giants play and practice. He saw Grange and Nevers and Nagurski and all the other greats of the day play. And the one Gallico called the "greatest football player in the world" was Benny Friedman, "the young Cleveland Jew, born of orthodox parents."

But Gallico offered an explanation for Benny's vaunted field generalship that was shrouded in malicious religious stereotype: "Behind that swart face that is sometimes almost a bitter mask is a lightning mind that plans the downfall of his opponents, that is continually probing of and analyzing their weaknesses, one that lures them with Oriental cunning and which strikes when the time is at hand."

Here was one of the eminent sportswriters of the day expressing anti-Semitic notions of the Jew as devious schemer—in a piece written, ostensibly, to laud the exploits of the "perfect football player," as Gallico described Benny.

Friedman's dismantling of Rockne's All-Stars culminated a fourth straight season in which Benny had essentially played in a league of his own. He completed 57 percent of his passes. His average completion netted nearly 11 yards. He passed for almost 1,300 yards, exceeding 1,000 yards for the fourth consecutive season. And he threw 13 touchdown passes, down from 20 in 1929 but still far beyond his nearest pursuers, none of whom cracked double figures. While leading the league in all of these passing categories by a mile, Benny gained 360 yards rushing, scored 6 touchdowns, and kicked 23 extra points. Once again, he was named to every All-Pro team, including one selected by Red Grange, who named his longtime rival the league's outstanding player for 1930.

From 1927, Benny's rookie season, through the 1930 campaign, he had thrown for 5,653 yards and 55 touchdowns. Over that same four-year period, the second-place totals accumulated by different men were 3,770 yards and 27 touchdowns.

Yet, once again, even though he'd finally won a game against the dreaded Packers and had steered the Giants to thirteen wins against just four losses, Benny—by mere percentage points—had missed out on the league championship.

And as 1931 dawned, Friedman wasn't sure he wanted to gear up for another run at it. Benny enjoyed playing football, but playing it as an avocation had not been his preference. He had jumped into the pro game in 1927 only after a great deal of equivocation and only because he needed the money to help support his family when his father became ill. Some of his friends, far less talented players who could not command his salary, had pursued legal or medical studies or had taken jobs in the business world and were on their way to productive, secure careers. Notwithstanding the fame and, relatively speaking in the world of football salaries, the fortune that had come his way, Friedman was beginning to feel he'd been wasting time.

Moreover, the sheer demands of playing the game were wearing on him. Friedman's unmatched ability always made him the favorite target of the opposition. Players, coaches, and writers routinely marveled at Benny's ability to take a blow from or deliver a blow to larger players and emerge from the collision unscathed while his victim often wasn't as fortunate. "When he is tackled by 210-pounders, Benny always gets up, but the tackler sometimes doesn't," Paul Gallico observed of the muscle-rippled five-foot-ten-inch, 180-pound Friedman. Art Arker, the coach of the football team at Chico State University in California, once related how he saw Benny rifle a thirty-yard touchdown pass from the ground after being creamed simultaneously by Bronko Nagurski and another large defender, and then get up and calmly dust himself off.

And no less an authority than Red Grange, who knew a little something about being the opposition's target, declared Friedman to be the toughest player he'd ever seen.

But all the pounding—in league games, non-league games, charity games, exhibitions—was starting to grate. And Benny was growing annoyed with the fans' refusal to allow him an occasional respite from the mayhem during a game, even though he surely understood that, more often than not, the only reason the fans were at the game was to see him play.

"I'd rather sit on the bench and watch others play," Benny growled early in 1931. "I've had enough of pro football. Playing an average of fifty minutes a game is a tough job. If you stay out for even a little while the crowd begins to boo and so you can't rest a minute . . . You can't go on forever that way. It's my future I'm thinking about and if football holds a future for me, it's not as a player."

In some respects, Benny's retirement musings were coming at an odd time. He was healthy, just twenty-five years of age, and at or near the peak of his skills. And the National Football League, in no small measure thanks to Friedman's decimation of Rockne's All-Stars and his popularity at the box office, was beginning to gain some real traction. League-wide attendance had jumped 8 percent in 1930, with the Giants themselves enjoying a 25 percent increase at the Polo Grounds.

In July 1930, Benny had met twenty-three-year-old Shirley Immerman, a Brooklyn girl. Petite and shapely, with short blonde hair and a ready smile that produced a trace of a twinkle in her eye, Shirley might have been a Broadway showgirl. Her bearing, if not quite regal, had a touch of glamour. Shirley's family, in fact, was a bit more patrician than Benny's. Joseph Immerman, Shirley's father, was a German Jew, more upper-crust in his mindset than the working-class Russian Jewish immigrants of the late nineteenth and early twentieth centuries that had included Lewis and Mayme Friedman. A granddaughter of Joseph Immerman recalled that he could be a bit snobbish and that Benny's football celebrity may have eased what otherwise might have been a rocky welcome for a son of a simple Russian tailor. News of Benny and Shirley's engagement began circulating in January 1931, with reports that they would marry in the spring.

Reports of potential coaching jobs for Benny also began circulating in the first few weeks of 1931. Positions at Yale, Penn, and the University of California were rumored, with the head coaching job at Cal emerging as Benny's most likely destination. The Golden Bears' coach, Clarence Price, had resigned in November amidst turmoil following Cal's season-ending 41–0 loss to their bitter rival Stanford. Benny hadn't spent much time on the West Coast, but Cal had a solid football tradition, and if the university president had anything to say about it, Benny's prospects looked good. "I will see that Friedman gets every consideration for the California football coaching job," Robert Sproul announced. "I cannot recommend him because that is a matter for the committee, and I do not desire to usurp their power, but I believe he would make an admirable coach."

Unfortunately for Friedman, the committee charged with selecting the new coach didn't see things that way. The job went to Bill Ingram, the same Bill Ingram who as the Navy's coach in 1926 had masterminded the Middies' huge upset of Benny and the Wolverines in Baltimore.

Nothing materialized for Benny at Penn, either, and so his focus returned to Yale. Benny's part-time coaching in 1930 had helped the Elis to a 5–2–1 season. Now Friedman pushed for a full-time position in New Haven.

Yale was a bit funny about hiring coaches who hadn't been Yalies. Yale alumni held strong sway over the university's football affairs, and they generally preferred their coaches to be their own kind. Grantland Rice, for one opinionated and generally well-informed authority on sporting matters, couldn't have cared less where Friedman went to college and clearly felt that it shouldn't matter to the Yale elite either. "If Benny Friedman goes to Yale as backfield coach, the Blue will get one of the smartest young instructors football has known in a long time," Rice wrote in his syndicated column.

Yale had hired outsiders before, albeit rarely. The current line coach was the great Notre Dame all-American Adam Walsh. And in early February, the announcement was made that Friedman, the outsider from Michigan, would be Yale's full-time backfield coach for the 1931 season. With that, Benny announced that that his playing days were over.

. . .

On February 12, more than two hundred guests watched Benny Friedman and Shirley Immerman exchange vows. The wedding, held at the Glen Oaks Golf and Country Club on Long Island, about fifteen miles east of Manhattan, had a bit of society flare. Benny's friend Guy Lombardo, the popular band leader, and his Royal Canadian Orchestra provided the music, and noted humorist Irvin Cobb provided the wisecracks.

Following the wedding, the Friedmans headed to a honeymoon in Miami and Havana. One photographer captured the couple relaxing on the beach in Miami. Wearing a robe and lounging next to his bride, Benny had the look of a man who wasn't going to miss spending his Sunday afternoons in the frozen muck of the Polo Grounds.

. . .

On March 31, 1931, in an early morning midwestern chill, Knute Rockne boarded a plane in Kansas City on his way to Los Angeles, where just a few months earlier the great coach had guided his beloved Notre Dame footballers to their stunning triumph over Southern Cal. Rockne was a pitchman for Studebaker, the automobile maker, and had some business to attend to for the company in California.

The Rock and the seven other people on board never made it there. High over the Kansas plains, in a sky shrouded in fog, the plane lost a wing and virtually split apart before going down in a fiery heap.

Rockne was just forty-three years of age. Unlike others in the highest echelon of coaching who would toil for nearly three decades or even longer, greats like Yost and Stagg and Zuppke, Rockne's coaching career spanned just thirteen years. Yet during his relatively brief tenure, Rockne established a legend that neither those three greats nor any others would ever match. Taking on the toughest schedules in the country year after year, Rockne's teams compiled a staggering mark of 105 wins, 5 ties, and just 12 losses. And they did it with a cerebral approach, something that Friedman especially appreciated. Donald Miller Jr., the son of Four Horseman Don Miller, spoke of the reverence reserved for Rockne by his father and his teammates: "My dad always said that Rockne was ten years ahead of every coach and if he had stayed alive he'd still be ten years ahead."

A number of the leading coaches of the time didn't have the best relationships with one another. It seems their competitiveness allowed for nothing warmer than a distant respectfulness. Yost and Rockne didn't manage even that much. There had been a good deal of backbiting between the two in the first decade of the century. Rockne believed that Yost resented Notre Dame's Catholic orientation. Yost hated Rockne's shift offense and didn't think much of the Irish's sportsmanship. Yost dropped Notre Dame from Michigan's schedule and lobbied other Big Ten teams to follow suit, and for a long while, the Irish, unable to get a game with Big Ten teams, had to head east for their major challenges. It wasn't unusual for the two coaches to trade long-distance barbs, as in 1925, following George Little's departure from Michigan, when Rockne asked: "Who will be Michigan's coach this year on the days that the team loses?" But despite the ill feelings between the two, Benny respected them both immensely. "My admiration for the man was intense," Benny said later of Rockne. "In meeting Rockne one could readily understood [sic] why he was successful," Benny said upon learning of Rockne's death. "Not only was he master at making the plays 'click' but he also created unusual confidence among his boys. I feel the loss deeply."

When Rockne, bundled against the winter and aching with phlebitis, had watched Benny thrash his boys in the Polo Grounds, he'd entertained notions of quitting the coaching business. After a couple of months' rest, however, he'd been rejuvenated and was very much anticipating a new season of drills and halftime oratory and, no doubt, a bundle of victories. But the tragedy over the skies of Kansas had turned the game against Friedman and the Giants into the last game Knute Rockne ever coached. Benny had also played in Fielding Yost's last game—making him the only man to play in the coaching finales of those two great coaches and antagonists.

A few weeks after Rockne's tragic passing, Benny joined a new brokerage firm called L. Filchheimer & Co. as a partner. He spent the spring trading stocks and shuttling to New Haven for Yale's spring practice. To go along with his brokerage and coaching pursuits and the joys and responsibilities of being a newlywed, Benny would also find time in 1931 to publish a short book, *The Passing Game,* a tutorial on his style and philosophy of passing spiced with recollections of noteworthy plays and his development as a player.

· · ·

When Benny was announced as Yale's backfield coach, there was more than a little suspicion that, titles notwithstanding, head coach Mal Stevens would in reality be Benny's assistant. There was some sense in New Haven that the Elis had been underachieving recently and that Friedman was the man to get Yale's players to start playing to their ability, particularly on offense. In essence, Stevens did turn the offense over to Benny and Adam Walsh, but the former Yale star was no pushover. Whatever the public perception may have been, Mal was still the head coach.

Yale's results early in the 1931 season were far from earth-shattering. They defeated two weak teams, Maine and the University of Chicago, but were outclassed badly, at home, by a powerful outfit from the University of Georgia. In their fourth game they met their traditional rival, the Army.

The Elis and the Cadets usually played close games, like the 7–7 tie the previous season. On October 24, seventy-five thousand fans crammed into the Yale Bowl and saw the rivals once again batter each other through an evenly matched contest that remained scoreless near the end of the third quarter.

Then the game exploded. The Army drove nearly seventy yards and finished off the march with a two-yard scoring run on the fourth quarter's second play. The Cadets missed the extra-point try and then kicked off to the Elis. Eighty-eight yards and a field strewn with would-be Army tacklers later, Yale's Bud Parker crossed the Army goal line with a game-tying touchdown. In a matter of seconds, the teams had scored twelve points in a game that had been threatening to put the big crowd to sleep.

Now that crowd was hysterical as they watched the Army, playing for field position, elect to kick off. A talented young Yale back named Bob Lassiter fielded the kick and bounded upfield for some modest yardage before disappearing in the usual pile of tacklers and blockers that end most kick returns. As the players disentangled and trotted off toward their respective sidelines, most of the crowd was at first too rapt in the pandemonium of the scoring explosion to notice that one player, a Cadet, remained prone on the ground. But Benny, on the Yale sideline, noticed the young man right away. He'd seen what had happened. He'd seen the Cadet dive in front of Lassiter, with his head down, and watched him crumple to the ground.

Several people attended to the young Army player in full view of the crowd, which by now had hushed. After a few minutes, Cadet Richard Sheridan was taken from the field on a stretcher, unconscious.

Sheridan never woke up. He'd broken his neck on the play and died two days later.

To Benny, the Sheridan tragedy was stark proof of the importance of players knowing how to protect themselves in the violent game of football. Some time later, Friedman related a story of a similar hit he'd once taken that had resulted in far less serious consequences.

"I made the same kind of a diving tackle to stop 'Pug' Manders of the Chicago Bears. The next thing I remember, my brother was trying to lead me under a shower in the dressing room. I had been knocked cold, but it hadn't hurt. I threw Manders back and all I lost was 15 minutes of my life.

"The reason I'm alive and kicking today and Dick Sheridan is dead is that I had drilled into me the correct habit of always keeping my head up and my neck 'bulled' when making a tackle. Sheridan in his youthful exuberance forgot the lesson that had been taught him. He hadn't made a habit of keeping his head up, and the result was fatal."

Benny's observations of the Sheridan tragedy reflected both a tendency to believe that, in football matters, he knew all there was to know and a proclivity for making others aware of his omniscience. At least in print, he could sound pedantic when analyzing the failure or refusal of other players to develop the "correct" habits. Pedantic or not, as a coach, he would be consumed with the safety of his players.

The Yale-Army game ended in a 6–6 tie, bringing the Elis' record at the season's halfway point to an unimpressive 2–1–1. While Yale had been running in place, back in New York the Giants were displaying similar mediocrity. A committee of quarterbacks assembled to replace Friedman— new pickups Red Smith and Mack Flenniken together with old reliable Hap Moran—had produced an unremarkable 3–3 record through October.

As the NFL schedule headed into November, the league's big story was the Portsmouth Spartans. The team that had struggled in their first year in the league in 1930 had vaulted to the head of the class in 1931. The Spartans were a perfect 8–0 as they readied themselves for a visit to the Polo Grounds to battle the Giants on November 1.

The two main components of the Spartans' stunning makeover were tailbacks Earl "Dutch" Clark and Glenn Presnell. Clark, a Rocky Mountain boy from Colorado, had traveled an unlikely road to the NFL. He had starred for Colorado College but didn't expect anybody connected with pro ball to find him at the tiny school. But an Associated Press reporter named Alan Gould had picked up on Clark's multiple talents and given the boy some national exposure. Spartans coach Potsy Clark, no relation to Earl, offered the young tailback $140 a game to play for the Spartans. The small-town star jumped at the chance to compete against football's best and, to his pleasant surprise, discovered that he more than belonged in the NFL. As Clark was guiding the Spartans to their midseason undefeated record, few people realized that he was blind in one eye.

Glenn Presnell's route to Portsmouth was unusual in a different way. Unlike Clark, Presnell didn't want for exposure coming out of college. As a senior in 1927 he was an all-American for midwestern powerhouse

Nebraska. The NFL wanted the strapping boy from the Nebraska plains, but he opted to sign with the Ironton Tanks, a strong Ohio Valley regional professional team that plied its trade outside the brighter lights of the NFL. Most of these teams were no match for the NFL's best, but Ironton, with Presnell at the helm, was an exception. In 1930, a few days after Benny's sensational appearance against Portsmouth, the Nebraska star had knocked off Friedman and the Giants virtually on his own, scoring on a long touchdown run and then, with no time left on the clock, rifling a fifty-yard touchdown pass and kicking the extra point to give the Tanks a 13–12 victory.

When the Depression swallowed the Tanks after the 1930 season, Presnell finally joined the NFL's ranks, hooking up with nearby Portsmouth. With Presnell, and Dutch Clark, and the iron-willed Potsy Clark doing the coaching, the Portsmouth Spartans had become one tough customer of a football club. One of their eight victories thus far in '31, back in September in Portsmouth, had come at the Giants' expense. In that game the Spartans had an easier time with the New York squad than they had had against Friedman in Portsmouth a year earlier.

Now, with the Spartans getting ready to invade the Polo Grounds, Tim Mara was looking to get Friedman back in a Giants uniform.

Nothing in Benny's contract with Yale prohibited him from playing while he was coaching. He wasn't thrilled about the commuting and the long hours such double duty would entail, but the nice money he'd make from the Giants wouldn't hurt. On October 26—the day Dick Sheridan passed away—Benny signed with the Giants for the rest of the season. The next day he was at practice at the Polo Grounds, preparing for the Portsmouth Spartans.

Friedman was a fanatic when it came to staying in shape, so he was in pretty good condition. But game condition was an entirely different level of fitness. Nearly a year had passed since Benny had played in a football game. Now he had three days to ready himself to last a game in the meat grinder that the league's leading team would have waiting for him.

As things turned out, Benny didn't need to last a game. It took him less than a half to bury the undefeated Spartans. The famous feather ball returned with no sign of rust. Short-, medium-, and long-range passes propelled the Giants to two second-quarter touchdowns and a 14–0 lead.

Shortly before the first half ended, Benny took a seat on the bench. He never returned to the game and he never had to, as an inspired Giants defense squashed Presnell and made the 14–0 score stand up. "Friedman retired soon after he had passed the Giants to victory and with his departure went New York's chances of scoring again," the *New York Times* declared. "But even playing less than half a game the Yale backfield coach had given New York a spark and a verve it had not shown all season."

Just as important as the victory, at least as far as Tim Mara was concerned, was the surge at the gate Friedman provided. Nearly thirty-three thousand fans, easily the season's largest crowd, had turned out to watch Benny wreak havoc with Portsmouth's unbeaten season.

Twenty-five thousand fans, half of them women taking advantage of the Giants' first-ever "Ladies Day" promotion, watched Benny stake the Maramen to a 13–0 halftime lead against the Frankford Yellow Jackets the following week. Then he rested for most of the second half as the Giants' defense quieted Frankford's offense.

A few days later, Benny was in Cleveland to bury his father. Lewis Friedman, the refugee from the shtetls of Russia whose son had become football's first great passer, had finally succumbed after years of ill health at the age of fifty-nine.

· · ·

Friedman returned to New York in time for the Giants' next game against the Bears. A portion of the ticket receipts from the game was to go to the Federation for the Support of Jewish Philanthropies, and it was a healthy gate—more than thirty thousand, including Mayor Jimmy Walker and former New York governor Al Smith. But Friedman's play and that of the Giants' didn't match the pomp and circumstance of the afternoon. Other than a nice thirty-yard run from scrimmage early on, Benny was missing the spark he'd shown in his comeback game against Portsmouth and then against Frankford. The Bears banged out a 12–6 win on the strength of Carl Brumbaugh's passing and the receiving of Garland Grange, Red's kid brother.

New York now had four losses, and their plight wasn't about to get any easier. The Green Bay Packers, Friedman's nemesis, were the next visitor due at the Polo Grounds.

Things did not start well for the Giants in a game they had to win to retain any hope of capturing the league title. One play after the Packers' Hardis McCrary returned the opening kickoff to midfield, Friedman—on the sideline to start the game—watched Red Dunn and Johnny Blood hook up on a fifty-yard scoring pass. Blood was an outstanding player against any opponent, but he seemed to specialize in making life miserable for the Giants.

Soon, Friedman entered the game and promptly passed the Giants to the doorstep of the Packers' end zone. Hap Moran finished off the march with a three-yard run and then kicked the extra point. A short while later, Moran and Ray Flaherty teamed up on a pass that surprised the Packers and transported the Giants deep into Green Bay territory. The drive stalled, but Moran was able to kick the Giants into a 10–7 halftime lead with a field goal.

In his games against Curly Lambeau's boys, Benny had usually been able to inflict some damage. But the Packers always seemed able to adjust and stanch the bleeding, and they did it again this day. New York's defense displayed an equal diligence, and neither team scored in the third quarter. Into the fourth, it seemed the Giants might hold on—until Red Dunn began driving the Pack down the field, pushing the Maramen's backs closer to their goal line with a stream of running plays. Then, from the Giants' 20, the clever Packer quarterback went to the air and found rookie Hank Bruder, who a year earlier had captained the Northwestern Wildcats, for a touchdown that with the extra point put Green Bay ahead 14–10.

Back came the Giants on the fleet legs of Len Sedbrook, who dashed sixty-five yards with the Packers' kickoff. Benny then inched the Giants toward the end zone, with time getting scarce. Only a few ticks remained as Friedman took the snap and faded back, looking to launch a game-winning floater as forty thousand fans screamed in hysteria. Standing at the Green

Bay fourteen-yard line, he desperately searched for Sedbrook or Badgro or Chris Cagle. And then, before he could find one of them, a wave of Packers engulfed him and drowned out the remnants of the Giants' 1931 championship hopes.

The Bears and the Packers had neutralized the adrenaline jolt Benny had given the Giants in his comeback game against Portsmouth. And four days after being gutted by the Packers, Ken Strong's Staten Island Stapletons whipped the dispirited New Yorkers on Thanksgiving Day. Three days after that, the Giants fell to 5–6–1, as they could manage only a scoreless tie with Providence at the Polo Grounds. Benny did guide the Giants to a convincing victory over the Brooklyn Dodgers and then a 25–6 thrashing of the Bears in a Wrigley Field freeze. The late spurt boosted the Giants back over .500, but 7–6–1 is far from what Tim Mara had in mind for his Giants at the start of the season.

Meanwhile, the Yale Elis hadn't seemed distracted by sharing their backfield coach with the Giants. They went 3–0–1 in the four games they played after Benny returned to the Giants, including a 3–0 win over Harvard in front of a madhouse at the Yale Bowl and a season-ending 51–14 walloping of a weak Princeton team.

Yale's 5–1–2 record and their palpable improvement in the passing game should have assured Benny an offer to return as backfield coach for the 1932 season. Yet something was amiss in New Haven. There had been some tension between Friedman and Yale's popular back, "Little Boy Blue" Albie Booth. There was undoubtedly some discomfort—on both sides—resulting from Benny splitting time between coaching in New Haven and playing in New York. And the original uneasiness about having a Michigan man running Yale's offense had never really gone away.

In mid-December, Yale announced the names of its football coaching staff for the 1932 season. Benny wasn't among them; moreover, he was the only coach from the '31 staff who would not be returning.

On his way out of New Haven, Friedman took an unnecessary parting shot at Booth that reflected both his frustration and that nagging imperiousness he sometimes just couldn't squelch. "The newspapers made Booth an outstanding star, when as a matter of fact Albie is highly overrated," Friedman was quoted as saying.

It mattered not at all that Benny might have been correct in his assessment of Booth's talent. It was simply poor form for a coach to degrade his own player so publicly. The fact that Booth was confined to bed, recovering from an injury, when Benny uttered the remarks made them that much more distasteful.

Despite missing nearly half the '31 season, Benny performed well enough to be named the quarterback on several All-Pro teams. And his return to action had produced an unmistakable surge at the gate in a year that was the best yet for the league as a whole.

Just a couple of years earlier, the Giants—the team in the nation's largest city—had hung from the precipice, one small shove from joining the Triangles and the Bisons and the Bulldogs on the NFL's scrap heap. Benny's drawing power didn't merely save Tim Mara's team; it turned it into a steadily profitable business enterprise, if not quite a cash cow. In the process, the quarterback and Mara had grown close, developing a bond way beyond the normal owner-player relationship.

Mara had paid his great quarterback well, better than any player in the league. Friedman wasn't unappreciative, but he also felt he deserved every penny he'd been paid. And now, after three profitable years at the gate and three successful years on the field (albeit without a championship), Benny thought it was time for a different compensation arrangement. Not long after the season ended, Friedman visited Mara in his Manhattan office and asked for an equity interest in the Giants.

The request stunned the big Irishman, but it didn't take him long to respond.

"You're a good friend and a great quarterback, and I hope you come back to us for years," Mara said to Benny. "If you cannot play any longer, we'll always have a place for you here. But this is a family business. The Giants are for my sons."

Now it was Benny who was stunned. He was convinced that his value to the team entitled him to the equity he'd requested, and he had been confident

Mara would agree. But Mara's unequivocal response made it clear that Benny had overreached.

Just a few weeks earlier, Friedman had been the backfield coach of a successful Yale squad, and the star, captain, and coach of the Giants. Now there was a very real chance that come the 1932 football season, he'd hold none of those titles.

EIGHTEEN

Transition

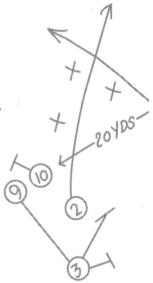

Benny was not looking to leave the Giants. He liked New York City. He liked playing for the league's marquee franchise. His home and his wife's family's home were in Brooklyn.

But Benny was as firm in his belief that he was due a piece of the Giants as Mara was in rebuffing his request. He had saved the Giants. Benny's pride simply wouldn't allow him to play for Mara—whom he loved and respected—any longer.

Benny had an offer from Papa Bear Halas. The Bears' patriarch had pounced when he learned of the rift between Friedman and Mara. Halas sensed an opportunity to finally have the quarterback playing on the Bears' side of the line of scrimmage.

The prospect of playing in the same backfield with Red Grange and the league's new line-plunging terror, Bronko Nagurski, tantalized Friedman. Here was an opportunity to play with the game's greatest open-field runner ever and its fiercest line smasher. Had the situation presented itself a couple of years earlier, Benny probably would have become a Chicago Bear. But Friedman was married now, and when Shirley Friedman resisted the idea of leaving New York, Halas's play for the quarterback crumbled.

Not long after Benny and Yale parted ways, rumors began to circulate that Chick Meehan, NYU's well-respected coach who had mentored Ken Strong to all-American honors, would be stepping down. Some reports declared Benny to be the favorite to replace Meehan. But when Meehan left to accept the head coaching job at Manhattan College, NYU passed on Benny and decided to keep the job in-house, handing the reins to Howard Cann, their outstanding basketball coach and former football star. Nothing came of the University of Iowa's rumored interest in Friedman either.

With no coaching jobs in the offing, Friedman explored his playing options. The most logical one was with the Brooklyn Dodgers. The Dodgers offered Benny a couple of things: the perfect location and an opportunity to build a team from scratch. The Dodgers were, in a word, awful. Formed in 1930 from the remnants of the Dayton Triangles and a few other defunct clubs, the Dodgers had performed well in their debut season, going 7–4–1, but they'd plummeted in '31 with a 2–12 mark.

Part of the Dodgers' problem was their owner, William Dwyer, a gent very much a product of the seamier side of Depression-era New York City. In the twenties, "Big Bill" Dwyer ran what was perhaps New York's most active bootlegging operation by day and relaxed at night at the Stork Club or other trendy speakeasies with friends and FBI poster boys such as Dutch Shultz, Legs Diamond, and Frank Costello. Dwyer emerged from a stint in a federal penitentiary in 1926 and straightened out—some—with legitimate business interests such as the Dodgers.

Dwyer approached Benny early in 1932, offering him a player-coach position with his football team, and Benny accepted. Several months later, in August, Benny, in his capacity as coach, attended the league's annual meeting in Atlantic City, New Jersey. Friedman and the other attendees were a bit startled when George Preston Marshall, the owner of the newly constituted Boston Redskins (comprised mostly of players from the defunct Newark Tornadoes), prattled on about changing the rules to encourage more passing and more scoring. Marshall, the owner of a laundry business, had no previous football experience and a forceful, even offensive manner—not the best prescription for convincing hard-bitten football lifers to change the rules of their venerable game. Marshall's long-winded pitch fizzled.

A month later, the Brooklyn Dodgers' new quarterback, captain, and coach took his team down to Lakewood, near the New Jersey Shore, to train for what Benny hoped would be a makeover season. Looking around the locker room, Friedman must have realized that his talented Giants teammates had spoiled him. There were no Tony Planskys or Steve Owens in evidence, no Red Badgros or Ray Flahertys or Len Sedbrooks. Friedman reached out to his old friend Bennie Oosterbaan for some help. "Are there any of the graduating football men who weigh 210 or thereabouts," Friedman wrote to Bennie in Ann Arbor, "who would like to play, and who you think would be an asset to me? . . . What are your own plans for this fall?"

Oosterbaan stayed put at Michigan, content with his position as assistant coach. Still, the Dodgers were not as devoid of talent as Benny's mildly panicked letter might have indicated. Benny's buddy from Glenville, Saul Mielziner, had come over from the Giants with Friedman. With Mielziner and former Packer All-Pro Jim Bowdoin and a six-foot-two-inch, 270-pound giant from Iowa named Harold Ely—whom Benny, probably in a burst of undue enthusiasm, likened to Cal Hubbard—the line looked solid. Friedman's old end from the Cleveland Bulldogs, Ossie Wiberg, came along as well. Rookies Paul Riblett from Penn, "Bull" Karcis, an aptly nicknamed five-foot-nine-inch, 220-pounder from Carnegie-Mellon, and Jack Grossman from Rutgers were attractive backfield prospects. Grossman, in particular, had the look of stardom about him; he was a fleet runner and pass receiver who could also throw.

And then, of course, there was Friedman himself. After absorbing the ravages of five years of pro ball, Benny was still healthy and just twenty-seven years old. He'd played well enough in '31—especially considering that he'd started in midseason—to suggest that he was ready to reprise his magic in Brooklyn.

But anyone taking a closer look at Friedman in the Dodgers' Lakewood camp might have detected some cracks in the foundation. The litheness of

Benny's early youth was eroding, ever so gradually. There was added thickness to his torso now, not from flab, to be sure, but a muscular thickness borne of maturity. That dreaded loss of a step that visits every player at some time or other seemed to be knocking on Benny's door.

Still, Brooklyn's first two games were shutout wins in Staten Island and in Boston. Against the Redskins, Benny's "disciple of Barnum" was rookie Ernie Pinckert, who had signed with Boston following two all-American seasons with USC. Pinckert, it seems, was near-sighted, a shortcoming that Benny exploited to the tune of two early touchdown passes that set the tone for a dominant Friedman performance. The fans and local media genuflected in awe as, with Pinckert's help, the Hebrew connection between Friedman and Grossman made like Friedman and Oosterbaan. In just two games under the new "Friedman regime," the Dodgers had equaled their victory total from a year ago.

Brooklyn's flying start injected Benny with a jolt of bravado. "I'll bet you that before the season's over, this will be the greatest club I've ever played with," he declared. "Why? Because we're off on the right foot, that's why. Boy, I've seen some prima donnas in this league, let me tell you. But there's none of that here. We practice every day, and I'm boss. We wouldn't get very far without discipline, and the fellows know it, too." For good measure, Friedman also puffed his Dodgers' chances of beating the defending champion Green Bay Packers in a couple of weeks.

Before their trip to Green Bay, however, they had to deal with Staten Island and the Giants. First the Stapes slapped Benny and the Dodgers with a dose of reality, nipping them 7–6. Then the Giants ruined Benny's notions of a triumphant return to the Polo Grounds by jumping out to a 14–0 first-quarter advantage and holding on in a bitterly fought game to win 20–12. Suddenly, with mighty Green Bay looming, the Dodgers were 2–2 and looking a lot less capable of the big things Benny had predicted.

On their way to Green Bay, the Dodgers stopped off in Cleveland to play a charity exhibition against Red Grange and the Chicago Bears. To help promote the game, Benny took Red with him on a visit to his alma mater,

Glenville High. Glenville students packed the auditorium at an assembly to welcome their famous alumnus and his famous rival.

Hal Lebovitz was then a sixteen-year-old junior member of the Tar-blooders football team. Lebovitz had a love of sports and a special ability to write about it that would lead to his becoming the longtime sports editor of the *Cleveland Plain Dealer* and a local sports icon. Over the course of a lengthy and distinguished career, Lebovitz would come to know many sporting greats and witness many legendary moments. He never forgot that assembly at Glenville High, when he and his classmates thrilled to the sight of the great Red Grange in their midst.

But for Lebovitz, and for most of the predominantly Jewish students there, the real treat that day was the presence of Benny Friedman, one of their own, who'd vaulted from the ghetto to the pinnacle of the sports world. For those students at Glenville and for countless others in schools in New York City's Lower East Side and Detroit's Hastings Street section and in Jewish neighborhoods across the nation, Benny was living, breathing inspiration that despite the restraints imposed by their own insular culture and despite the presence of anti-Semitism, there was a place for them in America. "He was our hero," Lebovitz recalled decades later.

. . .

Benny was nursing a sore shoulder and therefore didn't play much in Brooklyn's 13–0 loss to the Bears in the Cleveland exhibition. He wanted to be ready for the Packers in Green Bay a few days later. "Friedman is a great drawing card in the Badger state," declared the Packers' official program for the Dodgers game, but on this occasion there was no Friedman magic for the fans. Sitting out the exhibition helped Benny not at all as Green Bay crushed the Dodgers, 13–0, and the game was never even that close. Benny's passes were totally ineffective. His most remarkable "completions" were two lateral passes the Packers picked off that led to their two touchdowns.

For Brooklyn the highlight of the game came after the Packers crashed through Brooklyn's line to block Benny's attempted punt. The ball caromed into the arms of a Green Bay player, who took off toward the Brooklyn end zone with an escort of teammates leading interference. Friedman was the only Dodger between the Packer posse and the goal line, but he was so badly outnumbered that he had no hope of making a tackle. Just as the ball carrier was about to streak away, Benny stopped in his tracks.

"All right," Friedman barked at the Green Bay contingent. "Your ball." Then he turned his back and strolled away. The ball carrier and his blockers, on hearing Benny's proclamation, stopped in their tracks also. A moment later, the ball carrier touched the ball down in the middle of the field. Somehow, Benny's "concession" had convinced the Packers that the play was over. And when the Packer ball carrier touched the ball down, the play *was* over. Friedman's quick thinking, together with a collective Packer brain cramp, had saved a touchdown.

Benny missed a game a few days later when his father-in-law became ill. The Chicago Cardinals trounced Brooklyn in Wrigley Field, 27–7. Cardinals owner Charles Bidwell, who had promoted the game heavily on the assumption that Friedman would be playing, was none too happy when Benny suddenly traveled to New York a couple of days before the contest upon his father-in-law taking ill. Bidwell filed a formal complaint against Friedman with league president Joe Carr, who quickly ruled that Benny had acted properly in view of the medical emergency.

The Green Bay game showed that Benny's performance on the field was slipping. And for the remainder of the season, it never got much better. The Dodgers lost four of their last five games, including rematches with the Packers and the Giants. Their lone victory in that stretch was an ugly 3–0 win over the Cardinals on a Friedman field goal.

A combination of factors sabotaged Benny's performance in '32, not the least of which was inept play from his linemen. But the other factors had nothing to do with his teammates: a bit of aging; distractions from juggling ownership, coaching, and playing responsibilities; and perhaps a lingering frustration at having torpedoed his relationship with his good friend Tim Mara. And his apparent indifference in the season finale suggested he might also have started losing interest in playing. Twenty thousand fans showed their loyalty and excitement by coming out to Ebbets Field to watch their 3–8 Dodgers close out the season against the Boston Braves. Yet Benny did not start the game, and even with the Dodgers unable to mount any offense, he didn't enter the game until the fourth quarter. His belated efforts produced nothing, and Brooklyn was sent packing for the off-season with a 7–0 loss.

The Dodgers closed out the season with a 3–9 record. For the first time since he turned pro, Friedman was not named to even one All-Pro team. With the emergence of such stars as strong-armed Packer rookie Arnie Herber, Dutch Clark, Glenn Presnell, and the versatile Clark Hinkle, another Green Bay rookie, he now had company in the conversation about the league's best quarterback. And it looked like there would be another quarterback joining that group in 1933. Harry Newman, Benny's protégé, had just finished his senior year at Michigan, earning all-American and Big Ten Player of the Year honors while leading the Wolverines to the Big Ten title.

• • •

George Preston Marshall, now with a season of NFL ownership experience behind him, showed up at the league's annual meeting in February 1933 prepared to renew his pitch for a change in the rules. This time, to Marshall's delight, he'd picked up an important ally—George Halas. For years, Halas had seen Benny attract large crowds to watch him torch the Bears with passes from anywhere on the field, on first down or fourth down, his team ahead or behind. He'd seen Friedman rip holes in the best defenses in the league with a running attack made that much more effective because of the constant threat that he would pass. Marshall hadn't gotten much traction at the prior year's meeting, but Halas could see that the bombastic laundryman, inexperienced as he might be in football, was on target. The game needed to change. Attendance was stagnant. Scoring was down. Tie games abounded. The league's product was dull. It needed either more Friedmans or rules that would enable more players to do what Friedman had been doing.

Halas, the rules committee chairman, and Marshall took particular aim at the rule requiring forward passes to be thrown from a position at least five yards behind the line of scrimmage. The rule inhibited passers from deceiving defenses and from scrambling and creating plays. Halas and Marshall also pressed hard for a rule that would spot the ball ten yards in from the sideline if the ball had been out-of-bounds on the previous play. They also proposed moving the goalposts up to the goal line to encourage more field goals. A year earlier, Marshall had nearly been laughed out of the room when he lobbied for these changes. This time, with Halas on his side, the rules changes passed.

In August 1933, Bill Dwyer sold the Dodgers to Chris Cagle and Cagle's flamboyant Giants' teammate, John "Shipwreck" Kelly. The new owners brought in a new coach named John McEwan, the former head man at West Point with a hard-driving reputation. "Potsy Clark showed the boys the value of good coaching at Portsmouth," Cagle said shortly after hiring McEwan. "Man for man there were several teams in the league better than Portsmouth, but Portsmouth has always made a great showing because Clark handled the material correctly. I feel that the Dodgers have championship material and that McEwan will bring it out."

Whether Cagle's remarks constituted a swipe at Friedman's coaching performance in '32, or they were simply the enthusiastic words of a new owner promoting his new coach, it was clear that the complexion of this Dodgers team would be different from the '32 model. As the team readied to head up to Hopewell Junction, New York, for preseason training camp, the two former Giants signed a number of new players, with a heavy emphasis on improving the team's line play. Cagle unabashedly promoted his new team, predicting a championship—and Benny hadn't yet re-signed to play.

That changed in mid-September when Friedman, with no coaching jobs in the offing, signed a contract to play for the Dodgers in 1933. Cagle was delighted. "With Friedman in the fold, we figure to have one of the flashiest passing attacks in the league," he said. "Coach McEwan is busy designing several sets of series plays built around Friedman to enable us to make the most of Benny's great passing ability and his flair for booting those dropkicks through the uprights."

Cagle, of course, was well aware of Benny's capabilities, having witnessed his feats firsthand as Benny's teammate in New York. After watching his new quarterback in a training-camp exhibition game against a local pro outfit called the Paterson Hawks, McEwan became a believer too.

"That man is the smartest signal caller I have ever seen," McEwan gushed. "It's just too bad if any defensive men are out of position, for Benny will spot the mistake at once. He sizes up a situation quicker than any player I can recall. There is no doubt that he was handicapped last year by his many duties off and on the football field, and if anyone feels Friedman has slipped, he will discover his mistake this season. As far as his passing is concerned I don't think there is any doubt that we have yet to see his like."

Unfortunately for Brooklyn, Benny didn't get a chance to validate the hopes of his new owner and coach in the Dodgers' season opener against the Bears. While tackling the rugged Jack Manders in the first minutes of the game at Ebbets Field, Benny was knocked cold when Manders's knee slammed into his head. Friedman spent the rest of the game in the showers and then on the sideline, trying to remember his name.

Benny rebounded well from that knockout. The next week, against new league entry Cincinnati, Friedman passed the Reds silly, leading the Dodgers to a 27–0 romp. It was the perfect prelude to their next game, against the Giants, a battle with much more at stake than a mere game in the league standings.

For starters, there was the brewing New York–Brooklyn rivalry. It was a rivalry still in its infancy, to be sure, not yet having generated the passions stoked by the decades-old feud between the baseball Giants and Dodgers. But it was New York against Brooklyn, and it captured the attention of the New York sporting world.

Then there was the "revenge" angle. The circumstances surrounding Benny's departure from the Giants were no secret. Friedman still cared for

Tim Mara, but he was still bitter, too, and he wanted this game. So did former Giants Chris Cagle and Shipwreck Kelly.

And maybe the most intriguing angle was the duel between Benny Friedman and the Giants quarterback—none other than Harry Newman. Mara had signed Newman earlier that year following Harry's graduation from Michigan. The rookie had played spectacularly in his first few games for the Giants, inspiring comparisons to Benny. It was more than a little ironic that the promising scholastic quarterback Benny had mentored had followed Friedman first as an all-American quarterback and now as the leader and star of the New York Giants. And of course, the fact that Friedman and Newman were both Jewish proved irresistible to many writers covering the lead-up to the game, not to mention a good number of the thirty-five thousand New Yorkers who trekked to the Polo Grounds to watch it.

Both teacher and pupil lived up to their billing and their reputations. Newman sliced up the Dodgers with breathtaking runs and timely passes. Benny hit on thirteen of twenty-three throws and consistently crashed into the Giants' line for significant gains. But the pupil's supporting cast outstripped his teacher's. Red Badgro and Ray Flaherty and Glenn Campbell on the ends, Bo Molenda and Ken Strong, finally a Giant, in the backfield, and the irrepressible lineman Mel Hein were too much for Brooklyn. Benny managed a late touchdown pass to Paul Riblett, but it was too late and too little as the Giants defeated their interborough rival, 21–7.

Though not quite the otherworldly player he had been from '27 through '31, Friedman was still good enough to joust with Dutch Clark, Glenn Presnell, and Newman for the league's lead in passing for most of the season. Benny was the NFL players' overwhelming choice for their 1933 All-Pro team, over Newman and Clark and all the rest. Even the Giants went for Benny over Newman, their sensational rookie leader. "[If] Benny was placed behind the line of scrimmage in a wheelchair, he would still be the most dangerous man in the league," one Giant player declared. Another Giant expanded on that assessment:

"If anyone thinks he can tell ahead of time what Benny is going to do, he has another guess coming. Friedman is the smartest, most observing man that ever stepped on a football field. What is more important, he is the greatest passer the game has ever seen, and he has driven many a defensive back crazy trying to guess whether to play in close for a line play or to float out for a pass. There isn't a single doubt that Friedman is the best."

But his feeling that he was wasting his time playing pro ball was becoming harder to ignore. Thanks to Red Grange and Halas and Tim Mara and Lambeau—and Benny—the NFL was beginning, ever so subtly, to emerge from its dark ages. Strangely enough, the league was hanging on even as the Great Depression was battering so many other enterprises. For someone caught up in the middle of it, like Benny, it was tough to sense any progress. In a piece published in the November 25, 1933, issue of *Collier's*, Benny rambled on at length about the fleeting fame and glory of the college football star and warned future campus heroes to resist the attractive, but ultimately unfulfilling, seduction of professional football:

Consider my own experience. When I left college I wanted, more than anything else, to be a stockbroker. Instead I became a pro football player, in Chicago, in Cleveland and in Brooklyn. For the past six years I've made ten thousand dollars a year at pro football.

It's been fun, hard-earned fun; but where has it got me? I'm still in football, while scores of men I know have turned to other things. One of these was worth his 228 pounds in gold as a pro football player or as a boxing or wrestling gate-puller. Instead, he threw his All-America football glory aside and as an intern specialized in heart diseases. Now he's thriving in medical practice and thoroughly satisfied with life.

Money? I asked this ex-hero about that. He hasn't made a lot of money—not as much in the aggregate as I have. But his future is assured, while I, on the verge of thirty, still have to scout around for mine, with football rapidly becoming no pastime for an aging gent. My best advice to all gridders is to play the game as a college function—then forget it as a postgraduate career. The intelligence necessary . . . to make your degree in any recognized school is not something to be thrown away on professional sport unless you're a world-beater in the ring, which is most unlikely, or a wow of a baseball player—for that's the steadiest of all pro sports employment.

· · ·

Elected mayor in 1933, Fiorello LaGuardia immediately became New York City's beacon of light amidst the Depression's darkness. LaGuardia had a zest for his job that had been sorely lacking in Beau James Walker, his laconic predecessor, and he worked tirelessly to create jobs in the city. His irrepressible optimism and compassion for the underprivileged instilled hope in a time of despair. He had no patience or tolerance for organized crime or the corrupt Tammany Hall machine that had propped up Walker for so long. Though LaGuardia was nominally a Republican, his ideology was liberal, as evidenced by his support for such causes as labor unions and women's suffrage.

And with anti-Semitism increasing at home and Hitler rising to power in Germany, the outspoken mayor, whose mother was a Jewish immigrant from Italy, was at his outspoken best in voicing support for the Jews. A letter LaGuardia would write in September 1936 to the editor of a local Jewish periodical was but one of many expressions of his sympathies:

> As Mayor of the City of New York, and personally, it gives me pleasure to extend through your publication to the citizens of the Jewish Faith in New York City, my sincerest greetings on the Eve of the observance of the coming Holy Days . . .
>
> The world is now passing through a cycle of hatred inspired and fostered at its start by a demagogue whose only appeal was that of prejudice in seeking the support of the uneducated.
>
> Similar previous cycles are recorded in history. They have always been coincident with the rise to power of small-minded men, too minute in statesmanlike stature to have any confidence in their own ability to retain the heights for long. These puppets always have tried to retain their place in the sun by despotism and an appeal to the baser elements.
>
> None have successfully wielded their staffs of oppression for long. With their fall have passed the dark cycles. Enlightened public opinion saw to that and will again in the present crisis.
>
> The Jews of the world have contributed more than their share to civilization. Civilization will thwart the efforts of any tyrant to destroy this great people.

With this kind of kinship for and with the Jewish people, LaGuardia's desire for an improved football program at the "Jewish University of America," as City College was known, was no surprise. Now LaGuardia was eyeing Benny as the coach to build that program.

Shoehorned between Harlem's St. Nicholas Park to the west and Amsterdam Avenue to the east, the City College of New York (CCNY) was an urban oasis of opportunity for New York City kids who wanted to go to college but couldn't afford it. CCNY offered free tuition to all New Yorkers, and in the early 1930s, with the country reeling from the Depression, that was no small feature.

For New York's Jewish kids, CCNY was particularly attractive. There were no religious quotas at "City," unlike at Columbia, its upscale neighbor a few subway stops to the south. If you could meet the school's academic standards—which, if not onerous, were no pushover either—you were welcome there. And in the 1920s and '30s, droves of Jewish kids enrolled, most of them children of immigrants, taking the IRT train to Broadway and 137th Street and walking a few blocks up a steep hill to Amsterdam Avenue and their chance at an education.

The City students played football, too, and in the '20s, the Lavender had fielded some competitive teams; in 1930, as a matter of fact, the Lavender had posted a commendable 5–2–1 mark. Then the program plummeted, producing only five wins over the next three seasons. Attendance at home games, never huge at City in any case, dwindled with the spike in the number in the loss column. By the end of the dreadful 1933 campaign that saw City finish at 1–5–1, the 137th Street IRT station at rush hour attracted larger crowds than the games at Lewisohn Stadium, City's home park.

LaGuardia wasn't looking to build another Michigan or Notre Dame, but he did want the upper Manhattan school to return to respectability. Friedman, the popular mayor thought, was the man to get it there. He would galvanize the moribund program the moment he stepped foot on campus. His football knowledge and leadership skills were peerless. And, just like the majority of the football team and student body at large, Benny was Jewish.

Students, alumni, and the administration had begun campaigning for a replacement for longtime City coach Harold Parker back in November as the squad was staggering through the misery of its third consecutive losing season. It was then that LaGuardia approached Benny.

Maybe this wooing was the final push Benny needed to quit playing. He'd passed on a few exhibition games the Dodgers played following their league finale in early December 1933. On December 19, Benny announced his retirement as a player and his intention to seek a coaching position.

City's interest in Friedman was an open secret, and it was widely assumed that the coaching position Benny referred to was with the Lavender. LaGuardia was a tough man to turn down and Benny was interested in the job, but there still were the matters of salary and staffing. Benny wanted a $5,000 salary for himself and reasonable salaries for his handpicked assistants, Paul Riblett, Saul Mielziner, and Joe Alexander. With equipment needs and other expenses, the total budget for the 1934–1935 season would be in the neighborhood of $10,000. And City didn't have the money.

But with LaGuardia pushing for Friedman and the student body and alumni buzzing at the chance to have the famous quarterback as their coach, the parties found a way around the budgetary snag. The City College Advisory Football Committee, an alumni group intoxicated with the idea of a Friedman-led Lavender football renaissance, agreed to raise the necessary funds through solicitations from alumni. The school administration approved Benny's hiring on this basis, and in March 1934, Benny Friedman was announced as the new coach at CCNY.

A few days later, about a thousand CCNY students welcomed the new coach they'd been clamoring for at a pep rally at the Great Hall on campus. Benny told the students what they had come to hear: the dreary football situation in upper Manhattan was about to change. There would be spring practice for the first time in years. There would be a focus on fundamentals—no surprise given Fielding Yost's devotion to them. Benny would push New York City officials for a new practice field. There would be a major effort to cut back on injuries. And the team would have a two-week preseason training camp in late summer in the country, several hours away from Manhattan's distractions.

The next week some three hundred would-be Friedmans and Granges and Nagurskis reported for spring practice and tryouts. By contrast, only about ninety players had reported for spring tryouts in Benny's freshman year at Michigan. Of course, the vast majority of the three hundred "prospects" had no chance of sticking with the team. They were there for an up close experience with the famous Benny Friedman, even if only for a few days.

After an upbeat several weeks of spring practice, Benny and his staff whittled down the number of potential team members to about forty. That's when Friedman really began to understand the tall task ahead of him. Even among those forty, signs of real football ability were scarce. A good number of them had never even played before, and those who had weren't exactly all-American timber. And they were, with an exception here and there, undersized. Or, as Benny would put it some years later, "Many boys needed a good meal."

Lewisohn Stadium, where the Lavender both practiced and played their home games, needed some grass. The playing surface was a combination of stones, nails, broken glass—enough to support an annual "pebble picking contest" and fill a dump truck, according to Stan Brodsky, one of Benny's players. The Doric-columned stadium, designed in the style of an ancient amphitheater right down to the concrete bleachers, was the frequent site of concerts given by some of the music world's greatest luminaries. Thousands of spectators would be seated on the field for these shows and, with such repeated wear and tear, field maintenance became a virtual impossibility. It didn't help that daily football practice never gave the field a chance to breathe, either. "Lewisohn Stadium was a chore to play in," another of Friedman's players, Bill Silverman, said decades later.

As if a lack of players and a decent field weren't enough to deal with, Benny would also have to face the fact of life that basketball, under Coach Nat Holman, was king at City and would remain that way regardless of how strong a football program Benny might build. Holman had been coaching at City since 1919, and "Mr. Basketball," as he was known, had also been heralded as perhaps the sport's greatest player while playing for the original Boston Celtics during the 1920s. Holman's City teams were a New York powerhouse, and he could be a little proprietary about preserving his team's lofty status at the school. Bernard Slegel, a City basketball player, recalled how Holman politely but in no uncertain terms rebuffed Benny's attempt to recruit Slegel for the football team.

A school with a tradition of losing football, dreadful facilities, and no apparent prospects for a reversal of fortune would not seem a logical coaching destination for a two-time Michigan all-American and the greatest forward passer in the game's history. Benny's decision to coach at City may have been rooted in his Jewishness. The mayor chose Benny, a Jew, to resurrect a program at a school that was overwhelmingly Jewish. LaGuardia may not have been motivated primarily by religious considerations when he offered Friedman the job, and Benny may not have been motivated primarily by religious considerations when he agreed to take it. But he certainly could not have been blind to the circumstances and may have acted out of a sense of obligation, however subliminal, to his coreligionists.

The explanation for Benny's acceptance of the City job may also be, in part, that he felt he had no other coaching options. If so, that premise begs a question: why? Why had the man universally praised as a field general without peer, Fielding Yost's quarterback who "never made a mistake," been unable to land a job with a major program? Benny's Jewishness must be considered as a possible answer, even if it is unprovable empirically and even if Friedman himself would have been the last person to suggest it as an answer. Anti-Semitism in the 1930s could be virulent and unabashed, as with the rantings of Father Coughlin in America and Hitler in Europe. Or it could be far more subtle, the unspoken explanation for injustices great and small. While Friedman may well have been turned down at other schools strictly on a perceived lack of merit or because a given school may have honestly felt that other candidates were stronger, Benny's Jewishness cannot be discounted as a possible factor.

. . .

The thirty-six New York City–area boys Benny invited to training camp at the Wayne Country Club in Pennsylvania's Pocono Mountains likely hadn't spent much time in such a bucolic setting. The trip was a treat, to be sure, but it came with a price. Benny, along with Paul Riblett, Saul Mielziner, and Joe Alexander, had two weeks to teach the boys a lifetime of football fundamentals and get them into game condition, and the coaches drove the boys accordingly. The hard work seemed to be paying dividends: in a scrimmage played just before the close of training camp, the Beavers—the team's new nickname—dismantled an experienced local team of hardscrabble coal miners.

"City never has had a football team like this present edition . . . [Friedman] really has accomplished wonders with a group of boys who have little in the way of gridiron tradition behind them," the *New York Times* reported following the scrimmage.

Senior quarterback Adolph Cooper did have some gridiron experience behind him—all bad. Cooper had joined the team in 1931, just in time for its miserable three-year run. Benny quickly picked Cooper out as a real player. He could pass and run and punt with impressive accuracy that buried opponents in their own end. Friedman was also starting to like what he saw from several linemen, particularly a raw-boned, six-foot-two-inch, 192-pound football neophyte from Manhattan named Roy Ilowit. The beginner from Manhattan was strong and tough, and he proved to be a quick study when it came to football fundamentals. As the Beavers broke camp and headed back to Manhattan, Friedman had good reason to feel optimistic about the opener against rival Brooklyn College at Lewisohn Stadium on September 29.

A week before the game, the Brooklyn College freshman squad lost a game against Brooklyn's Erasmus Hall High School. Erasmus was led by a quarterback who for three seasons had been turning heads with his spectacular passing and outstanding running. Thick-chested and thick-legged and as tough as they come, it seemed like every college in the Northeast was preparing to open its doors to the Jewish boy from Brooklyn once he graduated. His name was Sid Luckman, and his idol was Benny Friedman.

. . .

City's four home games in 1933 drew a total of about seven thousand fans. The Beavers nearly matched that total on the wet, clammy evening of September 29, 1934. Five thousand rooters—City's largest opening-day crowd ever—filed into the concrete bleachers for Benny's CCNY debut despite a steady rain pelting down from the dark sky. Friedman disliked night games altogether—he thought the cool night air prevented players from perspiring—and the rain only made matters worse.

Brooklyn College, like CCNY, is one of a number of separately chartered colleges that comprise the broader City University of the City of New York. Like CCNY, its roster was heavily populated with Jewish players. The Kingsmen had fared better than CCNY in recent seasons, winning three games in 1932 and again in 1933. Curiously, though, they hadn't beaten City; two of the Beavers' three victories in the past two seasons had come against Brooklyn.

The Kingsmen looked poised to interrupt their losing streak with the Beavers when, early in the game, Cooper's punt was blocked near Brooklyn's forty-yard line. The fans in Lewisohn could have been excused for feeling they'd seen it all before. It was the type of sloppy play that had plagued City for years—the type of play that always seemed to instigate a total collapse. But the team steadied. They stopped Brooklyn on the Kingsmen's ensuing possession and, though pinned in their own end for most of the first half, kept Brooklyn off the scoreboard.

In the second half, the Beavers began reaping returns from the endless drills they'd slogged through in the Pennsylvania hills. Adolph Cooper began hitting passes and running through holes in the Brooklyn line. Before the half was done, the senior quarterback scored three touchdowns, including one on a seventy-yard kick return. Brooklyn's offense had no response. The Kingsmen limped out of Lewisohn Stadium for the bus ride back to Brooklyn on the short end of an 18–0 score and with their losing streak to City intact.

The Beavers won three of their next four games: a 31–0 thumping of the University of Baltimore at Lewisohn Stadium, a victory over Lowell, and a hard-fought 12–7 triumph over Drexel that reversed the 32–0 thrashing Drexel had given City a year earlier. Even City's only loss in that stretch, a 19–6 decision to a bigger, more talented Providence team led by future NFL star Hank Soar, showed the Beavers' marked improvement—their losses to Providence in the two previous seasons had been by scores of 39–6 and 46–0.

City's vastly improved play under Friedman earned them some local newsprint that was typically reserved for the likes of metropolitan powers Fordham, Columbia, and NYU. "[City] is the new football sensation of the Big Town," renowned columnist Joe Williams wrote. "I have heard more of City College in the last five weeks than in the seven years I have been a resident of this city." And as the *Brooklyn Times Union* declared:

At the box office, which is the best indication of a new football regime at any college, Friedman has done equally well. Despite rain at every one of the home games, City College drew an average attendance of 5,500 per game or a 3-game total of 17,000.

But it is not only in these things that Friedman has proved to be a real football magician. School spirit, the intangible something which only evidenced itself in the past at City College in the form of an occasional snake dance or pep rally, has become a real thing. Friedman, depending upon his dynamic personality and popularity, has aroused the book-worms and the grinds, and the horn-rimmed Phi Betas with his stirring weekly football talks to the point where they are perusing the football 'dope sheets' instead of their Schopenhauer, Kant, Milton and Spinoza and are using their knowledge of the very best Aristotelian logic to figure out next week's scores.

On campus and throughout the city, hope started to build that Benny's team might just upset powerful intra-city foes Manhattan College and NYU in their final two games. Friedman even joined in the giddiness. The fact that City hadn't defeated Manhattan in their annual battle since 1926 didn't stop Benny from displaying his usual bravado before the game. When reporters asked how he planned to deal with the tough Jaspers, he shot back with a query of his own: "What do you think folks would say if we beat Manhattan by 20 to 0?"

The Jaspers showed the fifteen thousand fans at Ebbets Field that the gulf separating the two football teams still had plenty of breadth despite City's obvious upgrade. As the Beavers had discovered against Providence, a weight differential averaging fifteen pounds per man is a difficult obstacle to surmount. The Jaspers' startling hundred-yard touchdown return of an intercepted Adolph Cooper pass had to be particularly annoying to Benny, who as a player always took special pride in never having had an interception of his returned for a touchdown. The Jaspers won, 21–0.

The following week, NYU had its turn against Benny's upstarts, trouncing the uptowners, 38–13, and giving coach Mal Stevens a nice win over Benny, his former assistant at Yale.

Disappointing as the two season-ending thumpings were, Benny had revitalized the woeful City football program. Working mostly with beginners and on a shoestring budget, he'd transformed an inept 1–5–1 group into a winning squad. The 4–3 Beavers weren't exactly Rose Bowl material, but Benny had given Fiorello LaGuardia the competitive team he was looking for.

In the days following the end of the season, the sense of pride and accomplishment around Convent Avenue was tempered by concern for a city player who had been injured during the NYU game. Twenty-one-year-old Aaron Greenwald, a junior reserve back, had sustained an abdominal injury that at first blush did not appear to be serious. But after attending classes for a few days after the game, the young man fell seriously ill and was rushed to Morrisania Hospital in the Bronx, near his home. Over the next several weeks, Benny, along with Greenwald's teammates, kept a vigil in his hospital room. They donated blood and did what they could, and the stricken player grimly held on.

On Thanksgiving eve, a couple of weeks after the NYU game, it was announced that Benny would play quarterback for the Brooklyn Dodgers in their Thanksgiving meeting with the Giants in Ebbets Field. For the 1934 season, the NFL had taken another step to unleash the potential of the passing game. "Influenced by Benny's success," George Halas wrote, "the rules committee moved to slenderize the 'prolate spheroid,' as the football was then described in the official manual." The sleeker ball, far easier to throw than the fat watermelon Benny had toiled with, would over the next decade facilitate the emergence of a number of talented young passers, including Sid Luckman; Harry Newman; Green Bay's Arnie Herber and Cecil Isbell; Clarence "Ace" Parker of the Brooklyn Dodgers; and a tall, razor-thin whippet from Texas with a slingshot for an arm that earned him his nickname—"Slingin'" Sammy Baugh. These outstanding quarterbacks would take that slimmer ball and fill the air with it throughout NFL stadiums in the 1930s and into the 1940s, as Benny had done with the fat ball a decade earlier. With more great passers came more great receivers, most notably Green Bay's Don Hutson, widely considered the greatest receiver of the league's first several decades and one of the greatest of any decade.

Fans would warm to the increased emphasis on the passing game. League-wide average attendance would approach twenty thousand fans per game. As the country would begin to escape the Depression's doldrums, NFL franchises would stabilize. In 1936, the NFL would institute an annual draft of college players that would raise the league's profile and standing in its ongoing fight for parity with the college game.

It is more than a little ironic that Benny, whose unique brilliance led to the adoption of the slimmer ball in 1934 as well as the adoption the year before of the new rules that favored the passing game, didn't stick around the NFL long enough to enjoy the benefits his brilliance had wrought. And unquestionably, from an ability standpoint, he could have. "I had some good years left," Benny said in commenting on his retirement, "but of course I didn't know pro football was going to progress as much as it did. If I had, I might have stayed in."

In the Dodgers-Giants 1934 Thanksgiving battle, Friedman would at least get one chance to throw the slimmed-down ball. Benny hadn't played in a game since walking off the field in Boston a year earlier. Still, Chris Cagle and Shipwreck Kelly thought Benny could help the Dodgers defeat the Giants, whom they were battling for the NFL's Eastern Division title.

Benny had told Kelly he'd seen all of the Giants' home games that fall and was totally familiar with their tendencies. And Cagle and Kelly knew that Benny had scrimmaged frequently with the Beavers and that, as always, he was in shape.

The Dodgers' player-owners found out, however, that scrimmaging with a midlevel local college team and playing against a highly motivated group of New York Giants were two different things entirely. Friedman ran with some success, but Mel Hein, Red Badgro, and Ken Strong were not an ideal group against which to shed a year's worth of rust. Benny did nothing with the slimmer ball; his passing was totally ineffective and the Giants routed the Dodgers, 27–0.

As it turned out, this would be the last National Football League game Benny would ever play.

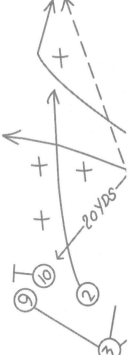

NINETEEN

Coach and Commander

O n December 9, a month after his devastating injury, Aaron Green-wald lost his valiant struggle. Greenwald's death plunged the CCNY community into mourning. But the tragedy did not blind the college's administration to Friedman's outstanding work in revitalizing the football program. The school rehired Benny and his staff for the 1935 and then the 1936 season, although alumni contributions were again necessary to fund Benny's salary. After Benny led the Beavers to respectable 4–3 and 4–4 marks in '35 and '36, the college finally made room for their coach in its budget for the 1937 campaign and granted him a tenured position as a hygiene (physical education) instructor.

What the college couldn't give Benny was much talent to work with. CCNY's focus on academics and the limited geographical area that supplied its students virtually guaranteed a paucity of skilled players. Friedman understood this as well as anyone. "All we need up here," Friedman cracked following his reappointment for the '37 season, "is seven linemen and four backs. We have the place."

City's roster for '37 actually may have been its strongest ever. The team featured a little more size than usual and a core of skilled veterans that

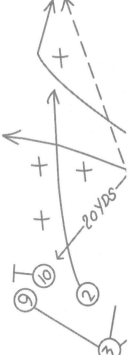

included linemen Bill Silverman and Jerry Stein and backs Walter Schi-
menty and Harry Stein. With this bigger, better team and with Benny developing City's passing attack, the Beavers marched to a 5–2 record—their
best ever. It didn't hurt, either, that City had dropped local brutes Manhattan and NYU from their schedule.

One strong team that City didn't drop was Providence College. The
Friars had routinely pushed around the Beavers over the years, and the '37
meeting figured to feature more of the same—and then some. Just a couple
of weeks earlier, Providence had lost a 7–0 squeaker to a Holy Cross team
that would go on to defeat national powers Georgia and Georgetown on its
way to an 8–0–2 record. Meanwhile, the Beavers were coming off a miserable 13–7 loss against Hobart in which they fumbled thirteen times.

Benny challenged his boys in practice that week, and against Providence in Lewisohn Stadium, they responded with maybe the best football
ever played by a Beavers squad. Benny's boys did more than hold on to the
ball. They whipped the stunned Friars, 8–6, employing an unyielding defense and just enough of the deception on offense that Benny had implemented for the game.

Friedman's success at City was borne of a coaching style that reflected
his overall personality—and not a little of Fielding Yost's philosophy. Fundamentals were stressed. Practice and preparation were paramount. Top
physical condition was a hallmark. "We ran and ran and ran and ran,"
quarterback Stanley Brodsky said, recalling the rigors of preseason training.
"By the time we were done with that training camp, we felt like we could
run through a brick wall." To Benny, the safety of his boys on the football
field was, according to halfback Harold Goldstein, "his main concern."

Always fit, well groomed, and, seemingly, always tan, Benny struck an
impressive figure—"like a Rodin," Brodsky said. He was a strong-willed
coach with an eye for detail, quick to address a player's errors and not beyond devoting entire practice sessions to lectures designed to ensure that a
poor performance would not be repeated. But he was not a screamer. "He
was very good at communicating and being friendly and so forth in a

coach's way with everyone on the team," lineman Bill Silverman said. "I never really saw him blow his top at anybody for an error or things like that."

Administrators at City seemed to share Silverman's view. "Mr. Friedman works very well with both students and his colleagues," administrators wrote in an evaluation. "He is exceedingly helpful in every way and particularly watchful of the health condition of those who come under his jurisdiction. He has a pleasing personality which he uses to good effect in his work."

The educators at City also liked that Friedman understood that football at City was secondary to education. "Of course we shall maintain our requirements of high scholarship for all students who wish to play," college president Frederick Robinson had said upon announcing Benny's reappointment for the 1935 season. "We shall not make any concession to athletics but will continue to encourage football as an amateur sport for young men whose prime purpose in life is to study. We are fortunate in having Mr. Friedman, a football expert who understands the relative importance of a football season and a whole college career."

Benny accepted football's secondary role at City, but he didn't stop yearning for a head coaching job at a big-time program. Back in January of '37, certain reports had named him as a leading candidate for the coaching position at the University of Texas. Nothing had come of it, but as 1937 drew to a close, the former Michigan all-American seemed to have a real shot at the job he coveted—the head coaching position at his alma mater. Harry Kipke, Michigan's great punter in the early '20s and head coach since 1929, was in trouble in Ann Arbor. Kipke had guided the Wolverines to two national championships and a slew of Big Ten titles in his first five years. Then the losses started flowing. Michigan finished at 1–7 in 1937, their second 1–7 mark in three seasons. Kipke was revered in Ann Arbor as one of the Wolverines' all-time great players, but Michigan's alumni and athletic powers-that-be had little tolerance for 1–7 seasons.

On December 9, 1937, Michigan's athletic board informed Kipke that his contract, due to expire in the spring, would not be renewed. Despite the storm that had been gathering above his head, Kipke professed to be shocked at his dismissal. Michigan, for its part, claimed that Harry had refused the school's offer to allow him to resign.

No sooner had Kipke's tenure ended than a number of Michigan alumni began boosting Benny as the Wolverines' next coach. Most prominent among these supporters was the influential Michigan Club of New York, which wrote in the December 1937 issue of its magazine: "Benny Friedman is still winning orchids from the sporting writers, 10 years after he played his last college football game. This time the newspapers are singing his praises as a miracle coach for the wonders he has done at City College under conditions that would break any man's heart." Coincidentally, the day after news of Kipke's firing had broken, Friedman attended a dinner in Manhattan given by the club. When Benny, acting as toastmaster, rose to preside over the festivities, the crowd broke into a prolonged chant of "Our next coach!" and showered him with a thunderous standing ovation. Benny was under contract with City College and so spoke only briefly about the prospects of the Michigan job. "Naturally I would like to coach Michigan," Friedman said. "Every football player's ambition is to return to his alma mater."

The administration at Michigan, however, was in no rush to coronate Friedman, or anyone else, for that matter. Few coaching jobs were as prestigious as the one now open in Ann Arbor, and the opening attracted a flood of candidates. The authorities at Michigan were determined to evaluate all of them. "No member of a school faculty should be selected with more painstaking care than the athletic coach," Fielding Yost, still Michigan's athletic director, had once said. Benny would have to wait, and despite the support of the New York alumni and reports published within days of Kipke's dismissal indicating that Benny had the inside track to the job, his initial prospects didn't look good. Michigan had compiled a list of eight "preferred" candidates, and Benny wasn't one of them. Some reports indicated that Michigan was looking for a coach older than Benny, who was just thirty-two. And another report asserted that the powers-that-be in Ann Arbor had decided they wanted a coach with no previous Michigan connection—a condition that obviously ruled out Benny.

A few days after basking in the adoration of New York's Michigan alums, Friedman attended another Manhattan "function" that was significantly less enjoyable. The setting wasn't a glitzy Manhattan ballroom. It was a dark-paneled, dimly lit Manhattan courtroom. The occasion was jury selection in the case of William P. Fleckenstein against Benny Friedman and P. F. Collier & Son.

The October 15, 1932, issue of *Collier's*, the popular national magazine, included a piece written by Benny with ghostwriter John B. Kennedy that rambled about the demands of pro football. Mixed into the piece was a choice paragraph that described Fleckenstein's penchant for creating mayhem:

Fleckenstein of Iowa, a big, tough 225-pound guard, played for the Chicago Bears, and when you ran into him you quickly realized that his idea of play was loser take all—on the chin. The Cleveland Bulldogs were about unanimous after one meeting with Mr. Fleckenstein that he was a specialist at infighting during scrimmages. As a committee of one I warned him about this before our return match. But Fleckenstein went on impartially pasting the boys when inspiration seized him. It just isn't part of the code to call attention to a rough gent who's discreet enough to slug under cover. We told Fleckenstein to his face. His reply was instant—sock upon sock . . .

Fleckenstein, it seems, took offense at Benny's depiction of his excessively exuberant play. He had sued Benny and *Collier's* for libel back in July 1933 in New York Supreme Court, alleging that the article had injured his "good name, credit and reputation," and had damaged him "in his business or profession of playing professional football." Friedman and *Collier's* pleaded the most straightforward legal defense to a libel claim—"justification," or, in layman's terms, truth.

Fleckenstein had pursued the suit relentlessly, and lawyers for Friedman and *Collier's* responded in kind. The parties had filed motion upon motion. One such filing, in which Fleckenstein sought a dismissal of the justification defense, even reached the Court of Appeals, New York's highest court. The court refused to dismiss the defense and in the process made Benny a party to a small piece of precedent-setting libel law jurisprudence.

When the lawyers weren't filing motions, they were busy taking deposi-
tions of the parties and a number of players who had had the misfortune to
line up across from Fleckenstein at one time or another. One such player
was Robert "Dozy" Howard, Benny's former teammate on the Detroit
Wolverines and the Giants. Howard testified in vivid detail as to how
Fleckenstein had broken his nose with a closed-hand smash in a game between the Wolverines and the Bears in 1928. Howard also described Wild
Bill's notorious sucker punch of the Giants' Cliff Ashburn at Wrigley Field
in 1929:

> After the game was over—the game was ended—and we were starting
> for our clubhouse, dressing room, both teams were going to their
> dressing rooms after the game was over, and Mr. Fleckenstein came
> from behind Clifford Ashburn, who was walking along with me, and
> struck him in the face . . .
>
> Then the majority . . . of our team started after Mr. Fleckenstein
> and ran him to the dugout which led to the dressing room of the
> Chicago Bears. There, after Mr. Fleckenstein outran every member of
> our team to the dugout, we were stopped by a number of policemen,
> where we were unable to enter the dugout leading to the Chicago
> Bears' dressing room.

Fleckenstein, in his deposition, denied being the dirty player portrayed
in the *Collier's* piece. He flatly denied striking either Howard or Ashburn
and even denied knowing them.

With such starkly contradictory versions of the events, this was a lawsuit that could not be resolved without a trial. And so there were Friedman
and Fleckenstein at the courthouse on that late December morning in
1937, digging in for a trial that would culminate more than four years of
combative litigation. For five days the jury and presiding judge Aron
Steuer, the son of famed New York trial attorney Max Steuer, watched and
listened as Fleckenstein and Friedman and their respective witnesses traded
verbal blows.

Friedman certainly couldn't have anticipated such an arduous saga.
The piece's portrayal of Fleckenstein was but a sliver of a long conversa-

tional discourse on pro football, and while the passages in question described Fleck's roughhousing, their tone was closer to playful than malicious. At the time the article was published, Fleckenstein had apparently retired after managing to play seven years, a long career by the standards of the day, particularly for a journeyman lineman. And Fleck's penchant for extracurricular physicality was hardly a secret around the league. It was difficult to imagine the article had caused any real injury to his "good name and reputation" or that he'd been "damaged in his business." In the end, that's how the jurors saw it. They handed Fleckenstein a pyrrhic victory, somehow finding that the article had libeled him—and awarding him damages in the princely sum of six cents.

Benny's article was an entertaining, candid piece on the trials and tribulations of the early days of pro ball, including its less refined elements as exemplified by the section on Fleckenstein. But with portions of the preceding four years spent reviewing legal documents and testifying in courthouses, Benny had paid a price for his candor.

Meanwhile, Fielding Yost and the Michigan athletic board remained tight-lipped about their ongoing search for Michigan's new coach. The leading candidate for the job seemed to change from day to day, depending on which rumor appeared most believable. In late January 1938, Benny, apparently writing off his dim chances for the Michigan job, sent a letter to the athletic manager at the University of Oregon expressing interest in the newly vacated head coaching position there.

On January 31, Oregon announced that their next coach would be University of Arizona coach Tex Oliver. Then on February 8, Michigan announced the hiring of Princeton coach Fritz Crisler as the Wolverines' next head man. Crisler also received a commitment from Michigan's athletic board that he would succeed Fielding Yost as athletic director when the Michigan patriarch was ready to retire. In Crisler, Michigan would be getting a coach with significant big-time experience: eight years assisting Amos Alonzo Stagg with the perennially strong football program at the University of Chicago, followed by two years as the head man at Minnesota and six seasons as head coach at Princeton during which the Tigers went 35–9–5.

Friedman was back to picking up nails from the Lewisohn Stadium dirt patch. Though it wasn't Ann Arbor, New York City wasn't a bad place to be if, like Benny, you had a little celebrity attached to your name. He hosted a Sunday morning radio show on WGN called *Sunday Morning Quarterback*. He appeared frequently as a guest on other radio programs, such as Ed Herlihy's *If I Had the Chance*. Wheaties came calling in 1937, making Benny one of the first athletes honored with what would become the gold standard for the athlete as pitchman when his likeness appeared on the company's cereal box. He was featured in newspaper and magazine ads endorsing a variety of products from Studebaker automobiles to Williams Shaving Cream, from coffee to Sulka ties.

In between all the radio shows and print ads, Benny began attending Brooklyn Law School. But the law degree that had been one of his goals since childhood remained elusive; for reasons that are unclear, Friedman withdrew after completing only a year and a half of the three-year program.

As always, Benny kept in top shape. He often practiced with his CCNY players, and he showed off his athleticism by playing squash. This racquet sport was typically the province of blue bloods from Harvard and Yale and Princeton and athletic bastions like the New York Athletic Club, where men with names like Friedman weren't welcome. But in New York there was a haven for athletic-minded Jewish men called the City Athletic Club. The CAC fielded a squash team that held its own in high-level tournament competition. Benny became a part of that team in 1937, playing in the middle and lower flights.

Friedman also worked the public speaking circuit during his time at City College. He had the name, good looks, confident bearing, and command of the subject matter required of a natural public speaker. And he had a midwestern-accented eloquence that was unusual for a footballer. As a lecturer on the Redpath Chautaqua circuit, a traveling cultural lecture circuit featuring prominent politicians, writers, entertainers, and athletes, Friedman spoke on such subjects as sport's place in broader society and its role as "a leveler of prejudice and intolerance." Schools and civic associations placed him high on their list of guest speakers, as did Jewish organizations such as B'nai B'rith and the committee organizing America's team for the first Maccabiah Games in Palestine. His appearances weren't always for weighty causes; often he would speak at nothing more elaborate than a men's club breakfast at a local temple.

And Manhattan did not want for football functions. At one affair at the Commodore Hotel, Benny, Sid Luckman, and Sammy Baugh, decked out in suits and ties and pocket squares, repaired to a guest room and proceeded to treat a herd of writers to an impromptu clinic on forward passing accuracy—complete with real footballs and real passes. First Benny gripped a pigskin and then, fading back behind a chair that served as his "line," fired at a doorknob across the room and launched one of his trademark leaping passes. Slingin' Sam scored a direct hit, knocking the "intended receiver"—a painting—off the wall. Luckman followed suit, nailing a designated spot across the room. It's safe to say that no greater exhibition of forward passing inside a hotel room has ever been given.

In 1939, in addition to his responsibilities at City, Benny became the coach and quarterback of a semiprofessional team called the Cedarhurst Wolverines, Cedarhurst being the Long Island town the team called home and "Wolverines" being an obvious nod to Benny's alma mater. The competition wasn't quite NFL-caliber, but the former pros and college players in the league (including a few of Benny's CCNY standouts such as Bill Silverman and Jerry Stein) played some serious football.

Initially, Benny joined the Wolverines only as coach, not intending to play, but an uneven 3–2–1 start in '39 changed his mind. He was now thirty-four years old and he hadn't played a game in more than five years, but on October 22, 1939, he led Cedarhurst to a 9–0 victory. Four straight victories followed, including 28–7 and 35–6 trouncings of the two teams that had beaten Cedarhurst earlier in the season before Benny's return to action. The Wolverines finished the '39 campaign at 8–2–1, winning every game after Benny began playing. Friedman played again for Cedarhurst in 1940, driving the Wolverines to a 7–1–1 mark. One of Benny's 1940 victims later recalled:

We were quite familiar with Friedman's career before we met him in 1940, when he was the quarterback of the Cedarhurst Wolverines . . . To this day, the ultimate satisfaction we have ever experienced in any athletic encounter was not only to participate against, but to witness, the football genius of Benny Friedman, at the time a semi-potbellied, forty-year-old coach of City College playing football on Sundays with a semipro club on Long Island.

When the game was over, there was not a grass stain on Friedman's gleaming white pants, and, perhaps for the thousandth time, he walked off the field without a trace of battle stress. He had continually tossed passes that were absolutely impossible to defend. This fattish, yet sturdy "old man" had calmly humiliated a tough and capable team.

We hated his guts that day, but we had consolation as we grouched off the field. We had faced one of the greatest football talents and technicians that had ever played the game, ten years past his prime and still incomparable.

· · ·

During his years at City, Benny became a fixture on the "Mourner's Bench," a weekly gathering of New York–area college football coaches organized by Manhattan College coach Chick Meehan. Benny's primary coaching duties were with CCNY, but he did a little moonlighting—he ran a football summer camp for boys in Cheshire, Connecticut, and for a time he coached the semipro Bay Parkways and New York Yankees of the American Football Association.

There was also the occasional charity or all-star game, such as the tilt between a collection of pros and a squad of all-black college stars coached by Friedman. One of Benny's players in that game would go on to earn heroic status while playing baseball for the Brooklyn Dodgers. His name was Jackie Robinson. In another all-star contest, in December 1938, Benny organized and coached a team of New York college stars in a game against the Brooklyn Dodgers to benefit refugees from Nazi Germany. It was quite a treat for Friedman—an opportunity to work, if only for a game, with a squad of college boys talented from top to bottom, including a couple of Benny's own boys from City. The cream of the all-stars, though, was Sid

Luckman. The sensation from Brooklyn's Erasmus High had just ended a spectacular college career at Columbia that had NFL owners salivating. Against the Dodgers, Luckman ignored a completely unprotected broken nose, and his outstanding passing and running kept things respectable for the college boys in a 27–14 loss to the pros.

That all-star game came at the end of another winning season at CCNY: the '38 Beavers team finished with a 4–3 mark. The '38 season, ending with City's 41–14 rout of Moravian College in the final game, was Friedman's high-water mark at the college. The Beavers' fortunes plummeted in 1939 and 1940, as they managed only two wins and a tie in fifteen outings. Brooklyn College, led by quarterback Allie Sherman, who would go on to play several seasons in the NFL and become the New York Giants' head coach, handed City a 14–6 defeat in the 1940 finale. Shortly after that game, a reporter for the *Jewish Digest* asked Friedman how he felt about the difficult season coming to an end. In responding, Benny didn't offer any positive spin or false bravado about how things would turn around next year. "Thank God," he said.

With the end of the '40 season, Benny once again searched for a bigger coaching job. He interviewed for the head coaching job at Ohio State, Michigan's archrival, and was rumored to be a candidate to coach the NFL's Detroit Lions. Neither position worked out, and Friedman re-signed with City for the '41 season.

Somehow, Benny coaxed a recovery out of his boys in '41, guiding them to a 4–4 mark. The grandest moment of the Beavers' return to respectability, if only for one season, was a season-ending 43–13 rout over Brooklyn and Allie Sherman.

Benny's contract with City for the 1941–1942 season ran through June. With World War II now raging, Benny wanted to join the service and do his part, as did many professional athletes of the time, and he didn't seem to give a second thought to the fact that, at thirty-seven, he was substantially older than most enlisted men. He informed CCNY officials of his intention to join the Navy. Friedman had fulfilled Fiorello LaGuardia's mission of restoring some luster to CCNY football. He was proud of his efforts and proud of the undersized and inexperienced boys who had played so hard for him. But he had had enough.

Benny's first posting in the Navy, in July of 1942, was as an officer-in-training at the United States Naval Reserve Midshipman's School, located at Abbot Hall on Northwestern University's Chicago campus. Two weeks later, Friedman was transferred to the Great Lakes Naval Training Station, about an hour north of Chicago on the shores of Lake Michigan.

The main mission at Great Lakes, the nation's largest naval training base at that time, was to get sailors ready for the bloody business of defeating Germany and Japan. "Mothers once reared their sons to be gentlemen but now they must rear them to be killers," Lieutenant Friedman told a civic group shortly after he arrived at Great Lakes. "We naturally don't like this idea, but it's kill or be killed and America isn't ready to die."

They played some football at the base too. In fact, the Great Lakes football team of 1918 that featured George Halas, Jimmy Conzelman, and the Northwestern all-American Paddy Driscoll compiled a 6–0–2 record against a monster schedule, defeating Illinois and Iowa and tying Northwestern and Notre Dame along the way. The mobilization of sailors at Great Lakes ceased with the end of World War I and so did the base's football program. But now, with a new world war raging and sailors again massing at Great Lakes, football returned. A team of former college players with a pro or two mixed in was assembled. Benny accepted head football coach Paul Hinkle's invitation to join his staff that included several other former college stars. One of them was Mickey Cochrane, the soon-to-be Hall of Fame baseball catcher who had been an outstanding back at Boston University in the early 1920s. Cochrane also coached the base's powerful baseball team that featured a slew of major leaguers, including the great pitcher Bob Feller and Yankees slugger Johnny Mize.

Friedman's first game on the sideline for the Great Lakes Bluejackets took place at Michigan Stadium against his beloved Wolverines and Bennie Oosterbaan, who was one of Fritz Crisler's assistants. Despite a 9–0 Michigan victory that day, Great Lakes went on to have a fine season, amassing eight wins and one tie—against Notre Dame—to go along with three losses. The Bluejackets did even better in 1943: a 10–2 record capped by a season-ending 19–14 upset over Notre Dame and their Heisman Trophy winner, Angelo Bertelli. More than twenty thousand delirious sailors at Great Lakes' home field watched their future shipmates ruin an undefeated season for famed coach Frank Leahy and his number-one-ranked Irish.

As exciting as it was to knock off a great Notre Dame team, Benny had not joined the Navy to coach football. He wanted combat duty. Working some connections, Friedman arranged a meeting in Washington with an officer in charge of aircraft carrier personnel who had been at the Naval Academy when Benny played against them. In June 1944, the personnel officer arranged for Friedman's transfer from Great Lakes to the naval training station in Newport, Rhode Island, often the last stateside stop for sailors about to ship out to the war zone. After training in Newport for three months, Lieutenant Benjamin Friedman was assigned to the newly commissioned aircraft carrier USS *Shangri-La* and shipped out on September 15, 1944.

Charles Crump, a shipmate friend of Benny's, recalled that he was reserved about his sporting celebrity. "He didn't promote himself, I can assure you of that," Crump drawled in his Tennessee accent, decades after the two had walked the deck of the *Shangri-La* together. Still, Benny's athletic celebrity preceded him on the ship, and on at least one occasion he flaunted it. On the *Shangri-La's* shakedown cruise, the carrier stopped at the Naval Academy in Annapolis. In the midst of some ribbing between Benny and some of his Naval Academy–graduate shipmates, Benny boasted that if they went ashore, the Academy football coach would ask him to work out with their football team. And Benny, although nearly forty years old, wasn't worried about how he would do. "I'll bet you each five bucks that I'll be the best man out there," Benny challenged his midshipmen buddies. Benny did go ashore, did work out with the Navy team, and, at least by his reckoning, was the best man on the field. It's unclear whether he ever collected on his bet. Regardless of that impromptu performance during the shakedown cruise, the Naval Academy alumni onboard the *Shangri-La*, some of whom had played in Navy's 10–0 ambush of the

Wolverines in 1926, never tired of reminding Benny of that game. Benny naturally preferred to discuss Michigan's 54–0 rout of Navy in 1925.

At the beginning of his tour on the *Shangri-La,* Benny's notions of seeing combat had very little to do with the reality of life at sea. He was the ship's athletic officer (even though the crew's main sporting diversion was volleyball, not football), and most of his time was occupied by mundane chores, hours of watch duty, and yearning for some good home cooking to replace the nearly inedible fare on the ship. "When you write of such things as gefilte fish, my mouth waters," Benny wrote in a letter home to his sister Florence. "It is inconceivable how long we have gone without a good meal."

Keeping his looks, it seems, was a constant concern of Benny's during his time at sea. Sunbathing, the better to keep his tan, was a favorite spare-time activity. Having turned forty in March 1945, his concern about his appearance seemed to match his devotion to maintaining top physical condition. "You might be interested in the fact that I manage to get a little exercise & also to eat very little & as a result maintain my figure," he wrote to his sister. "I can't keep the grey out of my hair or make hair grow on the bald spot, but I can straighten out my elbows at the table eating very little. I have a horror of looking my age—I feel it a good deal, but I don't want to look it."

When the *Shangri-La* steamed into the heart of the Navy's drive toward Japan in the spring of 1945, Lieutenant Friedman's positions—as a gunnery officer supervising a machine gun battery with direct responsibility for the safety of the ship's captain, and as officer of the deck—landed him much closer to the action he'd been seeking since the day he'd signed up. The carrier provided key combat air patrols and close air support during the battle of Okinawa, and her planes launched numerous strikes against the Japanese outer islands and the Japanese homeland itself. Benny was back in command, and he relished the responsibility. Years later he said:

> Well, I had qualified to be officer of the deck, which meant that I was again playing quarterback. I was the captain's representative when I

took over what's called the con, and that is, I was in charge of the whole ship, and that was, you know, quite something because you had a hundred and three aircraft aboard, you had twenty-five hundred men in the ship's company and five hundred in the air group, and I had the deck when we were striking, you know, sending planes off or bringing them back. It was a very interesting and rather exciting kind of duty.

Benny earned two combat medals and a promotion to the rank of lieutenant commander.

Shortly after Benny's discharge from the Navy in December 1945, the Friedmans moved to Detroit, where Benny operated a Jeep automobile dealership and, for the first time other than during his stretch in the Navy, found himself out of football. But in August 1946, football was very much on Benny's mind as he made the short trip from Detroit to Ann Arbor to attend the funeral of Fielding Harris Yost. The Old Man's physical health had been spotty for several years, and, in the years following his retirement in 1941 as Michigan's athletic director, he had a penchant for wandering around the Michigan campus, occasionally getting lost and needing a police escort to help him home. A sudden gall bladder attack had finally overwhelmed him, and he passed away at his Ann Arbor home on August 20 at the age of seventy-five. Three of Yost's former captains—Paul Goebel '22, Bob Brown '25 (captain of the team that Yost considered his best), and Bennie Oosterbaan '27—served as pallbearers for their beloved coach.

In the years to come, Benny would have many occasions to speak about his career as a football player and the game of football generally. Almost without exception, Benny's words on such occasions would pay homage to the old "Meeshegan" coach whom he revered.

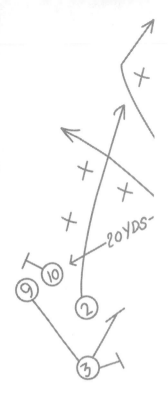

TWENTY

Brandeis

Back in 1925, around the same time that Illinois's Big Ten opponents were receiving weekly lessons on the football field from Red Grange, Red was receiving lessons in the classroom from a history professor named Abram Sachar. In the two decades since then, Sachar had distinguished himself as a chronicler of the history of the Jews and as a tireless activist at the forefront of such Jewish organizations as Hillel and B'nai B'rith.

When leaders of the American Jewish community set out to establish America's first Jewish-sponsored, non-sectarian university, Sachar was at the top of the list of candidates to serve as the fledgling university's first president. Sachar accepted the position, and in 1948, atop a hill on the southern edge of working-class Waltham, Massachusetts, just nine miles outside of Boston, Brandeis University opened its doors.

Named for the esteemed jurist Louis Dembitz Brandeis, the university's mission was, first and foremost, an academic one. The goal of the founders, a goal Sachar was charged to achieve, was the establishment of a small, selective liberal arts institution, but Sachar was not blind to the danger that an academically selective Jewish-sponsored university might come to be viewed as nothing more than a glorified yeshiva. He did not want Brandeis to founder on this well-worn stereotype before it even got started. As Sachar wrote years later, the solution was to add diversity—including athletics—to the school's intellectual rigors:

> If the university were ultimately to become diversified in its regional, ethnic, and economic character, it could not concentrate exclusively on hard-driving intellectuals who remained encysted among their books and in their laboratories. Pervasive also was the yearning of many of our most generous supporters to make sure that Brandeis, in addition to its intellectual standards and its national service, also projected the traditional American image of college as a center for wholesome physical fitness. For them, modestly organized athletic squads, whose schedules were limited to the smaller schools where intercollegiate athletics did not dominate, could give visibility to the pattern Brandeis was anxious to achieve.

To Sachar, Benny Friedman was the obvious choice to establish and lead an athletic program at Brandeis that would provide the sought-after balance to the school's academic rigors. Benny was the embodiment of the "tough Jew" that Sachar felt the university needed—someone who could identify with, and be identified with, the university's Jewish links, and who also had the athletic chops and reputation to attract players to the school. Friedman's name recognition wasn't quite at the level it had been during the height of his playing days, but he still had the cache that could furnish instant credibility to a budding athletic department. Beyond that, Sachar also saw in Benny the ingredients of a productive fund-raiser—a handsome, articulate, worldly celebrity with demonstrated public speaking skills.

Friedman was doing well with the Jeep agency in Detroit when Sachar approached him in 1949 and asked him to come to Brandeis. If he was looking for a coaching job, it wasn't at a brand-new, small school that didn't even own a football, much less have a football team or a field to play on. CCNY at least had been an established institution with a football history, albeit a lackluster one. Brandeis was a university infant. Benny was, to say the least, skeptical.

"How large is the student body?" Benny asked Sachar.

The fledgling university's president mustered his courage.

"Almost three hundred and fifty," Sachar boldly replied.

"Does that include girls?" Friedman wasn't kidding.

"Of course," Sachar barked, mindful that it is not good form for a university president to appear to be begging.

"Do you have an adequate playing field?" Benny asked.

"Not yet," Sachar responded. "I am quite sure that we will acquire one fairly soon after we announce our sports program and can say that Benny Friedman is its director."

Benny remained skeptical, but Sachar was not a man easily refused. With the preliminaries out of the way, the forceful Brandeis president got to the point. He made the proposal personal for Friedman. "Benny, you owe this to us," Sachar told him. "This is the first school founded by our own people. Everything we do has got to have quality. When we bring in a coach like Benny Friedman, it's like bringing in a Lenny Bernstein to head up our school of music."

And so for the second time in little more than a decade, Benny said yes to the chance—or perhaps a sense of obligation—to guide a football program with strong Jewish links out of the wilderness. Brandeis wasn't much more than a shell consisting of a few hundred students, a few dozen faculty members, and a small collection of buildings. The closest thing the school had to any athletic facilities was a gymnasium under construction. There were no fields. There was no sports equipment. And there were no football players either. "I knew when I first stood on Ferry Field at Michigan with Fielding Yost, there were ghosts all around," Benny said shortly after beginning at the Massachusetts school. "There are no ghosts at Brandeis."

So Friedman hit the recruiting trail. He reached out to boys all over New England, and he reached back to his old haunts in Manhattan and Brooklyn and the Bronx, too, selling what there was to sell—the chance for a first-rate education, along with the opportunity to one day be able to say that they had built a college football program from scratch.

The romance of such an opportunity was lost on many high-school stars who couldn't see past the advantages offered by established college football powers. But there were a few outstanding boys willing to forsake the Boston Universities and Boston Colleges and Northeasterns of the world and take the plunge at Brandeis. One such young star was Sid Goldfader, an all-state football and baseball player from Worcester in central Massachusetts. The 1950 Massachusetts High School Athlete of the Year, heavily recruited by dozens of established schools, took refuge in the innocence and anonymity offered by the new university in Waltham. "Once a school is in big time, it's a business," Goldfader said. "I've talked to a lot of the fellows who played with me and against me in high school. I know what I got here [at Brandeis]. Football's not a duty. It's a pleasure. I'm enjoying it. I'm not just another football player in a school."

Other high-school stars, like Ed Manganiello from Revere, hard by Boston's northern city limits, were sold on Benny himself. Manganiello and other Brandeis recruits like him had barely been born when Benny retired from the NFL. But they knew of his legendary gridiron feats, and that knowledge, combined with the impression that Benny could make when shaking a young football player's hand, was enough. "I love football and I think Benny Friedman can teach me a lot about it," Manganiello said.

By the fall of 1950, while the construction cranes and jackhammers were pounding out the Shapiro Gymnasium on the Brandeis campus, Benny had attracted enough players to cobble together a team. And using his reputation and considerable powers of persuasion, he arranged for a number of games against the freshman teams of local area schools. The first such battle was against none other than Harvard University at Soldiers Field in Cambridge. The unexpected result—a Brandeis victory—wasn't quite the upset of the century, but the triumph of the baby school was more than ample cause for celebration in Waltham. Years later, Abram Sachar wrote: "If a Pulitzer for literature or history had been announced in the next morning's press, it could not have made the impact on our constituency that the Brandeis victory did."

With his football pedigree, Friedman probably didn't find a victory over the Harvard freshmen as thrilling as Sachar. Benny surely would rather have been prowling the sideline in the entirely different opening day setting that October in Ann Arbor, where ninety-six thousand Wolverine loyalists in Michigan Stadium screamed themselves hoarse as they watched Michigan defeat Michigan State. But that privilege belonged to a different coach—none other than Bennie Oosterbaan. Oosterbaan had chosen a different path than Friedman, eschewing pro football and remaining at Michigan. His devoted and competent service as an assistant, first to Harry Kipke and then to Fritz Crisler, had earned him the appointment as Wolverines head coach in 1948 upon Crisler's retirement.

Meanwhile, Friedman was now in Waltham, Massachusetts, a universe removed from the pomp of Ann Arbor, and he was determined to meet the challenge of building a football team at Brandeis University. The victory over the Harvard freshmen propelled the Brandeis Judges to a strong 4–2 1950 campaign that, together with continued productive recruiting, allowed Benny to plan for varsity competition in 1951. Once again it took no small amount of arm-twisting by Benny to convince other coaches and athletic directors to play the upstart Judges. But he cajoled and schmoozed and badgered, and in the end, there were enough schools that simply could not say no to Benny Friedman.

In their first-ever varsity football game, the Brandeis Judges faced the University of New Hampshire, an experienced squad that had been ranked as the top small college team in New England in 1950. The Wildcats may have viewed the occasion as a burden rather than a distinction, for they had nothing to gain by beating a novice squad like Brandeis and everything to lose should the unthinkable occur. As the Judges took the field—their own field, which, though temporary, had finally been made ready for play— they had a few things going for them. One was an exuberant partisan crowd of 4,500. Another was Benny, who had convinced them during the week leading up to the game that they had as much chance to win as New

Hampshire. Before the game, the thing that had Benny most concerned was that his boys would be tight. If they could relax, he thought, they would be tough to beat. And finally, the Judges had the youthful enthusiasm one might expect from what was quite likely the only college football team in America composed solely of freshmen and sophomores.

The Judges were young and inexperienced, but they were not without some impressive talent and size. Freshman end Bill McKenna was a six-foot-two-inch, 175-pound high-school star from Salem, Massachusetts, with a ranginess and athleticism reminiscent of Bennie Oosterbaan. At the other end was sophomore Robert Griffin, who had starred at Boston's English High School and who, at six foot four and 210 pounds, would have been a load for the best pass defenders at the biggest schools. Billy Billups was a six-foot-three-inch, 190-pound quarterback with tree trunks for legs who could hurt you on the ground and in the air. Back Sid Goldfader had the athletic pedigree and look that said he could be a star anywhere. Detroth "Dee" Tyson, a freshman back with a sprinter's speed, was a threat to score whenever he touched the ball. Ed Manganiello and six-foot-one-inch, 225-pound Brooklynite Phil Goldstein anchored the lines.

When New Hampshire hit the locker room at halftime, the experienced small college champs were clinging to a 13–7 lead. A game that most had thought would serve as Brandeis's rude indoctrination to the world of varsity football had instead developed into an all-out brawl.

And if New Hampshire thought they would simply regroup at the half, return to the field, and put the upstart Judges in their place, Brandeis halfback Len Toomey quickly disabused the Wildcats of such a notion. On Brandeis's first possession of the third quarter, Toomey snared a screen pass from Billups, picked up textbook-crisp blocks from several teammates, and steamed seventy-five yards for a touchdown. When Gene Renzi added the extra point, the Brandeis University Judges held a 14–13 third-quarter lead over the vaunted University of New Hampshire Wildcats.

The Judges weren't through. Later in the third quarter, the sure-tackling Brandeis back Myron Uhlberg recovered a New Hampshire fumble on the Wildcats twenty-five-yard line. A few plays later, Bill McKenna snuck across the goal line with a Billups pass. Renzi booted the extra point and now Brandeis led 20–13.

That's when inexperience, injuries, fatigue, and New Hampshire's savvy and talent caught up with the Judges. The Wildcats were an unstoppable whirlwind in the last twenty minutes of the game. They began exploding through and around the weary, beaten-up Judges virtually at will, producing three touchdowns. At the same time, the Wildcats clamped down tight on defense, not allowing Brandeis to sniff the goal line again. New Hampshire had survived, 33–20, and the Wildcats couldn't get on their bus for the ride out of Waltham quickly enough.

The Judges had played well enough to suggest that their first triumph was not far off. And indeed, it wasn't. The very next week, in Hempstead, Long Island, Benny watched his boys whip Hofstra University by a score of 24–13. A bold headline in the *Boston Globe* trumpeted the news:

> B.C. Loses to Ole Miss, 34–7;
> B.U., Notre Dame, Brandeis Win

It had taken just two varsity outings for Brandeis to be mentioned in the same breath as powerhouses Boston University, Boston College, and the most exalted of all college programs—Notre Dame.

• • •

Bill McKenna, who would go on to play professional football for nearly ten seasons in the Canadian Football League, said no team he ever played for was better prepared than Benny's Brandeis squads. McKenna and his Brandeis mates had Fielding Yost to thank for that; the influence of the Old Man on Benny was manifest in Friedman's attention to detail; his emphasis on finding the opponent's suckers—their "disciples of Barnum" as Yost would have called them—and exploiting them without mercy; and his frequent invocation of Yost's name. But the closest he would come to any fiery, Yostian pregame oratory was a stock reminder to his players: "Boys,"

Benny would say, speaking as a professor might speak, not shouting like a coach might shout, "you've got to get up for the game, or you're going to get knocked ass over tea kettle."

More often than not, Benny maintained a certain gentility in the world of gridiron mayhem. There was an air of superiority about him that he seemed intent on fostering, a sort of informal caste system in which he was the Brahmin and his players were the untouchables. It was an air complemented by his fastidious dress, his perpetual bronze tan, and, though nearly fifty and with rapidly thinning hair, his still-striking good looks and toned body. "Benny to me was like a Hollywood character," Bob Weintraub remembered, years after his service as team manager. Friedman often addressed his players with phrases and words one might expect to hear from the headmaster of a tony prep school rather than from a football coach. If there was something he thought his players should do, he wouldn't simply tell them to do it; he'd tell them that it would "behoove them" to do it. On a particularly warm, sunny day, he wouldn't merely warn the players against soaking up too much sun; he'd tell his boys to take care not to become too "enervated" by the rays.

The net effect was to create a cocoon between him and his players, and it was a tough cocoon to crack. Billy McKenna, who along with quarterback Jim Stehlin were two of Friedman's best players, recalled years after his Brandeis days that Benny was a difficult man to get very close to.

"Benny, you didn't go to talk to," recalled running back Bob Domozych, who later enjoyed a long and successful career as a high-school coach. If a player had a minor problem, or just wanted a little friendly coach-and-player banter, he sought out one of Benny's very able assistant coaches: Irv Heller, formerly a star lineman at Boston University; George Keneally, an outstanding NFL lineman and playing contemporary of Benny's; the gregarious Emmanuel Flumere, known as "Foxy," who had been a standout three-sport athlete at Northeastern University in the 1930s and had also been the Huskies' head football coach for a time; and Harry Stein, one of Benny's star players at CCNY who had followed his mentor to Brandeis. The genial

Stein had the warmth, the ready smile, and the willingness to engage the players on an emotional level that Benny couldn't, or wouldn't, muster.

The players knew that when it came to serious matters, however, their coach was their protector. According to Dick Collins, when he was a local star at Waltham High grieving the recent loss of his parents, Benny offered him a full scholarship to Brandeis despite Collins's somewhat lacking academic record. Actually, Friedman arranged scholarships for a number of players with shaky academic skills that Brandeis's demanding classes quickly exposed. As Benny's 1956 team captain, Dick Baldacci, put it, when it came to academics, "There was nowhere to hide." Some were simply overwhelmed and flunked out or left the school after a year, or sooner. But Benny was able to shepherd a good number of other players through their academic difficulties by vigilantly checking on their progress, by forcing them to seek extra help, and, when necessary, by interceding with the university's faculty or administration to prevent academic probation from ripening into expulsion. Many players whose Brandeis degrees propelled them to successful careers would never have made it through even one semester had Friedman not watched over them. And Benny's task of building a football program at Brandeis was, undoubtedly, made easier by some of the players he helped get into Brandeis and helped stay in once they got there.

Injury was another matter that pierced Benny's cool exterior and exposed a caring core. As he had done at City College, he drilled his players incessantly on the importance of protecting themselves on the field. The players watched as Benny showed them how to fall and how to tackle. They watched him demonstrate the exaggerated follow-through on a forward pass that he mandated for his quarterbacks, occasionally unable to suppress some snickering at the odd-looking, unorthodox technique. But there was no denying that Benny's obsessiveness in this area saved them injuries they otherwise would have sustained.

And there was no snickering at the way their coach looked after them when they did suffer the occasional injuries that were inevitable regardless of Benny's precautions. In a road game against the University of Toledo, an opposing player delivered a cheap shot to the mouth of Brandeis guard Bill Orman that would have made Wild Bill Fleckenstein proud. The smash sprinkled pieces of Orman's teeth all over the field. Friedman accompanied Orman to a local emergency room and, both that night and upon the team's return home, personally arranged the best possible dental and plastic surgical care for his player. Decades later, the grateful Orman's voice quavered when he recalled Benny's attentiveness and assistance.

It didn't always take an injury or a nettlesome academic problem to produce a thaw in Benny's cool reserve. On a road trip to Detroit for a game against Wayne State University, Benny took his boys on a short detour—a field trip to Ann Arbor. The coach escorted his Brandeis crew onto Ferry Field. As Friedman strolled around the hallowed turf, lost in the memories of his youth and his love of Michigan, he treated his players to a rare glimpse of his soul. "To just watch him walk across that sod . . . it was just such reverence," Brandeis quarterback Tom Egan recalled years later.

Benny didn't talk much to his players about his own career, but he couldn't resist the occasional story, including one that concerned his legendary accuracy as a passer. On one specific play, Benny dropped back to pass and, finding no receiver open, decided to throw the ball away to avoid being tackled for a loss. He fired the ball toward no one in particular about thirty yards down the middle of the field, where it should have landed harmlessly incomplete. However, referee Tom Thorp called Benny for intentional grounding. Benny protested, but Thorp was having none of it. As far as the ref was concerned, other passers could legitimately throw incomplete passes. But if the uncannily accurate Friedman threw an incomplete pass, he had to have done so on purpose. "Anybody but you, Benny," Thorp said to Friedman. "Anybody but you."

Just as he would tell the occasional tale, Benny, who typically reacted to a player's mistake with a simple glare or a calm, low-volume dressing-down of the offending player, wasn't beyond the occasional flash of anger during a game. Halfback Dick Bergel, who came to Brandeis from his hometown in Providence, Rhode Island, remembers well what unfolded when his blown blocking assignment on a Brandeis punt nearly got star signal caller and Brandeis punter Jim Stehlin killed. As Bergel's man slipped by him on his way toward Stehlin, Bergel, near the Brandeis sideline, burst downfield to cover the play, hoping his error would somehow go unnoticed. It was then that the speedy halfback learned that his fifty-year-old coach was every bit as fast as he was. "Bergel, you son of a bitch! You son of a bitch! You son of a bitch!" Benny screamed as he tore down the sideline after his chagrined halfback, matching him stride for stride.

Benny's sprint after Bergel was prompted in part by his partiality to his quarterbacks, and he had a particular fondness for the talented Stehlin. The former Pennsylvania high-school star had transferred to Brandeis from Georgetown when that school dropped football following his freshman year in 1951. He was blessed with a powerful, accurate arm, but as far as Benny was concerned, that wasn't enough. "Jimmy, you've got talent," he told Stehlin, "but you've got to do something with it." Friedman was delighted when he realized that Stehlin's work ethic matched his considerable talent level. He tutored his young quarterback, imparting the finer points of playing the position—how to exploit a defense's weakness, how to avoid injury, how to deliver a pass on time and on target. "I'm not interested in how hard you can throw the ball," Benny would tell Stehlin. "I'm not interested in how far you can throw the ball. I'm interested in your delivery and your accuracy."

Stehlin had come to Brandeis specifically for the opportunity to work with Friedman, whose pioneering forward passing he had heard about from an uncle. And so the young man was only too willing to absorb the teachings from the master. "He had a charisma about him," Stehlin said years later, "that he made you feel, 'Gee, Benny Friedman's telling me this, so I know I'm going to be good at it.'" In fact Stehlin was good enough to be selected, along with McKenna, as a Little All-American, the highest individual honor available to a small-college player.

Years after his Brandeis days, Bill McKenna recalled the outstanding passers he had played with during his long pro career—passers such as Buffalo Bills All-Pro Jack Kemp and NFL All-Pro Joe Kapp, who once threw for a record seven touchdowns in an NFL game. None of them, McKenna said, threw as good a ball as Jimmy Stehlin.

"And," McKenna said, "Benny Friedman coached him."

• • •

Benny's mission at Brandeis was far more expansive than coaching his quarterback and his football team. Back in 1949, Abram Sachar, well aware of Benny's magic name and dynamic speaking ability, was more excited about his potential as a fund-raiser for Brandeis than as a football coach. Had frequent flier mileage been available in the 1950s, Friedman's fund-raising trips would have earned him a bundle of free first class tickets. Benny was constantly in the air or on the road, often leaving the team in the capable hands of his assistants on a Monday or Tuesday and returning in time to coach the boys in the game on Saturday. Sometimes with Sachar, sometimes alone, Benny wooed the big donors for the big money that Brandeis desperately needed to grow. Occasionally he would take some of his players with him, allowing them to put a young athlete's face on the pitch for funds. But it was Benny whom the people came out to see. Sachar, himself a prolific speaker and fund-raiser, recalled years later: "Benny was superb in addressing groups as well as on a one-to-one basis. He was an eloquent speaker, and he spoke with verve. He was a very great asset to us far beyond sports. This wasn't a job for him; it was a mission."

Friedman's primary interest at Brandeis was the football team and the athletic department, but he certainly understood that without a thriving university, there would be no football and no athletic department. His fund-raising efforts were indispensable to Brandeis's very existence as it groped its way through the 1950s and slowly but steadily built up and expanded its campus, while increasing its faculty and student body.

Brandeis also improved its athletic facilities, and not just its football facilities. Friedman's athletic director's hat called for him to develop other sports, too, and under his supervision, the university acquired a pool for the swimmers, a track (encircling a new football field) for the runners, and four new courts for the tennis players, who had been cramming in practices and matches on one old, decrepit court that had more cracks in it than the San Andreas Fault. With the new tennis courts came the opportunity to hire Brandeis's first tennis coach, and when word got out that Brandeis was looking for one, Benny received a phone call from a young sportswriter from the *Boston Globe* who had played a little college tennis himself.

"Benny, I understand you're looking for a [tennis] coach," the would-be Brandeis tennis mentor said.

"Yeah, we are," Benny replied. "Do you have any recommendations?"

The young writer thought about his obligations to the *Globe*. "How long is the season?"

"Oh, it's a pretty short season," Friedman said. "April and May."

"What does it pay?"

"Oh, we're going to pay $200," Benny said.

The young writer thought about how little money young writers made—but not for too long. "I'm your man!" Bud Collins said to Benny.

Collins would later become one of the most celebrated figures in the history of the sport—a pioneering broadcaster, a prolific and respected journalist and historian, and an all-around tennis aficionado who is guaranteed to bring a little extra color to any gathering with his unique sense of sartorial style.

During his five years in Waltham, Collins established a solid program that took its place within a well-rounded athletic program crafted by Friedman. Brandeis's basketball teams of the 1950s, coached by Harry Stein, were some of New England's best. Three Brandeis players—Len Winograd, James Houston, and Rudy Finderson—were drafted by National Basketball Association clubs. A large contingent of foreign exchange students helped build a competitive soccer team. A proud tradition of excellence in track and field and cross-country was born under the guidance of coach Norm Levine. Benny, who happened to be a fine golfer with a near-scratch handicap, even found time to coach the Brandeis golf team.

And at a time when women's intercollegiate sports were way back in the rearview mirror, Benny pushed hard to establish a women's program at Brandeis. Women's basketball and fencing, with outstanding coaching from Anna Nichols and Lisel Judge, respectively, became forces to be reckoned with in New England women's collegiate athletic circles.

Benny's football program grew and prospered too. With the help of Stehlin and McKenna and many other fine players, Friedman was able to field teams that, for most of the 1950s, were good enough to win more than they lost, against challenging competition that included schools far bigger and more experienced than Brandeis—schools such as Boston University, Boston College, Northeastern, and the University of Massachusetts.

In 1957, the Judges, led by All–New England stars Charlie Napoli and Morry Stein, posted a 6–1 record. Eight years after Abram Sachar and Benny had teamed up, it seemed as if their symbiotic goals were being realized. Though it was clear that the scale and quality of Brandeis football would never be confused with that of Michigan or Notre Dame, Benny had, in almost no time and completely from scratch, built a strong, reputable program that had assumed a proud place in the New England intercollegiate gridiron community. And Sachar, for his part, had seen Brandeis take major steps toward becoming the highly regarded academic institution and beacon for America's Jewish community he had envisioned. Brandeis's student body, just a few hundred at the school's inception, was now pushing one thousand. The school's faculty was growing in size and prestige. Lecture halls, laboratories, and dormitories were sprouting up all over campus, thanks in no small part to Friedman's prodigious fund-raising efforts. No longer considered a mere curiosity, Brandeis was evolving into a prestigious educational destination with an enhanced national profile. As Sachar had realized at the outset, the evolution likely could not have occurred had Benny's football program and the broader athletic program not enabled Brandeis to avoid a reputation as an insular, Jewish-based academic boutique that would have smothered it in its infancy.

• • •

Some people become victims of their own success. As the fifties drew to a close, it began to appear as if Benny, at Brandeis, was about to join the ranks of such unfortunates.

The establishment of a football factory had never been a part of Sachar's agenda, and although Benny's program was far from a factory, Sachar began to believe it was consuming an inordinate amount of time, money, and attention. Sachar and other administration officials also came to believe that too many places in each year's class were being reserved for football players of subpar academic ability at the expense of more academically qualified applicants. Sachar had tolerated this athletically-skewed imbalance earlier in the decade, when the university was taking its first breaths and he considered football a necessary oxygen mask. But with Brandeis's reputation and credibility in the world of higher education steadily rising, the number of applications for admissions was soaring, and as the administration was determined not to increase the size of the student body, places in each year's incoming class became precious. The administration began to seriously question the necessity and desirability of maintaining a football program.

Coincidentally, during the time that Benny's football program—and thus his job as football coach—had become imperiled, Bennie Oosterbaan's head coaching job at Michigan was also in deep trouble. Oosterbaan had accomplished the astounding feat of winning a Big Ten title—and a national championship—in his first season back in 1948. Since then he'd guided the Wolverines to two more conference crowns among a slew of winning seasons while solidifying his reputation as one of the most genial men in the business. But a losing record in '57 had sparked sentiment in Ann Arbor that perhaps the time for a new coach was at hand. That sentiment intensified when the Wolverines started slowly in '58. And when Northwestern shellacked Michigan, 54–25, in the season's fourth game, Oosterbaan's coaching demise at Michigan was all but certain. Following the Northwestern debacle, Michigan students hung the once-beloved Oosterbaan in effigy. Friedman was having his own troubles at Brandeis, but he came to his old friend's aid. In a letter to *Sports Illustrated,* he wrote:

> I understand that you are going to pick a Sportsman of the Year, and I would like to nominate my teammate at Michigan, Bennie Oosterbaan.
> This year Bennie has gone up and down the ladder of success . . . the students hung Bennie in effigy because Michigan had lost so badly

to Northwestern, but through all the vicissitudes, Bennie has kept his head above water and has maintained himself with a sense of dignity and sportsmanship that has made his critics very little people.

In this era of big time football, with the demands made on a coach for a winning team, Bennie has again maintained himself on a high level of character by refusing to be a party to the recruiting practices that are sometimes not a credit to the coaching profession.

I think that Bennie's record at the University of Michigan and his dignity, particularly this year, warrants his consideration for your award of the Sportsman of the Year.

Oosterbaan did not win the award; the honor went to the great decathlete Rafer Johnson. Bennie didn't keep his job either. The Wolverines' season-ending loss to Ohio State was Oosterbaan's last game at the Michigan helm. A few months later, in the spring of 1959, Bennie was feted by friends, coaches, and former teammates at a dinner in Detroit. Friedman didn't make it to the dinner but sent his regrets to the other half of the first great passer-receiver combination in football history: "I . . . would like to be one of those present to say 'well done' to a grand guy, a fine teammate and to one who happens to have a beautiful philosophy. This night will be a memorable one for you but not nearly as memorable as those Saturdays we spent together in 1925 and 1926."

By the fall of 1959, restlessness with the Brandeis football program had spread from the administration to the faculty and student body. With fewer quality players due to Sachar's stricter recruiting policy, the football team endured the misery of an 0–6–1 season in which, other than in the lone tie, they never came close to winning a game. But there was little sympathy to be found around campus. In a memo to Sachar, Dean of Faculty John Roche urged the university president to eliminate football: "I think you have here a magnificent opportunity for educational statesmanship. Your students and your faculty will look on you with augmented respect as the man who put an end to this moral absurdity."

Repeated articles in the *Justice,* the school's student newspaper, led a steady drumbeat of student discontent with the sport. Outspoken Brandeis students such as Abbie Hoffman, one of Bud Collins's tennis players who would later come to national prominence during the infamous 1968 Democratic Party convention in Chicago, railed against the continuation of football at Brandeis. Martin Peretz, who would later become a noted journalist and publisher at the *New Republic,* was another frequent student critic of the football program. Star lineman Charlie Napoli would engage Peretz in on-campus debates, but despite Napoli's best efforts, for Peretz and Hoffman and many other Brandeis students of like mind, football and the demands of running a football program had simply outgrown their place at a small, selective liberal arts university.

Benny vehemently protested against the impending doom of Brandeis football—and not, according to Sachar, without flashes of temper. Benny and Sachar—much of the time working together—had been Brandeis's two leading foot soldiers in the arduous process of building the university. But now, with Sachar leading the charge against Benny's football program, their relationship had cooled. Benny believed that Sachar was jealous because Benny's fund-raising prowess had outstripped the university president's. One memo, from Sachar to an administrator in February 1960 concerning a recent fund-raising trip by Friedman, seemed to reveal Sachar's growing distaste, perhaps even contempt, for football, if not for Benny himself: "I'm glad Benny raised $80,000 for us in San Diego. We can only reward him by letting him continue to play, over and over and over, the game with Ohio State that Michigan won, 3 to 0. Aren't we lucky?"

It's doubtful that Benny ever saw the memo. If he had, he might have reminded the historian Sachar that Michigan's victim in that 3–0 game had been Illinois, not Ohio State, and that Sachar had been teaching at Illinois at the time.

On May 16, 1960, Brandeis formally announced the end of its football program. The announcement emphasized the university's ongoing commitment to its other intercollegiate sports. It also declared that the decision to drop football had been made with the full approval of the athletic director. That statement was almost certainly a noble nod by Benny to political correctness. The truth of the matter is that the decision angered and embittered Friedman. Eleven years earlier, Abram Sachar had pleaded with Benny to come to Brandeis. "You owe this to us, Benny," Sachar had said, and Friedman had left his successful business and comfortable life in Detroit to help build America's first Jewish-sponsored non-sectarian university. Now that university had, in essence, told him that it owed him nothing. And perhaps it didn't. Perhaps Benny could have known or should have known—indeed, even did know—that this day would come. But he had come so far with football at Brandeis in so short a time, and he saw the potential of a program that would be strong for years to come— not a Michigan, perhaps, but a strong and worthy program nonetheless.

Benny stayed on at Brandeis for a time as athletic director and coach of the Judges' golf team. But without football, his heart wasn't in the job. Friedman tendered his letter of resignation in June 1962; the resignation was announced publicly the following April.

During the time Sachar had been weighing the fate of Brandeis football, he composed a list of "advantages" and "disadvantages" to the contemplated elimination of the sport. "End of warfare with student intellectuals" and the elimination of "Sabbath football" were among the advantages. "Enmity of BF" headed the list of disadvantages, and Sachar, and Brandeis, certainly received it. Following the announcement of his resignation, Friedman never set foot on the university's campus again.

Brandeis, at least according to Friedman, may have abandoned him. But as time would tell, a solid core of his players never would.

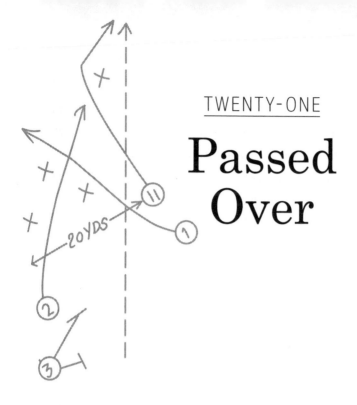

TWENTY-ONE

Passed Over

Benny's roller-coaster ride at Brandeis coincided with a dramatic rise in the popularity, and prosperity, of the National Football League—a rise owing, primarily, to the growing popularity and efficiency of the passing game. Inspired by Friedman's groundbreaking feats, the league had changed the rules and the ball and paved the way for outstanding passers such as Arnie Herber and Cecil Isbell, Davey O'Brien and Sid Luckman, and most of all, the great Sammy Baugh, to advance the passing game during the 1930s and '40s. These passers rendered obsolete the offensive formations of Benny's time—the single wing, double wing, and shift offenses—that were the hallmarks of football's anachronistic, grinding running game. The T formation now ruled the game, and during the '50s, the arms of such greats as Y. A. Tittle, Bob Waterfield, Eddie Lebaron, the fantastic Otto Graham, who passed the Cleveland Browns to seven league titles in ten years, and the storied Johnny Unitas elevated the passing game to even greater heights. Television responded to the excitement generated by these great throwers, and the league that very nearly vanished during the Depression was on its way to becoming the obsession of American sports fans that it is today.

Friedman was impressed with the things these modern-era passers could do with the football. But Benny wasn't content to settle for the role of pioneer and concede that his talents had been outstripped by his successors. In an article penned in 1953 for *Sport* magazine, Benny said:

> I feel sure I could play quarterback in professional football today. I'm 48 years old and have been out of the National Football League for 20 years but I'm confident I could do the job as well as, if not better than most present-day big-league quarterbacks, most of whom are half my age . . .
>
> The T-formation quarterback has a rocking-chair job . . . His duties are generally limited to taking the ball from center and handing it off to a runner or dropping back, protected by beefy linemen, to throw the ball . . .
>
> Many of the passing statistics and records which bring the boys fancy salaries and national prominence are misleading . . . How many times have you seen the passer-quarterback throw the ball to an end who has buttonhooked and is standing still? How many times have you seen him pass to a back, acting as a flanker, who just stands and faces the quarterback . . . ?
>
> I don't think it takes any special talent to complete such passes. Anybody ought to be able to hit a receiver standing at distances from five to 15 yards away. Yet these passes go down in the record books as completed, just like the ones that are thrown 25, 30 or 40 yards to a moving target . . .
>
> It's a pretty simple job any way you look at it. The quarterback in the National Football League simply takes the ball, hands it off to a back or keeps it and, protected by a wall of blockers, tosses it downfield to a stationary flanker. He doesn't even get his uniform dirty.
>
> It's a job I could handle right now. Any offers?

Benny's outsized ego notwithstanding, his place in the pantheon of football's greatest talents and transformational figures cannot be questioned. Nobody knew this better than his playing and coaching contemporaries. Red Grange called Benny the greatest quarterback he had ever played against. "They talk about great passers today," Grange said more than forty years after his first confrontation with Friedman in 1924. "But remember that the football has been changed three times since the early 1930s, and each time it has been made narrower and the axis pulled in.

Anybody could throw today's football. You go back to Benny Friedman playing with the New York Giants in the late 1920s and early '30s. He threw that old balloon. Now who's to tell what Benny Friedman might do with this modern football. He'd probably be the greatest passer that ever lived."

George Trafton said Friedman was the best passer he had ever seen, including the great Baugh. Ernie Pinckert, the nearsighted back whom Benny victimized in Boston in 1933, favored Baugh over Friedman, but only if a longer, harder pass was needed and only if you had receivers who could catch those bullets. "I always thought that for the majority of receivers, Friedman with his floater ball, which could thread a needle, was the greatest of them all," Pinckert said. "Friedman's accuracy was amazing," marveled Hall of Fame center Mel Hein, who played with Benny for a year with the Giants. "Over all the years I don't recall seeing him throw over or under a receiver. And he had the knack of leading a receiver down to what almost amounted to a science. When you consider the game was not so wide open in his time and the principles for protection of the passer were only loosely conceived, Friedman's performances take on added dimensions."

And Benny was known to sing his own praises now and then. Many years after his *Sport* magazine piece, Benny ran into John McVay, the newly appointed head coach of the Giants, at a New York football affair.

"Benny," McVay asked, "is it true that Tim Mara bought the whole Detroit team to get you to New York?"

"Yes," Friedman answered.

"You must have been a hell of a man."

Benny didn't parse his response to the impressed McVay.

"I was."

. . .

After leaving Brandeis, Benny focused on Camp Kohut, the coeducational summer camp in Maine he'd owned or operated since the mid-fifties. He was a ubiquitous presence on the grounds, doing everything from waking campers in the morning to picking up stray pieces of trash. Benny was fifty-eight when he left Brandeis, but a graying and rapidly balding head aside, he could have passed for a man twenty years younger. An exercise regimen that included water skiing and sets of push-ups that might have made a nineteen-year-old Marine recruit jealous kept Benny toned and fit. The vain Friedman typically bounded around the Kohut grounds shirtless. Every now and then the "Gray Eagle," as campers called Benny for his hair color and attention to the camp's smallest details, would demonstrate some of the unusual exercises he performed as a youngster to strengthen his hand and forearm, like grabbing a broom by its tip and lifting the heavily weighted bristled end with no more than the arching of his wrist.

In 1964, and again in 1965, Benny added a one-week camp for aspiring young quarterbacks to the regular two-month coed session. The quarterback camp was such a hit that Benny took his show on the road; he began operating sessions several times a year at sites throughout the country. High-school signal callers flocked to the camps to hear Benny expound on his familiar themes, themes that he'd learned from Fielding Yost four decades earlier: learning how to fall so as to avoid injury, and learning, like P. T. Barnum, to find the sucker in a defense and mercilessly exploit him.

The campers received up close and personal instruction from Benny on his unique throwing motion. Chuck Drimal, a high-school quarterback from Valley Stream, New York, recalled how astonished campers watched Friedman demonstrate the technique that had made him famous—the pronounced cocking of the arm; the careful aligning of the feet at a ninety-degree angle toward the intended target; the slight lifting of the front foot to initiate the throw, for balance; the pronounced wrist snap as the ball is released; and the exaggerated follow-through that brings the rear leg around and places the passer in a crouch.

When Drimal reported for high-school practice that fall and began passing the "Friedman way," he immediately got his coach's attention. "Where the hell did you get that throwing motion?" his incredulous coach bellowed. The quarterback enjoyed an award-winning senior year in high school and went on to letter in football for the University of Maryland.

Gary Wichard was another of Benny's campers to enjoy success at the college level. Wichard attracted national attention as an all-American quarterback at C.W. Post College on Long Island, where his outstanding passing outshone many talented quarterbacks who played for much larger schools. He was good enough to be drafted by the Baltimore Colts—"Hey, I got my Jewish quarterback," Colts' owner Carroll Rosenbloom said to him the day he was drafted—though he never played in the NFL. Wichard, a successful sports agent today, didn't take Benny's peculiar throwing motion home with him from his summer at the camp. Instead, he took Friedman's lessons about a quarterback's leadership, control, accountability, and making his teammates better—in essence, lessons on how to play the quarterback position, on how to *be* a quarterback. These were the same lessons that Fielding Yost had given to a young, quiet Benny Friedman that had helped develop Benny's peerless field generalship and leadership more than forty years earlier.

When he wasn't running his camps, Friedman spent most of his time in New York. As an insurance executive and occasional television color commentator for New York Jets and other NFL games, Benny was earning a comfortable enough living to sustain an elaborate six-room apartment on East Fifty-seventh Street in elegant Sutton Place. One of those rooms showcased the many trophies and other awards that Benny had received over his trailblazing career in football, including one of his favorites—if not the favorite: the Silver Football trophy he received as the Big Ten's most valuable player in 1926. ("There should have been two [Silver Football trophies]," Benny once told a friend, alluding to his belief that he should have won the award in 1925 as well.) Benny and Shirley were regulars on the Manhattan restaurant circuit, and the former football great and his wife usually didn't have to wait for a table. Their favorite haunt was probably Neary's Pub on Fifty-seventh Street, just a block from their door across First Avenue. Benny had met Jimmy Neary in 1954 at the popular New York saloon P. J. Moriarty's, where Neary was working as a bartender. The genial Neary opened his place in 1967 and quickly became one of New York's most popular restaurateurs and a friend to New York's political and athletic circles. Jimmy always made sure that Benny and Shirley could enjoy the friendly ambience of the place without much intrusion on their privacy.

In the winter, Benny and Shirley vacationed in Miami or at the Breakers Resort in Palm Beach. In the summer, they frequently drove to the resorts in New York's Catskill Mountains. Friedman's football clinics and appearances in the "Borscht Belt," as the area was called in recognition of its heavily Jewish clientele, were big hits.

Benny and Shirley were a devoted couple who indulged each other's joys. Shirley was a loyal football wife to "the Coach," as she often referred to her husband. She had supported Benny's coaching efforts at City College and Brandeis and enjoyed the celebrity that came with being Mrs. Benny Friedman. Benny, far more reserved than his wife in a family or social setting, indulged her enthusiasm and gift of gab. At dinner parties or Passover seders in their Sutton Place apartment, Benny would usually sit quietly and watch "Shoo Shoo," as the gregarious Shirley was known by friends, carry the conversation, unable or perhaps unwilling to get a word in himself. Benny also indulged Shirley's appetite for the finer things. "He treated her like a little princess," Benny's niece Jody Rosenbaum remembered. The daughter of a patrician German Jewish immigrant, Shirley was always dressed, coiffed, and bejeweled beautifully. In this department, Benny matched his glamorous wife. His friends, nieces and nephews, and former players, without exception, remember Benny as meticulously dressed, groomed—and tanned. "He used to sunbathe like nobody's business," Rosenbaum said.

Devoted as they were to each other, Benny and Shirley, by the '60s into their fourth decade of marriage, hadn't arrived there without some turbulence. Shirley spent many nights home alone while Benny was holding court at football functions at the Waldorf Astoria or the Downtown Athletic Club or some other fancy establishment. During Benny's years at Brandeis, Shirley usually stayed in New York while Benny coached the team during the week. Sometimes Benny would come back to New York on the weekend. Sometimes he wouldn't. Family members recall hearing of extramarital affairs by both spouses. "We've had a lot of give and take and there have been a lot of rough spots in it, and, as I say, the idea of divorce was rather . . . you know, too much, so you learned to . . . you know, to give and take . . . ," Benny recalled later. "We've had some . . . unfortunately some situations that were rather rugged, but we survived."

They had no children to help them through the rough patches. "We never felt the need of children and it just never came up to have children, and if either my wife or I had had the, you know, desire to have them, we would have," Benny said years later. "But, you know, very often as the years have gone by and we've seen all the nonsense that's in the world, we kind of feel rather happy that we didn't have them, you know? Because it's like shooting dice, you don't know what the hell you're going to come up with."

While no longer the New York celebrity he had been during his playing days with the Giants and Dodgers, Benny managed to stay in the news throughout the '60s as the subject of an occasional football retrospective or column. He seemed to cultivate a relationship with *New York Times* columnist Arthur Daley, as he had done some forty years earlier with *Detroit News* scribe Harry Salsinger. Daley wrote a number of columns that reminded the reader of Friedman's pioneering forward passing and ruminated on Fielding Yost, Tim Mara, passing mechanics, avoiding injury, and sundry other items that comprised the catalog of Benny's football life.

Nothing preoccupied Benny more than the Pro Football Hall of Fame in Canton, Ohio. He had been inducted in the National Football Foundation College Hall of Fame's charter class in 1951. But he had been left out of the pro football hall's charter class in 1963 that included Sammy Baugh, George Halas, Red Grange, Bronko Nagurski, and Ernie Nevers, among others. Benny was left out again in 1964, 1965, 1966, 1967, and 1968, while more of his pre-modern-era contemporaries, including George Trafton, Ed Healey, Arnie Herber, Cliff Battles, and Ken Strong, were elected. "I don't know what kept him out of Canton," said John Alexander, a Rutgers University teammate of the great Paul Robeson and, as maybe the first player to play what would come to be known as the linebacker position, a revolutionary footballer himself.

Daley's columns—with prodding from Friedman, according to Daley's *Times* colleague William N. Wallace—began to suggest, more politely than

Benny would have had he written them himself, that Friedman belonged in the Hall of Fame.

As the '60s gave way to the '70s, and a new class was admitted to the Canton shrine each year, Benny continued to be overlooked. For Friedman, never short on ego when it came to his football prowess, it was an increasingly painful slight. "He kept telling me all the time that he was a great, great football player," Benny's friend and *Scholastic Coach* editor Herman Maisin said, recalling Benny's constant entreaties to him concerning the Hall of Fame. "He absolutely was convinced that he was probably the greatest quarterback there ever was."

Benny didn't help his cause when, in 1970, he lambasted the National Football League Players Association for negotiating a pension plan with team owners that excluded pre-1958 players from benefits. "What gives the current players the license to draw the line at 1958?" a livid Friedman asked. "How can they exclude the older players? . . . There's no reason why we pioneers shouldn't benefit too." Benny threatened to bring a lawsuit to challenge the players union for an action he characterized as "brashness and arrogance beyond belief." Ultimately he let the matter lie, but not before doing further damage to his goodwill among the football powers-that-be.

Benny's bitterness spilled over into periodic criticism of modern-era quarterbacks. They didn't know how to protect themselves from injury. They didn't know how to throw the ball correctly. Things were too easy for them with the modern passer's "pocket," which gave them all day to pick out a receiver. "They" and "them" included Joe Namath, Terry Bradshaw, and just about every other quarterback in the league. There were a few exceptions: Bob Waterfield of the Rams; Eddie LeBaron of the Redskins; the Vikings' Fran Tarkenton; and Benny's favorite, the Packers' Bart Starr, generally regarded as one of the greats but whom Benny felt was unfairly eclipsed by the giant shadow of his coach, Vince Lombardi. These quarterbacks were of relatively small stature, able to wreak havoc on defenses with their brains and mobility as well as their outstanding passing. It's no coincidence that Benny strongly identified with them. And decades earlier, Friedman, like nearly everyone else, was awed by the talent of Sammy Baugh. "I thought I could pass until I saw Baugh today," Benny said back in 1937.

In February 1976, another class of enshrines, the fourteenth, was announced, and once again, Benny was left out. He was a month shy of turning seventy-one. It had been nearly forty years since he'd played his last NFL game. Most of Benny's playing contemporaries worthy of inclusion in the hall, if not all of them, had already been enshrined. With each passing year, his connection to the game and his chances for the honor he so desperately wanted were becoming increasingly remote. There were no more columns from Arthur Daley; he had passed away in 1974.

Benny picked up a pen and wrote his own letter to the *New York Times* on February 8, 1976:

> To the Sports Editor:
>
> The new inductees into the Pro Football Hall of Fame were recently announced, and again my name was not included. I wonder why. My exploits from 1927 through 1931 and my record put me on a par with or above many who are in the Hall now . . .
>
> The great sports writer Paul Gallico, who was sports editor of the *Daily News*, came to see me play at the Polo Grounds in 1929. What he saw caused him to write an article for *Liberty Magazine* titled "The Greatest Football Player in the World." George Halas, coach of the Bears, wrote an article in 1967 titled "Halas Calls Friedman Pioneer Passer—Rest Came By Design." He gave me the credit for revolutionizing the game with my passing and strategy . . .
>
> I suggest that those who vote for entrance to the Hall of Fame contact those greats of my era I played against, people like Ed Healey, Ernie Nevers, Bronko Nagurski and Ken Strong, among others.

There is a piercing poignancy to Benny's plea. Here was football's first great passer, the man who transformed the game, virtually begging for the game's ultimate recognition.

Why did it come to that? There was some resentment among the football establishment over Benny's protest against the Players Association. Friedman's self-promotion undoubtedly added to his plight. And some have speculated that anti-Semitism kept Benny out of Canton. Friedman was the first great Jewish football player, a man whose playing prime coincided with a rising tide of anti-Semitism in America. But evidence that anti-Semitism informed the hall's persistent rejection of Friedman has never surfaced, and while the influence of religious prejudice on men's actions can be quite subtle, Sid Luckman was enshrined in the hall's third class.

Over the years, writers pointed to the incomplete statistical record-keeping in Friedman's playing days—the NFL didn't begin to keep official passing statistics until 1932—as a possible explanation for his omission from the hall. The weakness in that argument, however, is that the hall continued to reject Benny long after football historians had started documenting statistics from his time. Benny's sixty-eight career touchdown passes stood as a league record for more than a decade, during which time passers threw the slimmed-down ball and were not hamstrung by the anti-passing rules of Benny's day. His record of twenty touchdown passes in a season set in 1929 withstood thirteen years of assault from Baugh, Luckman, Arnie Herber, Cecil Isbell, and others, until Isbell finally broke it in 1942. Baugh did not throw as many as twenty touchdown passes in a season until his seventh year in the league, when he had twenty-three. These statistics, along with the anecdotal and eyewitness evidence of Benny's revolutionary impact on the game, should have been too strong to ignore.

• • •

Benny's health failed him over the course of the '70s. First there was spinal surgery to remove a cancerous tumor that left him temporarily paralyzed. A few years later, there was back surgery to repair a disc, heart trouble, and diabetes. And in 1979, while Benny was crossing the street, an agonizing pain hit him in his left leg harder than George Trafton or Cal Hubbard or Wild Bill Fleckenstein ever had. The source of the pain was a blood clot, and doctors were forced to amputate the leg at the hip to keep Benny alive.

Friedman fought through the devastation of losing his leg. He kept exercising and stayed fit. With the aid of a prosthesis, a walker, and canes, he kept up his busy New York City life. Doormen and drivers would help him in and out of elevators and cars and help him get around to football functions, theaters, and restaurants. At Neary's Pub, Jimmy Neary would seat Benny so as to hide his hollow pants leg. He watched football on television and, for the most part, wasn't happy with what he saw: pampered players making huge sums of money who couldn't tolerate the pain of a hangnail and who would pass out at the mere thought of playing sixty minutes a game, as he did. He'd stopped writing letters to sports editors about the Hall of Fame, which seemed to have consigned him to the scrap heap of old players who'd fallen too far between the cracks.

Sometime around the middle of 1982, Benny's resolve began to waver. He couldn't seem to find a prosthesis he could tolerate. Diabetes had set in, and there were indications that Benny might lose his remaining leg. During Thanksgiving week, Benny's brother Jerry visited him. The younger Friedman was greeted by a shell of a man; the grandeur of the man who had once loomed so large over the football world was gone.

A couple of days later, Benny shot himself while sitting in his library, surrounded by the cornucopia of trophies and plaques that bore witness to his accomplishments. Shirley was in another room when she heard the shot that ended her husband's life.

Benny never did get that call from the Hall of Fame, the call he'd been waiting thirty-nine years to answer.

It was November 23, 1982, fifty-seven years to the day that Benny Friedman had been elected as the first Jewish captain of the Michigan Wolverines.

Epilogue

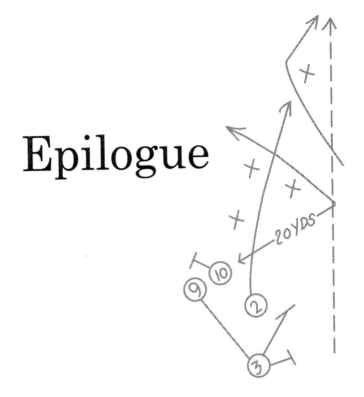

In 1998, I attended the Brandeis University Athletic Hall of Fame annual induction ceremony, which featured a special tribute to Benny Friedman. Produced by former football team manager Bob Weintraub and a large number of Benny's Brandeis players, the tribute included a short film depicting Friedman's spectacular achievements, as well as several moving speeches by his "boys."

The highlight of the evening was the unveiling of a life-size bust of Benny sculpted by Dick Baldacci, captain of Brandeis's 1956 football team. With Benny's help, Baldacci had persevered through early academic difficulty as a Brandeis student. His artistic talent ultimately emerged, and he graduated near the top of his class and went on to enjoy a long career as an art instructor. Baldacci's sculpture of the bust of his old coach was a work that "came from the soul," he said. The unveiling capped a tribute that was a beautiful testament to Benny's great life in football generally and to his indispensable contributions to Brandeis and his players in particular.

Benny's players were hoping that the Pro Football Hall of Fame selectors would take note. Sixteen years after his death, there still was no bust of

Friedman in Canton. He had long ago been relegated to "senior status," eligible for election only if he happened to be one of two candidates nominated each year by the hall's senior committee as an overall finalist. The enshrinees, at least three and no more than seven each year, are selected by vote of thirty-nine selectors who are prominent football writers from around the country. Benny had never even been selected as a finalist. The Brandeis players sent the selectors the materials they had assembled for the tribute, to no avail. Another five years passed without Benny so much as receiving a nomination as a finalist. He was sinking deeper and deeper into the Hall of Fame abyss.

Then, seemingly from nowhere, Friedman was nominated by the seniors' committee as one of the two senior finalists for the hall's class of 2005. Benny's Brandeis boys revved up again, lobbying the selectors with a fervor that Friedman himself would have been hard-pressed to equal.

The group of finalists in 2005 was impressive, headed by two modern-era quarterbacks, Dan Marino and Steve Young, who were virtually certain to be selected. And the other senior nominee, Fritz Pollard, one of the first two black players in the NFL and an outstanding runner, was a worthy pioneering candidate himself. Many speculated that the hall would not take both senior candidates in one year.

When the selectors convened in a Jacksonville, Florida, hotel on the morning of February 5, the day before the Super Bowl, and began voting on the finalists for the class of 2005, the speculation appeared to become reality. Benny didn't have the votes. Then, according to longtime selector and legendary *Los Angeles Times* football writer Bob Oates, two selectors who had originally voted no on Friedman changed their minds, pushing Benny over the top. Later that afternoon, the Pro Football Hall of Fame announced its class of 2005: Marino, Young, Pollard, and Benny Friedman.

• • •

The enshrinement of the Pro Football Hall of Fame Class of 2005 took place on August 7, 2005, just sixty miles from Cleveland, where Benny had been born one hundred years earlier. Canton's Fawcett Stadium was splendidly adorned for the occasion. A majestic stage, occupied by a number of past Hall of Famers, lay at one end of the field. The busts of the four inductees were perched on a table on the stage. Huge Hall of Fame banners framed the stage on either side. Large movie screens displayed highlights of the inductees. A sea of aquamarine created by Miami Dolphins jerseys, evidence of a huge turnout to honor Dan Marino, draped the packed grandstands on either side of the field.

In the VIP seats located on the field in front of the stage, a number of Benny's cousins, nieces, and nephews held a mini family reunion (Shirley had passed away in 1999, and Benny's siblings were also deceased by then). Just behind them were Benny's Brandeis boys, nearly thirty of them, proud of their efforts on behalf of their coach, but proudest most of all of him. It was a very hot, brilliantly sunny day, with not a cloud in the sky to interrupt the sun's rays, but they happily endured the heat. If Benny was whispering to them from above to be careful not to get too "enervated" by the sun, they weren't listening; they had waited a long time for this day.

"If Benny were alive now, he'd jump for joy," his old friend Herman Maisin said some time after his enshrinement in Canton. "The two things he wanted more than anything else in this world was to make the Hall of Fame and to have a book written about him."

ACKNOWLEDGMENTS

I'd had the idea of writing this book since the 1998 tribute to Benny Friedman at Brandeis, when I got my first inkling of just how transformative a figure in the world of sports he had been. Samuel Freedman, a distinguished author and professor at the Columbia University Graduate School of Journalism, breathed life into the idea when he accepted me into his renowned book writing seminar at Columbia. It was there that this project began and where Sam's expertise, critical eye, and encouragement guided me through the early stages. That was a rare opportunity for a first-time author for which I will always be grateful.

Sandy Padwe, also a distinguished author and journalism professor at Columbia, provided the kind of guidance in sports reporting and writing one might expect to receive from one of sports journalism's most highly respected practitioners. Another important influence at Columbia was Tim Harper, a veteran reporter and prolific author who gave me my first lessons in reporting and writing.

My agent, Stacey Glick of Dystel & Goderich Literary Management, didn't merely find a home for the book at PublicAffairs; her guidance throughout the process was of invaluable aid and great comfort. I will be forever grateful to PublicAffairs for giving me the platform to tell Benny's story. Thank you to publisher Susan Weinberg, project editor Meredith Smith, managing editor Melissa Raymond, art director Pete Garceau, and everyone else at PublicAffairs. I am especially indebted to my editor, Lindsay Jones—not just for her patience, energy, interest, and talent, all of which made this book better, but also for her unfailing kindness.

From the start of this project, "Benny's Boys," Friedman's Brandeis players, have been a great inspiration and, with their unique insights into their former coach, an indispensable resource. I will always remember the kindness and cooperation they showed me throughout this project, especially at Benny's Hall of Fame induction in Canton. On that glorious weekend they had worked so long and hard to help bring about, they weren't too busy to welcome an outsider into their midst. Special thanks to Jim Stehlin, Bill McKenna, Dick Bergel, Mike Uhlberg, Charlie Herman, Dick Baldacci, Tom Egan, Irv Heller, Bill Orman, Mike Long, Ed Manganiello, Marty Zelnick, Mel Nash, Leo Surrette, Martin Rachman, and Paul Levenson. Thank you to Bob Domozych, Dick Collins, George Doring, and Jackie Kirkwood, who sadly are no longer with us. And a very special thank-you to Bob Weintraub, the manager of Brandeis's mid-1950s football teams. Bob was my first Brandeis contact and throughout the project was always there with a name, a phone number, a helpful suggestion, an invitation to his home, an invitation to Canton.

Thanks to a few legendary journalists for sharing their memories: the late Hal Lebovitz, the dean of Cleveland sports journalists; Bob Oates, the great writer for the *Los Angeles Times* who thrilled me as he recounted seeing Benny play against the University of Minnesota some eighty-three years ago; and Herman Maisin, the editor-in-chief of *Scholastic Coach and Athletic Director* magazine for more than seven decades. Bud Collins graciously recalled the early days of Brandeis tennis and Benny's role in building the university's athletic department.

Bill Silverman was one of CCNY's star players who helped Benny bring respectability to the school's football program in the mid-1930s. I'm grateful to Bill, now into his ninth decade, for taking time to share his memories of Lewisohn Stadium, New York City college football, and his old coach. Thanks also to Stan Brodsky, Harold Goldstein, and David Weinreb, who played for Benny on his later CCNY teams. The late Irving Spanier, who as a CCNY baseball star met Benny in the mid-1930s and became Benny's attorney and lifelong friend, very kindly shared his recollections, including painful memories of Benny's death.

Special thanks to Marilyn Myers, Benny's grand-niece, for sharing her recollections and photographs and for her help in locating other family members. The late Tony Hattenbach, Benny's nephew, graciously gave me a number of family photographs as well as his time. Jody Rosenbaum, Benny's niece, welcomed me into her home to share memories of her uncle, and David Friedman and Larry Friedman, Benny's nephews, were generous with their time as well. Benny's friend and favorite restaurateur, Jimmy Neary, kindly shared his hospitality and memories. Marie Koenig of Cleveland, Glenville High Class of 1922, remembered how Benny Friedman, Glenville Class of '23, captivated the school with his football exploits.

A number of libraries and other instructions were most helpful throughout this project. Special thanks to Karen Jania and the staff at the University of Michigan's Bentley Historical Library; Karen Adler Abramson and the staff at the Robert D. Farber University Archives at Brandeis University; George Rugg, Charles Lamb, and the staff at the libraries of the University of Notre Dame; Sydney C. Van Nort at the City University of New York archives; Theresa Gonzalez, archivist at Great Lakes Naval Training Station; the staff at the Northwestern University archives; the staff at the New York Public Library, especially Michael Terry and the staff at the Dorot Jewish Division; Kent Stevens at the College Football Hall of Fame; Tom Murphy at the Green Bay Packers Hall of Fame; and the staffs at the archives of the Pro Football Hall of Fame, the Library of Congress, and the Western Reserve Historical Society in Cleveland.

Thanks to Grantland Rice, Wilfred Smith, Arthur Daley, Harry Salsinger, Joe Williams, Walter Eckersall, and the many other sportswriters of Benny's day who bore witness to the phenomenon that was Benny Friedman. Thanks, also, to the authors of the books noted in the bibliography that were so helpful in the writing of mine.

Thank you to the many other librarians and archivists, friends, players, Friedman family members, and others who shared their time with me and assisted me with this project.

My mother and father have been a rock for me in anything I've ever done. Their unwavering confidence in my ability to write this book has not been a surprise to me, but it has been a huge inspiration and comfort.

My daughters, Allie and Samantha, are two bright rays of sunshine who never ceased to encourage me even as they sacrificed and endured far more education about a Depression-era football player than any teenage girl should have to endure.

Thank you to my wife, Andrea, who has shared this dream of mine from the beginning and whose love and encouragement helped make it a reality.

NOTES

A Note on Sources

In writing this book I have drawn on interviews, newspaper, magazine, and journal articles, books, and other materials referenced in the chapter notes below and the bibliography. I would like to note here (in abbreviated format) some sources I found particularly valuable.

On Glenville and the history of the Jewish community in Cleveland: *The Encyclopedia of Cleveland History* and *Shul With A Pool: The "Synagogue Center" in American Jewish History*. On the role of football in the lives of young Jews: *King Football: Sports and Spectacle in the Golden Age of Radio, Newsreels, Movies and Magazines; Ellis Island to Ebbets Field; Jews and Sport: A Century of Retrospect; and Antisemitism in American Athletics.* On sports in Cleveland: *The Charity Game: The Story of Cleveland's Thanksgiving Day High School Football Classic; The Encyclopedia of Cleveland History; and Sports in Cleveland: An Illustrated History.*

On Jewish quotas: *Ellis Island to Ebbets Field.* On anti-Semitism, Henry Ford, and the Ku Klux Klan: *Henry Ford and the Jews: The Mass Production of Hate; The Death of American Anti-Semitism; Ellis Island to Ebbets Field; and Antisemitism in American Athletics.* On Red Grange and on Friedman's Michigan career: *The Big Nine; The Galloping Ghost: The Autobiography of Red Grange; Big Ten Football: Its Life and Times, Great Coaches, Players and Games; The Galloping Ghost: An Interview With Red Grange;* the *Michigan Daily;* the *Daily Illini; Big Ten Football Since 1895; Hail to the Victors.* On Fielding Yost: *Football's Greatest Coaches; Made in Detroit; Great College Football Coaches of the Twenties and Thirties;* "Building A Sports Empire."

On the development of the NFL through the 1920s and Friedman's NFL career: *Pro Football's Rag Days; The Giants of New York; Pigskin: The Early Years of Pro Football;* various articles from the Professional Football Researchers Association and *The Coffin Corner;* and *Big Leagues: Professional Baseball, Football and Basketball in National Memory.* On the charity game between the Giants and the Notre Dame All-Stars: the newsreel of Knute Rockne, Jimmy Walker, and assembly outside New York City Hall.

On Friedman's service in the Navy: *Dictionary of American Naval Fighting Ships; Chronology of the War at Sea 1939–1945;* and the military personnel record of Friedman provided by National Personnel Records Center, National Archives and Records Administration.

Newspaperarchive.com, with its supply of newspapers from locales throughout the country, was a most helpful database. The websites of the Pro Football Hall of

Fame, the Professional Football Researchers Association, and the University of Michigan's Bentley Historical Library provided helpful reference throughout this project.

Articles from contemporaneous issues of newspapers referenced in the chapter notes and bibliography were invaluable in describing the games that are recounted in this book. Those papers most valuable in this regard were the *Brooklyn Citizen, Brooklyn Times-Union, Chicago Daily Tribune, Cleveland Plain Dealer, Daily Illini, Detroit Free Press, Detroit News, Los Angeles Times, Michigan Daily, New York Daily News, New York Evening Journal, New York Evening Post, New York Herald-Tribune,* and *New York Times.*

Benny's articles in *Collier's* and *Scholastic Coach*; his book, *The Passing Game*; and his New York Public Library oral history interview were crucial sources on his unique passing motion and on the various phases and pursuits in his life.

Introduction

2   *"When he introduced himself"*: Author interview with Herman Maisin, December 7, 2006.

2   *"On the button"*: Ibid.

2   *"Herman . . . do you think anyone"*: Ibid.

3   *"Benny Friedman was responsible for changing"*: Cliff Gewecke, "At School with Benny the Convincer," *Los Angeles Times West Magazine,* November 26, 1967.

4   *"Has Mike Ditka been tipped off to the fact"*: "The Williams' Shuffle," CNN/SI .com, July 27, 1999, http://sportsillustrated.cnn.com/football/nfl/1999/preview /teams/news/1999/07/29/nfc_west_saints/.

4   *"The greatest football player in the world"*: Paul Gallico, "The Greatest Football Player in the World," *Liberty,* December 27, 1930, by permission of Liberty Library Corp.

Chapter 1

7   *"The polar opposites"*: Steven A. Riess, *Sports and the American Jew* (Syracuse, NY: Syracuse University Press, 1998), 15.

7   *"Not only are they undersized"*: Ibid.

8   *"I couldn't wait"*: Benny Friedman, interview by Elli Wohlgelernter, September 5 and October 6, 1980, The New York Public Library–American Jewish Committee Oral History Collection, by permission of Dorot Jewish Division, New York Public Library.

8   *"Pick it up . . . I won't pick it up"*: Friedman interview, 16.

9   *"We had an iron brick"*: Ibid., 4.

9   *"I'd stretch my hand"*: Ibid.

11   *"Just a little kid"*: Ibid., 2.

11   *"You're too small"*: Timothy L. Hudak, *The Charity Game: The Story of Cleveland's Thanksgiving Day High School Football Classic* (Cleveland, OH: Sports Heritage Specialty Publications, 2002), 19.

13   *"Bet you a dinner"*: "Friedman, Rated Dub, Is Now Star," *Kingston Daily Freeman,* December 4, 1925, http://www.newspaperarchive.com/PdfViewerTags .aspx?img=36847947&firstvisit=true&src=search&xurrentResult=0.

13   *"I had a field day"*: Friedman interview, 3.

16   *"We went into the game scared"*: Mitchell V. Charnley, *Play The Game: The Book of Sport* (New York: Viking Press, 1931), 100.

Chapter 2

24   *"The Michigan alumni in Cleveland decided"*: Friedman interview, 5.

26   *"Michigan isn't going to lose"*: John U. Bacon, "Building a Sports Empire," *Michigan History,* September/October 2000, http://www.michiganhistory magazine.com/portfoli/pdf/so00yos.pdf.

26   *"I remember Yost"*: Norman Beasley and George W. Stark, *Made in Detroit* (New York: G. P. Putnam's Sons, 1957), 64.

26   *"No, my father taught me"*: Edwin Pope, *Football's Greatest Coaches* (Atlanta: Tupper and Love, 1955), 311.

27   *"Willie Heston never had"*: Howard Roberts, *The Big Nine* (New York: G. P. Putnam's Sons, 1948), 40.

27   *"did not attempt to star"*: Ibid.

28   *"No sirree"*: Pope, *Football's Greatest Coaches,* 315.

28   *"Who are they . . . that they should beat"*: Bacon, "Building a Sports Empire."

29   *"Some people can drink"*: Pope, *Football's Greatest Coaches,* 318.

30   *"Cynics call our method"*: Roberts, *The Big Nine,* 50.

30   *"No good blocker and tackler"*: Official game program, Navy vs. Michigan, October 31, 1925.

30   *"Ye think we got all day?"*: Pope, *Football's Greatest Coaches,* 315.

Chapter 3

34   *"Stand a good chance"*: Mervin D. Hyman and Gordon S. White Jr., *Big Ten Football: Its Life and Times, Great Coaches, Players and Games* (New York: Macmillan, 1977), 165.

36   *"Grange runs as Nurmi runs"*: Ibid., 167.

37   *"Take those two dummies"*: Gallico, "The Greatest Football Player in the World."

37   *"I'm quitting"*: Arthur Daley, "The Education of Benny," *New York Times,* April 24, 1957.

39   *"My, I must have put down"*: Friedman interview, 9.

39   *"Friedman . . . any of his food"*: Ibid., 9–10.

39   *"To beat Illinoism"*: "Along the Sidelines," *Brooklyn Standard Union,* October 15, 1924.

39   *"Every time Grange takes the ball"*: Associated Press, *The Sports Immortals* (Englewood Cliffs, NJ: Prentice-Hall, 1972), 14.

40   *"You can't beat a coach"*: "Bunking the Line," *Daily Illini,* October 17, 1924.

42   *"There is absolutely no hope"*: "Michigan Tilt Ticket Orders Deluge Office," *Daily Illini,* October 15, 1924.

42   *"Anything in the rule book"*: Red Grange and Ira Morton, *The Galloping Ghost: The Autobiography of Red Grange* (Wheaton, IL: Crossroads Communications, 1953), 42.

43   *"Okay, fellas":* Ibid.

44   *"Yes, I know 'em . . . we may need you":* Friedman interview, 19.

48   *"I'm so dog-tired I can hardly stand":* Grange and Morton, *The Galloping Ghost,* 46.

48   *"Shoulda had another":* Ibid.

48   *"Fielding . . . why don't you":* Tim Cohane, *Great College Football Coaches of the Twenties and Thirties* (New Rochelle, NY: Arlington House, 1973), 237.

50   *"You!" Little bellowed:* Roberts, *The Big Nine,* 52.

Chapter 4

51   *"Give me a redheaded man":* "Yost Got His Athlete," *New York Sun,* October 20, 1924.

51   *"It may be some one else":* Grantland Rice, "The Star Performance," *New York Herald-Tribune,* October 28, 1924.

51   *"The second Jim Thorpe":* *Brooklyn Standard Union,* October 24, 1924.

51   *"Harold is a red-haired god":* "Red Grange," *Daily Illini,* October 26, 1924.

51   *"Michigan has some fleet-footed runners":* James Crusinberry, "Illinois Buries Wolverines 39 to 14," *Chicago Daily Tribune,* October 19, 1924.

52   *"Leading the long caravan":* H. F. Mahoney, "Gridiron Play Is Brilliant," *New York Sun,* October 20, 1924.

53   *"Bill . . . honestly, I'm on the varsity":* Friedman interview, 11.

53   *Discussion of Herbert Opitz:* "Electric Shock Fatal to Opitz, Badger Fullback," *Daily Illini,* October 24, 1924.

53   *Discussion of 1923 game:* Roberts, *The Big Nine,* 210–212.

54   *"Yes, Rockwell may have been downed":* Ibid., 212.

55   *Discussion of Tyson and broadcast of game:* "The Michigan Stadium Story: Michigan's Radio Football Announcers," Bentley Historical Library, http://bentley.umich.edu/~bhl/stadium/stadtext/mstadium.htm.

57   *"Friedman . . . we got a bigger":* Friedman interview, 12.

57   *Dialogue between Friedman and Hoyt:* Ibid.

57   *"Michigan Finds New Star":* "Michigan Finds New Star in Friedman as Wisconsin Falls, 21–0," *New York Herald-Tribune,* October 26, 1924.

58   *"FRIEDMAN STAR OF TILT":* *Daily Illini,* October 26, 1924.

58   *"Michigan whipped Wisconsin":* "Michigan Finds New Star . . . ," *New York Herald-Tribune,* October 26, 1924.

60   *Discussion of dropped passes and Friedman walking off field:* Friedman interview, 13.

61   *"Friedman, don't ever let me see you":* Ibid., 14.

61   *"You no-good":* Ibid.

62   *Discussion of Grange's injuries:* "Coach Says Grange Is Definitely Out," *New York Times,* November 17, 1924.

62   *"The leading student":* *Michigan Daily,* November 18, 1924.

Chapter 5

65   *"Anti-Semitism seems to have reached":* Neil Baldwin, *Henry Ford and the Jews: The Mass Production of Hate* (New York: PublicAffairs, 2001), 94.

66   *"Never before in the history of football":* Sidney S. Cohen, "The Jewish Football Stars: An All-American Team for 1925," *The Jewish Advocate,* December 17, 1925.

68   *"You don't even know"*: Roberts, *The Big Nine,* 52.

70   *"Benny Friedman appeared to be"*: Fred Turbyville, "Rockne Answers 1925's
      Question; Grange Falters," *Syracuse Herald,* October 5, 1925, evening edition,
      http://www.newspaperarchive.com/PdfViewerTags.aspx?img=22930699&
      firstvisit=true&src=search&currentResult=1.

70   *"Michigan's 39–0 victory cannot be assumed"*: "Potential Strength Shown By
      Michigan," *Detroit Free Press,* October 4, 1925.

71   *"Benny Friedman was the big noise"*: Frank H. Williams, "Few Surprises in U.S.
      Football," *Manitoba Free Press,* October 12, 1925, http://www.newspaperarchive
      .com/PdfViewerTags.aspx?img=41457977&firstvisit=true&src=search&current
      Result=0.

71   *"Benny Is Team By Himself"*: *Cleveland News,* October 11, 1925.

71   *"Statistics Show"*: "Indiana Team Fails in Face of Barrage of Yost's Gridmen," *In-
      diana Daily Student,* October 13, 1925.

71   *"The [Michigan State and Indiana] games"*: W. C. Richards, "Strength of Michi-
      gan Is Unknown," *Detroit Free Press,* October 12, 1925.

73   *"An impregnable defense"*: "Varsity Defense and Offense Gets Drill; 'Big Jawn'
      Watches," *Wisconsin Daily Cardinal,* October 16, 1925.

74   *"Hey, Coach"*: *Saturday Evening Post,* September 29, 1934.

74   *"In less than a minute"*: Bernard Postal, Jesse Silver, and Roy Silver, *Encyclopedia
      of Jews in Sports* (New York: Bloch Publishing Co., 1965), 245.

75   *"Benny Friedman, Benny Friedman:"* *Chicago Daily Tribune,* October 19, 1925,
      ProQuest Historical Newspapers.

75   *"We got the little Badgers' skins"*: Harry Bullion, "Michigan's Eleven Still Is
      Mystery," *Detroit Free Press,* October 19, 1925.

75   *"[I] left Ann Arbor"*: John D. McCallum, *Big Ten Football Since 1895* (Radnor,
      PA: Chilton Book Co., 1976), 37.

76   *"Ben Friedman of Michigan proved"*: Harry Conzel, "Sporting Column," *The
      Jewish Advocate,* October 15, 1925.

76   *"Benny Friedman, Michigan's quarterback, is simply"*: Harry Conzel, "Sporting
      Column," *The Jewish Advocate,* October 29, 1925.

76   *"Benny Friedman of Michigan Is All-American"*: Sidney S. Cohen, "Benny Fried-
      man of Michigan Is All-American Bound," *Brooklyn Jewish Chronicle,* October
      23, 1925.

76   *"A new hero has come"*: "Benny Friedman," *Chicago Chronicle,* October 23, 1925.

77   *"The background, heredity"*: Ibid.

77   *"Benny, short, stocky, 19"*: "Friedman, Hero of Wolverines, Peril to Grange,"
      Chicago Daily Tribune, October 19, 1925.

77   *"If Mr. Red Grange"*: Ibid.

Chapter 6

79   *"Benny . . . I'm scared to death"*: *Saturday Evening Post,* September 30, 1933.

79   *"Hell, Bennie, so am I"*: Ibid.

80   *"Outsmarted us to make the play"*: "Grange Picks Three Wolverines On Star
      Team Chosen From Players He Has Met," *Michigan Daily,* December 2, 1926.

80   *"Wolverine's Star Bests Grange"*: *Washington Post,* October 25, 1925.

80 *"The score [of the upcoming game]"*: University of Illinois football program, October 24, 1925.

80 *"Grange didn't gain enough ground"*: Pope, *Football's Greatest Coaches*, 315.

80 *"I particularly remember Benny Friedman"*: Grange and Morton, *The Galloping Ghost*, 56.

81 *"Friedman's worth to the Michigan team"*: Walter Eckersall, "Yost To Pit Star Back Against Navy's," *Chicago Daily Tribune*, October 28, 1925.

82 *"Pour it on"*: Grantland Rice, "When Michigan Sank Navy," *Newport Daily News*, September 15, 1953, http://www.newspaperarchive.com/PdfViewer Tags.aspx?img=55681460&firstvisit=true&src=search&currentResult=0.

84 *"The Navy, like every team"*: M. F. Druckenbrod, "Wolverines Prove Far Too Powerful," *Detroit Free Press*, November 1, 1925.

84 *"Haven't you any respect"*: "Yost's Answer to R. Lardner Is Neat Verse," *Michigan Daily*, November 3, 1925.

84 *"The forward pass is a useful thing"*: Ibid.

84 *"The secret of the feather ball"*: Benny Friedman, *The Passing Game* (New York: Steinfeld Inc., 1931), 33.

85 *"They concluded that all of the elements"*: Benny Friedman, "Forward Passing The Friedman Way," *Scholastic Coach* 36, no. 8 (April 1967): 90.

86 *"Michigan, mighty Michigan"*: Finney Briggs, "Crazy Quilt," *Southtown Economist*, November 3, 1925, http://www.newspaperarchive.com/PdfViewerTags .aspx?img=32164983&firstvisit=true&src=search&currentResult=6.

87 *"A school in any community"*: *Village of University Heights v. Cleveland Jewish Orphans' Home*, 20 F.2d, 745 (6th Cir. 1927).

87 *"[University Heights] . . . does not want"*: Stuart Meck, "Zoning and Anti-Semitism in the 1920s: The Case of Cleveland Jewish Orphan Home v. Village of University Heights and Its Aftermath," *Journal of Planning History* 4, no. 2 (May 2005): 105.

88 *Dialogue between Yost and Wilson on canceling the game*: George Beres, "NU and the Mud Cost Michigan the 1925 National Title," HailToPurple.Com, http:// www.hailtopurple.com/features/history1.html.

91 *"In my twenty-five years of football"*: Walter Eckersall, "Purple Brains And Lewis' Toe Sink Wolverines In Morass," *Chicago Daily Tribune*, November 11, 1925.

Chapter 7

96 *"We feel that due to Michigan's"*: "Wilson Lauds Wolverines," *Daily Northwestern*, November 25, 1925.

97 *"Your timely and unselfish concession"*: Charles F. Dellbridge, letter to Walter Dill Scott, December 1, 1925, Papers of Walter Dill Scott, by permission of Northwestern University Archives.

97 *"You are members of the greatest football team"*: "Friedman Announced As New Captain; President Scores Professionalism," *Michigan Daily*, November 24, 1925.

97 *"The modern Willie Heston"*: Richard Vidmer, "Michigan Crushes Navy Eleven, 54–0," *New York Times*, November 1, 1925.

97 *"He shoots passes"*: "Friedman, Hero Of Wolverines, Peril To Grange," *Chicago Daily Tribune*, October 19, 1925.

98   *"Sensation of the year":* Knute Rockne, "Notre Dame Mentor Selects Champion All-Western Team That He Would Willingly Back Against the Best in the East," *Syracuse Herald,* November 29, 1925, http://www.newspaperarchive.com /PdfViewerTags.aspx?img=22937260&firstvisit=true&src=search&current Result=1.

98   *"Friedman peeled off those yards":* Vidmer, "Michigan Crushes Navy Eleven."

98   *"He is the coolest man":* Stephen Fox, *Big Leagues: Professional Baseball, Football and Basketball in National Memory* (New York: William Morrow, 1994), 43.

98   *"To never make a mistake":* "Friedman, Benny," http://jewsinsports.org/profile .asp?sport=football&ID=5.

98   *"[I] was [Yost's] fair-haired boy":* Friedman interview, 14.

99   *"Right 'chere, right 'chere":* Ibid.

99   *"He is a genius at handling a team":* Cohen, "The Jewish Football Stars."

100 *"Be glad to see Grange do anything else":* Associated Press, "Yost Comments On Offers To Grange," *Michigan Daily,* November 19, 1925.

101 *"The Grange we know":* "Zuppke Rebukes Grange for Joining Pro Team," *Brooklyn Times Union,* November 24, 1925.

101 *"I tell you . . . that no other":* Ibid.

102 *"Not interested":* "M'Carty Gets Pro Bid; Turns It Down," *Chicago Daily Tribune,* November 26, 1925.

102 *Dialogue regarding captaincy:* Friedman interview, 38.

103 *"Benny Friedman at Full Tilt":* American Hebrew, December 18, 1925.

104 *"Have done the most for":* Jack Darcy, "The Five Big Jews of 1925: A Non-Jewish View of Which Five Jews Have Done The Most For America Within The Last Year," *American Jewish World,* January 1, 1926.

104 *"[Benny] is causing the members of his race":* Ibid.

104 *"Friedman's prowess as a football star":* Ibid.

104 *"This . . . Jewish prodigy":* Henry Paull, "'Benny' Friedman—Gridiron Hero," *American Hebrew,* December 18, 1925.

105 *"[Friedman] symbolizes a tolerance":* Ibid.

Chapter 8

106 *"Stagg is sixty-four and is still":* Fielding Yost, letter to C. D. King, December 15, 1925, by permission of Bentley Historical Library, University of Michigan.

107 *"As close to perfection as any":* Arthur Daley, "Trick Play," *New York Times,* November 5, 1963.

108 *"Unerring passing":* Associated Press, "Michigan Batters Oklahoma Aggies," *New York Times,* October 3, 1926.

111 *"The will to win . . . is not worth a nickel":* Time, "The Will to Prepare," November 7, 1955, http://www.time.com/time/magazine/article /0,9171,807959,00.html.

111 *"Apostle of Grief":* "Yost, Apostle of Grief, Sings Blues for Fans," *Chicago Daily Tribune,* October 29, 1926.

111 *"Last year's game is only a memory":* Ibid.

113 *"Those big Navy tackles":* Hyman and White, *Big Ten Football,* 198.

113 *"Benny, if it's all the same to you":* Ibid.

115   *"I never saw one penalty called"*: Grantland Rice, "When Michigan Sank Navy," *Newport Daily News,* September 15, 1953, http://www.newspaperarchive.com /PdfViewerTags.aspx?img=55681460&firstvisit=true&src=search&current Result=0.

115   *"We were quartered at"*: Hyman and White, *Big Ten Football,* 198.

117   *"The boys seemed to have the idea"*: Associated Press, "Benny Friedman Indignant When Name Is Used," *Salt Lake Tribune,* November 9, 1926, http://www.news paperarchive.com/PdfViewerTags.aspx?img=1024122488&firstvisit=true&src= search&currentResult=0.

Chapter 9

119   *"Football material that coaches get"*: Associated Press, "Big Ten Gets Two Big Shocks," *Washington Post,* November 1, 1926.

120   *"It is only natural to suppose that Capt. Benny"*: Irving Vaughn, "90,000 To Watch Michigan-Ohio Clash," *Chicago Daily Tribune,* November 13, 1926.

120   *"At this rate, they're going to drub us"*: McCallum, *Big Ten Football Since 1895,* 40.

121   *"Dammit, Wally"*: Ibid., 41.

123   *"Fake!"*: Roberts, *The Big Nine,* 54.

126   *"No soft ball here."*: Friedman, *Passing Game,* 45.

127   *"Benny Friedman passed all afternoon"*: "90,000 See Michigan Defeat Ohio State," *New York Times,* November 14, 1926.

128   *"I'm better now . . . Don't stay"*: "Benny Friedman Would Lead Michigan Teams To Title And Bring His Father Back To Health," *Akron Beacon Journal,* November 17, 1926.

Chapter 10

132   *"Come on Benny! You can do it!"*: McCallum, *Big Ten Football Since 1895,* 42.

133   *"For all-around football smartness and football ability"*: Grantland Rice, "The All-America Football Team," *Collier's,* December 11, 1926.

134   *"Pass as accurately as ever"*: Ibid.

134   *"The man whom Walter Eckersall, the Walter Camp of the Midwest"*: "The 1926 All-American All-Jewish Team," *American Jewish World,* November 26, 1926.

134   *"Break faith with the Old Man"*: Associated Press, "Friedman Turned Down Pro Offer," *Decatur Daily Review,* November 25, 1926, http://www.newspaper archive.com/PdfViewerTags.aspx?img=8468281&firstvisit=true&src=search& currentResult=3.

135   *"We wish to deal a death blow"*: Robert W. Peterson, *Pigskin: The Early Years of Pro Football* (New York: Oxford University Press, 1997), 92.

137   "To Benny Friedman: You were a bulwark": Fielding Yost to Benny Friedman, by permission of College Football Hall of Fame archives, South Bend, Indiana.

Chapter 11

145   *"I was the only chap"*: Bob Curran, *Pro Football's Rag Days* (Englewood Cliffs, NJ: 1969), 60. Copyright © 1969 by Bob Curran. Reprinted with permission of the R. S. Curran estate and the Foley Literary Agency.

145   *"I had to earn my spurs"*: Fox, *Big Leagues*, 34.

149   *"BENNY FRIEDMAN TO PLAY IN GREEN BAY"*: *Appleton Post-Crescent*, July 20, 1927, http://www.newspaperarchive.com/PdfViewerTags.aspx?img =47306288&firstvisit=true&src=search&currentResult=1.

149   *"Sunday is going to be"*: "'Benny Friedman Day' Will Be Observed Sunday When Packers Meet Clevelanders," *Wisconsin Rapids Daily Tribune*, September 22, 1927, http://www.newspaperarchive.com/PdfViewerTags.aspx?img =123673&firstvisit=true&src=search&currentResult=0.

149   *"Football fans in all parts of the country"*: "Packers Set For Feature Battle," *Appleton Post Crescent*, September 24, 1927, http://www.newspaperarchive.com /PdfViewerTags.aspx?img=4771676&firstvisit=true&src=search&current Result=8.

150   *"Keep your chin up, Benny" and ensuing dialogue:* Benny Friedman, "The Professional Touch," *Collier's*, October 15, 1932.

151   *"Precision, exactness, hard-hitting"*: Ibid.

Chapter 12

153   *"BENNY FRIEDMAN'S BULLDOGS"*: *Cleveland Plain Dealer*, September 30, 1927.

154   *"This is one sweet tough racket"*: Jack Sords, "Sords Points," *New Castle News*, October 20, 1927, http://www.newspaperarchive.com/PdfViewertags .aspx?img=568887888&firstvisit=true&src=search&currentResult=0.

154   *"He will be the sensation of the league"*: *Cleveland Plain Dealer*, September 27, 1927.

157   *"One of the greatest Jewish stars"*: "To Honor Friedman," *New York Times*, October 10, 1927.

158   *"I was all set to go"*: Associated Press, "Dooley, Friedman Engage In Joust Forward Passing," *Bridgeport Telegram*, October 14, 1927, http://www.newspaper archive.com/PdfViewerTags.aspx?img=12340123&firstvisit=true&src=search& currentResult=0.

160   *"Professional football drew only about"*: Walter Trumbull, "The Listening Post," *New York Evening Post*, October 17, 1927.

162   *"Perfect football"*: Wilfred Smith, "Benny's Passes Thrill; Visitors Lose on Safety," *Chicago Daily Tribune*, October 24, 1927.

163   *"Mr. Durfee, I'm not interested in Fielding Yost today"*: Curran, *Pro Football's Rag Days*, 61.

163   *"George, this isn't football"*: Dave Lewis, "Once Over Lightly," *The Independent*, December 2, 1951, http://www.newspaperarchive.com/PdfViewerTags .aspx?img=45670697&firstvisit=true&src=search&currentResult=0.

163   *"Friedman said that if you don't lay off"*: Ibid.

163 *"BENNY'S PASSES THRILL":* Chicago Daily Tribune, October 24, 1927.

163 *"The Bulldogs' touchdowns were gained":* Associated Press, "Bears Retain Lead," *New York Times,* October 24, 1927.

164 *"He tore our line to shreds":* Hugh Wyatt, "Ernie Nevers—Has There Ever Been Better?" http://www.coachwyatt.com/ernienevers.htm.

165 *"Until Friedman came along, the pass had been used":* George Halas, "Halas Calls Friedman Pioneer Passer—Rest Came By Design," *Daily News,* February 4, 1967.

166 *"I used to think of him . . . as a crusader":* Curran, *Pro Football's Rag Days,* 62.

166 *"[Ed] and I used to travel":* Ibid., 63.

166 *"Gertrude Ederle herself would have had":* Al Sommer, "Bulldogs Wallow to 15–0 Victory Over N.Y. Yanks," *Cleveland Plain Dealer,* November 7, 1927.

Chapter 13

173 *"He was the same old Benny":* Rud Rennie, "Friedman and His Wolverines Defeat Yankees," *New York Herald-Tribune,* October 15, 1928.

173 *"As splendid an individual performance as has been seen":* "Friedman Rampage Trims Pro Yankees," *New York Times,* October 15, 1928.

174 *"They all came from the cow country":* Friedman interview, 15.

174 *"Benny revolutionized football":* Barry Gottehrer, *The Giants of New York* (New York: G.P. Putnam's Sons, 1963), 65.

177 *"We fooled them by calling for a double pass":* Friedman, *Passing Game,* 45.

177 *"Benny was specially dangerous":* George Halas, with Gwen Morgan and Arthur Veysey, *Halas By Halas: The Autobiography of George Halas* (New York: McGraw-Hill, 1979), 152.

178 *"Benny as a forward passer and perfect field general":* Wilfred Smith, "Friedman The Passer Shines In New Role," *Chicago Daily Tribune,* October 29, 1928.

178 *"I did that lots of times":* George Sullivan, *Pro Football's Passing Game* (New York: Dodd, Mead & Co., 1972), 22.

178 *"Friedman remains today the best player":* H. G. Salsinger, "The Umpire," *Detroit News,* November 29, 1928.

182 *"After it was all over":* Rud Rennie, "Friedman Stars in Detroit's 19–19 Tie With Giants," *New York Herald-Tribune,* November 12, 1928.

183 *"We were in punt formation":* Friedman, *Passing Game,* 32.

185 *"Friedman has six threats instead of three":* Billy Evans, "Billy Evans Says," *Bismarck Tribune,* November 26, 1927, http://www.newspaperarchive.com /PdfViewerTags.aspx?img=581209&firstvisit=true&src=search&current Result=0.

Chapter 14

187 *"He made us believers":* Dave Klein, *The New York Giants: Yesterday, Today, and Tomorrow* (Chicago: Henry Regnery, 1973), 41.

189 *"Acquisition of Friedman is a ten strike":* Leonard Cohen, "Friedman Signed As Giant Captain," *New York Evening Post,* July 18, 1929.

190   *"The newspapers had gone to the top rabbi":* Hank Greenberg, *The Story of My Life,* ed. Ira Berkow (New York: Times Books, 1989), 59, by permisison of the William Morris Agency.

191   *"We are not a people apart":* Henry Rosenfeld, "Benny Friedman On Football," *Jewish Digest,* December 1940, 82.

191   *"I find myself wanting":* Greenberg, *The Story of My Life,* 62.

192   *"I might have gotten more being a Jew":* Friedman interview, 48.

193   *"The passing of Friedman had the crowd tingling":* "N.Y. Giants Beat Stapleton Eleven, 19–9," *New York Herald-Tribune,* October 14, 1929.

193   *"Benny really started the passing game":* letter from Ken Strong, February 28, 1966, Friedman file, Pro Football Hall of Fame, Canton, Ohio.

194   *"He was the decathalon champion":* Arthur Daley, "A Dissent From An Expert," *New York Times,* December 23, 1949.

196   *Giants-Bisons extract: Buffalo Evening News,* November 4, 1929.

197   *"Despite the one-sided aspect of the score":* Jack Laing, "Friedman, Hagerty, Plansky Star in Giants' 45–6 Win; Ryan Scores Local Tally," *Buffalo Courier Express,* November 6, 1929.

198   *"In the first place . . . all a professional player":* "Friedman Optimistic as He Brings Giants to Town For Test with Bison Gridders," *Buffalo Courier Express,* November 5, 1929.

198   *"When I played at the University of Michigan":* Ibid.

202   *"Wisconsinites Drub New York Eleven":* *New York Daily News,* November 25, 1929.

204   *"Benny Friedman is the quarterback and captain":* Wilfred Smith, "Packers, Giants Get 8 Places On All-Pro Eleven," *Chicago Daily Tribune,* December 22, 1929.

204   *"Usually the campus hero":* Frank Getty, "Speaking of Sport," *Ames Daily Tribune,* December 17, 1929, http://www.newspaperarchive.com/PdfViewer Tags.aspx?img=89573170&firstvisit=true&src=search&currentResult=1.

Chapter 15

207   *"Now, Mother, nothing vile":* Friedman interview, 20.

208   *"The greatest football brain":* Henry McCormick, "No Foolin' Now," *Wisconsin State Journal,* September 18, 1930, http://www.newspaperarchive.com/Pdf ViewerTags.aspx?img=1058723288&firstvisit=true&src=search&current Result=1?.

209   *"We had no problem with anyone else":* Klein, *The New York Giants,* 43.

210   *"I was living in Brooklyn that year":* Arthur Daley, "Food for Thought," *New York Times,* October 27, 1961.

210   *"I don't know how many, if any":* George Joel, "The Sporting World," *Jewish Advocate,* September 30, 1930.

210   *"Take it from any angle":* Hal Totten, "Newman, a Second Friedman, Leads Michigan Grid Hopes," *New York Evening Post,* October 28, 1930.

211   *"Friedman Is Coming":* *Portsmouth Times,* November 3, 1930.

212   *"Benny Friedman Performs Tonight":* *Portsmouth Times,* November 5, 1930.

212   *"Tonight is homecoming night":* Ibid.

212   *"David with his little slingshot"*: Lynn A. Wittenburg, "As The Giants Bounced The Spartans On Their Knees," *Portsmouth Times,* November 6, 1930.

214   *"It was an afternoon of thrills"*: Knute K. Rockne, "What Thrills A Coach," *Collier's,* December 6, 1930.

217   *"Cagle has greatly strengthened our team"*: "Giants Seek Title In Pro Grid Battle Against Green Bay," *New York Evening Post,* November 22, 1930.

Chapter 16

220   *"Our team will be one of the strongest"*: Marshall Hunt, "Rock Promises Plenty Of Opposition," *Detroit News,* December 11, 1930.

221   *"The greatest array of gridiron talent"*: Marshall Hunt, "Carideo, Brill, Savoldi Coming For Giant Game," *Daily News,* December 12, 1930.

222   *"There has been no occasion"*: Video of ceremony on steps of city hall, December 13, 1930, by permission of University of Notre Dame archives.

222   *"You'll never live to know the day"*: Ibid.

222   *"New York has always been"*: Ibid.

222   *"I was delightfully surprised"*: Ibid.

222   *"If Benny Friedman's boys"*: Ibid.

224   *"That's too bad"*: Curran, *Pro Football's Rag Days,* 64.

224   *"Fellows, these Giants are heavy but slow"*: Gottehrer, *The Giants of New York,* 81.

225   *"How many people are here today"*: Jerry Brondfield, *Rockne: The Coach, The Man, The Legend* (New York: Random House, 1976), 256.

227   *"I'm dropping back"*: Curran, *Pro Football's Rag Days,* 67.

229   *"Friedman played one of the greatest games"*: Tom Thorp, "Tilt Not True Comparison Of Players' Abilities," *New York Evening Journal,* December 15, 1930.

229   *"Who gave you the signals"*: Curran, *Pro Football's Rag Days,* 67.

229   *"One team in a thousand"*: Lewis Burton, "New York Turns Out to See Giants and 'Irish,'" *New York American,* December 15, 1930.

229   *"That was the greatest football machine"*: Gottehrer, *The Giants of New York,* 83.

229   "Today we saw the greatest football game": "Notre Dame Stars Praised At Dinner," *New York Times,* December 15, 1930.

Chapter 17

231   *"As a professional"*: Gallico, "The Greatest Football Player in the World."

232   *"greatest football player in the world"*: Ibid.

232   *"The young Cleveland Jew"*: Ibid.

232   *"Behind that swart face"*: Ibid.

233   *"When he is tackled by 210-pounders"*: Ibid.

234   *"I'd rather sit on the bench and watch"*: W. P. Minego, "Sparks From The Sport Anvil," *Portsmouth Times,* March 2, 1931, http://www.newspaperarchive.com /PdfViewerTags.aspx?img=56146330&firstvisit=true&src=search&current Result=1.

235   *"I will see that Friedman gets every consideration"*: "Benny Friedman Mentioned For Berkeley Post," *Modesto News-Herald,* January 6, 1931.

235   *"If Benny Friedman goes to Yale":* Grantland Rice, "The Sportlight," *Los Angeles Times,* February 6, 1931.

237   *"My dad always said that Rockne":* Author interview with Donald Miller Jr., May 17, 2004.

239   *"I made the same kind of stop":* W. J. Lee, "With Malice Toward None," *Hartford Courant,* April 18, 1941.

242   *"Friedman retired soon after he had passed the Giants to victory":* Arthur J. Daley, "Friedman's Passes Down Portsmouth," *New York Times,* November 2, 1931.

244   *"The newspapers made Booth an outstanding star":* Associated Press, "Booth Highly Overrated, Says Friedman," *Chicago Daily Tribune,* December 23, 1931.

245   *"You're a good friend":* Klein, *The New York Giants,* 70–71.

Chapter 18

249   *"Are there any of the graduating football men":* Benny Friedman, letter to Bennie Oosterbaan, April 14, 1932, Papers of Bennie Gaylord Oosterbaan, Bentley Historical Library, University of Michigan.

250   *Discussion of Pinckert:* Benny Friedman, "I Could Play Pro Football And I'm 48!" *Sport,* December 1953, 10, copyright © Sport Media Enterprises, www.thesportgallery.com.

250   *"I'll bet you that before the season's over":* Harold F. Parrot, "Friedman Calls Dodgers 'Potentially Strongest'; Predicts Packers' Fall," *Brooklyn Daily Eagle,* October 6, 1932.

251   *"He was our hero":* Author interview with Hal Lebovitz, April 10, 2003.

251   *"Friedman is a great drawing card":* Official game program, Brooklyn Dodgers vs. Green Bay Packers, October 23, 1932.

252   *"All right . . . Your ball":* "Benny Friedman Still Outfigures Grid Enemy," *San Antonio Light,* November 3, 1932, http://www.newspaperarchive.com/Pdf ViewerTags.aspx?img=59580437&firstvisit=true&src=search&currentResult=0.

254   *"Potsy Clark showed the boys the value":* "Cagle Confident Dodgers Will Win Football Title," *Brooklyn Times Union,* September 12, 1933.

254   *"With Friedman in the fold":* "Dodgers, Under New Deal, Due to Win Grid Crown," *Brooklyn Times Union,* September 19, 1933.

255   *"That man is the smartest signal caller":* "Benny Friedman Displays Old Skills Tossing Passes," *Brooklyn Times Union,* September 25, 1933.

257   *"If anyone thinks he can tell ahead of time":* Lou Niss, "Pro Football Players and Coaches Pick Friedman King of Quarterbacks," *Brooklyn Times Union,* December 6, 1933.

257   *"Consider my own experience":* Benny Friedman as told to John B. Kennedy, "Pro and Coin," *Collier's,* November 25, 1933.

258   *"As Mayor of the City of New York":* Fiorello LaGuardia, letter to Boris Fingerhood, September 9, 1936, Papers of Fiorello LaGuardia, courtesy of New York City Municipal Archives.

261   *"Many boys needed a good meal":* Postal, Silver, and Silver, *Encyclopedia of Jews in Sports,* 248.

261 *"Pebble picking contest":* Author interview with Stanley Brodsky, March 13, 2006.

261 *"Lewisohn Stadium was a chore to play in":* Author interview with Bill Silverman, March 7, 2006.

263 *"City never has had a football team like":* Arthur J. Daley, "New Gridiron Deal Scores At C.C.N.Y," *New York Times,* September 14, 1934.

265 *"[City] is the new football sensation of the Big Town":* Joe Williams, "Sports Roundup," *Syracuse Herald,* October 31, 1934, http://www.newspaperarchive .com/PdfViewerTags.aspx?img=41395124&firstvisit=true&src=search&current Result=0.

265 *"At the box office":* "Friedman Great Success At City," *Brooklyn Times Union,* October 31, 1934.

265 *"What do you think folks would say":* Bernard Brown, "Friedman Grooms City Grid Team to Surprise Jaspers," *Brooklyn Times Union,* November 1, 1934.

266 *"Influenced by Benny's success":* George Halas, "Halas Calls Friedman Pioneer Passer—Rest Came By Design," *New York Daily News,* February 4, 1967.

267 *"I had some good years left":* Curran, *Pro Football's Rag Days,* 72.

Chapter 19

269 *"All we need up here":* Eddie Brietz, "This And That From Here And There," *Lima News,* May 17, 1937, http://www.newspaperarchive.com/PdfViewer Tags.aspx?img=11207384&firstvisit=true&src=search&currentResult=0.

270 *"We ran and ran and ran":* Author interview with Stanley Brodsky.

270 *"His main concern":* Author interview with Harold Goldstein, May 8, 2003.

270 *"Like a Rodin":* Author interview with Stanley Brodsky.

270 *"He was very good at communicating":* Author interview with Bill Silverman, March 7, 2006.

271 *"Mr. Friedman works very well":* Recommendation for Reappointment with Tenure, City College Department of Hygiene, City University of New York Archives.

271 *"Of course we shall maintain our requirements":* The City College Alumnus 31, no. 4., April 1935.

272 *"Benny Friedman is still winning orchids":* Beach Conger, "New York Alumni Club Backs Friedman As The Ideal Coach," *Michigan Daily,* December 10, 1937.

272 *"Our next coach!":* "Graduates Here Boom Friedman As Kipke Successor at Michigan," *New York Times,* December 11, 1937.

272 *"Naturally I would like to coach Michigan":* UP, "Friedman Boosted To Succeed Kipke," *Oshkosh Northwestern,* December 11, 1937, http://www.newspaper archivPdfViewerTags.aspx?img=8942928&firstvisit=true&src=search&current Result=0e.com/.

272 *"No member of a school faculty should be selected":* "Yost Declares That Choice of Coach Should Be Made With Greatest Care," *Michigan Daily,* December 15, 1926.

273 *"Fleckenstein of Iowa"*: Benny Friedman, "The Professional Touch," *Collier's*, October 15, 1932.

273 *"Good name, credit and reputation"*: Fleckenstein v. Friedman, 266 NY, 22 (1934).

273 *"In his business or profession of playing professional football"*: Ibid.

274 *"After the game was over"*: Deposition of Robert Howard taken in case of *Fleckenstein v. Friedman.*

276 *"leveler of prejudice and intolerance"*: "Benny Friedman: Famed Sports Authority, Football Star, Coach and Speaker," Chicago: The Redpath Bureau, n.d., http://sdrcdata.lib.uiowa.edu/libsdrc/details.jsp?id=/friedman/1&page=2&ui=1.

278 *"We were quite familiar with Friedman's career"*: Eugene S. Tucker, letter to sports editor, "Pro Hall of Fame: Four Votes for Benny Friedman," *New York Times*, February 22, 1976.

279 *"Thank God"*: Henry Rosenfeld, "Benny Friedman On Football," *Jewish Digest*, December 1940, 82.

280 *"Mothers once reared their sons"*: John Whitaker, "Speculating in Sports," *Hammond Times*, October 23, 1942, http://www.newspaperarchive.com/Pdf ViewerTags.aspx?img=15080657&firstvisit=true&src=search&currentResult=2.

281 *"He didn't promote himself"*: Author interview with Charles Crump, May 17, 2004.

282 *"When you write of such things"*: Benny Friedman, letter to Florence Friedman, June 6, 1945, by permission of Marilyn Myers.

282 *"You might be interested in the fact"*: Benny Friedman, letter to Florence Friedman, May 25, 1945.

282 *"Well, I had qualified"*: Friedman interview, 105.

Chapter 20

286 *"How large is the student body?"*: Abram L. Sachar, *Brandeis University: A Host at Last*, rev. ed. (Hanover, NH: Brandeis University Press, 1995), 289. Copyright © University Press of New England, Hanover, NH. Reprinted with permission.

286 *"Benny, you owe this to us"*: William Simons, "Brandeis: Athletics at a Jewish Sponsored University," *American Jewish History* 83, no. 1 (1995): 68. Copyright © The American Jewish Historical Society. Reprinted with permission of the Johns Hopkins University Press.

286 *"I knew when I first stood on Ferry Field"*: Whitney Martin, "First Grid Season A Success for Nation's Newest University," *Wisconsin State Journal*, December 23, 1950, http://www.newspaperarchive.com/PdfViewerTags.aspx?img=99989060 &firstvisit=true&src=search&currentResult=0.

287 *"Once a school is in big time"*: Milton Gross, "Speaking Out," *New York Post*, November 12, 1951.

287 *"I love football and I think"*: Ibid.

287 *"If a Pulitzer for literature"*: Abram L. Sachar, *A Host at Last* (Boston: Little, Brown, 1976), 283.

290 *"B.C. Loses"*: *Boston Globe*, October 6, 1951.

290   *"Boys . . . you've got to get up for the game":* Author interview with Paul Levinson, March 18, 2008.

291   *"Benny to me was like a Hollywood character":* Author interview with Bob Weintraub, October 2003.

291   *"Benny, you didn't go to talk to":* Author interview with Robert Domozych, 2003.

292   *"There was nowhere to hide":* Author interview with Richard Baldacci, March 18, 2008.

293   *"To just watch him walk across that sod":* Author interview with Tom Egan, May 8, 2003.

294   *"Bergel, you son of a bitch!":* Author interview with Dick Bergel, 2003.

294   *"Jimmy, you've got talent":* Author interviews with Jim Stehlin, April 24 and October 2003.

294   *"I'm not interested in how hard you can throw":* Ibid.

294   *"He had a charisma about him":* Ibid.

295   *"And . . . Benny Friedman coached him":* Author interview with Bill McKenna, 2003.

295   *"Benny was superb in addressing groups":* Simons, "Brandeis," 70.

296   *"Benny, I understand you're looking":* Author interview with Bud Collins, October 29, 2005.

298   *"I understand that you are going to pick":* Benny Friedman, letter to *Sports Illustrated*, November 10, 1958, Papers of Bennie Gaylord Oosterbaan, by permission of Bentley Historical Library, University of Michigan.

299   *"I . . . would like to be one of those present":* Benny Friedman, letter to Bennie Oosterbaan, April 8, 1959, Papers of Bennie Gaylord Oosterbaan, by permission of Bentley Historical Library, University of Michigan.

299   *"I think you have here a magnificent opportunity":* John P. Roche, memorandum to Abram Sachar, December 31, 1959, Robert D. Farber University Archives and Special Collections Department, Brandeis University.

300   *"I'm glad Benny raised $80,000 for us":* Abram Sachar, memorandum February 23, 1960, Robert D. Farber University Archives and Special Collections Department, Brandeis University.

301   *"End of warfare with student intellectuals," elimination of "Sabbath football," and "enmity of BF":* Abram Sachar, notes, Robert D. Farber University Archives and Special Collections Department, Brandeis University.

Chapter 21

303   *"I feel sure I could play":* Friedman, "I Could Play Pro Football And I'm 48!" *Sport*, December 1953, 10.

303   *"But remember that the football had been changed":* Myron Cope, *The Game That Was: The Early Days of Pro Football* (Cleveland, OH: The World Publishing Co., 1970), 52.

304   *"I always thought that for the majority of receivers":* Maxwell Stiles, "Sammy Baugh's A Remarkable Player," *Long Beach Press-Telegram,* August 14, 1947, http://www.newspaperarchive.com/PdfViewerTags.aspx?img=36950603&first visit=true&src=search&currentResult=0.

304   *"Friedman's accuracy was amazing"*: Joe Williams, "Sports Roundup," *Syracuse Herald-Journal,* November 20, 1942, http://www.newspaperarchive.com/Pdf ViewerTags.aspx?img=22916394&firstvisit=true&src=search&currentResult=0.

304   *"Benny . . . is it true"*: Friedman interview, 29.

305   *"Where the hell did you get"*: Author interview with Chuck Drimal, March 18, 2008.

306   *"Hey, I got my Jewish quarterback"*: Author interview with Gary Wichard, April 9, 2008.

306   *"There should have been two"*: Author interview with anonymous Friedman friend, 2008.

307   *"He treated her like a little princess"*: Author interview with Jody Rosenbaum, November 17, 2004.

307   *"He used to sunbathe"*: Ibid.

307   *"We've had a lot of give and take"*: Friedman interview, 26.

308   *"We never felt the need of children"*: Ibid., 22.

308   *"I don't know what kept him out of Canton"*: Jim Campbell, "John Alexander, Pro Football Pioneer," Professional Football Researchers Association's *Coffin Corner* 16, no. 2 (1995), http://www.profootballresearchers.org/Coffin _Corner/16-02-558.pdf.

309   *"He kept telling me all the time"*: Author interview with Herman Maisin.

309   *"What gives the current players the license"*: Associated Press, "Friedman to Fight Old Pros' Exclusion From Pension Plan," *New York Times*, August 9, 1970.

310   *"I thought I could pass until"*: Gayle Talbot, Associated Press, "College Football Moved Up In Attendance and Receipts," *Ada Evening News,* December 6, 1937, http://www.newspaperarchive.com/PdfViewerTags.aspx?img=48769465 &firstvisit=true&src=search&currentResult=0.

310   *"To The Sports Editor"*: Friedman, letter to the editor, *New York Times,* February 8, 1976.

Epilogue

315   *"If Benny were alive now"*: Author interview with Herman Maisin, December 7, 2006.

BIBLIOGRAPHY

Books

Associated Press. *The Sports Immortals.* Englewood Cliffs, NJ: Prentice-Hall, 1972.

Baldwin, Neil. *Henry Ford and the Jews: The Mass Production of Hate.* New York: PublicAffairs, 2001.

Beasley, Norman, and George W. Stark. *Made In Detroit.* New York: G. P. Putnam's Sons, 1957.

Becker, Carl M. *Home and Away: The Rise and Fall of Professional Football on the Banks of the Ohio, 1919–1934.* Athens: Ohio University Press, 1998.

Behee, John. *Fielding Yost's Legacy to The University of Michigan.* Ann Arbor, MI: Uhlrich's Books, 1971.

Blakeslee, Spencer. *The Death of American Antisemitism.* Westport, CT: Praeger Publishers, 2000.

Broun, Heywood, and George Britt. *Christians Only: A Study in Prejudice.* New York: Da Capo Press, 1974.

Brown, Warren. *Rockne.* Chicago: Reilly and Lee, 1931.

Cantor, Judith Levin. *Jews in Michigan.* East Lansing: Michigan State University Press, 2001.

Charnley, Mitchell V. *Play the Game: The Book of Sport.* New York: Viking Press, 1931.

Claassen, Harold. *Football's Unforgettable Games.* New York: Ronald Press Co., 1963.

Cohane, Tim. *Great College Football Coaches of the Twenties and Thirties.* New Rochelle, NY: Arlington House, 1973.

Cohen, Richard M., J. A. Deutsch, and D. S. Neft. *The University of Michigan Football Scrapbook.* Indianapolis, IN: Bobbs-Merrill Company, Inc., 1978.

Curran, Bob. *Pro Football's Rag Days.* Englewood Cliffs, NJ: Prentice-Hall, 1969.

Danzig, Allison. *The History of American Football: Its Great Teams, Players, and Coaches.* Englewood Cliffs, NJ: Prentice-Hall, 1956.

DeVito, Carlo. *Wellington: The Maras, the Giants, and the City of New York.* Chicago: Triumph Books, 2006.

Donovan, Jim, Keith Marder, and Mark Spellen. *The Notre Dame Football Encyclopedia: The Ultimate Guide to America's Favorite College Team.* New York: Citadel Press, 2001.

Durant, John and Les Etter. *Highlights of College Football.* New York: Hasting House, 1970.

Eisenhammer, Fred, and Eric B. Sondheimer. *College Football's Most Memorable Games, 1913–1990: The Stories of 54 History-Making Contests.* Jefferson, NC: McFarland & Co., 1992.

Emmanuel, Greg. *The 100-Yard War: Inside the 100-Year-Old Michigan–Ohio State Football Rivalry.* Hoboken, NJ: John Wiley & Sons, 2004.

Eubanks, Lon. *The Fighting Illini: A Story of Illinois Football.* Huntsville, AL: Strode Publishers, 1976.

Falk, Gerhard. *Football and American Identity.* Binghamton, NY: Haworth Press, 2005.

Fass, Paula S. *The Damned and the Beautiful: American Youth in the 1920s.* New York: Oxford University Press, 1977.

Fitzgerald, Francis J., and Bob Rosiek. *Hail to the Victors: Greatest Moments in Michigan Football History.* Louisville, KY: AdCraft, 1995.

Fox, Stephen. *Big Leagues: Professional Baseball, Football, and Basketball in National Memory.* New York: William Morrow and Company, Inc., 1994.

Friedman, Benny. *The Passing Game.* New York: Steinfeld Inc. 1931.

Gildea, William, and Christopher Jennison. *The Fighting Irish.* Englewood Cliffs, NJ: Prentice-Hall, 1976.

Gorelick, Sherry. *City College and the Jewish Poor: Education in New York, 1880–1924.* New Brunswick, NJ: Rutgers University Press, 1981.

Gottehrer, Barry. *The Giants of New York: The History of Professional Football's Most Fabulous Dynasty.* New York: G. P. Putnam's Sons, 1963.

Grabowski, John J. *Sports in Cleveland: An Illustrated History.* Bloomington: Indiana University Press, 1992.

Grabowski, John J., and David D. Van Tassel, eds. *The Encyclopedia of Cleveland History.* Bloomington: Indiana University Press, 1996.

Grange, Harold. *The Galloping Ghost: The Autobiography of Red Grange.* As told to Ira Morton. Wheaton, IL: Crossroads Communications, 1953.

Greenberg, Hank. *Hank Greenberg: The Story of My Life.* New York: Times Books, 1989.

Halas, George Stanley. *Halas by Halas: The Autobiography of George Halas.* With Gwen Morgan and Arthur Veysey. New York: McGraw-Hill, 1979.

Hertzberg, Arthur. *The Jews in America: Four Centuries of an Uneasy Encounter: A History.* New York: Simon & Schuster, 1989.

Higham, John. *Send These to Me: Jews and Other Immigrants in Urban America.* New York: Atheneum, 1975.

Hudak, Timothy L. *The Charity Game: The Story of Cleveland's Thanksgiving Day High School Football Classic.* Cleveland, OH: Sports Heritage Specialty Publications, 2002.

Hyman, Mervin D., and Gordon S. White Jr. *Big Ten Football: Its Life and Times, Great Coaches, Players and Games.* New York: Macmillan, 1977.

Izenberg, Jerry. *New York Giants: Seventy-Five Years.* New York: Time-Life Books, 1999.

Kaufman, David. *Shul with a Pool: The "Synagogue Center" in American Jewish History.* Hanover, NH: University Press of New England, 1999.

Kaye, Ivan N. *Good Clean Violence: A History of College Football.* Philadelphia: J. B. Lippincott, 1973.

Klein, Dave. *The New York Giants: Yesterday, Today and Tomorrow.* Chicago: Henry Regnery Company, 1973.

Koger, Jim. *Football's Greatest Games: A Book Devoted to the Complete Story of the Most Famous Games in History.* Morros Publishing Co., 1966.

Levine, Peter. *Ellis Island to Ebbets Field: Sport and the American Jewish Experience.*
    New York: Oxford University Press, 1992.

Levy, Bill. *Three Yards and a Cloud of Dust: The Ohio State Football Story.* Cleveland,
    OH: World Publishing Co., 1966.

McCallum, John D. *Big Ten Football Since 1895.* Radnor, PA: Chilton Book Co., 1976.

Mooney, James L., ed. *Dictionary of American Naval Fighting Ships.* Vol. 6, *Historical
    Sketches: Letters R through S.* Washington: Naval History Division, Depart-
    ment of the Navy, 1976.

Neft, David S., Richard M. Cohen, and Rick Korch. *Football Encyclopedia: The Com-
    plete History of Professional NFL Football from 1892 to the Present.* New York:
    St. Martin's Press, 1994.

Oriard, Michael. *King Football: Sport and Spectacle in the Golden Age of Radio and
    Newsreels, Movies and Magazines, the Weekly and the Daily Press.* Chapel Hill:
    University of North Carolina Press, 2003.

Perrin, Tom. *Football: A College History.* Jefferson, NC: McFarland & Co., 1987.

Pesch, Ron, and Mark Okkonen. *100 Years of Football at Muskegon High School
    1895–1994.* Muskegon, MI: Muskegon Big Red Athletic Foundation.

Peterson, Robert W. *Pigskin: The Early Years of Pro Football.* New York: Oxford
    University Press, 1997.

Pope, Edwin. *Football's Greatest Coaches.* Atlanta: Tupper and Love, 1955.

Prell, Riv-Ellen. *Fighting to Become Americans: Assimilation and the Trouble between
    Jewish Women and Jewish Men.* Boston: Beacon Press, 1999.

Quirk, James, and Rodney Fort. *Pay Dirt: The Business of Professional Team Sports.*
    Princeton, NJ: Princeton University Press, 1992.

Ribalow, Harold U., and Meir Ribalow. *The Jew in American Sports.* New York:
    Hippocrene Books, 1985.

Roberts, Howard. *The Big Nine: The Story of Football in the Western Conference.* New
    York: G. P. Putnam's Sons, 1948.

Robinson, Ray. *Rockne of Notre Dame: The Making of a Football Legend.* New York:
    Oxford University Press, 1999.

Roff, Sandra, Anthony Cucchiara, and Barbara Dunlap. *From the Free Academy to
    CUNY: Illustrating Public Higher Education in New York City, 1847–1997.*
    New York: Fordham University Press, 2000.

Rowher, J., and G. Hummelchen. *Chronology of the War at Sea, 1939–1945.* Annapolis,
    MD: Naval Institute Press, 1972.

Rubinstein, Judah, with Jane Avner. *Merging Traditions: Jewish Life in Cleveland.* Rev.
    ed. Kent, Ohio: Kent State University Press, 2004.

Sachar, Abram L. *A Host at Last.* Boston: Little, Brown, 1976.

———. *Brandeis University: A Host at Last.* Rev. ed. Hanover, NH: University Press of
    New England, 1995.

Stuhldreher, Harry A. *Knute Rockne: Man Builder.* Philadelphia: Macrae Smith Co., 1931.

Sullivan, George. *Pro Football's Passing Game.* New York: Dodd, Mead, 1972.

Vincent, Sidney Z. *Personal and Professional: Memoirs of a Life in Community Service.*
    Cleveland, OH: Jewish Community Federation of Cleveland, 1982.

Wallace, Francis. *Notre Dame from Rockne to Parseghian.* New York: David McKay
    Co., 1967.

Watterson, John Sayle. *College Football: History, Spectacle, Controversy.* Baltimore: Johns Hopkins University Press, 2000.

Whittingham, Richard. *What Giants They Were.* Chicago: Triumph Books, 2000.

———. *Rites of Autumn: The Story of College Football.* New York: Free Press, 2001.

Willis, Chris. *Old Leather: An Oral History of Early Pro Football in Ohio, 1920–1935.* Lanham, MD: Scarecrow Press, 2005.

Articles and Oral History Interviews

Aston, Joe. "Benny Friedman's Toe Earns One-Point Margin." *The Lantern*, November 15, 1926, http://library.osu.edu/sites/archives/OSUvsMichigan/news/1926.htm.

"The Athletic Year: University of California, 1931–1932" (bulletin). Associated Students, University of California, May 1932.

Bacon, John U. "Building a Sports Empire." *Michigan History Magazine* (September/October 2000): 28–33.

Bellis, Milt. "Friedman quotes three Yost rules as 'soundest' football advice." *Stars and Stripes,* July 19, 1951, http://www.stripes.com/article.asp?section=126&article=29918&archive=true.

"Bennie Oosterbaan." http://www.mashf.com/1987_inductees.htm.

"Benny Friedman." http://jewsinsports.org/profile.asp?sport=football&ID=5.

"Benny Friedman." http://www.jt-sw.com/football/pro/players.nsf/ID/00820006.

Benson, Mark. "Ending Brandeis Football." *College Football Historical Society* 16, no. 4 (August 2003): 17–18 .

Brady, Tim. "A Difference in Tone." *Minnesota History Magazine* (January/February 2007), http://www.alumni.umn.edu/A_Difference_in_Tone.html.

"Brandeis Build-Up." *Newsweek,* May 15, 1950.

Brandeis University football press guides: 1952, 1953, 1954, 1955, 1957, 1958.

Cagle, Christian. "Football as a Vocation." *Outlook and Independent* 156, no. 15 (December 10, 1930): 572–573, 583, 585.

"Camp For Quarterbacks." *Sport,* October 1965: 50–53.

Campbell, Jim. "John Alexander, Pro Football Pioneer." *The Coffin Corner,* vol. 16, no. 2 (1995), http://www.profootballresearchers.org/Coffin_Corner/16-02-558.pdf.

———. "Benny Friedman." *The Coffin Corner,* vol. 20, no. 2 (1998), http://www.profootballresearchers.org/Coffin_Corner/20-02-746pdf.

Carroll, Bob. "Giants On The Gridiron: 1927." Professional Football Researchers Association, http://www.profootballresearchers.org/Articles/Giants_On_The_Gridiron.pdf.

———. "Steamrollered: 1928." Professional Football Researchers Association, http://profootballresearchers.org/Articles/Steamrollered.pdf.

———. "The Packers Crash Through: 1929." Professional Football Researchers Association, http://www.profootballresearchers.org/Articles/The_Packers_Crash_Through.pdf.

———. "The 1920s All-Pros In Retrospect." *The Coffin Corner,* vol. 7, no. 5 (1985), http://profootballresearchers.org/Coffin_Corner/07-05-233.pdf.

Carroll, John M. "The Impact of Red Grange on Pro Football in 1925." *The Coffin Corner*, vol. 20, no. 2 (1998), http://www.profootballresearchers.org/Coffin _Corner/20-02-742.pdf.

Cuneo, Ernest L. "I Remember Benny." *The Coffin Corner*, vol. 8, no. 8 (1986), http://www.profootballresearchers.org/Coffin_Corner/08-08-278.pdf.

Eckersall, Walter. "Foot Ball In The Middle West." *Spalding's Official Football Guide*, 1925, 1926, 1927.

———. "A Second to Think." *Liberty*, November 8, 1930.

Eisen, George. "Jews and Sport: A Century of Retrospect." *Journal of Sport History* 26, no. 2 (Summer 1999): 225–239.

Elias Sports Bureau and Pro Football Research Association Linescore Committee, Ken Pullis, Chairman. "1927 National Football League." http://www.profootball researchers.org/Linescores/1927.pdf.

———. "1928 National Football League." http://www.profootballresearchers.org /Linescores/1928.pdf.

———. "1929 National Football League." http://www.profootballresearchers.org /Linescores/1929.pdf.

———. "1930 National Football League." http://www.profootballresearchers.org /Linescores/1930.pdf.

———. "1931 National Football League." http://www.profootballresearchers.org /Linescores/1931.pdf.

———. "1932 National Football League." http://www.profootballresearchers.org /Linescores/1932.pdf.

———. "1933 National Football League." http://www.profootballresearchers.org /Linescores/1933.pdf.

———. "1934 National Football League." http://www.profootballresearchers.org /Linescores/1934.pdf.

Elliott, Lawrence. "Eight All Americans." *Coronet* 37, no. 2 (December 1954): 41–43.

Falk, Gerhard. "Football: The Jewish Experience." http://www.jbuff.com/c082103.htm.

"Football." *The City College Alumnus* 31, no. 4 (April 1935): 60.

"Freshman Coach." *People Today*, October 24, 1950.

Friedman, Benny. "The Professional Touch." *Collier's*, October 15, 1932.

———. "Pro and Coin." *Collier's*, November 25, 1933.

———. "Forward Passing The Friedman Way." *Scholastic Coach* vol. 36, no. 8 (1967): 54–58.

———. "Look! See! React." *Scholastic Coach* 38, no. 8 (1969): 36–37, 78.

———. Letter from Benny Friedman to George Sullivan, November 4, 1971. http://sports.ha.com/common/view_item.php?Sale_No=702&Lot _No=19414&src=pr#Photo.

———. Interview by Elli Wohlgelernter, September 5 and October 6, 1980. The New York Public Library, American Jewish Committee Oral History Collection, Dorot Jewish Division, NYPL.

"Friedman v. Dooley." *Time*, October 24, 1927.

Gallico, Paul. "The Greatest Football Player in the World." *Liberty*, December 27, 1930.

Gallagher, Robert S. "The Galloping Ghost: An Interview with Red Grange." *American Heritage Magazine,* December 1974, http://www.americanheritage.com/articles/magazine/ah/1974/1/1974_1_20.shtml.

Gewecke, Cliff. "At School With Benny The Convincer." *Los Angeles Times West Magazine,* November 26, 1967.

Gill, Bob. "Friedman's Last Hurrah." *The Coffin Corner,* vol. 8, no. 8 (1986), http://www.profootballresearchers.org/Coffin_Corner/08-08-277.pdf.

Gilleran, Ed, Jr. "Flatbush Kingsmen and Friends." *College Football Historical Society* 3, no. 3 (May 1990): 4–6, http://la84foundation.org/SportsLibrary/CFHSN/CFHSNv03/CFHSNv03n3b.pdf.

Goldberg, Samuel. "What's Wrong—Football in Mid-Season." *The City College Alumnus* 34, no. 8 (1938): 108.

Grange, Harold. "By Appointment Only." *Saturday Evening Post,* October 20, 1934.

Grosshandler, Stan. "The Brooklyn Dodgers." *The Coffin Corner,* vol. 12, no. 3 (1990), http://www.profootballresearchers.org/Coffin_Corner/12-03-399.pdf.

Hansen, Michael. "Shangri-La." In *Dictionary of American Naval Fighting Ships.* http://www.hazegray.org/danfs/carriers/cv38.htm.

Hehr, Russell Allon. "Luna Park, Cleveland, Ohio." In *The Encyclopedia of Cleveland History.* http://home.nyc.rr.com/johnmiller/luna.html.

Hirshberg, Al. "Brandeis' First Varsity Season." Official Program, Brandeis vs. New Hampshire, September 29, 1951. Lynn, MA: Stadium Programs Publishing Co.

"A History: The Adolph Lewisohn Plaza of Honor." http://www.ccny.cuny.edu/plazasite/plazahistory/history1.htm.

"Hubbard, 'Cal' (Robert Calvin)." HickockSports.com Sports Biographies, http://www.hickoksports.com/biograph/hubbardcal.shtml.

"The Incredible Jesse Owens." *Track and Field News.* http://www.trackandfieldnews.com/general/back_track/16.html.

"The International Jew: Anti-Semitism from the Roaring Twenties Revived on the Web." http://www.adl.org/special_reports/ij/print.asp.

"Intra Muros: Friedman Reappointed." *The City College Alumnus* 32, no. 4 (April 1936): 37,

Jaher, Frederic Cople. "Antisemitism in American Athletics." *Shofar* 20, no. 1 (2001): 61–73, http://muse.jhu.edu/journals/shofar/v020/20.1jaher.html.

Klinger, Jerry. "America was different. America is different." http://www.jewishmag.com/86mag/usa10/usa10.htm.

Kunderman, Brian. "Football's Forward Pass Turns 100 Years Old." News release, September 1, 2006. http://www.slu.edu/readstory/newlsink/7166.

Kyle, Robert K. "The Day Knute Rockne Died." *Indianapolis Star,* March 27, 1977, http://www.irishlegends.com/Pages/herbs/herbsarticle49.html.

Levenson, Paul E. Letter to *The Justice,* March 15, 2005. http://media.www.thejusticeonline.com/media/storage/paper573/news/2005/03/15/Forum/Letter.Alumnus.Reflects.Freidman.Unforgettable.Role.Model-894363.shtml.

Manus, Willard. "Battlin' Benny." *Alumnus* 97, no. 1 (Winter 2002): 8–9.

McCarty, Bernie. "Oberlander's 500-yard game." *College Football Historical Society* 3, no. 4 (August 1990): 17–18, www.la84foundation.org/SportsLibrary/CFHSN/CFHSNv03/CFHSNv03n4h.pdf.

Meck, Stuart. "Zoning and Anti-Semitism in the 1920s: The Case of *Cleveland Jewish Orphan Home v. Village of University Heights* and Its Aftermath." *Journal of Planning History*, vol. 4, no. 2 (May 2005): 91–128.

"The Michigan Stadium Story: Building the Big House." http://bentley.umich.edu/athdept/stadium/stadtext/stadbild.htm.

"The Michigan Stadium Story: Michigan's Radio Football Announcers." Bentley Historical Library, http://bentley.umich.edu/athdept/stadium/stadtext/radio.htm.

Microcosm (CCNY yearbook). 1933, 1935, 1936, 1941, 1942. Published annually.

"Notre Dame and Michigan—A History." http://www.ndnation.com/boards/showpost.php?b=hof;pid=457;d=this.

Official Football Review, University of Notre Dame, published annually.

"The Ohio Game." *Michigan Alumnus*, 1926, http://www.bentley.umich.edu/athdept/football/umosu/rivalrep/1926osu.htm.

Paull, Henry. "'Benny' Friedman—Gridiron Hero." *American Hebrew*, December 18, 1925.

Pickette, Jeffrey. "Band of Brothers." *The Justice*, May 20, 2008, http://media.www.thejusticeonline.com/media/storage/paper573/news/2008/02/05/Sports.

"Pictorial History of Ann Arbor 1920–1929: The Jazz Age in Ann Arbor." http://www.aadl.org/moaa/pictorial_history/1920-1929pg6.

Pro Football Hall of Fame. "Mr. Mara." *The Coffin Corner*, vol. 6, nos. 11 and 12 (1984), http://www.profootballresearchers.org/Coffin_Corner/06-11-199.pdf.

Pruter, Robert. "A Century of Intersectional and Interstate Football Contests." *Illinois H.S.toric*, http://www.ihsa.org/initiatives/hstoric/football_intersec.htm.

Rice, Grantland. "The All-America Football Team." *Collier's*, December 11, 1926.

Richards, William H. "Dedication Ceremony Marked by Simplicity." http://bentley.umich.edu/athdept/stadium/stadtext/fposu27.htm.

Ridgeway, Jim. "Remembering the Ironton Tanks." http://www.bvaughn.com/ironton_tanks.htm.

Rockne, Knute K. "What Thrills A Coach." *Collier's*, December 6, 1930.

Rosenfeld, Henry. "Benny Friedman On Football." *Jewish Digest* (December 1940): 82–84.

"The Royal Hotel." http://theidlehour.com/hotelfolder/royal.html.

Schmidt, Ray. "Changing Tides: College Football 1919–1930." *College Football Historical Society* 13, no. 3 (May 2000): 13–16.

Shalett, Sidney. "They're Working on a Big Idea at Brandeis," *Saturday Evening Post*, vol. 223, no. 48, May 26, 1951, 134.

Shapiro, Ezra. Interview by Sidney Vincent and Judah Rubinstein, February 26, 1972. The Judah Rubinstein Audiotape Oral History Project Collection at the Western Reserve Historical Society, Cleveland, OH.

Simons, William. "Brandeis: Athletics at a Jewish Sponsored University." *American Jewish History* 83, no. 1 (1995): 65–81.

Taft, Arthur. "125 Years of Sports at City College." *The City College Alumnus* (June 1973): 9.

"Traveling Culture: Circuit Chautauqua in the Twentieth Century." The University of Iowa Libraries, http://sdrcdata.lib.uiowa.edu/libsdrc/details.jsp?id=/friedman/1&page=2&ui=1.

Vertinsky, Patricia. "The Jew's Body: Anti-Semitism, Physical Culture and the Jew's Foot," NASSH Proceedings (1973–2003), http://www.la84foundation.org/SportsLibrary/NASSH_Proceedings/NP1994/NP1994e.pdf.

Weintraub, Bob. "A Tribute to Benny: More than Passing Greatness" (booklet prepared for the Brandeis tribute to Friedman), 1998.

Whalen, Jim, and C. C. Staph. "The Facts about Friedman." *The Coffin Corner*, vol. 8, no. 7 (1986), http://www.profootballresearchers.org/Coffin_Corner/08-07-276.pdf.

"The Will to Prepare." *Time,* November 7, 1955 http://www.time.com/time/magazine/article/0,9171,807959,00.html?promoid=googlep.

"The Williams' Shuffle." http://sportsillustrated.cnn.com/football/nfl/1999/preview/teams/news/1999/07/29/nfc_west_saints/.

Zucker, Henry L. Interview by Ferne Katleman, July 15, 1986. The Judah Rubinstein Audiotape Oral History Project Collection at the Western Reserve Historical Society, Cleveland, OH.

Game Programs

Official Program, Michigan vs. Illinois, October 24, 1925.

Official Program, Michigan vs. Navy, October 31, 1925.

Official Program, Michigan vs. Ohio State, November 13, 1926.

Official Program, Brooklyn Dodgers vs. Green Bay Packers, October 23, 1932.

Official Program, City College vs. St. Francis College, October 5, 1935.

Official Program, City College vs. Providence College, October 12, 1935.

Official Program, City College vs. Lowell Textile Institute, October 19, 1935.

Official Program, New York University vs. College of the City of New York, November 9, 1935.

Official Program, City College vs. St. Joseph's, November 6, 1937.

Official Program, City College vs. Buffalo, October 1, 1938.

Official Program, Brooklyn College vs. City College, November 16, 1940.

Official Program, City College vs. University of Buffalo, October 4, 1941.

Official Program, City College vs. Brooklyn College, November 15, 1941.

Souvenir Program, Great Lakes Naval Training Station vs. Pittsburgh, October 10, 1942.

Souvenir Program, Great Lakes Naval Training Station vs. Wisconsin, October 17, 1942.

Souvenir Program, Great Lakes Naval Training Station vs. Notre Dame, December 15, 1942.

Video and Sound Recordings

Benny Friedman Tribute, Brandeis University, October 16, 1998. The Benny Friedman Tribute Committee. Video.

"If I Had the Chance," featuring Benny Friedman and others. Radio broadcast, October 10, 1939. Library of Congress, Washington, DC.

Knute Rockne, Jimmy Walker, and assembly in plaza outside New York City Hall, December 13, 1930. University of Notre Dame Archives. Newsreel.

United States Armed Forces Radio and Television Service, 1968 sound recording featuring Benny Friedman and others. AFRTS Collection, Library of Congress, Washington, DC.

Manuscript and Archive Collections

Bentley Historical Library, University of Michigan, Benny Friedman scrapbook.

Bentley Historical Library, University of Michigan, papers of Bennie Gaylord Oosterbaan.

Bentley Historical Library, University of Michigan, papers of Fielding Harris Yost.

City College of New York, Archives and Special Collections Division (journals, yearbooks, programs, and papers relating to hiring of Friedman and the football program).

Great Lakes Naval Training Station Archives (programs, newspapers).

National Archives and Records Administration (records relating to Friedman's service in the Navy).

New York City Municipal Archives, papers of Fiorello LaGuardia.

New York City Municipal Archives, papers of James J. Walker.

The New York Public Library, American Jewish Committee Oral History Collection, Dorot Jewish Division, interview with Benny Friedman conducted by Elli Wohlgelernter, September 5 and October 6, 1980.

Northwestern University Archives (correspondence concerning 1925 Big Ten champion).

Robert D. Farber University Archives and Special Collections Department, Brandeis University (papers relating to Benny Friedman, Abram Sachar, and Brandeis football).

University of California Archives (correspondence concerning hiring of football coach in 1938).

University of Illinois Archives, 1925 Official Game Program, Michigan vs. Illinois.

University of Notre Dame Archives (materials relating to Notre Dame's 1930 football team and Knute Rockne, game programs and press kits, newsreel of Rockne's appearance at city hall).

University of Oregon Archives (records relating to hiring of football coach).

Western Reserve Historical Society, oral history interviews of Ezra Shapiro and Henry L. Zucker.

Newspapers

In addition to those cited in the notes, I consulted the following newspapers: *Amarillo Globe; Athens Messenger; The Bee; Berkshire Evening Eagle; Billings Gazette; Brainerd Daily Dispatch; Brooklyn Citizen; Burlington Daily News-Times; Capital Times; Charleroi Mail; Charleston Daily Mail; Chester Times; Chicago Defender; Chicago Herald Examiner; Chronicle Telegram; Cleveland Jewish Chronicle; Cleveland Jewish News and Observer; Coshocton Tribune; Davenport Democrat and Leader; Dayton Journal; Dunkirk Evening Observer; El Paso Herald; Excelsior Springs Daily Journal; Frederick Post; Fresno Bee; Galveston Daily News; Great Lakes Bulletin; Hamilton Evening Journal; Hayward Review; Indiana Daily Student; Iowa Press Citizen; Ironwood Daily Globe; Jewish*

Independent; Kingsport Times; La Crosse Tribune and Leader-Press; Lantern; Lincoln Star; Lowell Sun; Mansfield News; Nassau Herald; New York Amsterdam News; New York Evening Journal; New York Post; New York Telegram; Oakland Tribune; Ogden Standard-Examiner; Ohio Jewish Chronicle; Oregon Daily Emerald; Port Arthur News; Providence Journal; San Mateo Times; Sheboygan Press; Stevens Point Daily Journal; Van Wert Times-Bulletin; Vidette-Messenger; Wadsworth Banner-Press; Waterloo Evening Courier; Wisconsin Rapids Daily Tribune; Zanesville Signal.

INDEX

MURRAY GREENBERG is a former litigator and graduate of Brandeis University (where Benny Friedman was the first athletic director and only football coach), as well as Columbia University's Graduate School of Journalism. He lives with his wife, Andrea, and daughters, Allie and Samantha, in Hewlett Harbor, New York.

PublicAffairs is a publishing house founded in 1997. It is a tribute to the standards, values, and flair of three persons who have served as mentors to countless reporters, writers, editors, and book people of all kinds, including me.

I.F. STONE, proprietor of *I. F. Stone's Weekly*, combined a commitment to the First Amendment with entrepreneurial zeal and reporting skill and became one of the great independent journalists in American history. At the age of eighty, Izzy published *The Trial of Socrates*, which was a national bestseller. He wrote the book after he taught himself ancient Greek.

BENJAMIN C. BRADLEE was for nearly thirty years the charismatic editorial leader of *The Washington Post*. It was Ben who gave the *Post* the range and courage to pursue such historic issues as Watergate. He supported his reporters with a tenacity that made them fearless and it is no accident that so many became authors of influential, best-selling books.

ROBERT L. BERNSTEIN, the chief executive of Random House for more than a quarter century, guided one of the nation's premier publishing houses. Bob was personally responsible for many books of political dissent and argument that challenged tyranny around the globe. He is also the founder and longtime chair of Human Rights Watch, one of the most respected human rights organizations in the world.

• • •

For fifty years, the banner of Public Affairs Press was carried by its owner Morris B. Schnapper, who published Gandhi, Nasser, Toynbee, Truman, and about 1,500 other authors. In 1983, Schnapper was described by *The Washington Post* as "a redoubtable gadfly." His legacy will endure in the books to come.

Peter Osnos, *Founder and Editor-at-Large*